A VINDICATION OF THE
RIGHTS OF WOMAN

AN AUTHORITATIVE TEXT
BACKGROUNDS
THE WOLLSTONECRAFT DEBATE
CRITICISM

SECOND EDITION

A NORTON CRITICAL EDITION

MARY WOLLSTONECRAFT

A VINDICATION OF THE
RIGHTS OF WOMAN

AN AUTHORITATIVE TEXT
BACKGROUNDS
THE WOLLSTONECRAFT DEBATE
CRITICISM

SECOND EDITION

Edited by
CAROL H. POSTON

W · W · NORTON & COMPANY
New York · London

Library of Congress Cataloging-in-Publication Data
Wollstonecraft, Mary, 1759–1797.
  A vindication of the rights of woman.

  (A Norton critical edition)
  "The text . . . is the second 1792 London edition"—
Pref.
  Bibliography: p. 361
  1. Woman's rights—Great Britain. 2. Women—Education
—Great Britain. 3. Wollstonecraft, Mary, 1759–1797.
A vindication of the rights of woman. I. Poston,
Carol H. II. Title.
HQ1596.W6   1975c   305.4'0941   86-21802

ISBN 0-393-02427-X
ISBN 0-393-95572-9 {PBK}

W. W. Norton & Company, Inc.,
500 Fifth Avenue, New York, N.Y. 10110

W. W. Norton & Company Ltd.,
37 Great Russell Street, London WC1B 3NU

4 5 6 7 8 9 0

Contents

Criticism   277

Preface to the Second Edition

In the ten years since the first Norton Critical Edition of Mary Wollstonecraft's A Vindication of the Rights of Woman, interest in her work
has soared, with the result that the bibliography of works on her has
doubled in size. Not only has scholarly interest been invigorated; class-
room teaching of women writers has burgeoned as well. This increased
interest provides the environment for a new version of this Norton Critical Edition that includes more recent scholarly work and provides new
and clarifies old footnote information, updates the bibliography, and
puts into the hands of students and teachers a text that is useful, clear,
and up-to-date.

The Backgrounds section now goes back before 1700 to show how
long there has been a concern for reform of women's education. Materials by authors such as Catharine Macaulay have been amplified to
give more than a tempting tidbit, and each new author is now represented
by solid fare. The Criticism section retains the historically important
documents but also includes the best of the new work that has been
appearing in scholarly journals of the last decade. Excellent pieces had
to be excluded because they were not as useful to the student as other,
more general pieces or because they did not directly address the Vindication. Those works are pointed out to the student in the Bibliography,
which has been revised and updated.

Finally, a new section has been added: The Wollstonecraft Debate.
Modern students want to be apprised of the history of the whole feminist
struggle. The Debate is a gathering of materials that show how Mary
Wollstonecraft's reputation has veered over the years alongside the fortunes of the women's movement. It is a way to chart what has happened
in each generation to the "woman question." It is a chance to look at
one feminist's history, how her stock rose and fell in the idea market
because she wrote about the rights of women and lived them.

In my last edition, I included in the preface a plea for continuing aid
in locating Mary Wollstonecraft's sources, and I am happy to say that
the plea has been heard over the years. I want to thank Bernard Kogan
of the University of Illinois at Chicago, Richard F. Hettlinger of Kenyon
College, Dr. Jean Mather, and Nancy Wyatt Poston for help with footnotes. Librarians continue to be among the most helpful people alive,
and I thank here the staff of the Newberry Library and the libraries of
the University of Illinois at Chicago and Urbana-Champaign. I have
had the invaluable advice of professors Moira Ferguson and Mitzi Myers
in the preparation of this edition, for which I am deeply grateful.
Thanks to the National Museum of Women in the Arts, Washington,

D.C., and to Elizabeth Kattan. Finally, I want to thank my typist, George Popovich, for excellent work; my editor, John Benedict, for his geniality and continuing dedication to the cause of women's literature; my generous husband, Larry, and my daughters, Anne and Rachel, who are living out the promise all of us feminists have worked for.

Chicago, Illinois, 1986

Preface

In 1792 a book appeared in London which set out the claim, dramatically and classically, that true freedom necessitates the equality of women and men. Mary Wollstonecraft's *A Vindication of the Rights of Woman* was so provocative and popular that a second edition appeared in the same year, and Dublin, Paris, and American editions soon followed.

The history of the subsequent editions of *A Vindication of the Rights of Woman* closely parallels the vicissitudes of the women's movement: when feminism as a political cause comes to the fore, as it periodically does, Mary Wollstonecraft's work is one of the first to be reissued. Yet after nearly 175 years of republication and commentary, the book has never been annotated, nor has there been (save in the case of facsimile editions) an attempt to preserve Wollstonecraft's prose exactly as she wrote it.

The text used here is the second 1792 London edition. The first edition had been published by Joseph Johnson early in 1792, and later that same year sales justified a second edition. Since Wollstonecraft had a chance to revise her original work in those intervening months, it can be assumed that this version represents her final choice as to how the book should read.

A whole list of variants between the first two editions would be instructive, if only to demonstrate the author's possible change of attitude in the period of time between the first and second editions. In fact, however, the changes are by no means major, consisting mainly in punctuation, deletion of archaic word forms, and the substitution of the subjunctive verb form for the indicative in the second edition. Where seemingly significant changes in wording, spelling, or punctuation do occur, I have tried to indicate them in a footnote. I have made no attempt to change Wollstonecraft's spelling or punctuation; the only corrections I have made in the text are either obvious printer's errors or instances where the words have had to be changed to render a passage readable. A list of these follow in the Note on the Text.

The annotation which I have provided is designed to aid the student in understanding topical references, many of which are unfamiliar to a modern audience. I have tried, as well, to document every quotation or reference used by Wollstonecraft. The book is, unfortunately, a veritable compendium of tag lines from other authors, and the quotations are often only half-remembered or even, it seems, deliberately rearranged to suit Wollstonecraft's needs. I have therefore provided, in some cases, what can only be termed an educated guess, while in other cases the sources seem quite certain. A few references still elude me, and I will continue to welcome any aid from readers in locating them.

The Backgrounds and Criticism sections have been compiled with an eye to representative source material and criticism from various time periods so that the student may fully appreciate the intellectual victory that Mary Wollstonecraft's book represents. In the Criticism section I have given all references to *A Vindication of the Rights of Woman* to the present edition for the reader's convenience. And finally, for those interested, there is a selected Bibliography which lists additional reading in Wollstonecraft, her biographers, and her critics.

In preparing this text I have been indebted to many people. My thanks go to the personnel of the Rare Book Room of the Library of Congress, the University of Maryland Library, and the University of Nebraska-Lincoln Library, where the staff of the Interlibrary Loan section and the efforts of librarians Robert Boyce and Ormond Summerville have been especially helpful. Professor Hugh Luke oversaw my project when it was still at the dissertation stage, and Professors Ralph Wardle, Gina Luria, and Gary Kelly have been generous in their advice. It would be impossible to enumerate all the other people who, at various times, lent me their expertise, but I especially note the work of Professors Frederick M. Link, Robert F. Anderson, and Nelson Potter, and of Mary Ann Gauthier. Perhaps it is especially appropriate here, in this book about women, to thank Shirley McRae and Kathryn Boe for hours of free mothering they provided my daughter while I worked; to Peggy Briggs, a creative and tireless typist and proofreader; and, finally, to Larry Poston, one of the most supportive feminists I know.

Lincoln, Nebraska   CAROL H. POSTON

Note on the Text

Despite the fact that most of the changes Wollstonecraft made for the second edition are probably not of great consequence, she deleted one long passage which is worth noting. In the Letter to Talleyrand in the first edition, Wollstonecraft had addressed the French politician with a mixture of deference and apology. After "to induce you to," the passage originally read:

> read it with attention; and because I think that you will understand me, which I do not suppose many pert witlings will, who may ridicule the arguments they are unable to answer. But, Sir, I carry my respect for your understanding still farther; so far, that I am confident you will not

throw my work aside, and hastily conclude that I am in the wrong, because you did not view the subject in the same light yourself.— And, pardon my frankness, but I must observe, that you treated it in too cursory a manner, continued to consider it as it had been considered formerly, when the rights of man, not to advert to woman, were trampled on as chimerical—I call upon you, therefore, now to

The first edition then ends the sentence in the same manner as the second: "weigh what I have advanced respecting the rights of woman, and national education." By the time of the second edition, perhaps buoyed by her success, Wollstonecraft was less deferential and, by revising the whole passage, was showing a firmer grip on her own prose style. Interested students will no doubt want to look at the first 1792 edition which is now available in a modern reprint series.

The text which follows reproduces faithfully the second edition save for the following instances:

p. 31: The sentence which begins "But if" (;) > (,) for sense.
p. 33: "condered" > "considered"
p. 48: "vicegerents" > "viceregents"
p. 53, note 5: restore "to" in the last line of the Barbauld poem
p. 55: "you sport" > "your sport"
p. 81: "it it" > "it is"
p. 82: provide close quote after "obedience"
p. 87: remove end quote after "error"
p. 101: add begin quote to 'They are free
p. 123, note 4: "conserved" > "conversed"
p. 131: "become" > "becomes"
p. 175: "participate the" > "participate in the"

Finally, nonsubstantive changes in styling have been made to bring the eighteenth-century text into conformity with modern printing practices.

The Text of

A VINDICATION OF THE RIGHTS OF WOMAN

with Strictures on
Political and Moral Subjects

Contents

To
M. Talleyrand-Périgord,[1]

Late Bishop Of Autun

SIR,

Having read with great pleasure a pamphlet which you have lately published,[2] I dedicate this volume to you; to induce you to reconsider the subject, and maturely weigh what I have advanced respecting the rights of woman and national education: and I call with the firm tone of humanity; for my arguments, Sir, are dictated by a disinterested spirit—I plead for my sex—not for myself. Independence I have long considered as the grand blessing of life, the basis of every virtue—and independence I will ever secure by contracting my wants, though I were to live on a barren heath.

It is then an affection for the whole human race that makes my pen dart rapidly along to support what I believe to be the cause of virtue: and the same motive leads me earnestly to wish to see woman placed in a station in which she would advance, instead of retarding, the progress of those glorious principles that give a substance to morality. My opinion, indeed, respecting the rights and duties of woman, seems to flow so naturally from these simple principles, that I think it scarcely possible, but that some of the enlarged minds who formed your admirable constitution, will coincide with me.[3]

In France there is undoubtedly a more general diffusion of knowledge than in any part of the European world, and I attribute it, in a great measure, to the social intercourse which has long subsisted between the sexes.[4] It is true, I utter my sentiments with freedom, that in France the very essence of sensuality has been extracted to regale the voluptuary, and a kind of sentimental lust has prevailed, which, together with the system of duplicity that the whole tenour

---

1. Charles Maurice de Talleyrand-Périgord (1754–1838), famous French diplomat who managed, by means of a brilliant mind and conniving personality, to make himself useful during some of the most tumultuous history in French politics.

He had given up the bishopric of Autun in January 1791 on the grounds that his political activities did not allow him time for his diocese, though he had visited it but once during his tenure as bishop. In April 1791 he was formally excommunicated from the Church, because, after having resigned his bishopric, he nonetheless ordained three new bishops.

2. Talleyrand's report on public education to the Constituent Assembly, *Rapport sur L'Instruction Publique, fait au nom du Comité de Constitution* (Paris, 1791). France's present system of compul-sory free education owes a great deal to the model recommended over 150 years ago by Talleyrand.

3. Parts of the French Constitution of 1791 had been ratified as early as 1789. It had been commissioned as a result of the Tennis Court Oath of June 20, 1789, when the National Assembly vowed not to dissolve until the country had a new constitution.

4. Wollstonecraft may have in mind the Paris *salons* which were ruled by brilliant and powerful women who, in Duff Cooper's words, "were the arbiters not only of elegance, but of ethics, of politics, and of all the arts. No man could rise to prominence except against the background of a salon, and over every salon a woman ruled" (*Talleyrand* [New York, 1932], p. 19).

of their political and civil government taught, have given a sinister sort of sagacity to the French character, properly termed finesse; from which naturally flow a polish of manners that injures the substance, by hunting sincerity out of society. —And, modesty, the fairest garb of virtue! has been more grossly insulted in France than even in England, till their women have treated as *prudish* that attention to decency, which brutes instinctively observe.[5]

Manners and morals are so nearly allied that they have often been confounded; but, though the former should only be the natural reflection of the latter, yet, when various causes have produced factitious and corrupt manners, which are very early caught, morality becomes an empty name. The personal reserve, and sacred respect for cleanliness and delicacy in domestic life, which French women almost despise, are the graceful pillars of modesty; but, far from despising them, if the pure flame of patriotism have reached their bosoms, they should labour to improve the morals of their fellow-citizens, by teaching men, not only to respect modesty in women, but to acquire it themselves, as the only way to merit their esteem.

Contending for the rights of woman, my main argument is built on this simple principle, that if she be not prepared by education to become the companion of man, she will stop the progress of knowledge and virtue; for truth must be common to all, or it will be inefficacious with respect to its influence on general practice. And how can woman be expected to co-operate unless she know why she ought to be virtuous? unless freedom strengthen her reason till she comprehend her duty, and see in what manner it is connected with her real good? If children are to be educated to understand the true principle of patriotism, their mother must be a patriot; and the love of mankind, from which an orderly train of virtues spring, can only be produced by considering the moral and civil interest of mankind; but the education and situation of woman, at present, shuts her out from such investigations.

In this work I have produced many arguments, which to me were conclusive, to prove that the prevailing notion respecting a sexual character was subversive of morality, and I have contended, that to render the human body and mind more perfect, chastity must more universally prevail, and that chastity will never be respected in the male world till the person of a woman is not, as it were, idolized, when little virtue or sense embellish it with the grand traces of mental beauty, or the interesting simplicity of affection.

Consider, Sir, dispassionately, these observations—for a glimpse of this truth seemed to open before you when you observed, 'that to see one half of the human race excluded by the other from all par-

---

5. The allusion is to sexual fidelity, if not monogamy, for "brutes" usually adhere to one mate at least long enough to raise the young. The French had no such scrupulosity.

ticipation of government, was a political phænomenon that, according to abstract principles, it was impossible to explain.'[6] If so, on what does your constitution rest?[7] If the abstract rights of man will bear discussion and explanation, those of woman, by a parity of reasoning, will not shrink from the same test: though a different opinion prevails in this country, built on the very arguments which you use to justify the oppression of woman—prescription.

Consider, I address you as a legislator, whether, when men contend for their freedom, and to be allowed to judge for themselves respecting their own happiness, it be not inconsistent and unjust to subjugate women, even though you firmly believe that you are acting in the manner best calculated to promote their happiness? Who made man the exclusive judge, if woman partake with him the gift of reason?

In this style, argue tyrants of every denomination, from the weak king to the weak father of a family; they are all eager to crush reason; yet always assert that they usurp its throne only to be useful. Do you not act a similar part, when you *force* all women, by denying them civil and political rights, to remain immured in their families groping in the dark? for surely, Sir, you will not assert, that a duty can be binding which is not founded on reason? If indeed this be their destination, arguments may be drawn from reason: and thus augustly supported, the more understanding women acquire, the more they will be attached to their duty—comprehending it— for unless they comprehend it, unless their morals be fixed on the same immutable principle as those of man, no authority can make them discharge it in a virtuous manner. They may be convenient slaves, but slavery will have its constant effect, degrading the master and the abject dependent.

But, if women are to be excluded, without having a voice, from a participation of the natural rights of mankind, prove first, to ward off the charge of injustice and inconsistency, that they want reason —else this flaw in your NEW CONSTITUTION will ever shew that man must, in some shape, act like a tyrant, and tyranny, in whatever part of society it rears its brazen front, will ever undermine morality.

I have repeatedly asserted, and produced what appeared to me irrefragable arguments drawn from matters of fact, to prove my assertion, that women cannot, by force, be confined to domestic concerns; for they will, however ignorant, intermeddle with more weighty affairs, neglecting private duties only to disturb, by cunning tricks, the orderly plans of reason which rise above their comprehension.

6. Possibly a liberal translation from Talleyrand's *Rapport, op. cit.*, p. 9: "sur quel principe l'un des deux pourroit-il en être déshérité par la Societé protectrice des droits de tous?"

7. In France's Constitution of 1791 only males over twenty-five were citizens. Women were not to get the vote until 1944.

Besides, whilst they are only made to acquire personal accomplishments, men will seek for pleasure in variety, and faithless husbands will make faithless wives; such ignorant beings, indeed, will be very excusable when, not taught to respect public good, nor allowed any civil rights, they attempt to do themselves justice by retaliation.

The box of mischief thus opened in society,[8] what is to preserve private virtue, the only security of public freedom and universal happiness?

Let there be then no coercion *established* in society, and the common law of gravity prevailing, the sexes will fall into their proper places. And, now that more equitable laws are forming your citizens, marriage may become more sacred: your young men may choose wives from motives of affection, and your maidens allow love to root out vanity.

The father of a family will not then weaken his constitution and debase his sentiments, by visiting the harlot, nor forget, in obeying the call of appetite, the purpose for which it was implanted. And, the mother will not neglect her children to practise the arts of coquetry, when sense and modesty secure her the friendship of her husband.

But, till men become attentive to the duty of a father, it is vain to expect women to spend that time in their nursery which they, 'wise in their generation,'[9] choose to spend at their glass; for this exertion of cunning is only an instinct of nature to enable them to obtain indirectly a little of that power of which they are unjustly denied a share: for, if women are not permitted to enjoy legitimate rights, they will render both men and themselves vicious, to obtain illicit privileges.

I wish, Sir, to set some investigations of this kind afloat in France; and should they lead to a confirmation of my principles, when your constitution is revised the Rights of Woman may be respected, if it be fully proved that reason calls for this respect, and loudly demands JUSTICE for one half of the human race.

> I am, SIR,
> Your's respectfully,
> M. W.

Advertisement

When I began to write this work, I divided it into three parts, supposing that one volume would contain a full discussion of the

8. In Greek myth Pandora was the first woman. Out of curiosity she opened the box containing all the evils of humankind, thus loosing them on the world.

9. Luke 16:8: "For the children of this world are in their generation wiser than the children of light."

arguments which seemed to me to rise naturally from a few simple principles; but fresh illustrations occurring as I advanced, I now present only the first part to the public.

Many subjects, however, which I have cursorily alluded to, call for particular investigation, especially the laws relative to women, and the consideration of their peculiar duties. These will furnish ample matter for a second volume, which in due time will be published, to elucidate some of the sentiments, and complete many of the sketches begun in the first.[1]

Introduction

After considering the historic page, and viewing the living world with anxious solicitude, the most melancholy emotions of sorrowful indignation have depressed my spirits, and I have sighed when obliged to confess, that either nature has made a great difference between man and man, or that the civilization which has hitherto taken place in the world has been very partial. I have turned over various books written on the subject of education, and patiently observed the conduct of parents and the management of schools; but what has been the result?—a profound conviction that the neglected education of my fellow-creatures is the grand source of the misery I deplore; and that women, in particular, are rendered weak and wretched by a variety of concurring causes, originating from one hasty conclusion. The conduct and manners of women, in fact, evidently prove that their minds are not in a healthy state; for, like the flowers which are planted in too rich a soil, strength and usefulness are sacrificed to beauty; and the flaunting leaves, after having pleased a fastidious eye, fade, disregarded on the stalk, long before the season when they ought to have arrived at maturity.—One cause of this barren blooming I attribute to a false system of education, gathered from the books written on this subject by men who, considering females rather as women than human creatures, have been more anxious to make them alluring mistresses than affectionate wives and rational mothers; and the understanding of the sex has been so bubbled by this specious homage, that the civilized women of the present century, with a few exceptions, are only anxious to inspire love, when they ought to cherish a nobler ambition, and by their abilities and virtues exact respect.

In a treatise, therefore, on female rights and manners, the works which have been particularly written for their improvement must not be overlooked; especially when it is asserted, in direct terms, that the minds of women are enfeebled by false refinement; that

---

1. Only one volume was ever published, and so far as is known from Wollstonecraft's papers, she never began the other volume.

the books of instruction, written by men of genius, have had the same tendency as more frivolous productions; and that, in the true style of Mahometanism, they are treated as a kind of subordinate beings,[2] and not as a part of the human species, when improveable reason is allowed to be the dignified distinction which raises men above the brute creation, and puts a natural sceptre in a feeble hand.

Yet, because I am a woman, I would not lead my readers to suppose that I mean violently to agitate the contested question respecting the equality or inferiority of the sex; but as the subject lies in my way, and I cannot pass it over without subjecting the main tendency of my reasoning to misconstruction, I shall stop a moment to deliver, in a few words, my opinion.—In the government of the physical world it is observable that the female in point of strength is, in general, inferior to the male. This is the law of nature; and it does not appear to be suspended or abrogated in favour of woman. A degree of physical superiority cannot, therefore, be denied—and it is a noble prerogative![3] But not content with this natural pre-eminence, men endeavour to sink us still lower, merely to render us alluring objects for a moment; and women, intoxicated by the adoration which men, under the influence of their senses, pay them, do not seek to obtain a durable interest in their hearts, or to become the friends of the fellow creatures who find amusement in their society.

I am aware of an obvious inference: —from every quarter have I heard exclamations against masculine women; but where are they to be found? If by this appellation men mean to inveigh against their ardour in hunting, shooting, and gaming, I shall most cordially join in the cry; but if it be against the imitation of manly virtues, or, more properly speaking, the attainment of those talents and virtues, the exercise of which ennobles the human character, and which raise females in the scale of animal being, when they are comprehensively termed mankind;—all those who view them with a philosophic eye must, I should think, wish with me, that they may every day grow more and more masculine.

This discussion naturally divides the subject. I shall first consider women in the grand light of human creatures, who, in common with men, are placed on this earth to unfold their faculties; and afterwards I shall more particularly point out their peculiar designation.

---

2. In the Mohammedan religion women did not have souls and were not permitted an afterlife.
3. First edition reads ". . . the female, in general, is inferior to the male. The male pursues, the female yields—this is the law of nature; and it does not appear to be suspended or abrogated in favour of woman. This physical superiority cannot be denied—and it is noble prerogative!"

I wish also to steer clear of an error which many respectable writers have fallen into; for the instruction which has hitherto been addressed to women, has rather been applicable to *ladies*, if the little indirect advice, that is scattered through Sandford and Merton,[4] be excepted; but, addressing my sex in a firmer tone, I pay particular attention to those in the middle class, because they appear to be in the most natural state.[5] Perhaps the seeds of false-refinement, immorality, and vanity, have ever been shed by the great. Weak, artificial beings, raised above the common wants and affections of their race, in a premature unnatural manner, undermine the very foundation of virtue, and spread corruption through the whole mass of society! As a class of mankind they have the strongest claim to pity; the education of the rich tends to render them vain and helpless, and the unfolding mind is not strengthened by the practice of those duties which dignify the human character. —They only live to amuse themselves, and by the same law which in nature invariably produces certain effects, they soon only afford barren amusement.

But as I purpose taking a separate view of the different ranks of society, and of the moral character of women, in each, this hint is, for the present, sufficient; and I have only alluded to the subject, because it appears to me to be the very essence of an introduction to give a cursory account of the contents of the work it introduces.

My own sex, I hope, will excuse me, if I treat them like rational creatures, instead of flattering their *fascinating* graces, and viewing them as if they were in a state of perpetual childhood, unable to stand alone. I earnestly wish to point out in what true dignity and human happiness consists—I wish to persuade women to endeavour to acquire strength, both of mind and body, and to convince them that the soft phrases, susceptibility of heart, delicacy of sentiment, and refinement of taste, are almost synonymous with epithets of weakness, and that those beings who are only the objects of pity and that kind of love, which has been termed its sister, will soon become objects of contempt.

Dismissing then those pretty feminine phrases, which the men condescendingly use to soften our slavish dependence, and despising that weak elegancy of mind, exquisite sensibility, and sweet docility of manners, supposed to be the sexual characteristics of the weaker vessel, I wish to shew that elegance is inferior to virtue, that the first object of laudable ambition is to obtain a character as a human

---

4. *Sandford and Merton*, by Thomas Day (London, published in three volumes, 1786–89), is the story of Tommy Merton, a spoiled wealthy child, who is befriended by Harry Sandford, a poor but principled lad. Their instruction by the tutor, Mr. Barlow, often includes moral tales, one of which is mentioned approvingly by Wollstonecraft in Chapter III.

5. "Natural" here suggests that the middle classes had not been corrupted by generations of titles, property, and wealth and were thus, as Addison and Steele also asserted, the most educable class.

being, regardless of the distinction of sex; and that secondary views should be brought to this simple touchstone.

This is a rough sketch of my plan; and should I express my conviction with the energetic emotions that I feel whenever I think of the subject, the dictates of experience and reflection will be felt by some of my readers. Animated by this important object, I shall disdain to cull my phrases or polish my style;—I aim at being useful, and sincerity will render me unaffected; for, wishing rather to persuade by the force of my arguments, than dazzle by the elegance of my language, I shall not waste my time in rounding periods,[6] or in fabricating the turgid bombast of artificial feelings, which, coming from the head, never reach the heart.—I shall be employed about things, not words!—and, anxious to render my sex more respectable members of society, I shall try to avoid that flowery diction which has slided from essays into novels, and from novels into familiar letters and conversation.

These pretty superlatives, dropping glibly from the tongue, vitiate the taste, and create a kind of sickly delicacy that turns away from simple unadorned truth; and a deluge of false sentiments and over-stretched feelings, stifling the natural emotions of the heart, render the domestic pleasures insipid, that ought to sweeten the exercise of those severe duties, which educate a rational and immortal being for a nobler field of action.

The education of women has, of late, been more attended to than formerly; yet they are still reckoned a frivolous sex, and ridiculed or pitied by the writers who endeavour by satire or instruction to improve them. It is acknowledged that they spend many of the first years of their lives in acquiring a smattering of accomplishments; meanwhile strength of body and mind are sacrificed to libertine notions of beauty, to the desire of establishing themselves,— the only way women can rise in the world,—by marriage. And this desire making mere animals of them, when they marry they act as such children may be expected to act:—they dress; they paint, and nickname God's creatures.[7]—Surely these weak beings are only fit for a seraglio!—Can they be expected to govern a family with judgment, or take care of the poor babes whom they bring into the world?

If then it can be fairly deduced from the present conduct of the sex, from the prevalent fondness for pleasure which takes place of ambition and those nobler passions that open and enlarge the soul; that the instruction which women have hitherto received has only tended, with the constitution of civil society, to render them insig-

---

6. Formulating balanced sentences.
7. Hamlet speaks to Ophelia: "You jig, you amble, and you lisp, and nickname God's creatures, and make your wantonness your ignorance." *Hamlet* III.i.150.

nificant objects of desire—mere propagators of fools!—if it can be proved that in aiming to accomplish them, without cultivating their understandings, they are taken out of their sphere of duties, and made ridiculous and useless when the short-lived bloom of beauty is over,[8] I presume that *rational* men will excuse me for endeavouring to persuade them to become more masculine and respectable.

Indeed the word masculine is only a bugbear: there is little reason to fear that women will acquire too much courage or fortitude; for their apparent inferiority with respect to bodily strength, must render them, in some degree, dependent on men in the various relations of life; but why should it be increased by prejudices that give a sex to virtue, and confound simple truths with sensual reveries?

Women are, in fact, so much degraded by mistaken notions of female excellence, that I do not mean to add a paradox when I assert, that this artificial weakness produces a propensity to tyrannize, and gives birth to cunning, the natural opponent of strength, which leads them to play off those contemptible infantine airs that undermine esteem even whilst they excite desire. Let men become more chaste and modest, and if women do not grow wiser in the same ratio, it will be clear that they have weaker understandings. It seems scarcely necessary to say, that I now speak of the sex in general. Many individuals have more sense than their male relatives; and, as nothing preponderates where there is a constant struggle for an equilibrium, without it has[9] naturally more gravity, some women govern their husbands without degrading themselves, because intellect will always govern.

Chap. I

The Rights and Involved Duties of Mankind Considered

In the present state of society it appears necessary to go back to first principles in search of the most simple truths, and to dispute with some prevailing prejudice every inch of ground. To clear my way, I must be allowed to ask some plain questions, and the answers will probably appear as unequivocal as the axioms on which reasoning is built; though, when entangled with various motives of action, they are formally contradicted, either by the words or conduct of men.

---

8. "A lively writer, I cannot recollect his name, asks what business women turned of forty have to do in the world?" [Wollstonecraft's note]. Perhaps Wollstonecraft is referring to a passage in Fanny Burney's popular novel *Evelina* spoken by the li- centious Lord Merton: "I don't know what the devil a woman lives for after thirty: she is only in other folks' way" (*Evelina* [London and New York, 1958], p. 253).

9. We would probably say, "without its having."

In what does man's pre-eminence over the brute creation consist? The answer is as clear as that a half is less than the whole; in Reason.

What acquirement exalts one being above another? Virtue; we spontaneously reply.

For what purpose were the passions implanted? That man by struggling with them might attain a degree of knowledge denied to the brutes; whispers Experience.

Consequently the perfection of our nature and capability of happiness, must be estimated by the degree of reason, virtue, and knowledge, that distinguish the individual, and direct the laws which bind society: and that from the exercise of reason, knowledge and virtue naturally flow, is equally undeniable, if mankind be viewed collectively.

The rights and duties of man thus simplified, it seems almost impertinent to attempt to illustrate truths that appear so incontrovertible; yet such deeply rooted prejudices have clouded reason, and such spurious qualities have assumed the name of virtues, that it is necessary to pursue the course of reason as it has been perplexed and involved in error, by various adventitious circumstances, comparing the simple axiom with casual deviations.

Men, in general, seem to employ their reason to justify prejudices, which they have imbibed, they can scarcely trace how, rather than to root them out. The mind must be strong that resolutely forms its own principles; for a kind of intellectual cowardice prevails which makes many men shrink from the task, or only do it by halves. Yet the imperfect conclusions thus drawn, are frequently very plausible, because they are built on partial experience, on just, though narrow, views.

Going back to first principles, vice skulks, with all its native deformity, from close investigation; but a set of shallow reasoners are always exclaiming that these arguments[1] prove too much, and that a measure rotten at the core may be expedient. Thus expediency is continually contrasted with simple principles, till truth is lost in a mist of words, virtue, in forms, and knowledge rendered a sounding nothing, by the specious prejudices that assume its name.

That the society is formed in the wisest manner, whose constitution is founded on the nature of man,[2] strikes, in the abstract, every thinking being so forcibly, that it looks like presumption to endeavour to bring forward proofs; though proof must be brought, or the strong hold of prescription will never be forced by reason; yet to urge prescription as an argument to justify the depriving men (or

---

1. Those based on principled reason. 2. The nature of human beings is to be rational.

women) of their natural rights, is one of the absurd sophisms which daily insult common sense.

The civilization of the bulk of the people of Europe is very partial; nay, it may be made a question, whether they have acquired any virtues in exchange for innocence, equivalent to the misery produced by the vices that have been plastered over unsightly ignorance, and the freedom which has been bartered for splendid slavery. The desire of dazzling by riches, the most certain pre-eminence that man can obtain, the pleasure of commanding flattering sycophants, and many other complicated low calculations of doting self-love, have all contributed to overwhelm the mass of mankind, and make liberty a convenient handle for mock patriotism. For whilst rank and titles are held of the utmost importance, before which Genius "must hide its diminished head,"[3] it is, with a few exceptions, very unfortunate for a nation when a man of abilities, without rank or property, pushes himself forward to notice.—Alas! what unheard of misery have thousands suffered to purchase a cardinal's hat for an intriguing obscure adventurer, who longed to be ranked with princes, or lord it over them by seizing the triple crown![4]

Such, indeed, has been the wretchedness that has flowed from hereditary honours, riches, and monarchy, that men of lively sensibility have almost uttered blasphemy in order to justify the dispensations of providence. Man has been held out as independent of his power who made him, or as a lawless planet darting from its orbit to steal the celestial fire of reason; and the vengeance of heaven, lurking in the subtile flame, like Pandora's pent up mischiefs,[5] sufficiently punished his temerity, by introducing evil into the world.

Impressed by this view of the misery and disorder which pervaded society, and fatigued with jostling against artificial fools, Rousseau became enamoured of solitude, and, being at the same time an optimist, he labours with uncommon eloquence to prove that man was naturally a solitary animal.[6] Misled by his respect for the goodness of God, who certainly—for what man of sense and feeling can doubt it!—gave life only to communicate happiness, he considers

---

3. Milton, *Paradise Lost* IV.34–35: "At whose sight all the stars / Hide their diminish'd heads."

4. Cardinal Dubois (1656–1723) was the chief advisor to Louis XV; the "triple crown" is the traditional tiara worn by popes, suggesting Dubois's papal ambitions.

5. In Greek myth Prometheus stole fire to give to man, even though Zeus had forbidden it. Zeus' revenge was to give man Pandora, the first woman, who soon proved man's downfall by opening the box containing all the world's ills.

6. Jean Jacques Rousseau (1712–78), French philosopher, had one of the seminal minds of the eighteenth century. In his second essay, "A Discourse on the Origin of Inequality," Rousseau describes the state of nature as necessarily solitary; man inevitably grows more wicked as he grows more sociable. In the personal sphere, Rousseau himself preferred solitude, partly out of shyness, partly because of a urinary tract ailment. Book IX of the *Confessions* details the most joyful—and solitary—time of his life, at the Hermitage of Madame d'Épinay.

evil as positive, and the work of man; not aware that he was exalting one attribute at the expence of another, equally necessary to divine perfection.[7]

Reared on a false hypothesis his arguments in favour of a state of nature are plausible, but unsound. I say unsound; for to assert that a state of nature is preferable to civilization, in all its possible perfection, is, in other words, to arraign supreme wisdom; and the paradoxical exclamation, that God has made all things right, and that error has been introduced by the creature, whom he formed, knowing what he formed, is as unphilosophical as impious.[8]

When that wise Being who created us and placed us here, saw the fair idea, he willed, by allowing it to be so, that the passions should unfold our reason, because he could see that present evil would produce future good. Could the helpless creature whom he called from nothing break loose from his providence, and boldly learn to know good by practising evil, without his permission? No. —How could that energetic advocate for immortality[9] argue so inconsistently? Had mankind remained for ever in the brutal state of nature, which even his magic pen cannot paint as a state in which a single virtue took root, it would have been clear, though not to the sensitive unreflecting wanderer, that man was born to run the circle of life and death, and adorn God's garden for some purpose which could not easily be reconciled with his attributes.

But if, to crown the whole, there were to be rational creatures produced, allowed to rise in excellence by the exercise of powers implanted for that purpose; if benignity itself thought fit to call into existence a creature above the brutes,[1] who could think and improve himself, why should that inestimable gift, for a gift it was, if man was so created as to have a capacity to rise above the state in which sensation produced brutal ease, be called, in direct terms, a curse? A curse it might be reckoned, if the whole of our existence were bounded by our continuance in this world; for why should the

7. For Rousseau God is consummate goodness, so evil has to be man-made, a product of human society; it is "positive" because humans can choose to do evil or good by virtue of free will. Wollstonecraft takes the view that God is not only good but omniscient: while He could see that man would sin, He did not actually set it up for him to do so. Rousseau, then, exalts God's benevolence over His omniscience.
8. Rousseau's *Émile* begins: "God makes all things good; man meddles with them and they become evil." Jean Jacques Rousseau, *Émile*, trans. Barbara Foxley (London, 1911), p. 5. All future references are to this edition.

9. Rousseau, that is. His religious beliefs are found in "The Creed of a Savoyard Priest" in Book IV, *Émile*.
1. "Contrary to the opinion of anatomists, who argue by analogy from the formation of the teeth, stomach, and intestines, Rousseau will not allow a man to be a carnivorous animal. And, carried away from nature by a love of system, he disputes whether man be a gregarious animal, though the long and helpless state of infancy seems to point him out as particularly impelled to pair, the first step towards herding" [Wollstonecraft's note]. *Émile*, pp. 118–20 and 182.

gracious fountain of life give us passions, and the power of reflecting, only to imbitter our days and inspire us with mistaken notions of dignity? Why should he lead us from love of ourselves to the sublime emotions which the discovery of his wisdom and goodness excites, if these feelings were not set in motion to improve our nature, of which they make a part,[2] and render us capable of enjoying a more godlike portion of happiness? Firmly persuaded that no evil exists in the world that God did not design to take place, I build my belief on the perfection of God.

Rousseau exerts himself to prove that all *was* right originally: a crowd of authors that all *is* now right: and I, that all will *be* right.

But, true to his first position, next to a state of nature, Rousseau celebrates barbarism, and apostrophizing the shade of Fabricius,[3] he forgets that, in conquering the world, the Romans never dreamed of establishing their own liberty on a firm basis, or of extending the reign of virtue. Eager to support his system, he stigmatizes, as vicious, every effort of genius; and, uttering the apotheosis of savage virtues, he exalts those to demi-gods, who were scarcely human— the brutal Spartans,[4] who, in defiance of justice and gratitude, sacrificed, in cold blood, the slaves who had shewn themselves heroes to rescue their oppressors.

Disgusted with artificial manners and virtues, the citizen of Geneva,[5] instead of properly sifting the subject, threw away the wheat with the chaff, without waiting to inquire whether the evils which his ardent soul turned from indignantly, were the consequence of civilization or the vestiges of barbarism. He saw vice tramping on virtue, and the semblance of goodness taking place of the reality; he saw talents bent by power to sinister purposes, and never thought of tracing the gigantic mischief up to arbitrary power, up to the hereditary distinctions that clash with the mental superiority that naturally raises a man above his fellows. He did not

2. "What would you say to a mechanic whom you had desired to make a watch to point out the hour of the day, if, to show his ingenuity, he added wheels to make it a repeater, &c. that perplexed the simple mechanism; should he urge, to excuse himself—had you not touched a certain spring, you would have known nothing of the matter, and that he should have amused himself by making *an experiment* without doing you any harm: would you not retort fairly upon him, by insisting that if he had not added those needless wheels and springs, the accident could not have happened?" [Wollstonecraft's note]. It would be unthinkable that God would give human beings the ability to reason to his power and beauty if they were, at the end, to be mortal. God's perfect plan includes mankind's

discovery and use of reason to reach for—though never attain—godlike happiness. Because God gave man free will, however, error and evil exist.
3. In Rousseau's first work, *A Discourse on the Sciences and the Arts* (1750), he resurrects the ghost of Gaius Fabricius (3rd century B.C.) who criticizes the effeminacy of late Rome and urges its citizens to return to the business of conquering the world. Fabricius was an exemplar of the virtue of incorruptibility; he would not be bribed in public office.
4. Rousseau, in the discourse cited above, hails Sparta because it banished the arts and castigates Athens for harboring the learned.
5. Rousseau, that is: he was born in Geneva in 1712.

perceive that regal power, in a few generations, introduces idiotism into the noble stem, and holds out baits to render thousands idle and vicious.

Nothing can set the regal character in a more contemptible point of view, than the various crimes that have elevated men to the supreme dignity.—Vile intrigues, unnatural crimes, and every vice that degrades our nature, have been the steps to this distinguished eminence; yet millions of men have supinely allowed the nerveless limbs of the posterity of such rapacious prowlers to rest quietly on their ensanguined thrones.[6]

What but a pestilential vapour can hover over society when its chief director is only instructed in the invention of crimes, or the stupid routine of childish ceremonies? Will men never be wise?—will they never cease to expect corn from tares, and figs from thistles?[7]

It is impossible for any man, when the most favourable circumstances concur, to acquire sufficient knowledge and strength of mind to discharge the duties of a king, entrusted with uncontrouled power; how then must they be violated when his very elevation is an insuperable bar to the attainment of either wisdom or virtue; when all the feelings of a man are stifled by flattery, and reflection shut out by pleasure! Surely it is madness to make the fate of thousands depend on the caprice of a weak fellow creature, whose very station sinks him *necessarily* below the meanest of his subjects! But one power should not be thrown down to exalt another—for all power inebriates weak man; and its abuse proves that the more equality there is established among men, the more virtue and happiness will reign in society. But this and any similar maxim deduced from simple reason, raises an outcry—the church or the state is in danger, if faith in the wisdom of antiquity is not implicit; and they who, roused by the sight of human calamity, dare to attack human authority, are reviled as despisers of God, and enemies of man. These are bitter calumnies, yet they reached one of the best of

6. "Could there be a greater insult offered to the rights of man than the beds of justice in France, when an infant was made the organ of the detestable Dubois!" [Wollstonecraft's note]. "Beds of justice" are the *lits de justice,* the solemn meeting of king and Parliament in France to determine common policy. The "infant" Wollstonecraft is referring to is Philippe, Duc d'Orleans, who became regent of France in 1715 until Louis XV (who had become king at five) came of age. The regent's chief adviser and former tutor was Guillaume Dubois (1656–1723), a politically sophisticated religious who later became a cardinal. Wollstonecraft

had reviewed *Vie Privée du Cardinal Dubois* in August, 1789, and had said of the Cardinal's influence on the future regent: "So little alive was he to the restriction of conscience, so dead to the voice of honour, that he indulged the Duke in his favourite vice, an unbridled passion for women" (*Analytical Review,* IV, 405).
7. Matthew 7:16. "Ye shall know them by their fruits. Do men gather grapes of thorns, or figs of thistles?" and Luke 6:44: "For every tree is known by his own fruit. For of thorns men do not gather figs, nor of a bramble bush gather they grapes." ("Tares" are weeds.)

men,[8] whose ashes still preach peace, and whose memory demands a respectful pause, when subjects are discussed that lay so near his heart.—

After attacking the sacred majesty of Kings, I shall scarcely excite surprise by adding my firm persuasion that every profession, in which great subordination of rank constitutes its power, is highly injurious to morality.

A standing army, for instance, is incompatible with freedom; because subordination and rigour are the very sinews of military discipline; and despotism is necessary to give vigour to enterprizes that one will directs. A spirit inspired by romantic notions of honour, a kind of morality founded on the fashion of the age, can only be felt by a few officers, whilst the main body must be moved by command, like the waves of the sea; for the strong wind of authority pushes the crowd of subalterns forward, they scarcely know or care why, with headlong fury.

Besides, nothing can be so prejudicial to the morals of the inhabitants of country towns as the occasional residence of a set of idle superficial young men, whose only occupation is gallantry, and whose polished manners render vice more dangerous, by concealing its deformity under gay ornamental drapery. An air of fashion, which is but a badge of slavery, and proves that the soul has not a strong individual character, awes simple country people into an imitation of the vices, when they cannot catch the slippery graces, of politeness. Every corps is a chain of despots, who, submitting and tyrannizing without exercising their reason, become dead weights of vice and folly on the community. A man of rank or fortune, sure of rising by interest, has nothing to do but to pursue some extravagant freak; whilst the needy *gentleman*, who is to rise, as the phrase turns, by his merit, becomes a servile parasite or vile pander.

Sailors, the naval gentlemen, come under the same description, only their vices assume a different and a grosser cast. They are more positively indolent, when not discharging the ceremonials of their station; whilst the insignificant fluttering of soldiers may be termed active idleness. More confined to the society of men, the former acquire a fondness for humour and mischievous tricks; whilst the latter, mixing frequently with well-bred women, catch a sentimental cant.—But mind is equally out of the question, whether they indulge the horse-laugh, or polite simper.

May I be allowed to extend the comparison to a profession where more mind is certainly to be found; for the clergy have superior

8. "Dr. Price" [Wollstonecraft's note]. A friend of Wollstonecraft's and a minister, Dr. Richard Price (1723–91) was a well-known moral and political philosopher and advocate of the American colonial cause.

opportunities of improvement, though subordination almost equally cramps their faculties? The blind submission imposed at college to forms of belief serves as a novitiate to the curate, who must obsequiously respect the opinion of his rector or patron, if he mean to rise in his profession. Perhaps there cannot be a more forcible contrast than between the servile dependent gait of a poor curate and the courtly mien of a bishop. And the respect and contempt they inspire render the discharge of their separate functions equally useless.

It is of great importance to observe that the character of every man is, in some degree, formed by his profession. A man of sense may only have a cast of countenance that wears off as you trace his individuality, whilst the weak, common man has scarcely ever any character, but what belongs to the body; at least, all his opinions have been so steeped in the vat consecrated by authority, that the faint spirit which the grape of his own vine yields cannot be distinguished.

Society, therefore, as it becomes more enlightened, should be very careful not to establish bodies of men who must necessarily be made foolish or vicious by the very constitution of their profession.

In the infancy of society, when men were just emerging out of barbarism, chiefs and priests, touching the most powerful springs of savage conduct, hope and fear, must have had unbounded sway. An aristocracy, of course, is naturally the first form of government. But, clashing interests soon losing their equipoise, a monarchy and hierarchy break out of the confusion of ambitious struggles, and the foundation of both is secured by feudal tenures. This appears to be the origin of monarchical and priestly power, and the dawn of civilization. But such combustible materials cannot long be pent up; and, getting vent in foreign wars and intestine insurrections,[9] the people acquire some power in tumult, which obliges their rulers to gloss over their oppression with a shew of right. Thus, as wars, agriculture, commerce, and literature, expand the mind, despots are compelled, to make covert corruption hold fast the power which was formerly snatched by open force.[1] And this baneful lurking gangrene is most quickly spread by luxury and superstition, the sure dregs of ambition. The indolent puppet of a court first becomes a luxurious monster, or fastidious sensualist, and then makes the contagion which his unnatural state spread, the instrument of tyranny.

It is the pestiferous purple[2] which renders the progress of civilization a curse, and warps the understanding, till men of sensibility

9. Internal strife.
1. "Men of abilities scatter seeds that grow up and have a great influence on the forming opinion; and when once the public opinion preponderates, through the exertion of reason, the overthrow of arbitrary power is not very distant" [Wollstonecraft's note].
2. The color of royalty or high rank.

doubt whether the expansion of intellect produces a greater portion of happiness or misery. But the nature of the poison points out the antidote; and had Rousseau mounted one step higher in his investigation, or could his eye have pierced through the foggy atmosphere, which he almost disdained to breathe, his active mind would have darted forward to contemplate the perfection of man in the establishment of true civilization, instead of taking his ferocious flight back to the night of sensual ignorance.

Chap. II

The Prevailing Opinion of a Sexual Character Discussed

To account for, and excuse the tyranny of man, many ingenious arguments have been brought forward to prove, that the two sexes, in the acquirement of virtue, ought to aim at attaining a very different character: or, to speak explicitly, women are not allowed to have sufficient strength of mind to acquire what really deserves the name of virtue. Yet it should seem, allowing them to have souls, that there is but one way appointed by Providence to lead *mankind* to either virtue or happiness.

If then women are not a swarm of ephemeron triflers, why should they be kept in ignorance under the specious name of innocence? Men complain, and with reason, of the follies and caprices of our sex, when they do not keenly satirize our headstrong passions and groveling vices. —Behold, I should answer, the natural effect of ignorance! The mind will ever be unstable that has only prejudices to rest on, and the current will run with destructive fury when there are no barriers to break its force. Women are told from their infancy, and taught by the example of their mothers, that a little knowledge of human weakness, justly termed cunning, softness of temper, *outward* obedience, and a scrupulous attention to a puerile kind of propriety, will obtain for them the protection of man; and should they be beautiful, every thing else is needless, for, at least, twenty years of their lives.

Thus Milton describes our first frail mother; though when he tells us that women are formed for softness and sweet attractive grace,[1] I cannot comprehend his meaning, unless, in the true Mahometan strain, he meant to deprive us of souls,[2] and insinuate that we were beings only designed by sweet attractive grace, and docile blind obedience, to gratify the senses of man when he can no longer soar on the wing of contemplation.

1. *Paradise Lost* IV.297–99: "For contemplation he and valor form'd, / For softness she and sweet attractive grace; / He for God only, she for God in him."

2. Islam (the religion whose chief prophet was Mohammed) did not allow women to go to heaven and denied them souls.

How grossly do they insult us who thus advise us only to render ourselves gentle, domestic brutes! For instance, the winning softness so warmly, and frequently, recommended, that governs by obeying. What childish expressions, and how insignificant is the being—can it be an immortal one? who will condescend to govern by such sinister methods! 'Certainly,' says Lord Bacon, 'man is of kin to the beasts by his body; and if he be not of kin to God by his spirit, he is a base and ignoble creature!'[3] Men, indeed, appear to me to act in a very unphilosophical manner when they try to secure the good conduct of women by attempting to keep them always in a state of childhood. Rousseau was more consistent when he wished to stop the progress of reason in both sexes, for if men eat of the tree of knowledge, women will come in for a taste; but, from the imperfect cultivation which their understandings now receive, they only attain a knowledge of evil. [4]

Children, I grant, should be innocent; but when the epithet is applied to men, or women, it is but a civil term for weakness. For if it be allowed that women were destined by Providence to acquire human virtues, and by the exercise of their understandings, that stability of character which is the firmest ground to rest our future hopes upon, they must be permitted to turn to the fountain of light, and not forced to shape their course by the twinkling of a mere satellite. Milton, I grant, was of a very different opinion; for he only bends to the indefeasible right of beauty, though it would be difficult to render two passages which I now mean to contrast, consistent. But into similar inconsistencies are great men often led by their senses.

'To whom thus Eve with *perfect beauty* adorn'd.
'My Author and Disposer, what thou bidst
'*Unargued* I obey; So God ordains;
'God is *thy law, thou mine:* to know no more
'Is Woman's *happiest* knowledge and her *praise.*'[5]

These are exactly the arguments that I have used to children; but I have added, your reason is now gaining strength, and, till it arrives at some degree of maturity, you must look up to me for advice—then you ought to *think*, and only rely on God.

Yet in the following lines Milton seems to coincide with me; when he makes Adam thus expostulate with his Maker.

'Hast thou not made me here thy substitute,
'And these inferior far beneath me set?
'Among *unequals* what society

<hr>

3. Francis Bacon, Essay XVI, "Of Atheism."
4. Both Adam and Eve ate the fruit from the tree of knowledge of good and evil in the garden of Eden. In the fallen state both men and women need to work at virtue, but according to Wollstone-craft, women have been denied the education, and thus the means, to attain it.
5. *Paradise Lost* IV.634–38. The italics are Wollstonecraft's.

'Can sort, what harmony or true delight?
'Which must be mutual, in proportion due
'Giv'n and receiv'd; but in *disparity*
'The one intense, the other still remiss
'Cannot well suit with either, but soon prove
'Tedious alike: of *fellowship* I speak
'Such as I seek, fit to participate
'All rational delight— [6]

In treating, therefore, of the manners of women, let us, disregarding sensual arguments, trace what we should endeavour to make them in order to co-operate, if the expression be not too bold, with the supreme Being.

By individual education, I mean, for the sense of the word is not precisely defined, such an attention to a child as will slowly sharpen the senses, form the temper, regulate the passions as they begin to ferment, and set the understanding to work before the body arrives at maturity; so that the man may only have to proceed, not to begin, the important task of learning to think and reason.

To prevent any misconstruction, I must add, that I do not believe that a private education can work the wonders which some sanguine writers have attributed to it. Men and women must be educated, in a great degree, by the opinions and manners of the society they live in. In every age there has been a stream of popular opinion that has carried all before it, and given a family character, as it were, to the century. It may then fairly be inferred, that, till society be differently constituted, much cannot be expected from education. It is, however, sufficient for my present purpose to assert, that, whatever effect circumstances have on the abilities, every being may become virtuous by the exercise of its own reason; for if but one being was created with vicious inclinations, that is positively bad, what can save us from atheism? or if we worship a God, is not that God a devil?

Consequently, the most perfect education, in my opinion, is such an exercise of the understanding as is best calculated to strengthen the body and form the heart. Or, in other words, to enable the individual to attain such habits of virtue as will render it independent. In fact, it is a farce to call any being virtuous whose virtues do not result from the exercise of its own reason. This was Rousseau's opinion respecting men: I extend it to women, and confidently assert that they have been drawn out of their sphere by false refinement, and not by an endeavour to acquire masculine qualities. Still the regal homage which they receive is so intoxicating, that till the manners of the times are changed, and formed on more reasonable principles, it may be impossible to convince them that the illegitimate power, which they obtain, by degrading themselves, is a curse,

6. *Paradise Lost* VIII.381–92. The italics are Wollstonecraft's.

and that they must return to nature and equality, if they wish to secure the placid satisfaction that unsophisticated affections impart. But for this epoch we must wait—wait, perhaps, till kings and nobles, enlightened by reason, and, preferring the real dignity of man to childish state, throw off their gaudy hereditary trappings: and if then women do not resign the arbitrary power of beauty—they will prove that they have *less* mind than man.

I may be accused of arrogance; still I must declare what I firmly believe, that all the writers who have written on the subject of female education and manners from Rousseau to Dr. Gregory,[7] have contributed to render women more artificial, weak characters, than they would otherwise have been; and, consequently, more useless members of society. I might have expressed this conviction in a lower key; but I am afraid it would have been the whine of affectation, and not the faithful expression of my feelings, of the clear result, which experience and reflection have led me to draw. When I come to that division of the subject, I shall advert to the passages that I more particularly disapprove of, in the works of the authors I have just alluded to; but it is first necessary to observe, that my objection extends to the whole purport of those books, which tend, in my opinion, to degrade one half of the human species, and render women pleasing at the expense of every solid virtue.

Though, to reason on Rousseau's ground, if man did attain a degree of perfection of mind when his body arrived at maturity, it might be proper, in order to make a man and his wife *one*, that she should rely entirely on his understanding; and the graceful ivy, clasping the oak that supported it, would form a whole in which strength and beauty would be equally conspicuous. But, alas! husbands, as well as their helpmates, are often only overgrown children; nay, thanks to early debauchery, scarcely men in their outward form —and if the blind lead the blind, one need not come from heaven to tell us the consequence.[8]

Many are the causes that, in the present corrupt state of society, contribute to enslave women by cramping their understandings and sharpening their senses. One, perhaps, that silently does more mischief than all the rest, is their disregard of order.

To do every thing in an orderly manner, is a most important precept, which women, who, generally speaking, receive only a disorderly kind of education, seldom attend to with that degree of exactness that men, who from their infancy are broken into method, observe. This negligent kind of guess-work, for what other epithet can be used to point out the random exertions of a sort of instinctive common sense, never brought to the test of reason? prevents

7. Dr. John Gregory (1724–73), Scottish physician whose A *Father's Legacy to His Daughters* (1774) was one of the most popular treatises on female education of the time.

8. Matthew 15:14: "And if the blind lead the blind, both shall fall into the ditch." The "one . . . from heaven" is Jesus.

their generalizing matters of fact—so they do to-day, what they did yesterday, merely because they did it yesterday.

This contempt of the understanding in early life has more baneful consequences than is commonly supposed; for the little knowledge which women of strong minds attain, is, from various circumstances, of a more desultory kind than the knowledge of men, and it is acquired more by sheer observations on real life, than from comparing what has been individually observed with the results of experience generalized by speculation. Led by their dependent situation and domestic employments more into society, what they learn is rather by snatches; and as learning is with them, in general, only a secondary thing, they do not pursue any one branch with that persevering ardour necessary to give vigour to the faculties, and clearness to the judgment. In the present state of society, a little learning is required to support the character of a gentleman; and boys are obliged to submit to a few years of discipline. But in the education of women, the cultivation of the understanding is always subordinate to the acquirement of some corporeal accomplishment; even while enervated by confinement and false notions of modesty, the body is prevented from attaining that grace and beauty which relaxed half-formed limbs never exhibit. Besides, in youth their faculties are not brought forward by emulation; and having no serious scientific study, if they have natural sagacity it is turned too soon on life and manners. They dwell on effects, and modifications, without tracing them back to causes; and complicated rules to adjust behaviour are a weak substitute for simple principles.

As a proof that education gives this appearance of weakness to females, we may instance the example of military men, who are, like them, sent into the world before their minds have been stored with knowledge or fortified by principles. The consequences are similar; soldiers acquire a little superficial knowledge, snatched from the muddy current of conversation, and, from continually mixing with society, they gain, what is termed a knowledge of the world; and this acquaintance with manners and customs has frequently been confounded with a knowledge of the human heart. But can the crude fruit of casual observation, never brought to the test of judgment, formed by comparing speculation and experience, deserve such a distinction? Soldiers, as well as women, practice the minor virtues with punctilious politeness. Where is then the sexual difference, when the education has been the same? All the difference that I can discern, arises from the superior advantage of liberty, which enables the former to see more of life.

It is wandering from my present subject, perhaps, to make a political remark; but, as it was produced naturally by the train of my reflections, I shall not pass it silently over.

Standing armies can never consist of resolute, robust men; they may be well disciplined machines, but they will seldom contain men under the influence of strong passions, or with very vigorous faculties. And as for any depth of understanding, I will venture to affirm, that it is as rarely to be found in the army as amongst women; and the cause, I maintain, is the same. It may be further observed, that officers are also particularly attentive to their persons, fond of dancing, crowded rooms, adventures, and ridicule.[9] Like the *fair* sex, the business of their lives is gallantry.—They were taught to please, and they only live to please. Yet they do not lose their rank in the distinction of sexes, for they are still reckoned superior to women, though in what their superiority consists, beyond what I have just mentioned, it is difficult to discover.

The great misfortune is this, that they both acquire manners before morals, and a knowledge of life before they have, from reflection, any acquaintance with the grand ideal outline of human nature. The consequence is natural; satisfied with common nature, they become a prey to prejudices, and taking all their opinions on credit, they blindly submit to authority. So that, if they have any sense, it is a kind of instinctive glance, that catches proportions, and decides with respect to manners; but fails when arguments are to be pursued below the surface, or opinions analyzed.

May not the same remark be applied to women? Nay, the argument may be carried still further, for they are both thrown out of a useful station by the unnatural distinctions established in civilized life. Riches and hereditary honours have made cyphers of women to give consequence to the numerical figure; and idleness has produced a mixture of gallantry and despotism into society, which leads the very men who are the slaves of their mistresses to tyrannize over their sisters, wives, and daughters. This is only keeping them in rank and file, it is true. Strengthen the female mind by enlarging it, and there will be an end to blind obedience; but, as blind obedience is ever sought for by power, tyrants and sensualists are in the right when they endeavour to keep women in the dark, because the former only want slaves, and the latter a play-thing. The sensualist, indeed, has been the most dangerous of tyrants, and women have been duped by their lovers, as princes by their ministers, whilst dreaming that they reigned over them.

I now principally allude to Rousseau, for his character of Sophia[1] is, undoubtedly, a captivating one, though it appears to me grossly unnatural; however it is not the superstructure, but the foundation of her character, the principles on which her education was built, that I mean to attack; nay, warmly as I admire the genius of that able writer, whose opinions I shall often have occasion to cite,

9. "Why should women be censured with petulant acrimony, because they seem to have a passion for a scarlet coat? Has not education placed them more on a level with soldiers than any other class of men?" [Wollstonecraft's note].
1. Book V of *Émile* is entitled "Sophy, or Woman" and contains the germ of Rousseau's ideas about women.

indignation always takes place of admiration, and the rigid frown of insulted virtue effaces the smile of complacency, which his eloquent periods are wont to raise, when I read his voluptuous reveries. Is this the man, who, in his ardour for virtue, would banish all the soft arts of peace, and almost carry us back to Spartan discipline? Is this the man who delights to paint the useful struggles of passion, the triumphs of good dispositions, and the heroic flights which carry the glowing soul out of itself?—How are these mighty sentiments lowered when he describes the pretty foot and enticing airs of his little favourite! But, for the present, I wave[2] the subject, and, instead of severely reprehending the transient effusions of overweening sensibility, I shall only observe, that whoever has cast a benevolent eye on society, must often have been gratified by the sight of a humble mutual love, not dignified by sentiment, or strengthened by a union in intellectual pursuits. The domestic trifles of the day have afforded matters for cheerful converse, and innocent caresses have softened toils which did not require great exercise of mind or stretch of thought: yet, has not the sight of this moderate felicity excited more tenderness than respect? An emotion similar to what we feel when children are playing, or animals sporting,[3] whilst the contemplation of the noble struggles of suffering merit has raised admiration, and carried our thoughts to that world where sensation will give place to reason.

Women are, therefore, to be considered either as moral beings, or so weak that they must be entirely subjected to the superior faculties of men.

Let us examine this question. Rousseau declares that a woman should never, for a moment, feel herself independent, that she should be governed by fear to exercise her natural cunning, and made a coquetish slave in order to render her a more alluring object of desire, a *sweeter* companion to man, whenever he chooses to relax himself. He carries the arguments, which he pretends to draw from the indications of nature, still further, and insinuates that truth and fortitude, the corner stones of all human virtue, should be cultivated with certain restrictions, because, with respect to the female character, obedience is the grand lesson which ought to be impressed with unrelenting rigour.[4]

2. A common spelling for "waive" in the eighteenth century.
3. "Similar feelings has Milton's pleasing picture of paradisiacal happiness ever raised in my mind; yet, instead of envying the lovely pair, I have, with conscious dignity, or Satanic pride, turned to hell for sublimer objects. In the same style, when viewing some noble monument of human art, I have traced the emanation of the Deity in the order I admired, till, descending from that giddy height, I have caught myself contemplating the grandest of all human sights;—for fancy quickly placed, in some solitary recess, an outcast of fortune, rising superior to passion and discontent" [Wollstonecraft's note]. Wollstonecraft is referring to the portrait of Adam and Eve in Book IV of Milton's *Paradise Lost* and stating what has since become critical commonplace, that Milton's Eden, for all its bliss, is not as compelling as his suffering Satan.
4. *Émile*, p. 333: "What is most wanted in a woman is gentleness; formed to obey a creature so imperfect as man, a creature often vicious and always faulty, she should early learn to submit to injustice and to suffer the wrongs inflicted on her by her husband without complaint."

What nonsense! when will a great man arise with sufficient strength of mind to puff away the fumes which pride and sensuality have thus spread over the subject! If women are by nature inferior to men, their virtues must be the same in quality, if not in degree, or virtue is a relative idea; consequently, their conduct should be founded on the same principles, and have the same aim.

Connected with man as daughters, wives, and mothers, their moral character may be estimated by their manner of fulfilling those simple duties; but the end, the grand end of their exertions should be to unfold their own faculties and acquire the dignity of conscious virtue. They may try to render their road pleasant; but ought never to forget, in common with man, that life yields not the felicity which can satisfy an immortal soul. I do not mean to insinuate, that either sex should be so lost in abstract reflections or distant views, as to forget the affections and duties that lie before them, and are, in truth, the means appointed to produce the fruit of life; on the contrary, I would warmly recommend them, even while I assert, that they afford most satisfaction when they are considered in their true, sober light.

Probably the prevailing opinion, that woman was created for man, may have taken its rise from Moses's poetical story;[5] yet, as very few, it is presumed, who have bestowed any serious thought on the subject, ever supposed that Eve was, literally speaking, one of Adam's ribs, the deduction must be allowed to fall to the ground; or, only be so far admitted as it proves that man, from the remotest antiquity, found it convenient to exert his strength to subjugate his companion, and his invention to shew that she ought to have her neck bent under the yoke, because the whole creation was only created for his convenience or pleasure.

Let it not be concluded that I wish to invert the order of things; I have already granted, that, from the constitution of their bodies, men seem to be designed by Providence to attain a greater degree of virtue.[6] I speak collectively of the whole sex; but I see not the shadow of a reason to conclude that their virtues should differ in respect to their nature. In fact, how can they, if virtue has only one eternal standard? I must therefore, if I reason consequentially, as strenuously maintain that they have the same simple direction, as that there is a God.

It follows then that cunning should not be opposed to wisdom, little cares to great exertions, or insipid softness, varnished over with the name of gentleness, to that fortitude which grand views alone can inspire.

5. See Genesis 2:21–23 for one account of the creation of woman. Moses was thought to be the author of the first five books of the Old Testament (the Pentateuch).
6. Being physically inferior can lead to women's being morally inferior: not just physical size but their worldly pursuits allow men a greater opportunity to make moral choices and thus attain virtue.

I shall be told that woman would then lose many of her peculiar graces, and the opinion of a well known poet might be quoted to refute my unqualified assertion. For Pope has said, in the name of the whole male sex,

> 'Yet ne'er so sure our passion to create,
> 'As when she touch'd the brink of all we hate.' [7]

In what light this sally places men and women, I shall leave to the judicious to determine; meanwhile I shall content myself with observing, that I cannot discover why, unless they are mortal, females should always be degraded by being made subservient to love or lust.

To speak disrespectfully of love is, I know, high treason against sentiment and fine feelings; but I wish to speak the simple language of truth, and rather to address the head than the heart. To endeavour to reason love out of the world, would be to out Quixote Cervantes, [8] and equally offend against common sense; but an endeavour to restrain this tumultuous passion, and to prove that it should not be allowed to dethrone superior powers, or to usurp the sceptre which the understanding should ever coolly wield, appears less wild.

Youth is the season for love in both sexes; but in those days of thoughtless enjoyment provision should be made for the more important years of life, when reflection takes place of sensation. But Rousseau, and most of the male writers who have followed his steps, have warmly inculcated that the whole tendency of female education ought to be directed to one point:—to render them pleasing.

Let me reason with the supporters of this opinion who have any knowledge of human nature, do they imagine that marriage can eradicate the habitude of life? The woman who has only been taught to please will soon find that her charms are oblique sunbeams, and that they cannot have much effect on her husband's heart when they are seen every day, when the summer is passed and gone. Will she then have sufficient native energy to look into herself for comfort, and cultivate her dormant faculties? or, is it not more rational to expect that she will try to please other men; and, in the emotions raised by the expectation of new conquests, endeavour to forget the mortification her love or pride has received? When the husband ceases to be a lover—and the time will inevitably come, her desire of pleasing will then grow languid, or become a spring of bitterness; and love, perhaps, the most evanescent of all passions, gives place to jealousy or vanity.

I now speak of women who are restrained by principle or preju-

---

7. Alexander Pope, *Moral Essays* II.51–52.
8. The hero of Cervantes' satiric romance, *Don Quixote*, tries ineffectually to rid the world of evil.

dice; such women, though they would shrink from an intrigue with real abhorrence, yet, nevertheless, wish to be convinced by the homage of gallantry that they are cruelly neglected by their husbands; or, days and weeks are spent in dreaming of the happiness enjoyed by congenial souls till their health is undermined and their spirits broken by discontent. How then can the great art of pleasing be such a necessary study? it is only useful to a mistress; the chaste wife, and serious mother, should only consider her power to please as the polish of her virtues, and the affection of her husband as one of the comforts that render her task less difficult and her life happier.—But, whether she be loved or neglected, her first wish should be to make herself respectable, and not to rely for all her happiness on a being subject to like infirmities with herself.

The worthy Dr. Gregory fell into a similar error. I respect his heart; but entirely disapprove of his celebrated Legacy to his Daughters.[9]

He advises them to cultivate a fondness for dress, because a fondness for dress, he asserts, is natural to them.[1] I am unable to comprehend what either he or Rousseau mean, when they frequently use this indefinite term.[2] If they told us that in a pre-existent state the soul was fond of dress, and brought this inclination with it into a new body, I should listen to them with a half smile, as I often do when I hear a rant about innate elegance.—But if he only meant to say that the exercise of the faculties will produce this fondness—I deny it.—It is not natural; but arises, like false ambition in men, from a love of power.

Dr. Gregory goes much further; he actually recommends dissimulation, and advises an innocent girl to give the lie to her feelings, and not dance with spirit, when gaiety of heart would make her feel eloquent without making her gestures immodest. In the name of truth and common sense, why should not one woman acknowledge that she can take more exercise than another? or, in other words, that she has a sound constitution; and why, to damp innocent vivacity, is she darkly to be told that men will draw conclusions which she little thinks of?[3]—Let the libertine draw what inference he pleases; but, I hope, that no sensible mother will restrain the natural frankness of youth by instilling such indecent cautions. Out of the abundance of the heart the mouth speaketh;[4] and a wiser than Solomon

---

9. Dr. John Gregory's A *Father's Legacy to His Daughters*, first published in 1774, was widely read in the eighteenth century. The edition referred to hereafter is the modern facsimile of the first edition, ed. Gina Luria (New York: Garland Publishing Co., 1974).
1. "The love of dress is natural to you, and therefore it is proper and reasonable." Gregory, p. 55.
2. I.e., "natural."

3. For this and the previous sentence see Gregory, pp. 57–58: "I would have you to dance with spirit; but never allow yourselves to be so far transported with mirth, as to forget the delicacy of your sex.— Many a girl dancing in the gaiety and innocence of her heart, is thought to discover a spirit she little dreams of."
4. Matthew 12:34.

hath said, that the heart should be made clean, [5] and not trivial ceremonies observed, which it is not very difficult to fulfill with scrupulous exactness when vice reigns in the heart.

Women ought to endeavour to purify their heart; but can they do so when their uncultivated understandings make them entirely dependent on their senses for employment and amusement, when no noble pursuit sets them above the little vanities of the day, or enables them to curb the wild emotions that agitate a reed over which every passing breeze has power? To gain the affections of a virtuous man is affectation necessary? Nature has given woman a weaker frame than man; but, to ensure her husband's affections, must a wife, who by the exercise of her mind and body whilst she was discharging the duties of a daughter, wife, and mother, has allowed her constitution to retain its natural strength, and her nerves a healthy tone, is she, I say, to condescend to use art and feign a sickly delicacy in order to secure her husband's affection? Weakness may excite tenderness, and gratify the arrogant pride of man; but the lordly caresses of a protector will not gratify a noble mind that pants for, and deserves to be respected. Fondness is a poor substitute for friendship!

In a seraglio, I grant, that all these arts are necessary; the epicure must have his palate tickled, or he will sink into apathy; but have women so little ambition as to be satisfied with such a condition? Can they supinely dream life away in the lap of pleasure, or the languor of weariness, rather than assert their claim to pursue reasonable pleasures and render themselves conspicuous by practising the virtues which dignify mankind? Surely she has not an immortal soul who can loiter life away merely employed to adorn her person, that she may amuse the languid hours, and soften the cares of a fellow-creature who is willing to be enlivened by her smiles and tricks, when the serious business of life is over.

Besides, the woman who strengthens her body and exercises her mind will, by managing her family and practising various virtues, become the friend, and not the humble dependent of her husband; and if she, by possessing such substantial qualities, merit his regard, she will not find it necessary to conceal her affection, nor to pretend to an unnatural coldness of constitution to excite her husband's passions. In fact, if we revert to history, we shall find that the women who have distinguished themselves have neither been the most beautiful nor the most gentle of their sex.

Nature, or, to speak with strict propriety, God, has made all things right; but man has sought him out many inventions to mar

5. The "wiser than Solomon" is Jesus, who, in Mark 7:18–23 and Matthew 23:25–28, speaks of purifying the inner self rather than simply observing the pharasaical law. See also Milton, *Paradise Regained* II.205–6: "But he whom we attempt is wiser far than Solomon."

the work. I now allude to that part of Dr. Gregory's treatise, where he advises a wife never to let her husband know the extent of her sensibility or affection.[6] Voluptuous precaution, and as ineffectual as absurd.—Love, from its very nature, must be transitory. To seek for a secret that would render it constant, would be as wild a search as for the philosopher's stone,[7] or the grand panacea: and the discovery would be equally useless, or rather pernicious to mankind. The most holy band of society is friendship. It has been well said, by a shrewd satirist, "that rare as true love is, true friendship is still rarer."[8]

This is an obvious truth, and the cause not lying deep, will not elude a slight glance of inquiry.

Love, the common passion, in which chance and sensation take place of choice and reason, is, in some degree, felt by the mass of mankind; for it is not necessary to speak, at present, of the emotions that rise above or sink below love. This passion, naturally increased by suspense and difficulties, draws the mind out of its accustomed state, and exalts the affections; but the security of marriage, allowing the fever of love to subside, a healthy temperature is thought insipid, only by those who have not sufficient intellect to substitute the calm tenderness of friendship, the confidence of respect, instead of blind admiration, and the sensual emotions of fondness.

This is, must be, the course of nature.—Friendship or indifference inevitably succeeds love.—And this constitution seems perfectly to harmonize with the system of government which prevails in the moral world. Passions are spurs to action, and open the mind; but they sink into mere appetites, become a personal and momentary gratification, when the object is gained, and the satisfied mind rests in enjoyment. The man who had some virtue whilst he was struggling for a crown, often becomes a voluptuous tyrant when it graces his brow; and, when the lover is not lost in the husband, the dotard, a prey to childish caprices, and fond jealousies, neglects the serious duties of life, and the caresses which should excite confidence in his children are lavished on the overgrown child, his wife.

In order to fulfil the duties of life, and to be able to pursue with vigour the various employments which form the moral character, a master and mistress of a family ought not to continue to love each other with passion. I mean to say, that they ought not to indulge those emotions which disturb the order of society, and engross the thoughts that should be otherwise employed. The mind that has

6. Gregory, pp. 86–87: "If you love him, let me advise you never to discover to him the full extent of your love, no, not although you marry him."
7. The legendary substance sought by alchemists which could turn matter into gold.

8. La Rochefoucauld (1613–80, French noble and master of the epigram), Les Maximes, No. 473: "Quelque rare que soit que la véritable amour, il l'est encore moins que la véritable amitié."

never been engrossed by one object wants vigour—if it can long be so, it is weak.

A mistaken education, a narrow, uncultivated mind, and many sexual prejudices, tend to make women more constant than men; but, for the present, I shall not touch on this branch of the subject. I will go still further, and advance, without dreaming of a paradox, that an unhappy marriage is often very advantageous to a family, and that the neglected wife is, in general, the best mother.[9] And this would almost always be the consequence if the female mind were more enlarged: for, it seems to be the common dispensation of Providence, that what we gain in present enjoyment should be deducted from the treasure of life, experience; and that when we are gathering the flowers of the day and revelling in pleasure, the solid fruit of toil and wisdom should not be caught at the same time. The way lies before us, we must turn to the right or left; and he who will pass life away in bounding from one pleasure to another, must not complain if he acquire neither wisdom nor respectability of character.

Supposing, for a moment, that the soul is not immortal, and that man was only created for the present scene,—I think we should have reason to complain that love, infantine fondness, ever grew insipid and palled upon the sense. Let us eat, drink, and love, for to-morrow we die, would be, in fact, the language of reason, the morality of life; and who but a fool would part with a reality for a fleeting shadow? But, if awed by observing the improbable[1] powers of the mind, we disdain to confine our wishes or thoughts to such a comparatively mean field of action; that only appears grand and important, as it is connected with a boundless prospect and sublime hopes, what necessity is there for falsehood in conduct, and why must the sacred majesty of truth be violated to detain a deceitful good that saps the very foundation of virtue? Why must the female mind be tainted by coquetish arts to gratify the sensualist, and prevent love from subsiding into friendship, or compassionate tenderness, when there are not qualities on which friendship can be built? Let the honest heart shew itself, and *reason* teach passion to submit to necessity; or, let the dignified pursuit of virtue and knowledge raise the mind above those emotions which rather imbitter than sweeten the cup of life, when they are not restrained within due bounds.

I do not mean to allude to the romantic passion, which is the

9. The rather inverted meaning here is that the woman who is not absorbed in, and absorbing to, her husband does not spend all her time in dalliance and has, therefore, sufficient time to devote to her children. Despite the tone of this passage Wollstonecraft always argues that a mature affec-tion between parents is a good thing for the children.
1. The first edition reads "improvable" rather than "improbable." The former makes more sense in context.

concomitant of genius.—Who can clip its wing? But that grand passion not proportioned to the puny enjoyments of life, is only true to the sentiment, and feeds on itself. The passions which have been celebrated for their durability have always been unfortunate. They have acquired strength by absence and constitutional melancholy. —The fancy has hovered round a form of beauty dimly seen—but familiarity might have turned admiration into disgust; or, at least, into indifference, and allowed the imagination leisure to start fresh game. With perfect propriety, according to this view of things, does Rousseau make the mistress of his soul, Eloisa, love St. Preux, when life was fading before her;[2] but this is no proof of the immortality of the passion.

Of the same complexion is Dr. Gregory's advice respecting delicacy of sentiment, which he advises a woman not to acquire, if she have determined to marry.[3] This determination, however, perfectly consistent with his former advice, he calls *indelicate*, and earnestly persuades his daughters to conceal it, though it may govern their conduct;—as if it were indelicate to have the common appetites of human nature.

Noble morality! and consistent with the cautious prudence of a little soul that cannot extend its views beyond the present minute division of existence. If all the faculties of woman's mind are only to be cultivated as they respect her dependence on man; if, when a husband be obtained, she have arrived at her goal, and meanly proud rests satisfied with such a paltry crown, let her grovel contentedly, scarcely raised by her employments above the animal kingdom; but, if, struggling for the prize of her high calling, she look beyond the present scene, let her cultivate her understanding without stopping to consider what character the husband may have whom she is destined to marry. Let her only determine, without being too anxious about present happiness, to acquire the qualities that ennoble a rational being, and a rough inelegant husband may shock her taste without destroying her peace of mind. She will not model her soul to suit the frailties of her companion, but to bear with them: his character may be a trial, but not an impediment to virtue.

If Dr. Gregory confined his remark to romantic expectations of constant love and congenial feelings, he should have recollected that experience will banish what advice can never make us cease to wish for, when the imagination is kept alive at the expence of reason.

---

2. In Rousseau's *La Nouvelle Héloïse* (1761), the heroine, Julie, reveals her long-held passionate love for St. Preux as she is dying, even though she has been a faithful wife to Wolmar throughout the novel.
3. Gregory, pp. 116–18: "But if you find that marriage is absolutely essential to your happiness . . . shun . . . reading and conversation that warms the imagination, which engages and softens the heart, and raises the taste above the level of common life . . . [otherwise] you may be tired with insipidity and dullness; shocked with indelicacy, or mortified by indifference."

I own it frequently happens that women who have fostered a romantic unnatural delicacy of feeling, waste their[4] lives in *imagining* how happy they should have been with a husband who could love them with a fervid increasing affection every day, and all day. But they might as well pine married as single—and would not be a jot more unhappy with a bad husband than longing for a good one. That a proper education; or, to speak with more precision, a well stored mind, would enable a woman to support a single life with dignity, I grant; but that she should avoid cultivating her taste, lest her husband should occasionally shock it, is quitting a substance for a shadow. To say the truth, I do not know of what use is an improved taste, if the individual be not rendered more independent of the casualties of life; if new sources of enjoyment, only dependent on the solitary operations of the mind, are not opened. People of taste, married or single, without distinction, will ever be disgusted by various things that touch not less observing minds. On this conclusion the argument must not be allowed to hinge; but in the whole sum of enjoyment is taste to be denominated a blessing?

The question is, whether it procures most pain or pleasure? The answer will decide the propriety of Dr. Gregory's advice, and shew how absurd and tyrannic it is thus to lay down a system of slavery; or to attempt to educate moral beings by any other rules than those deduced from pure reason, which apply to the whole species.

Gentleness of manners, forbearance and long-suffering, are such amiable Godlike qualities, that in sublime poetic strains the Deity has been invested with them; and, perhaps, no representation of his goodness so strongly fastens on the human affections as those that represent him abundant in mercy and willing to pardon.[5] Gentleness, considered in this point of view, bears on its front all the characteristics of grandeur, combined with the winning graces of condescension; but what a different aspect it assumes when it is the submissive demeanour of dependence, the support of weakness that loves, because it wants protection; and is forbearing, because it must silently endure injuries; smiling under the lash at which it dare not snarl. Abject as this picture appears, it is the portrait of an accomplished woman, according to the received opinion of female excellence, separated by specious reasoners from human excellence. Or, they[6] kindly restore the rib, and make one moral being of a man and woman; not forgetting to give her all the 'submissive charms.'[7]

4. "For example, the herd of Novelists." [Wollstonecraft's note].
5. Isaiah 55:7: "And he will have mercy upon him; and to our God, for he will abundantly pardon."
6. "Vide Rousseau, and Swedenborg" [Wollstonecraft's note]. Rousseau insisted that man and wife comprised one moral unit; that is, a wife could not act with moral certainty by herself. Emanuel Swedenborg (1688–1772), Swedish scientist and theologian, believed in conjugality for all eternity, though the marriages in heaven resulted in but one angel, of which the husband was the understanding and the wife the will.
7. *Paradise Lost* IV.497–99: "he in delight / Both of her Beauty and submissive charms / Smil'd with superior love."

How women are to exist in that state where there is to be neither marrying nor giving in marriage, we are not told. For though moralists have agreed that the tenor of life seems to prove that *man* is prepared by various circumstances for a future state, they constantly concur in advising *woman* only to provide for the present. Gentleness, docility, and a spaniel-like affection are, on this ground, consistently recommended as the cardinal virtues of the sex; and, disregarding the arbitrary economy of nature, one writer has declared that it is masculine for a woman to be melancholy.[8] She was created to be the toy of man, his rattle, and it must jingle in his ears whenever, dismissing reason, he chooses to be amused.

To recommend gentleness, indeed, on a broad basis is strictly philosophical. A frail being should labour to be gentle. But when forbearance confounds right and wrong, it ceases to be a virtue; and, however convenient it may be found in a companion—that companion will ever be considered as an inferior, and only inspire a vapid tenderness, which easily degenerates into contempt. Still, if advice could really make a being gentle, whose natural disposition admitted not of such a fine polish, something towards the advancement of order would be attained; but if, as might quickly be demonstrated, only affectation be produced by this indiscriminate counsel, which throws a stumbling-block in the way of gradual improvement, and true melioration of temper, the sex is not much benefited by sacrificing solid virtues to the attainment of superficial graces, though for a few years they may procure the individuals regal sway.

As a philosopher, I read with indignation the plausible epithets which men use to soften their insults; and, as a moralist, I ask what is meant by such heterogeneous associations, as fair defects, amiable weaknesses, &c.?[9] If there be but one criterion of morals, but one archetype for man, women appear to be suspended by destiny, according to the vulgar tale of Mahomet's coffin;[1] they have neither the unerring instinct of brutes, nor are allowed to fix the eye of reason on a perfect model. They were made to be loved, and must not aim at respect, lest they should be hunted out of society as masculine.

But to view the subject in another point of view. Do passive indolent women make the best wives? Confining our discussion to the present moment of existence, let us see how such weak creatures perform their part? Do the women who, by the attainment of a few superficial accomplishments, have strengthened the prevailing prejudice, merely contribute to the happiness of their husbands? Do they

8. This reference possibly originates from Edmund Burke's *A Philosophical Inquiry into the Origin of Our Ideas of the Sublime and the Beautiful*, where he allies melancholy with the non-beautiful, the non-sublime, and, by a process of categories, the non-feminine.
9. *Paradise Lost* X.891–92: "This fair defect / Of nature"; and Pope, *Moral Essays* II.44: "Fine by defect, and delicately weak."
1. Although entirely without foundation, popular lore had it that Mahomet's coffin hung in the middle of his tomb, suspended by some magic of magnetism.

display their charms merely to amuse them? And have women, who have early imbibed notions of passive obedience, sufficient character to manage a family or educate children? So far from it, that, after surveying the history of woman, I cannot help, agreeing with the severest satirist, considering the sex as the weakest as well as the most oppressed half of the species. What does history disclose but marks of inferiority, and how few women have emancipated themselves from the galling yoke of sovereign man?—So few, that the exceptions remind me of an ingenious conjecture respecting Newton: that he was probably a being of a superior order, accidentally caged in a human body.[2] Following the same train of thinking, I have been led to imagine that the few extraordinary women who have rushed in eccentrical directions out of the orbit prescribed to their sex, were *male* spirits, confined by mistake in female frames. But if it be not philosophical to think of sex when the soul is mentioned, the inferiority must depend on the organs; or the heavenly fire, which is to ferment the clay, is not given in equal portions.

But avoiding, as I have hitherto done, any direct comparison of the two sexes collectively, or frankly acknowledging the inferiority of woman, according to the present appearance of things, I shall only insist that men have increased that inferiority till women are almost sunk below the standard of rational creatures. Let their faculties have room to unfold, and their virtues to gain strength, and then determine where the whole sex must stand in the intellectual scale. Yet let it be remembered, that for a small number of distinguished women I do not ask a place.

It is difficult for us purblind mortals to say to what height human discoveries and improvements may arrive when the gloom of despotism subsides, which makes us stumble at every step; but, when morality shall be settled on a more solid basis, then, without being gifted with a prophetic spirit, I will venture to predict that woman will be either the friend or slave of man. We shall not, as at present, doubt whether she is a moral agent, or the link which unites man with brutes.[3] But, should it then appear, that like the brutes they were principally created for the use of man, he will let them patiently bite the bridle, and not mock them with empty praise; or, should their rationality be proved, he will not impede their improvement merely to gratify his sensual appetites. He will not, with all

---

2. A possible reference to Pope's *Essay on Man* II.31–34: "Superior beings, when of late they saw / A mortal Man unfold all Nature's law, / Admir'd such wisdom in an earthly shape, / And shew'd a NEWTON as we shew an Ape."
3. Rousseau doubted that a woman, of herself, was a moral agent. There had been a long dispute about the question of woman being part of humankind. In the *Summa Theologica* (Question XVII, Art. 1) St. Thomas Aquinas concedes, with Aristotle, that the "production of woman comes from a defect in the active power, or from some material indisposition, or even from some external influence, such as that of a south wind, which is moist" (English Dominican translation of St. Thomas, edited by Anton C. Pegis, *The Basic Writings of Saint Thomas Aquinas* [New York, 1945], I, 880).

the graces of rhetoric, advise them to submit implicitly their under-standing to the guidance of man. He will not, when he treats of the education of women, assert that they ought never to have the free use of reason, nor would he recommend cunning and dissimulation to beings who are acquiring, in like manner as himself, the virtues of humanity.

Surely there can be but one rule of right, if morality has an eter-nal foundation, and whoever sacrifices virtue, strictly so called, to present convenience, or whose *duty* it is to act in such a manner, lives only for the passing day, and cannot be an accountable crea-ture.

The poet then should have dropped his sneer when he says,

> "If weak women go astray,
> "The stars are more in fault than they." [4]

For that they are bound by the adamantine chain of destiny is most certain, if it be proved that they are never to exercise their own reason, never to be independent, never to rise above opinion, or to feel the dignity of a rational will that only bows to God, and often forgets that the universe contains any being but itself and the model of perfection to which its ardent gaze is turned, to adore attributes that, softened into virtues, may be imitated in kind, though the degree overwhelms the enraptured mind.

If, I say, for I would not impress by declamation when Reason offers her sober light, if they be really capable of acting like rational creatures, let them not be treated like slaves; or, like the brutes who are dependent on the reason of man, when they associate with him; but cultivate their minds, give them the salutary, sublime curb of principle, and let them attain conscious dignity by feeling them-selves only dependent on God. Teach them, in common with man, to submit to necessity, instead of giving, to render them more pleas-ing, a sex to morals.

Further, should experience prove that they cannot attain the same degree of strength of mind, perseverance, and fortitude, let their virtues be the same in kind, though they may vainly struggle for the same degree; and the superiority of man will be equally clear, if not clearer; and truth, as it is a simple principle, which admits of no modification, would be common to both. Nay, the order of society as it is at present regulated would not be inverted, for woman would then only have the rank that reason assigned her, and arts could not be practised to bring the balance even, much less to turn it.

These may be termed Utopian dreams.—Thanks to that Being who impressed them on my soul, and gave me sufficient strength of

4. Matthew Prior, "Hans Carvel," lines 11–12.

mind to dare to exert my own reason, till, becoming dependent only on him for the support of my virtue, I view, with indignation, the mistaken notions that enslave my sex.

I love man as my fellow; but his scepter, real, or usurped, extends not to me, unless the reason of an individual demands my homage; and even then the submission is to reason, and not to man. In fact, the conduct of an accountable being must be regulated by the operations of its own reason; or on what foundation rests the throne of God?

It appears to me necessary to dwell on these obvious truths, because females have been insulated, as it were; and, while they have been stripped of the virtues that should clothe humanity, they have been decked with artificial graces that enable them to exercise a short-lived tyranny. Love, in their bosoms, taking place of every nobler passion, their sole ambition is to be fair, to raise emotion instead of inspiring respect; and this ignoble desire, like the servility in absolute monarchies, destroys all strength of character. Liberty is the mother of virtue, and if women be, by their very constitution, slaves, and not allowed to breathe the sharp invigorating air of freedom, they must ever languish like exotics, and be reckoned beautiful flaws in nature.

As to the argument respecting the subjection in which the sex has ever been held, it retorts on man. The many have always been enthralled by the few; and monsters, who scarcely have shewn any discernment of human excellence, have tyrannized over thousands of their fellow-creatures. Why have men of superiour endowments submitted to such degradation? For, is it not universally acknowledged that kings, viewed collectively, have ever been inferior, in abilities and virtue, to the same number of men taken from the common mass of mankind—yet, have they not, and are they not still treated with a degree of reverence that is an insult to reason? China is not the only country where a living man has been made a God.[5] *Men* have submitted to superior strength to enjoy with impunity the pleasure of the moment—*women* have only done the same, and therefore till it is proved that the courtier, who servilely resigns the birthright of a man, is not a moral agent, it cannot be demonstrated that woman is essentially inferior to man because she has always been subjugated.

Brutal force has hitherto governed the world, and that the science of politics is in its infancy, is evident from philosophers scrupling to give the knowledge most useful to man that determinate distinction.

---

5. This could be either a reference to ancestor worship among most Chinese or an allusion to the emperor who is the vice-regent of heaven on earth.

I shall not pursue this argument any further than to establish an obvious inference, that as sound politics diffuse liberty, mankind, including woman, will become more wise and virtuous.

Chap. III

The Same Subject Continued

Bodily strength from being the distinction of heroes is now sunk into such unmerited contempt that men, as well as women, seem to think it unnecessary: the latter, as it takes from their feminine graces, and from that lovely weakness the source of their undue power; and the former, because it appears inimical to the character of a gentleman.

That they have both by departing from one extreme run into another, may easily be proved; but first it may be proper to observe, that a vulgar error has obtained a degree of credit, which has given force to a false conclusion, in which an effect has been mistaken for a cause.

People of genius have, very frequently, impaired their constitutions by study or careless inattention to their health, and the violence of their passions bearing a proportion to the vigour of their intellects, the sword's destroying the scabbard has become almost proverbial,[1] and superficial observers have inferred from thence, that men of genius have commonly weak, or, to use a more fashionable phrase, delicate constitutions. Yet the contrary, I believe, will appear to be the fact; for, on diligent inquiry, I find that strength of mind has, in most cases, been accompanied by superior strength of body,—natural soundness of constitution,—not that robust tone of nerves and vigour of muscles, which arise from bodily labour, when the mind is quiescent, or only directs the hands.

Dr. Priestley has remarked, in the preface to his biographical chart, that the majority of great men have lived beyond forty-five.[2] And, considering the thoughtless manner in which they have lavished their strength, when investigating a favourite science they have wasted the lamp of life, forgetful of the midnight hour; or, when, lost in poetic dreams, fancy has peopled the scene, and the soul has been disturbed, till it shook the constitution, by the passions that meditation had raised; whose objects, the baseless fabric of a vision,[3] faded before the exhausted eye, they must have had

---

1. Rousseau, *The Confessions* (trans. anon. [London, 1931], I, 200): "It is sometimes said that the sword wears out the scabbard. That is my history."
2. Joseph Priestley's A *Description of a Chart of Biography* (London, 1785), p. 34. The chart itself is simply a list of historical names, showing overlapping and comparative information; the preface explains the procedure and purpose of the chart.
3. *The Tempest* IV.i.151: "Like the baseless fabric of this vision."

iron frames. Shakspeare never grasped the airy dagger[4] with a nerve-less hand, nor did Milton tremble when he led Satan far from the confines of his dreary prison.[5]—These were not the ravings of imbecility, the sickly effusions of distempered brains; but the exuberance of fancy, that 'in a fine phrenzy'[6] wandering, was not continually reminded of its material shackles.

I am aware that this argument would carry me further than it may be supposed I wish to go; but I follow truth, and, still adhering to my first position, I will allow that bodily strength seems to give man a natural superiority over woman; and this is the only solid basis on which the superiority of the sex can be built. But I still insist, that not only the virtue, but the *knowledge* of the two sexes should be the same in nature, if not in degree, and that women, considered not only as moral, but rational creatures, ought to endeavour to acquire human virtues (or perfections) by the *same* means as men, instead of being educated like a fanciful kind of *half* being—one of Rousseau's wild chimeras.[7]

But, if strength of body be, with some shew of reason, the boast of men, why are women so infatuated as to be proud of a defect?

---

4. *Macbeth* III.iv.62–63: "This is the air-drawn dagger which, you said, led you to Duncan."
5. I.e., Milton's release of Satan in *Paradise Lost* to replay his fatal role in the fall of man was but an imaginative exercise.
6. *A Midsummer Night's Dream* V.i.12: "The poet's eye, in a fine frenzy rolling."
7. " 'Researches into abstract and speculative truths, the principles and axioms of sciences, in short, every thing which tends to generalize our ideas, is not the proper province of women; their studies should be relative to points of practice; it belongs to them to apply those principles which men have discovered; and it is their part to make observations, which direct men to the establishment of general principles. All the ideas of women, which have not the immediate tendency to points of duty, should be directed to the study of men, and to the attainment of those agreeable accomplishments which have taste for their object; for as to works of genius, they are beyond their capacity; neither have they sufficient precision or power of attention to succeed in sciences which require accuracy: and as to physical knowledge, it belongs to those only who are most active, most inquisitive; who comprehend the greatest variety of objects: in short, it belongs to those who have the strongest powers, and who exercise them most, to judge of the relations between sensible beings and the laws of nature. A woman who is naturally weak, and does not carry her ideas to any great extent, knows how to judge and make a proper estimate of those movements which she sets to work, in order to aid her weakness; and these movements are the passions of men. The mechanism she employs is much more powerful than ours; for all her levers move the human heart. She must have the skill to incline us to do every thing which her sex will not enable her to do herself, and which is necessary or agreeable to her; therefore she ought to study the mind of man thoroughly, not the mind of man in general, abstractedly, but the dispositions of those men to whom she is subject, either by the laws of her country or by the force of opinion. She should learn to penetrate into their real sentiments from their conversation, their actions, their looks, and gestures. She should also have the art, by her own conversation, actions, looks, and gestures, to communicate those sentiments which are agreeable to them, without seeming to intend it. Men will argue more philosophically about the human heart; but women will read the heart of man better than they. It belongs to women, if I may be allowed the expression, to form an experimental morality, and to reduce the study of man to a system. Women have most wit, men have most genius; women observe, men reason: from the concurrence of both we derive the clearest light and the most perfect knowledge, which the human mind is, of itself, capable of attaining. In one word, from hence we acquire the most intimate acquaintance, both with ourselves and others, of which our nature is capable; and it is thus that art has a constant tendency to perfect those endowments which nature has bestowed,—The world is the book of women.' Rousseau's Emilius. I hope my readers still remember the comparison, which I have brought forward, between women and officers" [Wollstonecraft's note]. The quotation is from *Émile*, pp. 349–50.

Rousseau has furnished them with a plausible excuse, which could only have occurred to a man, whose imagination had been allowed to run wild, and refine on the impressions made by exquisite senses; —that they might, forsooth, have a pretext for yielding to a natural appetite without violating a romantic species of modesty, which gratifies the pride and libertinism of man.

Women, deluded by these sentiments, sometimes boast of their weakness, cunningly obtaining power by playing on the *weakness* of men; and they may well glory in their illicit sway, for, like Turkish bashaws,[8] they have more real power than their masters: but virtue is sacrificed to temporary gratifications, and the respectability of life to the triumph of an hour.

Women, as well as despots, have now, perhaps, more power than they would have if the world, divided and subdivided into kingdoms and families, were governed by laws deduced from the exercise of reason; but in obtaining it, to carry on the comparison, their character is degraded, and licentiousness spread through the whole aggregate of society. The many become pedestal to the few. I, therefore, will venture to assert, that till women are more rationally educated, the progress of human virtue and improvement in knowledge must receive continual checks. And if it be granted that woman was not created merely to gratify the appetite of man, or to be the upper servant, who provides his meals and takes care of his linen, it must follow, that the first care of those mothers or fathers, who really attend to the education of females, should be, if not to strengthen the body, at least, not to destroy the constitution by mistaken notions of beauty and female excellence; nor should girls ever be allowed to imbibe the pernicious notion that a defect can, by any chemical process of reasoning, become an excellence. In this respect, I am happy to find, that the author of one of the most instructive books, that our country has produced for children, coincides with me in opinion; I shall quote his pertinent remarks to give the force of his respectable authority to reason.[9]

---

8. Turkish officers or governors of high rank.

9. "A respectable old man gives the following sensible account of the method he pursued when educating his daughter. 'I endeavoured to give both to her mind and body a degree of vigour, which is seldom found in the female sex. As soon as she was sufficiently advanced in strength to be capable of the lighter labours of husbandry and gardening, I employed her as my constant companion. Selene, for that was her name, soon acquired a dexterity in all these rustic employments, which I considered with equal pleasure and admiration. If women are in general feeble both in body and mind, it arises less from nature than from education. We encourage a vicious indolence and inactivity, which we falsely call delicacy; instead of hardening their minds by the severer principles of reason and philosophy, we breed them to useless arts, which terminate in vanity and sensuality. In most of the countries which I had visited, they are taught nothing of an higher nature than a few modulations of the voice, or useless postures of the body; their time is consumed in sloth or trifles, and trifles become the only pursuits capable of interesting them. We seem to forget, that it is upon the qualities of the female sex that our own domestic comforts and the education of our children must depend. And what are the comforts or the education which a race of beings, corrupted from their infancy, and unacquainted with all the duties

But should it be proved that woman is naturally weaker than man, whence does it follow that it is natural for her to labour to become still weaker than nature intended her to be? Arguments of this cast are an insult to common sense, and savour of passion. The *divine right* of husbands, like the divine right of kings, may, it is to be hoped, in this enlightened age, be contested without danger, and, though conviction may not silence many boisterous disputants, yet, when any prevailing prejudice is attacked, the wise will consider, and leave the narrow-minded to rail with thoughtless vehemence at innovation.

The mother, who wishes to give true dignity of character to her daughter, must, regardless of the sneers of ignorance, proceed on a plan diametrically opposite to that which Rousseau has recommended with all the deluding charms of eloquence and philosophical sophistry: for his eloquence renders absurdities plausible, and his dogmatic conclusions puzzle, without convincing, those who have not ability to refute them.

Throughout the whole animal kingdom every young creature requires almost continual exercise, and the infancy of children, conformable to this intimation, should be passed in harmless gambols, that exercise the feet and hands, without requiring very minute direction from the head, or the constant attention of a nurse. In fact, the care necessary for self-preservation is the first natural exercise of the understanding, as little inventions to amuse the present moment unfold the imagination. But these wise designs of nature are counteracted by mistaken fondness or blind zeal. The child is not left a moment to its own direction, particularly a girl, and thus rendered dependent—dependence is called natural.

To preserve personal beauty, woman's glory! the limbs and faculties are cramped with worse than Chinese bands,[1] and the sedentary life which they are condemned to live, whilst boys frolic in the open air, weakens the muscles and relaxes the nerves.—As for Rousseau's remarks, which have since been echoed by several writers,

---

of life, are fitted to bestow? To touch a musical instrument with useless skill, to exhibit their natural or affected graces to the eyes of indolent and debauched young men, to dissipate their husband's patrimony in riotous and unnecessary expences, these are the only arts cultivated by women in most of the polished nations I had seen. And the consequences are uniformly such as may be expected to proceed from such polluted sources, private misery and public servitude.

" 'But Selene's education was regulated by different views, and conducted upon severer principles; if that can be called severity which opens the mind to a sense of moral and religious duties, and most effectually arms it against the inevitable evils of life.' Mr. Day's *Sandford and Merton*, Vol. III" [Wollstonecraft's note].

The quoted selection is from "The Conclusion of the Story of Sophron and Tigranes." One of several didactic narratives in Day's work, this one is about a wise old man, Chares, who, after a life of adventure, settles down to domesticity. He explains how his only child, a daughter, is to be raised.

1. The Chinese practice of binding girls' feet led to their being disproportionately small. Wollstonecraft may have read of the practice in John Locke's *Some Thoughts Concerning Education*, Art. 12.

that they have naturally, that is from their birth, independent of education, a fondness for dolls, dressing, and talking[2]—they are so puerile as not to merit a serious refutation. That a girl, condemned to sit for hours together listening to the idle chat of weak nurses, or to attend at her mother's toilet, will endeavour to join the conversation, is, indeed, very natural; and that she will imitate her mother or aunts, and amuse herself by adorning her lifeless doll, as they do in dressing her, poor innocent babe! is undoubtedly a most natural consequence. For men of the greatest abilities have seldom had sufficient strength to rise above the surrounding atmosphere; and, if the page of genius have always been blurred by the prejudices of the age, some allowance should be made for a sex, who, like kings, always see things through a false medium.

Pursuing these reflections, the fondness for dress, conspicuous in women, may be easily accounted for, without supposing it the result of a desire to please the sex on which they are dependent. The absurdity, in short, of supposing that a girl is naturally a coquette, and that a desire connected with the impulse of nature to propagate the species,[3] should appear even before an improper education has, by heating the imagination, called it forth prematurely, is so unphilosophical, that such a sagacious observer as Rousseau would not have adopted it, if he had not been accustomed to make reason give way to his desire of singularity, and truth to a favourite paradox.

Yet thus to give a sex to mind was not very consistent with the principles of a man who argued so warmly, and so well, for the immortality of the soul.[4] —But what a weak barrier is truth when it stands in the way of an hypothesis! Rousseau respected—almost adored virtue—and yet he allowed himself to love with sensual fondness.[5] His imagination constantly prepared inflammable fewel[6] for his inflammable senses; but, in order to reconcile his respect for self-denial, fortitude, and those heroic virtues, which a mind like his could not coolly admire, he labours to invert the law of nature, and broaches a doctrine pregnant with mischief and derogatory to the character of supreme wisdom.[7]

2. "The doll is the girl's special plaything; this shows her instinctive bent towards her life's work" (*Émile*, pp. 330–31); "Even the tiniest little girls love finery; they are not content to be pretty, they must be admired . . . their heads are full of this idea" (p. 329); "Women have ready tongues; they talk earlier, more easily, and more pleasantly than men" (p. 339).
3. "Woman is a coquette by profession, but her coquetry varies with her aims; let these aims be in accordance with those of nature, and a woman will receive a fitting education." *Émile*, p. 329.
4. In Book IV of *Émile*, "The Creed of a Savoyard Priest" summarizes Rousseau's argument for the immortality of the soul.
5. Probably a reference to Thérèse Le Vasseur who was Rousseau's lifelong mistress. Near the end of his life they were married in a civil ceremony of Rousseau's creation, but no legal documents were signed to testify to its validity.
6. A common eighteenth-century variant for "fuel."
7. Wollstonecraft's charge here seems to be that Rousseau, because he himself had passions which he found hard to discipline, needed to think that women were natural coquettes in order to justify his own selfish, sensual use of them.

His ridiculous stories, which tend to prove that girls are *naturally* attentive to their persons, without laying any stress on daily example, are below contempt.—And that a little miss should have such a correct taste as to neglect the pleasing amusement of making O's, merely because she perceived that it was an ungraceful attitude, should be selected with the anecdotes of the learned pig.[8]

I have, probably, had an opportunity of observing more girls in their infancy than J. J. Rousseau[9]—I can recollect my own feelings, and I have looked steadily around me; yet, so far from coinciding with him in opinion respecting the first dawn of the female character, I will venture to affirm, that a girl, whose spirits have not been damped by inactivity, or innocence tainted by false shame, will always be a romp, and the doll will never excite attention unless confinement allows her no alternative. Girls and boys, in short, would play harmlessly together, if the distinction of sex was not inculcated long before nature makes any difference.—I will go further, and affirm, as an indisputable fact, that most of the women, in the circle of my observation, who have acted like rational creatures, or shewn any vigour of intellect, have accidentally been allowed to run wild—as some of the elegant formers of the fair sex would insinuate.

The baneful consequences which flow from inattention to health during infancy, and youth, extend further than is supposed—dependence of body naturally produces dependence of mind; and how can she be a good wife or mother, the greater part of whose time is employed to guard against or endure sickness? Nor can it be expected that a woman will resolutely endeavour to strengthen her constitution and abstain from enervating indulgencies, if artificial notions of beauty, and false descriptions of sensibility, have been early entangled with her motives of action. Most men are sometimes obliged to bear with bodily inconveniencies, and to endure, occasionally, the inclemency of the elements; but genteel women

8. " 'I once knew a young person who learned to write before she learned to read, and began to write with her needle before she could use a pen. At first, indeed, she took it into her head to make no other letter than the O: this letter she was constantly making of all sizes, and always the wrong way. Unluckily, one day, as she was intent on this employment, she happened to see herself in the looking-glass; when, taking a dislike to the constrained attitude in which she sat while writing, she threw away her pen, like another Pallas, and determined against making the O any more. Her brother was also equally adverse to writing: it was the confinement, however, and not the constrained attitude, that most disgusted him.' *Rousseau's Emilius*" [Wollstonecraft's note]. The quotation is from *Émile*, p. 332.

The "learned pig" was an animal apparently shown around England in the 1780s because of its more than porcine intelligence. Chapter IX of Sarah Trimmer's popular *Fabulous Histories* (1784) describes the pig as picking out the letters of the alphabet to spell a word suggested from the audience and telling time by pointing its snout to the proper numerals of a large clock provided for the purpose. See also the reference in James Boswell, *Life of Johnson* [(London, 1909), II, 578], where Miss (Anna) Seward tells Dr. Johnson of seeing the animal at Nottingham.

9. If one recollects Wollstonecraft's history as not only the eldest sister in a family having three girls, but also as a governess and as the headmistress in a girls' school, this claim seems to be an understatement, if anything.

are, literally speaking, slaves to their bodies, and glory in their subjection.

I once knew a weak woman of fashion, who was more than commonly proud of her delicacy and sensibility. She thought a distinguishing taste and puny appetite the height of all human perfection, and acted accordingly.—I have seen this weak sophisticated being neglect all the duties of life, yet recline with self-complacency on a sofa, and boast of her want of appetite as a proof of delicacy that extended to, or, perhaps, arose from, her exquisite sensibility: for it is difficult to render intelligible such ridiculous jargon.—Yet, at the moment, I have seen her insult a worthy old gentlewoman, whom unexpected misfortunes had made dependent on her ostentatious bounty, and who, in better days, had claims on her gratitude. Is it possible that a human creature could have become such a weak and depraved being, if, like the Sybarites,[1] dissolved in luxury, every thing like virtue had not been worn away, or never impressed by precept, a poor substitute, it is true, for cultivation of mind, though it serves as a fence against vice?

Such a woman is not a more irrational monster than some of the Roman emperors, who were depraved by lawless power. Yet, since kings have been more under the restraint of law, and the curb, however weak, of honour, the records of history are not filled with such unnatural instances of folly and cruelty, nor does the despotism that kills virtue and genius in the bud, hover over Europe with that destructive blast which desolates Turkey,[2] and renders the men, as well as the soil, unfruitful.

Women are every where in this deplorable state; for, in order to preserve their innocence, as ignorance is courteously termed, truth is hidden from them, and they are made to assume an artificial character before their faculties have acquired any strength. Taught from their infancy that beauty is woman's sceptre, the mind shapes itself to the body, and, roaming round its gilt cage, only seeks to adorn its prison. Men have various employments and pursuits which engage their attention, and give a character to the opening mind; but women, confined to one, and having their thoughts constantly directed to the most insignificant part of themselves, seldom extend their views beyond the triumph of the hour. But were their understanding once emancipated from the slavery to which the pride and sensuality of man and their short-sighted desire, like that of dominion in tyrants, of present sway, has subjected them, we should probably read of their weaknesses with surprise. I must be allowed to pursue the argument a little farther.

1. Inhabitants of Sybaris, an ancient Greek city located in southern Italy, famed for its life of ease and voluptuousness.

2. The dry south wind, laden with dust, known as the simoom or samūm.

Perhaps, if the existence of an evil being were allowed, who, in the allegorical language of scripture, went about seeking whom he should devour,[3] he could not more effectually degrade the human character than by giving a man absolute power.

This argument branches into various ramifications.—Birth, riches, and every extrinsic advantage that exalt a man above his fellows, without any mental exertion, sink him in reality below them. In proportion to his weakness, he is played upon by designing men, till the bloated monster has lost all traces of humanity. And that tribes of men, like flocks of sheep, should quietly follow such a leader, is a solecism that only a desire of present enjoyment and narrowness of understanding can solve. Educated in slavish dependence, and enervated by luxury and sloth, where shall we find men who will stand forth to assert the rights of man;—or claim the privilege of moral beings, who should have but one road to excellence? Slavery to monarchs and ministers, which the world will be long in freeing itself from, and whose deadly grasp stops the progress of the human mind, is not yet abolished.

Let not men then in the pride of power, use the same arguments that tyrannic kings and venal ministers have used, and fallaciously assert that woman ought to be subjected because she has always been so.—But, when man, governed by reasonable laws, enjoys his natural freedom, let him despise woman, if she do not share it with him; and, till that glorious period arrives, in descanting on the folly of the sex, let him not overlook his own.

Women, it is true, obtaining power by unjust means, by practising or fostering vice, evidently lose the rank which reason would assign them, and they become either abject slaves or capricious tyrants. They lose all simplicity, all dignity of mind, in acquiring power, and act as men are observed to act when they have been exalted by the same means.

It is time to effect a revolution in female manners—time to restore to them their lost dignity—and make them, as a part of the human species, labour by reforming themselves to reform the world. It is time to separate unchangeable morals from local manners.—If men be demi-gods—why let us serve them! And if the dignity of the female soul be as disputable as that of animals—if their reason does not afford sufficient light to direct their conduct whilst unerring instinct is denied—they are surely of all creatures the most miserable! and, bent beneath the iron hand of destiny, must submit to be a *fair defect* in creation. But to justify the ways of Providence respecting them,[4] by pointing out some irrefragable reason for thus

---

3. 1 Peter 5:8: "Be sober, be vigilant; because your adversary the devil, as a roaring lion, walketh about, seeking whom he may devour."

4. *Paradise Lost* I.25–26: "I may assert Eternal Providence, / And justify the ways of God to men."

making such a large portion of mankind accountable and not accountable, would puzzle the subtilest casuist.

The only solid foundation for morality appears to be the character of the supreme Being; the harmony of which arises from a balance of attributes;—and, to speak with reverence, one attribute seems to imply the *necessity* of another. He must be just, because he is wise, he must be good, because he is omnipotent. For to exalt one attribute at the expence of another equally noble and necessary, bears the stamp of the warped reason of man—the homage of passion. Man, accustomed to bow down to power in his savage state, can seldom divest himself of this barbarous prejudice, even when civilization determines how much superior mental is to bodily strength; and his reason is clouded by these crude opinions, even when he thinks of the Deity.—His omnipotence is made to swallow up, or preside over his other attributes, and those mortals are supposed to limit his power irreverently, who think that it must be regulated by his wisdom.

I disclaim that specious humility which, after investigating nature, stops at the author.—The High and Lofty One, who inhabiteth eternity, doubtless possesses many attributes of which we can form no conception; but reason tells me that they cannot clash with those I adore—and I am compelled to listen to her voice.

It seems natural for man to search for excellence, and either to trace it in the object that he worships, or blindly to invest it with perfection, as a garment. But what good effect can the latter mode of worship have on the moral conduct of a rational being? He bends to power; he adores a dark cloud, which may open a bright prospect to him, or burst in angry, lawless fury, on his devoted head —he knows not why. And, supposing that the Deity acts from the vague impulse of an undirected will, man must also follow his own, or act according to rules, deduced from principles which he disclaims as irreverent. Into this dilemma have both enthusiasts and cooler thinkers fallen, when they laboured to free men from the wholesome restraints which a just conception of the character of God imposes.

It is not impious thus to scan the attributes of the Almighty: in fact, who can avoid it that exercises his faculties? For to love God as the fountain of wisdom, goodness, and power, appears to be the only worship useful to a being who wishes to acquire either virtue or knowledge. A blind unsettled affection may, like human passions, occupy the mind and warm the heart, whilst, to do justice, love mercy, and walk humbly with our God, is forgotten.[5] I shall pursue

5. Micah 6:8: "What doth the Lord require of thee, but to do justly, and to love mercy, and to walk humbly with thy God?"

this subject still further, when I consider religion in a light opposite to that recommended by Dr. Gregory, who treats it as a matter of sentiment or taste.[6]

To return from this apparent digression. It were to be wished that women would cherish an affection for their husbands, founded on the same principle that devotion ought to rest upon. No other firm base is there under heaven—for let them beware of the fallacious light of sentiment; too often used as a softer phrase for sensuality. It follows then, I think, that from their infancy women should either be shut up like eastern princes, or educated in such a manner as to be able to think and act for themselves.

Why do men halt between two opinions, and expect impossibilities? Why do they expect virtue from a slave, from a being whom the constitution of civil society has rendered weak, if not vicious?

Still I know that it will require a considerable length of time to eradicate the firmly rooted prejudices which sensualists have planted; it will also require some time to convince women that they act contrary to their real interest on an enlarged scale, when they cherish or affect weakness under the name of delicacy, and to convince the world that the poisoned source of female vices and follies, if it be necessary, in compliance with custom, to use synonymous terms in a lax sense, has been the sensual homage paid to beauty:—to beauty of features; for it has been shrewdly observed by a German writer, that a pretty woman, as an object of desire, is generally allowed to be so by men of all descriptions; whilst a fine woman, who inspires more sublime emotions by displaying intellectual beauty, may be overlooked or observed with indifference, by those men who find their happiness in the gratification of their appetites. I foresee an obvious retort—whilst man remains such an imperfect being as he appears hitherto to have been, he will, more or less, be the slave of his appetites; and those women obtaining most power who gratify a predominant one, the sex is degraded by a physical, if not by a moral necessity.

This objection has, I grant, some force; but while such a sublime precept exists, as, 'be pure as your heavenly Father is pure;'[7] it would seem that the virtues of man are not limited by the Being who alone could limit them; and that he may press forward without considering whether he steps out of his sphere by indulging such a noble ambition. To the wild billows it has been said, 'thus far shalt thou go, and no further; and here shall thy proud waves be stayed.'[8] Vainly then do they beat and foam, restrained by the power that confines the struggling planets in their orbits, matter

6. "Religion is rather a matter of sentiment than reasoning." Gregory, p. 13.

7. Matthew 5:48: "Be ye therefore perfect, even as your Father which is in heaven is perfect."

8. Job 38:11.

yields to the great governing Spirit.—But an immortal soul, not restrained by mechanical laws and struggling to free itself from the shackles of matter, contributes to, instead of disturbing, the order of creation, when, co-operating with the Father of spirits, it tries to govern itself by the invariable rule that, in a degree, before which our imagination faints, regulates the universe.

Besides, if women be educated for dependence; that is, to act according to the will of another fallible being, and submit, right or wrong, to power, where are we to stop? Are they to be considered as viceregents allowed to reign over a small domain, and answerable for their conduct to a higher tribunal, liable to error?

It will not be difficult to prove that such delegates will act like men subjected by fear, and make their children and servants endure their tyrannical oppression. As they submit without reason, they will, having no fixed rules to square their conduct by, be kind, or cruel, just as the whim of the moment directs; and we ought not to wonder if sometimes, galled by their heavy yoke, they take a malignant pleasure in resting it on weaker shoulders.

But, supposing a woman, trained up to obedience, be married to a sensible man, who directs her judgment without making her feel the servility of her subjection, to act with as much propriety by this reflected light as can be expected when reason is taken at second hand, yet she cannot ensure the life of her protector; he may die and leave her with a large family.

A double duty devolves on her; to educate them in the character of both father and mother; to form their principles and secure their property. But, alas! she has never thought, much less acted for herself. She has only learned to please[9] men, to depend gracefully on them; yet, encumbered with children, how is she to obtain another protector—a husband to supply the place of reason? A rational

---

9. " 'In the union of the sexes, both pursue one common object, but not in the same manner. From their diversity in this particular, arises the first determinate difference between the moral relations of each. The one should be active and strong, the other passive and weak: it is necessary the one should have both the power and the will, and that the other should make little resistance.

" 'This principle being established, it follows that woman is expressly formed to please the man: if the obligation be reciprocal also, and the man ought to please in his turn, it is not so immediately necessary: his great merit is in his power, and he pleases merely because he is strong. This, I must confess, is not one of the refined maxims of love; it is, however, one of the laws of nature, prior to love itself.

" 'If woman be formed to please and be subjected to man, it is her place, doubtless, to render herself agreeable to him, instead of challenging his passion. The violence of his desires depends on her charms; it is by means of these she should urge him to the exertion of those powers which nature hath given him. The most successful method of exciting them, is, to render such exertion necessary by resistance; as, in that case, self-love is added to desire, and the one triumphs in the victory which the other obliged to acquire. Hence arise the various modes of attack and defence between the sexes; the boldness of one sex and the timidity of the other; and, in a word, that bashfulness and modesty with which nature hath armed the weak, in order to subdue the strong.' *Rousseau's Emilius.* I shall make no other comment on this ingenious passage, than just to observe, that it is the philosophy of lasciviousness" [Wollstonecraft's note]. The quotation is from *Émile*, p. 322.

man, for we are not treading on romantic ground, though he may think her a pleasing docile creature, will not choose to marry a *family* for love, when the world contains many more pretty creatures. What is then to become of her? She either falls an easy prey to some mean fortune-hunter, who defrauds her children of their paternal inheritance, and renders her miserable; or becomes the victim of discontent and blind indulgence. Unable to educate her sons, or impress them with respect; for it is not a play on words to assert, that people are never respected, though filling an important station, who are not respectable; she pines under the anguish of unavailing impotent regret. The serpent's tooth[1] enters into her very soul, and the vices of licentious youth bring her with sorrow, if not with poverty also, to the grave.

This is not an overcharged picture; on the contrary, it is a very possible case, and something similar must have fallen under every attentive eye.

I have, however, taken it for granted, that she was well-disposed, though experience shews, that the blind may as easily be led into a ditch as along the beaten road. But supposing, no very improbable conjecture, that a being only taught to please must still find her happiness in pleasing;—what an example of folly, not to say vice, will she be to her innocent daughters! The mother will be lost in the coquette, and, instead of making friends of her daughters, view them with eyes askance, for they are rivals—rivals more cruel than any other, because they invite a comparison, and drive her from the throne of beauty, who has never thought of a seat on the bench of reason.

It does not require a lively pencil, or the discriminating outline of a caricature, to sketch the domestic miseries and petty vices which such a mistress of a family diffuses. Still she only acts as a woman ought to act, brought up according to Rousseau's system. She can never be reproached for being masculine, or turning out of her sphere; nay, she may observe another of his grand rules, and, cautiously preserving her reputation free from spot, be reckoned a good kind of woman. Yet in what respect can she be termed good? She abstains, it is true, without any great struggle, from committing gross crimes; but how does she fulfil her duties? Duties!—in truth she has enough to think of to adorn her body and nurse a weak constitution.

With respect to religion, she never presumed to judge for herself; but conformed, as a dependent creature should, to the ceremonies of the church which she was brought up in, piously believing that wiser heads than her own have settled that business:—and not to

---

1. *King Lear* I.iv.310–11: "How sharper than a serpent's tooth it is / To have a thankless child!"

doubt is her point of perfection.[2] She therefore pays her tythe of mint and cummin[3]—and thanks her God that she is not as other women are. These are the blessed effects of a good education! These the virtues of man's help-mate![4]

I must relieve myself by drawing a different picture.

Let fancy now present a woman with a tolerable understanding, for I do not wish to leave the line of mediocrity, whose constitution, strengthened by exercise, has allowed her body to acquire its full vigour; her mind, at the same time, gradually expanding itself to comprehend the moral duties of life, and in what human virtue and dignity consist.

Formed thus by the discharge of the relative duties of her station, she marries from affection, without losing sight of prudence, and looking beyond matrimonial felicity, she secures her husband's respect before it is necessary to exert mean arts to please him and feed a dying flame, which nature doomed to expire when the object became familiar, when friendship and forbearance take place of a more ardent affection.—This is the natural death of love, and domestic peace is not destroyed by struggles to prevent its extinction. I also suppose the husband to be virtuous; or she is still more in want of independent principles.

Fate, however, breaks this tie.—She is left a widow, perhaps, without a sufficient provision; but she is not desolate! The pang of nature is felt; but after time has softened sorrow into melancholy resignation, her heart turns to her children with redoubled fondness, and anxious to provide for them, affection gives a sacred heroic cast to her maternal duties. She thinks that not only the eye sees her virtuous efforts from whom all her comfort now must flow, and whose approbation is life; but her imagination, a little abstracted and exalted by grief, dwells on the fond hope that the eyes which her trembling hand closed, may still see how she subdues every wayward passion to fulfil the double duty of being the father as well as the mother of her children. Raised to heroism by misfortunes, she represses the first faint dawning of a natural inclination, before it ripens into love, and in the bloom of life forgets her sex—forgets the pleasure of an awakening passion, which might again have been inspired and returned. She no longer thinks of pleasing, and conscious dignity prevents her from priding herself on account of the

2. In *Émile*, p. 359 ff., Sophy is taught to defer to her husband in religious matters.
3. Matthew 23:23: "Woe unto you, scribes and Pharisees, hypocrites! for ye pay tithe of mint and anise and cummin, and have omitted the weightier matters of the law, judgment, mercy, and faith."
4. " 'O how lovely,' exclaims Rousseau, speaking of Sophia, 'is her ignorance! Happy is he who is destined to instruct her! She will never pretend to be the tutor of her husband, but will be content to be his pupil. Far from attempting to subject him to her taste, she will accommodate herself to his. She will be more estimable to him, than if she was learned: he will have a pleasure in instructing her.' *Rousseau's Emilius*. I shall content myself with simply asking, how friendship can subsist, when love expires, between the master and his pupil?" [Wollstonecraft's note]. The quotation is from *Émile*, p. 373.

praise which her conduct demands. Her children have her love, and her brightest hopes are beyond the grave, where her imagination often strays.

I think I see her surrounded by her children, reaping the reward of her care. The intelligent eye meets hers, whilst health and innocence smile on their chubby cheeks, and as they grow up the cares of life are lessened by their grateful attention. She lives to see the virtues which she endeavoured to plant on principles, fixed into habits, to see her children attain a strength of character sufficient to enable them to endure adversity without forgetting their mother's example.

The task of life thus fulfilled, she calmly waits for the sleep of death, and rising from the grave, may say—Behold, thou gavest me a talent—and here are five talents.[5]

I wish to sum up what I have said in a few words, for I here throw down my gauntlet, and deny the existence of sexual virtues, not excepting modesty. For man and woman, truth, if I understand the meaning of the word, must be the same; yet the fanciful female character, so prettily drawn by poets and novelists, demanding the sacrifice of truth and sincerity, virtue becomes a relative idea, having no other foundation than utility, and of that utility men pretend arbitrarily to judge, shaping it to their own convenience.

Women, I allow, may have different duties to fulfil; but they are *human* duties, and the principles that should regulate the discharge of them, I sturdily maintain, must be the same.

To become respectable, the exercise of their understanding is necessary, there is no other foundation for independence of character; I mean explicitly to say that they must only bow to the authority of reason, instead of being the *modest* slaves of opinion.

In the superior ranks of life how seldom do we meet with a man of superior abilities, or even common acquirements? The reason appears to me clear, the state they are born in was an unnatural one. The human character has ever been formed by the employments the individual, or class, pursues; and if the faculties are not sharpened by necessity, they must remain obtuse. The argument may fairly be extended to women; for, seldom occupied by serious business, the pursuit of pleasure gives that insignificancy to their character which renders the society of the *great* so insipid. The same want of firmness, produced by a similar cause, forces them both to fly from themselves to noisy pleasures, and artificial passions, till vanity takes place of every social affection, and the characteristics of

5. In the parable of the talents (Matthew 25:15–28), a master distributes talents to his servants, to each according to his ability. The servant who receives the most—five talents—invests them wisely and doubles their value, while the servant given one talent foolishly buries it. The parable illustrates the wise use of God's gifts.

humanity can scarcely be discerned. Such are the blessings of civil governments, as they are at present organized, that wealth and female softness equally tend to debase mankind, and are produced by the same cause; but allowing women to be rational creatures, they should be incited to acquire virtues which they may call their own, for how can a rational being be ennobled by any thing that is not obtained by its *own* exertions?

Chap. IV

Observations on the State of Degradation to Which Woman Is Reduced by Various Causes

That woman is naturally weak, or degraded by a concurrence of circumstances, is, I think, clear. But this position I shall simply contrast with a conclusion, which I have frequently heard fall from sensible men in favour of an aristocracy: that the mass of mankind cannot be anything, or the obsequious slaves, who patiently allow themselves to be driven forward, would feel their own consequence, and spurn their chains. Men, they further observe, submit every where to oppression, when they have only to lift up their heads to throw off the yoke; yet, instead of asserting their birthright, they quietly lick the dust, and say, let us eat and drink, for to-morrow we die. Women, I argue from analogy, are degraded by the same propensity to enjoy the present moment; and, at last, despise the freedom which they have not sufficient virtue to struggle to attain. But I must be more explicit.

With respect to the culture of the heart, it is unanimously allowed that sex is out of the question; but the line of subordination in the mental powers is never to be passed over.[1] Only 'absolute in loveliness,'[2] the portion of rationality granted to woman, is, indeed, very scanty; for, denying her genius and judgment, it is scarcely possible to divine what remains to characterize intellect.

The stamen[3] of immortality, if I may be allowed the phrase, is the perfectibility of human reason; for, were man created perfect, or did a flood of knowledge break in upon him, when he arrived at maturity, that precluded error, I should doubt whether his existence would be continued after the dissolution of the body. But, in the present state of things, every difficulty in morals that escapes from human discussion, and equally baffles the investigation of profound

1. "Into what inconsistencies do men fall when they argue without the compass of principles. Women, weak women, are compared with angels; yet, a superior order of beings should be supposed to possess more intellect than man; or, in what does their superiority consist? In the same strain, to drop the sneer, they are allowed to possess more goodness of heart, piety, and benevolence.—I doubt the fact, though it be courteously brought forward, unless ignorance be allowed to be the mother of devotion; for I am firmly persuaded that, on an average, the proportion between virtue and knowledge, is more upon a par than is commonly granted" [Wollstonecraft's note].
2. *Paradise Lost* VIII. 547–48. "So absolute she seems / And in herself complete."
3. Essence or fundamental element.

thinking, and the lightning glance of genius, is an argument on which I build my belief of the immortality of the soul. Reason is, consequentially, the simple power of improvement; or, more properly speaking, of discerning truth. Every individual is in this respect a world in itself. More or less may be conspicuous in one being than another; but the nature of reason must be the same in all, if it be an emanation of divinity, the tie that connects the creature with the Creator; for, can that soul be stamped with the heavenly image, that is not perfected by the exercise of its own reason?[4] Yet outwardly ornamented with elaborate care, and so adorned to delight man, 'that with honour he may love,'[5] the soul of woman is not allowed to have this distinction, and man, ever placed between her and reason, she is always represented as only created to see through a gross medium, and to take things on trust. But dismissing these fanciful theories, and considering woman as a whole, let it be what it will, instead of a part of man, the inquiry is whether she have reason or not. If she have, which, for a moment, I will take for granted, she was not created merely to be the solace of man, and the sexual should not destroy the human character.

Into this error men have, probably, been led by viewing education in a false light; not considering it as the first step to form a being advancing gradually towards perfection;[6] but only as a preparation for life. On this sensual error, for I must call it so, has the false system of female manners been reared, which robs the whole sex of its dignity, and classes the brown and fair with the smiling flowers that only adorn the land. This has ever been the language of men, and the fear of departing from a supposed sexual character, has made even women of superiour sense adopt the same sentiments.[7] Thus understanding, strictly speaking, has been denied

4. " 'The brutes,' says Lord Monboddo, 'remain in the state in which nature has placed them, except in so far as their natural instinct is improved by the culture we bestow upon them.' " [Wollstonecraft's note]. The quotation is from James Burnett, Lord Monboddo, *Of the Origin and Progress of Language* (Edinburgh, 1774), p. 137. Wollstonecraft quotes Monboddo out of context and unfairly, since he had an uncommon respect for brutes, especially orangutangs. He goes on to say that he cannot "exactly determine how far the brute might be carried by culture and education."
5. "Vide Milton" [Wollstonecraft's note]. *Paradise Lost* VIII.57–58: "O when meet now / Such pairs, in love and mutual Honour join'd?"
6. "This word is not strictly just, but I cannot find a better" [Wollstonecraft's note].
7. " 'Pleasure's the portion of th' *inferior* kind; / But glory, virtue, Heaven for *man* design'd.' After writing these lines, how could Mrs. Barbauld write the following ignoble comparison:

To a Lady, with some painted flowers.

Flowers to the fair: to you these flowers I bring,
And strive to greet you with an earlier spring.

Flowers SWEET, *and gay, and* DELICATE LIKE YOU;
Emblems of innocence, and beauty too.
With flowers the Graces bind their yellow hair,
And flowery wreaths consenting lovers wear.
Flowers, the sole luxury which nature knew,
In Eden's pure and guiltless garden grew.
To loftier forms are rougher tasks assign'd;
The sheltering oak resists the stormy wind,
The tougher yew repels invading foes,
And the tall pine for future navies grows;
But this soft family, to cares unknown,
Were born for pleasure and delight ALONE.
Gay without toil, and lovely without art,
They spring to CHEER *the sense, and* GLAD *the*
heart.
Nor blush, my fair, to own you copy these;
Your BEST, *your* SWEETEST *empire is*—TO PLEASE.'
So the men tell us; but virtue, says reason, must be acquired by *rough* toils, and useful struggles with worldly *cares*" [Wollstonecraft's note]. The first couplet is from a poem by Mrs. Barbauld called "To Mrs. P********", with some Drawings of Birds and Insects." The citation is confusing because, given Wollstonecraft's context, "th' inferior kind"

to woman; and instinct, sublimated into wit and cunning, for the purposes of life, has been substituted in its stead.

The power of generalizing ideas, of drawing comprehensive conclusions from individual observations, is the only acquirement, for an immortal being, that really deserves the name of knowledge. Merely to observe, without endeavouring to account for any thing, may (in a very incomplete manner) serve as the common sense of life; but where is the store laid up that is to clothe the soul when it leaves the body?

This power has not only been denied to women; but writers have insisted that it is inconsistent, with a few exceptions, with their sexual character. Let men prove this, and I shall grant that woman only exists for man. I must, however, previously remark, that the power of generalizing ideas, to any great extent, is not very common amongst men or women. But this exercise is the true cultivation of the understanding; and every thing conspires to render the cultivation of the understanding more difficult in the female than the male world.

I am naturally led by this assertion to the main subject of the present chapter, and shall now attempt to point out some of the causes that degrade the sex, and prevent women from generalizing their observations.

I shall not go back to the remote annals of antiquity to trace the history of woman; it is sufficient to allow that she has always been either a slave, or a despot, and to remark, that each of these situations equally retards the progress of reason. The grand source of female folly and vice has ever appeared to me to arise from narrowness of mind; and the very constitution of civil governments has put almost insuperable obstacles in the way to prevent the cultivation of the female understanding:—yet virtue can be built on no other foundation! The same obstacles are thrown in the way of the rich, and the same consequences ensue.

Necessity has been proverbially termed the mother of invention —the aphorism may be extended to virtue. It is an acquirement, and an acquirement to which pleasure must be sacrificed—and who sacrifices pleasure when it is within the grasp, whose mind has not been opened and strengthened by adversity, or the pursuit of knowledge goaded on by necessity?—Happy is it when people have the cares of life to struggle with; for these struggles prevent their becoming a prey to enervating vices, merely from idleness! But, if from their birth men and women be placed in a torrid zone, with

---

might be assumed to be women, whereas in Barbauld's poem they are feathered and crawly creatures. The second selection is quoted above in its entirety.

the meridian sun of pleasure darting directly upon them, how can they sufficiently brace their minds to discharge the duties of life, or even to relish the affections that carry them out of themselves?

Pleasure is the business of woman's life, according to the present modification of society, and while it continues to be so, little can be expected from such weak beings. Inheriting, in a lineal descent from the first fair defect in nature,[8] the sovereignty of beauty, they have, to maintain their power, resigned the natural rights, which the exercise of reason might have procured them, and chosen rather to be short-lived queens than labour to obtain the sober pleasures that arise from equality. Exalted by their inferiority (this sounds like a contradiction), they constantly demand homage as women, though experience should teach them that the men who pride themselves upon paying this arbitrary insolent respect to the sex, with the most scrupulous exactness, are most inclined to tyrannize over, and despise, the very weakness they cherish. Often do they repeat Mr. Hume's sentiments; when, comparing the French and Athenian character, he alludes to women. 'But what is more singular in this whimsical nation, say I to the Athenians, is, that a frolick of yours during the Saturnalia, when the slaves are served by their masters, is seriously continued by them through the whole year, and through the whole course of their lives; accompanied too with some circumstances, which still further augment the absurdity and ridicule. Your sport only elevates for a few days those whom fortune has thrown down, and whom she too, in sport, may really elevate for ever above you. But this nation gravely exalts those, whom nature has subjected to them, and whose inferiority and infirmities are absolutely incurable. The women, though without virtue, are their masters and sovereigns.'[9]

Ah! why do women, I write with affectionate solicitude, condescend to receive a degree of attention and respect from strangers, different from that reciprocation of civility which the dictates of humanity and the politeness of civilization authorise between man and man? And, why do they not discover, when 'in the noon of beauty's power,'[1] that they are treated like queens only to be

8. *Paradise Lost* (X.891–92) refers to woman as "this fair defect / Of nature."
9. This passage occurs in "A Dialogue," which first appeared in the 1777 posthumous edition of "An Enquiry Concerning the Principles of Morals," Hume's famous ethical work. David Hume (1711–76) was an English empirical philosopher, historian, and religious skeptic. The "Dialogue" is not to be found in all editions of the "Enquiry," but appears in David Hume, *Enquiries*, ed. L. A. Selby-Bigge (Oxford, 2nd ed., 1962), pp. 324–43.

1. Wollstonecraft used this phrase when reviewing a translation of Adam Beuvius' *Henrietta of Gerstenfeld* (*Analytical Review*, I, 209). The phrase is related to the "meridian sun of pleasure" (l. 3 in text above) and may have been inspired by Beuvius' comment that "the beauty of Henrietta obscures that of her mother as much as the meridian splendours of the sun outshine the light of the moon" (Beuvius, *Henrietta of Gerstenfeld* [Dublin, 1788], II, 24).

deluded by hollow respect, till they are led to resign, or not assume, their natural prerogatives? Confined then in cages like the feathered race, they have nothing to do but to plume themselves, and stalk with mock majesty from perch to perch. It is true they are provided with food and raiment, for which they neither toil nor spin;[2] but health, liberty, and virtue, are given in exchange. But, where, amongst mankind, has been found sufficient strength of mind to enable a being to resign these adventitious prerogatives; one who, rising with the calm dignity of reason above opinion, dared to be proud of the privileges inherent in man? And it is vain to expect it whilst hereditary power chokes the affections and nips reason in the bud.

The passions of men have thus placed women on thrones, and, till mankind become more reasonable, it is to be feared that women will avail themselves of the power which they attain with the least exertion, and which is the most indisputable. They will smile,—yes, they will smile, though told that—

> 'In beauty's empire is no mean,
> 'And woman, either slave or queen,
> 'Is quickly scorn'd when not ador'd.'[3]

But the adoration comes first, and the scorn is not anticipated.

Lewis the XIVth, in particular, spread factitious manners, and caught, in a specious way, the whole nation in his toils; for, establishing an artful chain of despotism, he made it the interest of the people at large, individually to respect his station and support his power. And women, whom he flattered by a puerile attention to the whole sex, obtained in his reign that prince-like distinction so fatal to reason and virtue.[4]

A king is always a king—and a woman always a woman:[5] his authority and her sex, ever stand between them and rational converse. With a lover, I grant, she should be so,[6] and her sensibility will naturally lead her to endeavour to excite emotion, not to gratify her vanity, but her heart. This I do not allow to be coquetry, it is the artless impulse of nature, I only exclaim against the sexual desire of conquest when the heart is out of the question.

This desire is not confined to women; 'I have endeavoured,' says Lord Chesterfield, 'to gain the hearts of twenty women, whose persons I would not have given a fig for.'[7] The libertine, who, in a gust of passion, takes advantage of unsuspecting tenderness, is a saint

2. Matthew 6:28; Luke 12:27.
3. Anna Laetitia Barbauld, "Song V," lines 16–18, in her *Works* (London, 1825), I, 84.
4. The despotism of France's Louis XIV (1638–1715) was already a legend. Despite its being a brilliant period of art and literature, his reign showed the king was the state personified.
5. "And a wit, always a wit, might be added; for the vain fooleries of wits and beauties to obtain attention, and make conquests, are much upon a par" [Wollstonecraft's note].
6. "She should be so" means being the female stereotype: emotional rather than rational.
7. Wollstonecraft is misquoting Chesterfield's *Letters to His Son*, Letter CCXCIV (November 16, 1752): "And, moreover, I will own to you, under the secrecy of confession, that my vanity has very often made me take pains to make a woman in

when compared with this cold-hearted rascal; for I like to use significant words. Yet only taught to please, women are always on the watch to please, and with true heroic ardour endeavour to gain hearts merely to resign or spurn them, when the victory is decided, and conspicuous.

I must descend to the minutiae of the subject.

I lament that women are systematically degraded by receiving the trivial attentions, which men think it manly to pay to the sex, when, in fact, they are insultingly supporting their own superiority. It is not condescension to bow to an inferior. So ludicrous, in fact, do these ceremonies appear to me, that I scarcely am able to govern my muscles, when I see a man start with eager, and serious solicitude, to lift a handkerchief, or shut a door, when the *lady* could have done it herself, had she only moved a pace or two.

A wild wish has just flown from my heart to my head, and I will not stifle it though it may excite a horse-laugh.—I do earnestly wish to see the distinction of sex confounded in society, unless where love animates the behaviour. For this distinction is, I am firmly persuaded, the foundation of the weakness of character ascribed to woman; is the cause why the understanding is neglected, whilst accomplishments are acquired with sedulous care: and the same cause accounts for their preferring the graceful before the heroic virtues.

Mankind, including every description, wish to be loved and respected by *something*; and the common herd will always take the nearest road to the completion of their wishes. The respect paid to wealth and beauty is the most certain, and unequivocal; and, of course, will always attract the vulgar eye of common minds. Abilities and virtues are absolutely necessary to raise men from the middle rank of life into notice; and the natural consequence is notorious, the middle rank contains most virtue and abilities. Men have thus, in one station, at least an opportunity of exerting themselves with dignity, and of rising by the exertions which really improve a rational creature; but the whole female sex are, till their character is formed, in the same condition as the rich: for they are born, I now speak of a state of civilization, with certain sexual privileges, and whilst they are gratuitously granted them, few will ever think of works of supererogation, to obtain the esteem of a small number of superiour people.

When do we hear of women who, starting out of obscurity, boldly claim respect on account of their great abilities or daring virtues? Where are they to be found?—'To be observed, to be

---

love with me, if I could, for whose person I would not have given a pinch of snuff."

Philip Dormer Stanhope, 4th Earl of Chesterfield (1694–1773), was a politician whose famous epistles to his illegitimate son, Philip, were an attempt to advance him to a respectful place in the world.

attended to, to be taken notice of with sympathy, complacency, and approbation, are all the advantages which they seek.'[8]—True! my male readers will probably exclaim; but let them, before they draw any conclusion, recollect that this was not written originally as descriptive of women, but of the rich. In Dr. Smith's Theory of Moral Sentiments, I have found a general character of people of rank and fortune, that, in my opinion, might with the greatest propriety be applied to the female sex. I refer the sagacious reader to the whole comparison; but must be allowed to quote a passage to enforce an argument that I mean to insist on, as the one most conclusive against a sexual character. For if, excepting warriors, no great men, of any denomination, have ever appeared amongst the nobility, may it not be fairly inferred that their local situation swallowed up the man, and produced a character similar to that of women, who are *localized*, if I may be allowed the word, by the rank they are placed in, by *courtesy*? Women, commonly called Ladies, are not to be contradicted in company, are not allowed to exert any manual strength; and from them the negative virtues only are expected, when any virtues are expected, patience, docility, good-humour, and flexibility; virtues incompatible with any vigorous exertion of intellect. Besides, by living more with each other, and being seldom absolutely alone, they are more under the influence of sentiments than passions. Solitude and reflection are necessary to give to wishes the force of passions, and to enable the imagination to enlarge the object, and make it the most desirable. The same may be said of the rich; they do not sufficiently deal in general ideas, collected by impassioned thinking, or calm investigation, to acquire that strength of character on which great resolves are built. But hear what an acute observer says of the great.

'Do the great seem insensible of the easy price at which they may acquire the publick admiration; or do they seem to imagine that to them, as to other men, it must be the purchase either of sweat or of blood? By what important accomplishments is the young nobleman instructed to support the dignity of his rank, and to render himself worthy of that superiority over his fellow-citizens, to which the virtue of his ancestors had raised them? Is it by knowledge, by industry, by patience, by self-denial, or by virtue of any kind? As all his words, as all his motions are attended to, he learns an habitual regard to every circumstance of ordinary behaviour, and studies to perform all those small duties with the most exact propriety. As he is conscious how much he is observed, and how much mankind are disposed to favour all his inclinations, he acts, upon the most indifferent occasions, with that freedom and elevation which the

8. Adam Smith, *The Theory of Moral Sentiments* (Glasgow, 1809 [first published 1759), p. 86. Smith (1723–90), a Scottish thinker and political economist, is most famous for his *Wealth of Nations*.

thought of this naturally inspires. His air, his manner, his deportment, all mark that elegant and graceful sense of his own superiority, which those who are born to inferior station can hardly ever arrive at. These are the arts by which he proposes to make mankind more easily submit to his authority, and to govern their inclinations according to his own pleasure: and in this he is seldom disappointed. These arts, supported by rank and pre-eminence, are, upon ordinary occasions, sufficient to govern the world. Lewis XIV during the greater part of his reign, was regarded, not only in France, but over all Europe, as the most perfect model of a great prince. But what were the talents and virtues by which he acquired this great reputation? Was it by the scrupulous and inflexible justice of all his undertakings, by the immense dangers and difficulties with which they were attended, or by the unwearied and unrelenting application with which he pursued them? Was it by his extensive knowledge, by his exquisite judgment, or by his heroic valour? It was by none of these qualities. But he was, first of all, the most powerful prince in Europe, and consequently held the highest rank among kings; and then, says his historian, "he surpassed all his courtiers in the gracefulness of his shape, and the majestic beauty of his features. The sound of his voice, noble and affecting, gained those hearts which his presence intimidated. He had a step and a deportment which could suit only him and his rank, and which would have been ridiculous in any other person. The embarrassment which he occasioned to those who spoke to him, flattered that secret satisfaction with which he felt his own superiority." These frivolous accomplishments, supported by his rank, and, no doubt too, by a degree of other talents and virtues, which seems, however, not to have been much above mediocrity, established this prince in the esteem of his own age, and have drawn, even from posterity, a good deal of respect for his memory. Compared with these, in his own times, and in his own presence, no other virtue, it seems, appeared to have any merit. Knowledge, industry, valour, and beneficence, trembled, were abashed, and lost all dignity before them.'[9]

Woman also thus 'in herself complete,'[1] by possessing all these *frivolous* accomplishments, so changes the nature of things

> ————'That what she wills to do or say
> 'Seems wisest, virtuousest, discreetest, best;
> 'All higher knowledge in her *presence* falls
> 'Degraded. Wisdom in discourse with her
> 'Loses discountenanc'd, and, like Folly, shows;
> 'Authority and Reason on her wait.'[2]

---

9. Adam Smith, *op. cit.*, pp. 90–91.
1. *Paradise Lost* VIII. 548.

2. *Paradise Lost* VIII. 549–54. The italics are Wollstonecraft's.

And all this is built on her loveliness!

In the middle rank of life, to continue the comparison, men, in their youth, are prepared for professions, and marriage is not considered as the grand feature in their lives; whilst women, on the contrary, have no other scheme to sharpen their faculties. It is not business, extensive plans, or any of the excursive flights of ambition, that engross their attention; no, their thoughts are not employed in rearing such noble structures. To rise in the world, and have the liberty of running from pleasure to pleasure, they must marry advantageously, and to this object their time is sacrificed, and their persons often legally prostituted. A man when he enters any profession has his eye steadily fixed on some future advantage (and the mind gains great strength by having all its efforts directed to one point), and, full of his business, pleasure is considered as mere relaxation; whilst women seek for pleasure as the main purpose of existence. In fact, from the education, which they receive from society, the love of pleasure may be said to govern them all; but does this prove that there is a sex in souls? It would be just as rational to declare that the courtiers in France, when a destructive system of despotism had formed their character, were not men, because liberty, virtue, and humanity, were sacrificed to pleasure and vanity.—Fatal passions, which have ever domineered over the *whole* race!

The same love of pleasure, fostered by the whole tendency of their education, gives a trifling turn to the conduct of women in most circumstances: for instance, they are ever anxious about secondary things; and on the watch for adventures, instead of being occupied by duties.

A man, when he undertakes a journey, has, in general, the end in view; a woman thinks more of the incidental occurrences, the strange things that may possibly occur on the road; the impression that she may make on her fellow-travellers; and, above all, she is anxiously intent on the care of the finery that she carries with her, which is more than ever a part of herself, when going to figure on a new scene; when, to use an apt French turn of expression, she is going to produce a sensation.—Can dignity of mind exist with such trivial cares?

In short, women, in general, as well as the rich of both sexes, have acquired all the follies and vices of civilization, and missed the useful fruit. It is not necessary for me always to premise, that I speak of the condition of the whole sex, leaving exceptions out of the question. Their senses are inflamed, and their understandings neglected, consequently they become the prey of their senses, delicately termed sensibility, and are blown about by every momentary gust of feeling. Civilized women are, therefore, so weakened by false refinement, that, respecting morals, their condition is much below what it would be were they left in a state nearer to nature. Ever restless and anxious, their over exercised sensibility not only renders them uncomfortable themselves, but troublesome, to use a soft phrase, to others. All their thoughts turn on things calculated to excite emotion; and feeling, when they should reason, their conduct is unstable, and their opinions are wavering—not the wavering produced by deliberation or progressive views, but by contradictory emotions. By fits and starts they are warm in many pursuits; yet this warmth, never concentrated into perseverance, soon exhausts itself; exhaled by its own heat, or meeting with some other fleeting passion, to which reason has never given any specific gravity, neutrality ensues. Miserable, indeed, must be that being whose cultivation of mind has only tended to inflame its passions! A distinction should be made between inflaming and strengthening them. The passions thus pampered, whilst the judgment is left unformed, what can be expected to ensue?—Undoubtedly, a mixture of madness and folly!

This observation should not be confined to the *fair* sex; however, at present, I only mean to apply it to them.

Novels, music, poetry, and gallantry, all tend to make women the creatures of sensation, and their character is thus formed in the mould of folly during the time they are acquiring accomplishments, the only improvement they are excited, by their station in society, to acquire. This overstretched sensibility naturally relaxes the other powers of the mind, and prevents intellect from attaining that sovereignty which it ought to attain to render a rational creature useful to others, and content with its own station: for the exercise of the understanding, as life advances, is the only method pointed out by nature to calm the passions.

Satiety has a very different effect, and I have often been forcibly struck by an emphatical description of damnation:—when the spirit is represented as continually hovering with abortive eagerness round the defiled body, unable to enjoy any thing without the organs of sense. Yet, to their senses, are women made slaves, because it is by their sensibility that they obtain present power.

And will moralists pretend to assert, that this is the condition in which one half of the human race should be encouraged to remain with listless inactivity and stupid acquiescence? Kind instructors! what were we created for? To remain, it may be said, innocent; they mean in a state of childhood.—We might as well never have been born, unless it were necessary that we should be created to enable man to acquire the noble privilege of reason, the power of discerning good from evil, whilst we lie down in the dust from whence we were taken, never to rise again.—

It would be an endless task to trace the variety of meannesses, cares, and sorrows, into which women are plunged by the prevailing opinion, that they were created rather to feel than reason, and that all the power they obtain, must be obtained by their charms and weakness:

'Fine by defect, and amiably weak!'[3]

And, made by this amiable weakness entirely dependent, excepting what they gain by illicit sway, on man, not only for protection, but advice, is it surprising that, neglecting the duties that reason alone points out, and shrinking from trials calculated to strengthen their minds, they only exert themselves to give their defects a graceful covering, which may serve to heighten their charms in the eye of the voluptuary, though it sink them below the scale of moral excellence?

Fragile in every sense of the word, they are obliged to look up to man for every comfort. In the most trifling dangers they cling to their support, with parasitical tenacity, piteously demanding succour; and their *natural* protector extends his arm, or lifts up his voice, to guard the lovely trembler—from what? Perhaps the frown of an old cow, or the jump of a mouse; a rat, would be a serious danger. In the name of reason, and even common sense, what can save such beings from contempt; even though they be soft and fair?

These fears, when not affected, may produce some pretty attitudes; but they shew a degree of imbecility which degrades a rational creature in a way women are not aware of—for love and esteem are very distinct things.

I am fully persuaded that we should hear of none of these infantine airs, if girls were allowed to take sufficient exercise, and not confined in close rooms till their muscles are relaxed, and their powers of digestion destroyed. To carry the remark still further, if fear in girls, instead of being cherished, perhaps, created, were treated in the same manner as cowardice in boys, we should quickly see women with more dignified aspects. It is true, they could not then with equal propriety be termed the sweet flowers that smile in the walk of man; but they would be more respectable members of society, and discharge the important duties of life by the light of their own reason. 'Educate women like men,' says Rousseau, 'and the more they resemble our sex the less power will they have over us.'[4] This is the very point I aim at. I do not wish them to have power over men; but over themselves.

In the same strain have I heard men argue against instructing the poor; for many are the forms that aristocracy assumes. 'Teach them to read and write,' say they, 'and you take them out of the station

3. A misquotation of Pope, *Moral Essays* II.44: "Fine by defect, and delicately weak."
4. *Émile*, p. 327. Rousseau, of course, is not advocating equal education: he has made the point that women have sexual power over men. If women were educated, they would lose their sway, presumably an undesirable state of affairs for them.

assigned them by nature.' An eloquent Frenchman has answered them, I will borrow his sentiments. But they know not, when they make man a brute, that they may expect every instant to see him transformed into a ferocious beast.[5] Without knowledge there can be no morality!

Ignorance is a frail base for virtue! Yet, that it is the condition for which woman was organized, has been insisted upon by the writers who have most vehemently argued in favour of the superiority of man; a superiority not in degree, but essence; though, to soften the argument, they have laboured to prove, with chivalrous generosity, that the sexes ought not to be compared; man was made to reason, woman to feel: and that together, flesh and spirit, they make the most perfect whole, by blending happily reason and sensibility into one character.

And what is sensibility? 'Quickness of sensation; quickness of perception; delicacy.' Thus is it defined by Dr. Johnson;[6] and the definition gives me no other idea than of the most exquisitely polished instinct. I discern not a trace of the image of God in either sensation or matter. Refined seventy times seven,[7] they are still material; intellect dwells not there; nor will fire ever make lead gold!

I come round to my old argument; if woman be allowed to have an immortal soul, she must have, as the employment of life, an understanding to improve. And when, to render the present state more complete, though every thing proves it to be but a fraction of a mighty sum, she is incited by present gratification to forget her grand destination, nature is counteracted, or she was born only to procreate and rot. Or, granting brutes, of every description, a soul, though not a reasonable one, the exercise of instinct and sensibility may be the step, which they are to take, in this life, towards the attainment of reason in the next; so that through all eternity they will lag behind man, who, why we cannot tell, had the power given him of attaining reason in his first mode of existence.

When I treat of the peculiar duties of women, as I should treat of the peculiar duties of a citizen or father, it will be found that I do not mean to insinuate that they should be taken out of their families, speaking of the majority. 'He that hath wife and children,' says Lord Bacon, 'hath given hostages to fortune; for they are impediments to great enterprises, either of virtue or mischief. Certainly

---

5. Since Wollstonecraft was deeply absorbed in the French political cause at this time, she could possibly be referring to the great French statesman Mirabeau's remark to Abbé Siéyès who had just met with discourtesy on the floor of the Constituent Assembly in 1790. Mirabeau is supposed to have chided him by saying, "My dear abbé, you have loosed the bull: do you expect he is not to make use of his horns?"

6. Samuel Johnson's *Dictionary* of 1755, the first of its kind in English, was the arbiter of linguistic correctness.

7. Matthew 18:22: "Jesus saith unto him, I say not unto thee, Until seven times: but, Until seventy times seven."

the best works, and of greatest merit for the public, have proceeded from the unmarried or childless men.'[8] I say the same of women. But, the welfare of society is not built on extraordinary exertions; and were it more reasonably organized, there would be still less need of great abilities, or heroic virtues.

In the regulation of a family, in the education of children, understanding, in an unsophisticated sense, is particularly required: strength both of body and mind; yet the men who, by their writings, have most earnestly laboured to domesticate women, have endeavoured, by arguments dictated by a gross appetite, which satiety had rendered fastidious, to weaken their bodies and cramp their minds. But, if even by these sinister methods they really *persuaded* women, by working on their feelings, to stay at home, and fulfil the duties of a mother and mistress of a family, I should cautiously oppose opinions that led women to right conduct, by prevailing on them to make the discharge of such important duties the main business of life, though reason were insulted. Yet, and I appeal to experience, if by neglecting the understanding they be as much, nay, more detached from these domestic employments, than they could be by the most serious intellectual pursuit, though it may be observed, that the mass of mankind will never vigorously pursue an intellectual object,[9] I may be allowed to infer that reason is absolutely necessary to enable a woman to perform any duty properly, and I must again repeat, that sensibility is not reason.

The comparison with the rich still occurs to me; for, when men neglect the duties of humanity, women will follow their example; a common stream hurries them both along with thoughtless celerity. Riches and honours prevent a man from enlarging his understanding, and enervate all his powers by reversing the order of nature, which has ever made true pleasure the reward of labour. Pleasure—enervating pleasure is, likewise, within women's reach without earning it. But, till hereditary possessions are spread abroad, how can we expect men to be proud of virtue? And, till they are, women will govern them by the most direct means, neglecting their dull domestic duties to catch the pleasure that sits lightly on the wing of time.

'The power of the woman,' says some author, 'is her sensibility;'[1] and men, not aware of the consequence, do all they can to make this power swallow up every other. Those who constantly employ their sensibility will have most: for example; poets, painters, and composers.[2] Yet, when the sensibility is thus increased at the ex-

8. Francis Bacon, Essay VIII, "Of Marriage and the Single Life."
9. "The mass of mankind are rather the slaves of their appetites than of their passions" [Wollstonecraft's note].
1. The sentiment is a commonplace, but Wollstonecraft may be referring to Edmund Burke's phrase: "The beauty of women is considerably ow-

ing to their weakness, or delicacy . . ." (Edmund Burke, *A Philosophical Enquiry into the Origin of Our Ideas of the Sublime and Beautiful* [London, 1759 (repr. The Scolar Press, 1970)], p. 219.
2. "Men of these descriptions pour it into their compositions, to amalgamate the gross materials; and, moulding them with passion, give to the inert body a soul; but, in woman's imagination, love

pence of reason, and even the imagination, why do philosophical men complain of their fickleness? The sexual attention of man particularly acts on female sensibility, and this sympathy has been exercised from their youth up. A husband cannot long pay those attentions with the passion necessary to excite lively emotions, and the heart, accustomed to lively emotions, turns to a new lover, or pines in secret, the prey of virtue or prudence. I mean when the heart has really been rendered susceptible, and the taste formed; for I am apt to conclude, from what I have seen in fashionable life, that vanity is oftener fostered than sensibility by the mode of education, and the intercourse between the sexes, which I have reprobated; and that coquetry more frequently proceeds from vanity than from that inconstancy, which overstrained sensibility naturally produces.

Another argument that has had great weight with me, must, I think, have some force with every considerate benevolent heart. Girls who have been thus weakly educated, are often cruelly left by their parents without any provision; and, of course, are dependent on, not only the reason, but the bounty of their brothers. These brothers are, to view the fairest side of the question, good sort of men, and give as a favour, what children of the same parents had an equal right to. In this equivocal humiliating situation, a docile female may remain some time, with a tolerable degree of comfort. But, when the brother marries, a probable circumstance, from being considered as the mistress of the family, she is viewed with averted looks as an intruder, an unnecessary burden on the benevolence of the master of the house, and his new partner.[3]

Who can recount the misery, which many unfortunate beings, whose minds and bodies are equally weak, suffer in such situations —unable to work, and ashamed to beg? The wife, a cold-hearted, narrow-minded, woman, and this is not an unfair supposition; for the present mode of education does not tend to enlarge the heart any more than the understanding, is jealous of the little kindness which her husband shews to his relations; and her sensibility not rising to humanity, she is displeased at seeing the property of *her* children lavished on an helpless sister.

These are matters of fact, which have come under my eye again and again. The consequence is obvious, the wife has recourse to cunning to undermine the habitual affection, which she is afraid openly to oppose; and neither tears nor caresses are spared till the spy is worked out of her home, and thrown on the world, unprepared for its difficulties; or sent, as a great effort of generosity, or from some regard to propriety, with a small stipend, and an uncultivated mind, into joyless solitude.

---

alone concentrates these ethereal beams" [Wollstonecraft's note].

3. Wollstonecraft may have in mind the situation of her sister Everina who, before Mary Wollstonecraft helped to make her independent, had been living off their brother Edward.

These two women may be much upon a par, with respect to reason and humanity; and changing situations, might have acted just the same selfish part; but had they been differently educated, the case would also have been very different. The wife would not have had that sensibility, of which self is the centre, and reason might have taught her not to expect, and not even to be flattered by, the affection of her husband, if it led him to violate prior duties. She would wish not to love him merely because he loved her, but on account of his virtues; and the sister might have been able to struggle for herself instead of eating the bitter bread of dependence.

I am, indeed, persuaded that the heart, as well as the understanding, is opened by cultivation; and by, which may not appear so clear, strengthening the organs; I am not now talking of momentary flashes of sensibility, but of affections. And, perhaps, in the education of both sexes, the most difficult task is so to adjust instruction as not to narrow the understanding, whilst the heart is warmed by the generous juices of spring, just raised by the electric fermentation of the season; nor to dry up the feelings by employing the mind in investigations remote from life.

With respect to women, when they receive a careful education, they are either made fine ladies, brimful of sensibility, and teeming with capricious fancies; or mere notable women.[4] The latter are often friendly, honest creatures, and have a shrewd kind of good sense joined with worldly prudence, that often render them more useful members of society than the fine sentimental lady, though they possess neither greatness of mind nor taste. The intellectual world is shut against them; take them out of their family or neighbourhood, and they stand still; the mind finding no employment, for literature affords a fund of amusement which they have never sought to relish, but frequently to despise. The sentiments and taste of more cultivated minds appear ridiculous, even in those whom chance and family connections have led them to love; but in mere acquaintance they think it all affectation.

A man of sense can only love such a woman on account of her sex, and respect her, because she is a trusty servant. He lets her, to preserve his own peace, scold the servants, and go to church in clothes made of the very best materials. A man of her own size of understanding would, probably, not agree so well with her; for he might wish to encroach on her prerogative, and manage some domestic concerns himself. Yet women, whose minds are not enlarged by cultivation, or the natural selfishness of sensibility expanded by reflection, are very unfit to manage a family; for, by an undue stretch of power, they are always tyrannizing to support a superiority that only rests on the arbitrary distinction of fortune. The evil is sometimes more serious, and domestics are deprived of

4. "Notable" women are industrious and energetic housewives.

innocent indulgences, and made to work beyond their strength, in order to enable the notable woman to keep a better table, and outshine her neighbours in finery and parade. If she attend to her children, it is, in general, to dress them in a costly manner—and, whether this attention arise from vanity or fondness, it is equally pernicious.

Besides, how many women of this description pass their days; or, at least, their evenings, discontentedly. Their husbands acknowledge that they are good managers, and chaste wives; but leave home to seek for more agreeable, may I be allowed to use a significant French word, *piquant* society; and the patient drudge, who fulfils her task, like a blind horse in a mill, is defrauded of her just reward; for the wages due to her are the caresses of her husband; and women who have so few resources in themselves, do not very patiently bear this privation of a natural right.

A fine lady, on the contrary, has been taught to look down with contempt on the vulgar employments of life; though she has only been incited to acquire accomplishments that rise a degree above sense; for even corporeal accomplishments cannot be acquired with any degree of precision unless the understanding has been strengthened by exercise. Without a foundation of principles taste is superficial, grace must arise from something deeper than imitation. The imagination, however, is heated, and the feelings rendered fastidious, if not sophisticated; or, a counterpoise of judgment is not acquired, when the heart still remains artless, though it becomes too tender.

These women are often amiable; and their hearts are really more sensible to general benevolence, more alive to the sentiments that civilize life, than the square-elbowed family drudge; but, wanting a due proportion of reflection and self-government, they only inspire love; and are the mistresses of their husbands, whilst they have any hold on their affections; and the platonic friends of his male acquaintance. These are the fair defects in nature; the women who appear to be created not to enjoy the fellowship of man, but to save him from sinking into absolute brutality, by rubbing off the rough angles of his character; and by playful dalliance to give some dignity to the appetite that draws him to them.—Gracious Creator of the whole human race! hast thou created such a being as woman, who can trace thy wisdom in thy works, and feel that thou alone art by thy nature exalted above her,—for no better purpose?—Can she believe that she was only made to submit to man, her equal, a being, who, like her, was sent into the world to acquire virtue?— Can she consent to be occupied merely to please him; merely to adorn the earth, when her soul is capable of rising to thee?—And can she rest supinely dependent on man for reason, when she ought to mount with him the arduous steeps of knowledge?—

Yet, if love be the supreme good, let women be only educated to inspire it, and let every charm be polished to intoxicate the senses;

but, if they be moral beings, let them have a chance to become intelligent; and let love to man be only a part of that glowing flame of universal love, which, after encircling humanity, mounts in grateful incense to God.

To fulfil domestic duties much resolution is necessary, and a serious kind of perseverance that requires a more firm support than emotions, however lively and true to nature. To give an example of order, the soul of virtue, some austerity of behaviour must be adopted, scarcely to be expected from a being who, from its infancy, has been made the weathercock of its own sensations. Whoever rationally means to be useful must have a plan of conduct; and, in the discharge of the simplest duty, we are often obliged to act contrary to the present impulse of tenderness or compassion. Severity is frequently the most certain, as well as the most sublime proof of affection; and the want of this power over the feelings, and of that lofty, dignified affection, which makes a person prefer the future good of the beloved object to a present gratification, is the reason why so many fond mothers spoil their children, and has made it questionable whether negligence or indulgence be most hurtful, but I am inclined to think, that the latter has done most harm.

Mankind seem to agree that children should be left under the management of women during their childhood. Now, from all the observation that I have been able to make, women of sensibility are the most unfit for this task, because they will infallibly, carried away by their feelings, spoil a child's temper. The management of the temper, the first, and most important branch of education, requires the sober steady eye of reason; a plan of conduct equally distant from tyranny and indulgence: yet these are the extremes that people of sensibility alternately fall into; always shooting beyond the mark. I have followed this train of reasoning much further, till I have concluded, that a person of genius is the most improper person to be employed in education, public or private. Minds of this rare species see things too much in masses, and seldom, if ever, have a good temper. That habitual cheerfulness, termed good-humour, is, perhaps, as seldom united with great mental powers, as with strong feelings. And those people who follow, with interest and admiration, the flights of genius; or, with cooler approbation suck in the instruction which has been elaborately prepared for them by the profound thinker, ought not to be disgusted, if they find the former choleric, and the latter morose; because liveliness of fancy, and a tenacious comprehension of mind, are scarcely compatible with that pliant urbanity which leads a man, at least, to bend to the opinions and prejudices of others, instead of roughly confronting them.

But, treating of education or manners, minds of a superior class are not to be considered, they may be left to chance; it is the multitude, with moderate abilities, who call for instruction, and catch the colour of the atmosphere they breathe. This respectable concourse, I contend, men and women, should not have their sensations heightened in the hot-bed of luxurious indolence, at the expence of their understanding; for, unless there be a ballast of understanding, they will never become either virtuous or free: an aristocracy, founded on property, or sterling talents, will ever sweep before it, the alternately timid, and ferocious, slaves of feeling.

Numberless are the arguments, to take another view of the subject, brought forward with a shew of reason, because supposed to be deduced from nature, that men have used morally and physically, to degrade the sex. I must notice a few.

The female understanding has often been spoken of with contempt, as arriving sooner at maturity than the male. I shall not answer this argument by alluding to the early proofs of reason, as well as genius, in Cowley, Milton, and Pope,[5] but only appeal to experience to decide whether young men, who are early introduced into company (and examples now abound), do not acquire the same precocity. So notorious is this fact, that the bare mentioning of it must bring before people, who at all mix in the world, the idea of a number of swaggering apes of men, whose understandings are narrowed by being brought into the society of men when they ought to have been spinning a top or twirling a hoop.

It has also been asserted, by some naturalists, that men do not attain their full growth and strength till thirty; but that women arrive at maturity by twenty.[6] I apprehend that they reason on false ground, led astray by the male prejudice, which deems beauty the perfection of woman—mere beauty of features and complexion, the vulgar acceptation of the word, whilst male beauty is allowed to have some connection with the mind. Strength of body, and that character of countenance, which the French term a *physionomie*,[7] women do not acquire before thirty, any more than men. The little artless tricks of children, it is true, are particularly pleasing and attractive; yet, when the pretty freshness of youth is worn off, these artless graces become studied airs, and disgust every person of taste. In the countenance of girls we only look for vivacity and bashful modesty; but, the spring-tide of life over, we look for soberer sense in the face, and for traces of passion, instead of the dimples of animal spirits; expecting to see individuality of character, the only

5. "Many other names might be added" [Wollstonecraft's note]. Abraham Cowley (1618–67) putatively began writing verses at age ten; John Milton (1608–74) studied passionately at an early age and wrote poetry by age ten; and Alexander Pope (1688–1744) wrote his first epic between the ages of thirteen and fifteen. Wollstonecraft probably read of all three in Dr. Samuel Johnson's *The Lives of the Most Eminent English Poets* (1779–81).
6. See the remark of Buffon, one of the most famous naturalists of the time: "But, in women, the body sooner attains this symmetry. As their size is smaller, and their muscles, and other parts, less strong, compact, and solid, than those of men, they arrive more early at a state of maturity. A woman at twenty years is as perfectly formed as a man at thirty" (Georges Buffon, *Natural History*, trans. William Smellie [Edinburgh, 1780], II, 436).
7. Cast of the features that reveal one's special character.

fastener of the affections.[8] We then wish to converse, not to fondle; to give scope to our imaginations as well as to the sensations of our hearts.

At twenty the beauty of both sexes is equal; but the libertinism of man leads him to make the distinction, and superannuated coquettes are commonly of the same opinion; for, when they can no longer inspire love, they pay for the vigour and vivacity of youth. The French, who admit more of mind into their notions of beauty, give the preference to women of thirty. I mean to say that they allow women to be in their most perfect state, when vivacity gives place to reason, and to that majestic seriousness of character, which marks maturity;—or, the resting point. In youth, till twenty, the body shoots out, till thirty the solids are attaining a degree of density; and the flexible muscles, growing daily more rigid, give character to the countenance; that is, they trace the operations of the mind with the iron pen of fate, and tell us not only what powers are within, but how they have been employed.

It is proper to observe, that animals who arrive slowly at maturity, are the longest lived, and of the noblest species. Men cannot, however, claim any natural superiority from the grandeur of longevity; for in this respect nature has not distinguished the male.

Polygamy is another physical degradation; and a plausible argument for a custom, that blasts every domestic virtue, is drawn from the well-attested fact, that in the countries where it is established, more females are born than males. This appears to be an indication of nature, and to nature, apparently reasonable speculations must yield. A further conclusion obviously presented itself; if polygamy be necessary, woman must be inferior to man, and made for him.

With respect to the formation of the fetus in the womb, we are very ignorant; but it appears to me probable, that an accidental physical cause may account for this phenomenon, and prove it not to be a law of nature.[9] I have met with some pertinent observations on the subject in Forster's Account of the Isles of the South-Sea, that will explain my meaning. After observing that of the two sexes amongst animals, the most vigorous and hottest constitution always prevails, and produces its kind; he adds,—'If this be applied to the inhabitants of Africa, it is evident that the men there, accustomed to polygamy, are enervated by the use of so many women, and therefore less vigorous; the women, on the contrary, are of a hotter constitution, not only on account of their more irritable nerves, more sensible organization, and more lively fancy; but likewise because they are deprived in their matrimony of that share of physi-

8. "The strength of an affection is, generally, in the same proportion as the character of the species in the object beloved, is lost in that of the individual" [Wollstonecraft's note].

9. Wollstonecraft is referring to whether the fetus will be male or female. We know now that the "accidental physical cause" is a matter of x and y chromosomes.

cal love which, in a monogamous condition, would all be theirs; and thus, for the above reasons, the generality of children are born females.

'In the greater part of Europe it has been proved by the most accurate lists of mortality, that the proportion of men to women is nearly equal, or, if any difference takes place, the males born are more numerous, in the proportion of 105 to 100.'[1]

The necessity of polygamy, therefore, does not appear; yet when a man seduces a woman, it should, I think, be termed a *left-handed*[2] marriage, and the man should be *legally* obliged to maintain the woman and her children, unless adultery, a natural divorcement, abrogated the law. And this law should remain in force as long as the weakness of women caused the word seduction to be used as an excuse for their frailty and want of principle; nay, while they depend on man for a subsistence, instead of earning it by the exertion of their own hands or heads. But these women should not, in the full meaning of the relationship, be termed wives, or the very purpose of marriage would be subverted, and all those endearing charities that flow from personal fidelity, and give a sanctity to the tie, when neither love nor friendship unites the hearts, would melt into selfishness. The woman who is faithful to the father of her children demands respect, and should not be treated like a prostitute; though I readily grant that if it be necessary for a man and woman to live together in order to bring up their offspring, nature never intended that a man should have more than one wife.

Still, highly as I respect marriage, as the foundation of almost every social virtue, I cannot avoid feeling the most lively compassion for those unfortunate females who are broken off from society, and by one error torn from all those affections and relationships that improve the heart and mind. It does not frequently even deserve the name of error; for many innocent girls become the dupes of a sincere, affectionate heart, and still more are, as it may emphatically be termed, *ruined* before they know the difference between virtue and vice:—and thus prepared by their education for infamy, they become infamous. Asylums and Magdalenes[3] are not the proper remedies for these abuses. It is justice, not charity, that is wanting in the world!

A woman who has lost her honour, imagines that she cannot fall lower, and as for recovering her former station, it is impossible; no

1. John Reinhold Forster, *Observations Made During a Voyage Round the World* (London, 1778), pp. 425–26. Forster traveled the South Seas with Captain Cook's voyage. After the passage quoted by Wollstonecraft, he notes that in the Easter Islands the crew found only about 900 people, 50 of those being women, despite the fact that if the theory quoted here were true, more males should be being born.

2. Illegal, or "morganatic," marriage in which the groom gives his left hand instead of right. Offspring of such marriages would have no legal rights, since the marriage was usually undertaken by a man in an exalted rank and a woman in a lower station with the provision that the children be supported but not be permitted to claim the rank or possessions of the titled father.

3. Institutions for the reformation of prostitutes.

exertion can wash this stain away. Losing thus every spur, and having no other means of support, prostitution becomes her only refuge, and the character is quickly depraved by circumstances over which the poor wretch has little power, unless she possesses an uncommon portion of sense and loftiness of spirit. Necessity never makes prostitution the business of men's lives; though numberless are the women who are thus rendered systematically vicious. This, however, arises, in a great degree, from the state of idleness in which women are educated, who are always taught to look up to man for a maintenance, and to consider their persons as the proper return for his exertions to support them. Meretricious airs, and the whole science of wantonness, have then a more powerful stimulus than either appetite or vanity; and this remark gives force to the prevailing opinion, that with chastity all is lost that is respectable in woman. Her character depends on the observance of one virtue, though the only passion fostered in her heart—is love. Nay, the honour of a woman is not made even to depend on her will.

When Richardson [4] makes Clarissa tell Lovelace that he had robbed her of her honour, he must have had strange notions of honour and virtue. For, miserable beyond all names of misery is the condition of a being, who could be degraded without its own consent! This excess of strictness I have heard vindicated as a salutary error. I shall answer in the words of Leibnitz—'Errors are often useful; but it is commonly to remedy other errors.' [5]

Most of the evils of life arise from a desire of present enjoyment that outruns itself. The obedience required of women in the marriage state comes under this description; the mind, naturally weakened by depending on authority, never exerts its own powers, and the obedient wife is thus rendered a weak indolent mother. Or, supposing that this is not always the consequence, a future state of existence is scarcely taken into the reckoning when only negative virtues are cultivated. For, in treating of morals, particularly when women are alluded to, writers have too often considered virtue in a very limited sense, and made the foundation of it *solely* worldly utility; nay, a still more fragile base has been given to this stupendous fabric, and the wayward fluctuating feelings of men have been made the standard of virtue. Yes, virtue as well as religion, has been subjected to the decisions of taste.

It would almost provoke a smile of contempt, if the vain absurdities of man did not strike us on all sides, to observe, how eager men

---

4. "Dr. Young supports the same opinion, in his plays, when he talks of the misfortune that shunned the light of day" [Wollstonecraft's note]. Mandane's speech in Edward Young's *Busiris, King of Egypt*: "So black a story well might shun the day" (Edward Young, *Works* [London, 1762], II, 13). Lovelace is the rake in Samuel Richardson's novel *Clarissa*; he seduces the heroine, Clarissa Har-

lowe.
5. From the Preface to the German philosopher's famous religious work, *Theodicy* (G. W. Leibniz, *Theodicy*, ed. Austin Farrer, trans. E. M. Huggard [New Haven, 1952], p. 56). Leibniz (1646–1716) is probably most famous for his doctrine of the "pre-established harmony" of the universe.

are to degrade the sex from whom they pretend to receive the chief pleasure of life; and I have frequently with full conviction retorted Pope's sarcasm on them;[6] or, to speak explicitly, it has appeared to me applicable to the whole human race. A love of pleasure or sway seems to divide mankind, and the husband who lords it in his little haram thinks only of his pleasure or his convenience. To such lengths, indeed, does an intemperate love of pleasure carry some prudent men, or worn out libertines, who marry to have a safe bed-fellow, that they seduce their own wives.—Hymen[7] banishes modesty, and chaste love takes its flight.

Love, considered as an animal appetite, cannot long feed on itself without expiring. And this extinction in its own flame, may be termed the violent death of love. But the wife who has thus been rendered licentious, will probably endeavour to fill the void left by the loss of her husband's attentions; for she cannot contentedly become merely an upper servant after having been treated like a goddess. She is still handsome, and, instead of transferring her fondness to her children, she only dreams of enjoying the sunshine of life. Besides, there are many husbands so devoid of sense and parental affection, that during the first effervescence of voluptuous fondness they refuse to let their wives suckle their children. They are only to dress and live to please them: and love—even innocent love, soon sinks into lasciviousness when the exercise of a duty is sacrificed to its indulgence.

Personal attachment is a very happy foundation for friendship; yet, when even two virtuous young people marry, it would, perhaps, be happy if some circumstances checked their passion; if the recollection of some prior attachment, or disappointed affection, made it on one side, at least, rather a match founded on esteem. In that case they would look beyond the present moment, and try to render the whole of life respectable, by forming a plan to regulate a friendship which only death ought to dissolve.

Friendship is a serious affection; the most sublime of all affections, because it is founded on principle, and cemented by time. The very reverse may be said of love. In a great degree, love and friendship cannot subsist in the same bosom; even when inspired by different objects they weaken or destroy each other, and for the same object can only be felt in succession. The vain fears and fond jealousies, the winds which fan the flame of love, when judiciously or artfully tempered, are both incompatible with the tender confidence and sincere respect of friendship.

Love, such as the glowing pen of genius has traced, exists not on earth, or only resides in those exalted, fervid imaginations that have

6. Alexander Pope, *Moral Essays* II.207–10: "In Men are various Ruling Passions find, / In Women, two almost divide the Kind, / Those only fix'd, they first or last obey; / The Love of Pleasure, and the Love of Sway."
7. Greek god of marriage.

sketched such dangerous pictures. Dangerous, because they not only afford a plausible excuse, to the voluptuary who disguises sheer sensuality under a sentimental veil; but as they spread affectation, and take from the dignity of virtue. Virtue, as the very word imports, should have an appearance of seriousness, if not of austerity; and to endeavour to trick her out in the garb of pleasure, because the epithet has been used as another name for beauty, is to exalt her on a quicksand; a most insidious attempt to hasten her fall by apparent respect. Virtue and pleasure are not, in fact, so nearly allied in this life as some eloquent writers have laboured to prove. Pleasure prepares the fading wreath, and mixes the intoxicating cup; but the fruit which virtue gives, is the recompence of toil: and, gradually seen as it ripens, only affords calm satisfaction; nay, appearing to be the result of the natural tendency of things, it is scarcely observed. Bread, the common food of life, seldom thought of as a blessing, supports the constitution and preserves health; still feasts delight the heart of man, though disease and even death lurk in the cup or dainty that elevates the spirits or tickles the palate. The lively heated imagination likewise, to apply the comparison, draws the picture of love, as it draws every other picture, with those glowing colours, which the daring hand will steal from the rainbow that is directed by a mind, condemned in a world like this, to prove its noble origin by panting after unattainable perfection; ever pursuing what it acknowledges to be a fleeting dream. An imagination of this vigorous cast can give existence to insubstantial forms, and stability to the shadowy reveries which the mind naturally falls into when realities are found vapid. It can then depict love with celestial charms, and dote on the grand ideal object—it can imagine a degree of mutual affection that shall refine the soul, and not expire when it has served as a 'scale to heavenly;'[8] and, like devotion, make it absorb every meaner affection and desire. In each others arms, as in a temple, with its summit lost in the clouds, the world is to be shut out, and every thought and wish, that do not nurture pure affection and permanent virtue.—Permanent virtue! alas! Rousseau, respectable visionary! thy paradise would soon be violated by the entrance of some unexpected guest. Like Milton's it would only contain angels, or men sunk below the dignity of rational creatures. Happiness is not material, it cannot be seen or felt! Yet the eager pursuit of the good which every one shapes to his own fancy, proclaims man the lord of this lower world, and to be an intelligential creature, who is not to receive, but acquire happiness. They, therefore, who complain of the delusions of passion, do not recollect that they are exclaiming against a strong proof of the immortality of the soul.

But leaving superior minds to correct themselves, and pay dearly

---

8. *Paradise Lost* IV.354–55: "and in th' ascending scale / Of Heav'n the stars that usher Evening rose."

for their experience, it is necessary to observe, that it is not against strong, persevering passions; but romantic wavering feelings that I wish to guard the female heart by exercising the understanding: for these paradisiacal reveries are oftener the effect of idleness than of a lively fancy.

Women have seldom sufficient serious employment to silence their feelings; a round of little cares, or vain pursuits frittering away all strength of mind and organs, they become naturally only objects of sense.—In short, the whole tenour of female education (the education of society) tends to render the best disposed romantic and inconstant; and the remainder vain and mean. In the present state of society this evil can scarcely be remedied, I am afraid, in the slightest degree; should a more laudable ambition ever gain ground they may be brought nearer to nature and reason, and become more virtuous and useful as they grow more respectable.

But, I will venture to assert that their reason will never acquire sufficient strength to enable it to regulate their conduct, whilst the making an appearance in the world is the first wish of the majority of mankind. To this weak wish the natural affections, and the most useful virtues are sacrificed. Girls marry merely to *better themselves*, to borrow a significant vulgar phrase, and have such perfect power over their hearts as not to permit themselves to *fall in love* till a man with a superiour fortune offers. On this subject I mean to enlarge in a future chapter; it is only necessary to drop a hint at present, because women are so often degraded by suffering the selfish prudence of age to chill the ardour of youth.

From the same source[9] flows an opinion that young girls ought to dedicate great part of their time to needle-work; yet, this employment contracts their faculties more than any other that could have been chosen for them, by confining their thoughts to their persons. Men order their clothes to be made, and have done with the subject; women make their own clothes, necessary or ornamental, and are continually talking about them; and their thoughts follow their hands. It is not indeed the making of necessaries that weakens the mind; but the frippery of dress. For when a woman in the lower rank of life makes her husband's and children's clothes, she does her duty, this is her part of the family business; but when women work only to dress better than they could otherwise afford, it is worse than sheer loss of time. To render the poor virtuous they must be employed, and women in the middle rank of life, did they not ape the fashions of the nobility, without catching their ease, might employ them, whilst they themselves managed their families, instructed their children, and exercised their own minds. Gardening, experimental philosophy, and literature, would afford them subjects to think of and matter for conversation, that in some degree would

9. Society's idea of female education, that is.

exercise their understandings. The conversation of French women, who are not so rigidly nailed to their chairs to twist lappets, [1] and knot ribands, is frequently superficial; but, I contend, that it is not half so insipid as that of those English women whose time is spent in making caps, bonnets, and the whole mischief of trimmings, not to mention shopping, bargain-hunting, &c. &c.: and it is the decent, prudent women, who are most degraded by these practices; for their motive is simply vanity. The wanton who exercises her taste to render her passion alluring, has something more in view.

These observations all branch out of a general one, which I have before made, and which cannot be too often insisted upon, for, speaking of men, women, or professions, it will be found that the employment of the thoughts shapes the character both generally and individually. The thoughts of women ever hover round their persons, and is it surprising that their persons are reckoned most valuable? Yet some degree of liberty of mind is necessary even to form the person; and this may be one reason why some gentle wives have so few attractions beside that of sex. Add to this, sedentary employments render the majority of women sickly—and false notions of female excellence make them proud of this delicacy, though it be another fetter, that by calling the attention continually to the body, cramps the activity of the mind.

Women of quality seldom do any of the manual part of their dress, consequently only their taste is exercised, and they acquire, by thinking less of the finery, when the business of their toilet is over, that ease, which seldom appears in the deportment of women, who dress merely for the sake of dressing. In fact, the observation with respect to the middle rank, the one in which talents thrive best, extends not to women; for those of the superior class, by catching, at least, a smattering of literature, and conversing more with men, on general topics, acquire more knowledge than the women who ape their fashions and faults without sharing their advantages. With respect to virtue, to use the word in a comprehensive sense, I have seen most in low life. Many poor women maintain their children by the sweat of their brow, and keep together families that the vices of the fathers would have scattered abroad; but gentlewomen are too indolent to be actively virtuous, and are softened rather than refined by civilization. Indeed, the good sense which I have met with, among the poor women who have had few advantages of education, and yet have acted heroically, strongly confirmed me in the opinion that trifling employments have rendered woman a trifler. Man, taking her [2] body, the mind is left to rust; so that while physical love enervates man, as being his favourite recreation, he will endeav-

1. To plait ribbons attached to womens' caps and hats.
2. " 'I take her body,' says Ranger" [Wollstonecraft's note]. Ranger, the dissolute rake in Benja-min Hoadly's play, "The Suspicious Husband," comes into his chambers from a night of carousing and reads from one of William Congreve's *Poems on Several Occasions* entitled simply, "Song": "You

our to enslave woman:—and, who can tell, how many generations may be necessary to give vigour to the virtue and talents of the freed posterity of abject slaves?[3]

In tracing the causes that, in my opinion, have degraded woman, I have confined my observations to such as universally act upon the morals and manners of the whole sex, and to me it appears clear that they all spring from want of understanding. Whether this arise from a physical or accidental weakness of faculties, time alone can determine; for I shall not lay any great stress on the example of a few women[4] who, from having received a masculine education, have acquired courage and resolution; I only contend that the men who have been placed in similar situations, have acquired a similar character—I speak of bodies of men, and that men of genius and talents have started out of a class, in which women have never yet been placed.

Chap. V

Animadversions on Some of the Writers Who Have Rendered Women Objects of Pity, Bordering on Contempt.

The opinions speciously supported, in some modern publications on the female character and education, which have given the tone to most of the observations made, in a more cursory manner, on the sex, remain now to be examined.

SECT. I

I shall begin with Rousseau, and give a sketch of his character of woman, in his own words, interspersing comments and reflections.

think she's false. I'm sure she's kind, / I take her body, you her mind; / Which has the better bargain?"
3. " 'Supposing that women are voluntary slaves—slavery of any kind is unfavourable to human happiness and improvement.' *Knox's Essays*" [Wollstonecraft's note]. The quoted matter appears in Vicesimus Knox's *Essays, Moral and Literary*, Essay No. 5, "On the Fear of Appearing Singular," and reads: "The subjects of these self-erected tyrants [i.e., those who establish what norm of human affairs will be, either "some rich, gross, unphilosophical man, or some titled frivolous lady, distinguished for boldness, but not for excellence"] are most truly slaves, though voluntary slaves; but as slavery of any kind is unfavourable to human happiness and improvement, I will venture to offer a few suggestions, which may induce the subjugated tribes to revolt, and claim their invaluable birthright, their natural liberty." Knox's subject throughout is conforming human beings, not sim-

ply women and, though Knox was eminently a champion of women, he never calls them "slaves" in the *Essays*. Wollstonecraft here is suiting a quotation to her own purposes.
4. "Sappho, Eloisa, Mrs. Macaulay, the Empress of Russia, Madame d'Eon, &c. These, and many more, may be reckoned exceptions; and, are not all heroes, as well as heroines, exceptions to general rules? I wish to see women neither heroines nor brutes; but reasonable creatures" [Wollstonecraft's note]. Sappho, the Greek poet; Eloisa, lover of Peter Abelard and intellectual in her own right; Catharine Macaulay, Wollstonecraft's contemporary, a historian; Catherine the Great of Russia, "enlightened" and brilliant despot; Chevalier d'Eon, the French secret agent who disguised himself as a woman and, even when ordered by the king in 1777 to dress according to his/her sex, still wore woman's dress—an autopsy in 1810 certified him male. It is probable that Wollstonecraft was unaware at this time of d'Eon's sex.

My comments, it is true, will all spring from a few simple principles, and might have been deduced from what I have already said; but the artificial structure has been raised with so much ingenuity, that it seems necessary to attack it in a more circumstantial manner, and make the application myself.

Sophia, says Rousseau, should be as perfect a woman as Emilius is a man, and to render her so, it is necessary to examine the character which nature has given to the sex.[1]

He then proceeds to prove that woman ought to be weak and passive, because she has less bodily strength than man; and hence infers, that she was formed to please and to be subject to him; and that it is her duty to render herself *agreeable* to her master—this being the grand end of her existence.[2] Still, however, to give a little mock dignity to lust, he insists that man should not exert his strength, but depend on the will of the woman, when he seeks for pleasure with her.

'Hence we deduce a third consequence from the different constitutions of the sexes; which is, that the strongest should be master in appearance, and be dependent in fact on the weakest; and that not from any frivolous practice of gallantry or vanity of protectorship, but from an invariable law of nature, which, furnishing woman with a greater facility to excite desires than she has given man to satisfy them, makes the latter dependent on the good pleasure of the former, and compels him to endeavour to please in his turn, *in order to obtain her consent that he should be strongest*.[3] On these occasions, the most delightful circumstance a man finds in his victory is, to doubt whether it was the woman's weakness that yielded to his superior strength, or whether her inclinations spoke in his favour: the females are also generally artful enough to leave this matter in doubt. The understanding of women answers in this respect perfectly to their constitution: so far from being ashamed of their weakness, they glory in it; their tender muscles make no resistance; they affect to be incapable of lifting the smallest burthens, and would blush to be thought robust and strong. To what purpose is all this? Not merely for the sake of appearing delicate, but through an artful precaution: it is thus they provide an excuse beforehand, and a right to be feeble when they think it expedient.'[4]

I have quoted this passage, lest my readers should suspect that I warped the author's reasoning to support my own arguments. I have already asserted that in educating women these fundamental principles lead to a system of cunning and lasciviousness.

Supposing woman to have been formed only to please, and be

---

1. *Émile*, p. 321.
2. "I have already inserted the passage, page 99" [Wollstonecraft's note]. See p. 48 in the present edition.
3. "What nonsense!" [Wollstonecraft's note].
4. *Émile*, p. 323.

subject to man, the conclusion is just, she ought to sacrifice every other consideration to render herself agreeable to him: and let this brutal desire of self-preservation be the grand spring of all her actions, when it is proved to be the iron bed of fate,[5] to fit which her character should be stretched or contracted, regardless of all moral or physical distinctions. But, if, as I think, may be demonstrated, the purposes, of even this life, viewing the whole, be subverted by practical rules built upon this ignoble base, I may be allowed to doubt whether woman was created for man: and, though the cry of irreligion, or even atheism, be raised against me, I will simply declare, that were an angel from heaven to tell me that Moses's beautiful, poetical cosmogony, and the account of the fall of man,[6] were literally true, I could not believe what my reason told me was derogatory to the character of the Supreme Being: and, having no fear of the devil before mine eyes, I venture to call this a suggestion of reason, instead of resting my weakness on the broad shoulders of the first seducer of my frail sex.

'It being once demonstrated,' continues Rousseau, 'that man and woman are not, nor ought to be, constituted alike in temperament and character, it follows of course that they should not be educated in the same manner. In pursuing the directions of nature, they ought indeed to act in concert, but they should not be engaged in the same employments: the end of their pursuits should be the same, but the means they should take to accomplish them, and of consequence their tastes and inclinations, should be different.'[7]

·   ·   ·   ·   ·   ·   ·   ·   ·   ·   ·   ·   ·

'Whether I consider the peculiar destination of the sex, observe their inclinations, or remark their duties, all things equally concur to point out the peculiar method of education best adapted to them. Woman and man were made for each other; but their mutual dependence is not the same. The men depend on the women only on account of their desires; the women on the men both on account of their desires and their necessities: we could subsist better without them than they without us.'

·   ·   ·   ·   ·   ·   ·   ·   ·   ·   ·   ·   ·

'For this reason, the education of the women should be always relative to the men. To please, to be useful to us, to make us love and esteem them, to educate us when young, and take care of us when grown up, to advise, to console us, to render our lives easy and agreeable: these are the duties of women at all times, and what

5. A reference to the Greek legend of Procrustes, who tailored guests to fit his great iron bed: if too short, they were stretched, and if too long, they were chopped off to fit.

6. It was assumed in the eighteenth century that Moses had written Genesis.

7. *Émile*, p. 326.

they should be taught in their infancy. So long as we fail to recur to this principle, we run wide of the mark, and all the precepts which are given them contribute neither to their happiness nor our own.'[8]

. . . .

'Girls are from their earliest infancy fond of dress. Not content with being pretty, they are desirous of being thought so; we see, by all their little airs, that this thought engages their attention; and they are hardly capable of understanding what is said to them, before they are to be governed by talking to them of what people will think of their behaviour. The same motive, however, indiscreetly made use of with boys, has not the same effect: provided they are let pursue their amusements at pleasure, they care very little what people think of them. Time and pains are necessary to subject boys to this motive.

'Whencesoever girls derive this first lesson, it is a very good one. As the body is born, in a manner, before the soul, our first concern should be to cultivate the former; this order is common to both sexes, but the object of that cultivation is different. In the one sex it is the developement of corporeal powers; in the other, that of personal charms: not that either the quality of strength or beauty ought to be confined exclusively to one sex; but only that the order of the cultivation of both is in that respect reversed. Women certainly require as much strength as to enable them to move and act gracefully, and men as much address as to qualify them to act with ease.'[9]

. . . .

'Children of both sexes have a great many amusements in common; and so they ought; have they not also many such when they are grown up? Each sex has also its peculiar taste to distinguish in this particular. Boys love sports of noise and activity; to beat the drum, to whip the top, and to drag about their little carts: girls, on the other hand, are fonder of things of show and ornament; such as mirrours, trinkets, and dolls: the doll is the peculiar amusement of the females; from whence we see their taste plainly adapted to their destination. The physical part of the art of pleasing lies in dress; and this is all which children are capacitated to cultivate of that art.'[1]

. . . .

'Here then we see a primary propensity firmly established, which you need only to pursue and regulate. The little creature will doubtless be very desirous to know how to dress up her doll, to make its

8. The foregoing two selections are from *Émile*, p. 328.

9. Ibid., p. 329.

1. Ibid., p. 330–31.

sleeve-knots, its flounces, its head-dress, &c. she is obliged to have so much recourse to the people about her, for their assistance in these articles, that it would be much more agreeable to her to owe them all to her own industry. Hence we have a good reason for the first lessons that are usually taught these young females: in which we do not appear to be setting them a task, but obliging them, by instructing them in what is immediately useful to themselves. And, in fact, almost all of them learn with reluctance to read and write; but very readily apply themselves to the use of their needles. They imagine themselves already grown up, and think with pleasure that such qualifications will enable them to decorate themselves.'[2]

This is certainly only an education of the body; but Rousseau is not the only man who has indirectly said that merely the person of a *young* woman, without any mind, unless animal spirits come under that description, is very pleasing. To render it weak, and what some may call beautiful, the understanding is neglected, and girls forced to sit still, play with dolls and listen to foolish conversations;—the effect of habit is insisted upon as an undoubted indication of nature. I know it was Rousseau's opinion that the first years of youth should be employed to form the body, though in educating Emilius he deviates from this plan; yet, the difference between strengthening the body, on which strength of mind in a great measure depends, and only giving it an easy motion, is very wide.

Rousseau's observations, it is proper to remark, were made in a country where the art of pleasing was refined only to extract the grossness of vice.[3] He did not go back to nature, or his ruling appetite disturbed the operations of reason, else he would not have drawn these crude inferences.

In France boys and girls, particularly the latter, are only educated to please, to manage their persons, and regulate their exterior behaviour; and their minds are corrupted, at a very early age, by the wordly and pious cautions they receive to guard them against immodesty. I speak of past times. The very confessions which mere children were obliged to make, and the questions asked by the holy men,[4] I assert these facts on good authority, were sufficient to impress a sexual character; and the education of society was a school of coquetry and art. At the age of ten or eleven; nay, often much sooner, girls began to coquet, and talked, unreproved, of establishing themselves in the world by marriage.

In short, they were treated like women, almost from their very birth, and compliments were listened to instead of instruction. These, weakening the mind, Nature was supposed to have acted like a step-mother, when she formed this after-thought of creation.

2. Ibid., p. 331.
3. Though born in Geneva, Rousseau spent most of his life in France, and *Émile* was published in 1762 in Paris.
4. In the Catholic confessional the priest could ask about certain transgressions.

Not allowing them understanding, however, it was but consistent to subject them to authority independent of reason; and to prepare them for this subjection, he gives the following advice:

'Girls ought to be active and diligent; nor is that all; they should also be early subjected to restraint. This misfortune, if it really be one, is inseparable from their sex; nor do they ever throw it off but to suffer more cruel evils. They must be subject, all their lives, to the most constant and severe restraint, which is that of decorum: it is, therefore, necessary to accustom them early to such confinement, that it may not afterwards cost them too dear; and to the suppression of their caprices, that they may the more readily submit to the will of others. If, indeed, they be fond of being always at work, they should be sometimes compelled to lay it aside. Dissipation, levity, and inconstancy, are faults that readily spring up from their first propensities, when corrupted or perverted by too much indulgence. To prevent this abuse, we should teach them, above all things, to lay a due restraint on themselves. The life of a modest woman is reduced, by our absurd institutions, to a perpetual conflict with herself: not but it is just that this sex should partake of the sufferings which arise from those evils it hath caused us.'[5]

And why is the life of a modest woman a perpetual conflict? I should answer, that this very system of education makes it so. Modesty, temperance, and self-denial, are the sober offspring of reason; but when sensibility is nurtured at the expence of the understanding, such weak beings must be restrained by arbitrary means, and be subjected to continual conflicts; but give their activity of mind a wider range, and nobler passions and motives will govern their appetites and sentiments.

'The common attachment and regard of a mother, nay, mere habit, will make her beloved by her children, if she do nothing to incur their hate. Even the constraint she lays them under, if well directed, will increase their affection, instead of lessening it; because a state of dependence being natural to the sex, they perceive themselves formed for obedience.'[6]

This is begging the question; for servitude not only debases the individual, but its effects seem to be transmitted to posterity. Considering the length of time that women have been dependent, is it surprising that some of them hug their chains, and fawn like the spaniel? 'These dogs,' observes a naturalist, 'at first kept their ears erect; but custom has superseded nature, and a token of fear is become a beauty.'[7]

'For the same reason,' adds Rousseau, 'women have, or ought to have, but little liberty; they are apt to indulge themselves exces-

5. *Émile*, p. 332.
6. Ibid., p. 333.
7. The naturalist Buffon generally took the attitude that the dog in its natural state has erect ears; spaniels, as house and lap dogs, have been degenerated by man's culture. See in Buffon, op. cit., IV, "The Natural History of the Dog."

sively in what is allowed them. Addicted in every thing to extremes, they are even more transported at their diversions than boys.'[8]

The answer to this is very simple. Slaves and mobs have always indulged themselves in the same excesses, when once they broke loose from authority.—The bent bow recoils with violence, when the hand is suddenly relaxed that forcibly held it; and sensibility, the play-thing of outward circumstances, must be subjected to authority, or moderated by reason.

'There results,' he continues, 'from this habitual restraint a tractableness which women have occasion for during their whole lives, as they constantly remain either under subjection to the men, or to the opinions of mankind; and are never permitted to set themselves above those opinions. The first and most important qualification in a woman is good-nature or sweetness of temper: formed to obey a being so imperfect as man, often full of vices, and always full of faults, she ought to learn betimes even to suffer injustice, and to bear the insults of a husband without complaint; it is not for his sake, but her own, that she should be of a mild disposition. The perverseness and ill-nature of the women only serve to aggravate their own misfortunes, and the misconduct of their husbands; they might plainly perceive that such are not the arms by which they gain the superiority.'[9]

Formed to live with such an imperfect being as man, they ought to learn from the exercise of their faculties the necessity of forbearance; but all the sacred rights of humanity are violated by insisting on blind obedience; or, the most sacred rights belong *only* to man.

The being who patiently endures injustice, and silently bears insults, will soon become unjust, or unable to discern right from wrong. Besides, I deny the fact, this is not the true way to form or meliorate the temper; for, as a sex, men have better tempers than women, because they are occupied by pursuits that interest the head as well as the heart; and the steadiness of the head gives a healthy temperature to the heart. People of sensibility have seldom good tempers. The formation of the temper is the cool work of reason, when, as life advances, she mixes with happy art, jarring elements. I never knew a weak or ignorant person who had a good temper, though that constitutional good humour, and that docility, which fear stamps on the behaviour, often obtains the name. I say behaviour, for genuine meekness never reached the heart or mind, unless as the effect of reflection; and that simple restraint produces a number of peccant humours in domestic life, many sensible men will allow, who find some of these gentle irritable creatures, very troublesome companions.

'Each sex,' he further argues, 'should preserve its peculiar tone and manner; a meek husband may make a wife impertinent; but

8. *Émile*, p. 333.   9. Ibid.

mildness of disposition on the woman's side will always bring a man back to reason, at least if he be not absolutely a brute, and will sooner or later triumph over him.'[1] Perhaps the mildness of reason might sometimes have this effect; but abject fear always inspires contempt; and tears are only eloquent when they flow down fair cheeks.

Of what materials can that heart be composed, which can melt when insulted, and instead of revolting at injustice, kiss the rod? Is it unfair to infer that her virtue is built on narrow views and selfishness, who can caress a man, with true feminine softness, the very moment when he treats her tyrannically? Nature never dictated such insincerity;—and, though prudence of this sort be termed a virtue, morality becomes vague when any part is supposed to rest on falsehood. These are mere expedients, and expedients are only useful for the moment.

Let the husband beware of trusting too implicitly to this servile obedience; for if his wife can with winning sweetness caress him when angry, and when she ought to be angry, unless contempt had stifled a natural effervescence, she may do the same after parting with a lover. These are all preparations for adultery; or, should the fear of the world, or of hell, restrain her desire of pleasing other men, when she can no longer please her husband, what substitute can be found by a being who was only formed, by nature and art, to please man? what can make her amends for this privation, or where is she to seek for a fresh employment? where find sufficient strength of mind to determine to begin the search, when her habits are fixed, and vanity has long ruled her chaotic mind?

But this partial moralist recommends cunning systematically and plausibly.

'Daughters should be always submissive; their mothers, however, should not be inexorable. To make a young person tractable, she ought not to be made unhappy, to make her modest she ought not to be rendered stupid. On the contrary, I should not be displeased at her being permitted to use some art, not to elude punishment in case of disobedience, but to exempt herself from the necessity of obeying. It is not necessary to make her dependence burdensome, but only to let her feel it. Subtilty is a talent natural to the sex; and, as I am persuaded, all our natural inclinations are right and good in themselves, I am of opinion this should be cultivated as well as the others: it is requisite for us only to prevent its abuse.'[2]

'Whatever is, is right,'[3] he then proceeds triumphantly to infer. Granted;—yet, perhaps, no aphorism ever contained a more paradoxical assertion. It is a solemn truth with respect to God. He, rev-

1. Ibid., p. 334.
2. Ibid.

3. Pope, *An Essay on Man* I.294: "One truth is clear, whatever IS, is RIGHT."

erentially I speak, sees the whole at once, and saw its just proportions in the womb of time; but man, who can only inspect disjointed parts, finds many things wrong; and it is a part of the system, and therefore right, that he should endeavour to alter what appears to him to be so, even while he bows to the Wisdom of his Creator, and respects the darkness he labours to disperse.

The inference that follows is just, supposing the principle to be sound. 'The superiority of address, peculiar to the female sex, is a very equitable indemnification for their inferiority in point of strength: without this, woman would not be the companion of man; but his slave: it is by her superiour art and ingenuity that she preserves her equality, and governs him while she affects to obey. Woman has every thing against her, as well our faults, as her own timidity and weakness; she has nothing in her favour, but her subtilty and her beauty. Is it not very reasonable, therefore, she should cultivate both?'[4] Greatness of mind can never dwell with cunning, or address; for I shall not boggle about words, when their direct signification is insincerity and falsehood, but content myelf with observing, that if any class of mankind be so created that it must necessarily be educated by rules not strictly deducible from truth, virtue is an affair of convention. How could Rousseau dare to assert, after giving this advice, that in the grand end of existence the object of both sexes should be the same, when he well knew that the mind, formed by its pursuits, is expanded by great views swallowing up little ones, or that it becomes itself little?

Men have superiour strength of body; but were it not for mistaken notions of beauty, women would acquire sufficient to enable them to earn their own subsistence, the true definition of independence; and to bear those bodily inconveniencies and exertions that are requisite to strengthen the mind.

Let us then, by being allowed to take the same exercise as boys, not only during infancy, but youth, arrive at perfection of body, that we may know how far the natural superiority of man extends. For what reason or virtue can be expected from a creature when the seed-time of life is neglected? None—did not the winds of heaven casually scatter many useful seeds in the fallow ground.

'Beauty cannot be acquired by dress, and coquetry is an art not so early and speedily attained. While girls are yet young, however, they are in a capacity to study agreeable gesture, a pleasing modulation of voice, an easy carriage and behaviour; as well as to take the advantage of gracefully adapting their looks and attitudes to time, place, and occasion. Their application, therefore, should not be solely confined to the arts of industry and the needle, when they come to display other talents, whose utility is already apparent.'[5]

4. *Émile*, pp. 334–35.   5. Ibid., p. 336.

'For my part, I would have a young Englishwoman cultivate her agreeable talents, in order to please her future husband, with as much care and assiduity as a young Circassian cultivates her's, to fit her for the Haram of an Eastern bashaw.'[6]

To render women completely insignificant, he adds—'The tongues of women are very voluble; they speak earlier, more readily, and more agreeably, than the men; they are accused also of speaking much more: but so it ought to be, and I should be very ready to convert this reproach into a compliment; their lips and eyes have the same activity, and for the same reason. A man speaks of what he knows, a woman of what pleases her; the one requires knowledge, the other taste; the principal object of a man's discourse should be what is useful, that of a woman's what is agreeable. There ought to be nothing in common between their different conversation but truth.

'We ought not, therefore, to restrain the prattle of girls, in the same manner as we should that of boys, with that severe question; *To what purpose are you talking?* but by another, which is no less difficult to answer, *How will your discourse be received?* In infancy, while they are as yet incapable to discern good from evil, they ought to observe it, as a law, never to say any thing disagreeable to those whom they are speaking to: what will render the practice of this rule also the more difficult, is, that it must ever be subordinate to the former, of never speaking falsely or telling an untruth.'[7] To govern the tongue in this manner must require great address indeed; and it is too much practised both by men and women.—Out of the abundance of the heart how few speak![8] So few, that I, who love simplicity, would gladly give up politeness for a quarter of the virtue that has been sacrificed to an equivocal quality which at best should only be the polish of virtue.

But, to complete the sketch. 'It is easy to be conceived, that if male children be not in a capacity to form any true notions of religion, those ideas must be greatly above the conception of the females: it is for this very reason, I would begin to speak to them the earlier on this subject; for if we were to wait till they were in a capacity to discuss methodically such profound questions, we should run a risk of never speaking to them on this subject as long as they lived. Reason in women is a practical reason, capacitating them artfully to discover the means of attaining a known end, but which would never enable them to discover that end itself. The social relations of the sexes are indeed truly admirable: from their union there results a moral person, of which woman may be termed the eyes,

6. Ibid., p. 337. Circassia is a Caucasus mountain country where women traditionally held a low place and were often sold into the harems of Oriental potentates.

7. Ibid., p. 339.
8. Matthew 12:34: ". . . for out of the abundance of the heart the mouth speaketh."

and man the hand, with this dependence on each other, that it is from the man that the woman is to learn what she is to see, and it is of the woman that man is to learn what he ought to do. If woman could recur to the first principles of things as well as man, and man was capacitated to enter into their *minutiæ* as well as woman, always independent of each other, they would live in perpetual discord, and their union could not subsist. But in the present harmony which naturally subsists between them, their different faculties tend to one common end; it is difficult to say which of them conduces the most to it: each follows the impulse of the other; each is obedient, and both are masters.

'As the conduct of a woman is subservient to the public opinion, her faith in matters of religion should, for that very reason, be subject to authority. *Every daughter ought to be of the same religion as her mother, and every wife to be of the same religion as her husband: for, though such religion should be false, that docility which induces the mother and daughter to submit to the order of nature, takes away, in the sight of God, the criminality of their error.*[9] As they are not in a capacity to judge for themselves, they ought to abide by the decision of their fathers and husbands as confidently as by that of the church.

'As authority ought to regulate the religion of the women, it is not so needful to explain to them the reasons for their belief, as to lay down precisely the tenets they are to believe: for the creed, which presents only obscure ideas to the mind, is the source of fanaticism; and that which presents absurdities, leads to infidelity.'[1]

Absolute, uncontroverted authority, it seems, must subsist somewhere: but is not this a direct and exclusive appropriation of reason? The *rights* of humanity have been thus confined to the male line from Adam downwards. Rousseau would carry his male aristocracy still further, for he insinuates, that he should not blame those, who contend for leaving woman in a state of the most profound ignorance, if it were not necessary in order to preserve her chastity and justify the man's choice, in the eyes of the world, to give her a little knowledge of men, and the customs produced by human passions; else she might propagate at home without being rendered less voluptuous and innocent by the exercise of her understanding: excepting, indeed, during the first year of marriage, when she might employ it to dress like Sophia. 'Her dress is extremely modest in appearance, and yet very coquettish in fact: she does not make a display of her charms, she conceals them; but in concealing them, she knows how to affect your imagination. Every one who

---

9. "What is to be the consequence, if the mother's and husband's opinion should *chance* not to agree? An ignorant person cannot be reasoned out of an error—and when *persuaded* to give up one prejudice for another the mind is unsettled. Indeed, the husband may not have any religion to teach her, though in such a situation she will be in great want of a support to her virtue, independent of worldly considerations" [Wollstonecraft's note].

1. *Émile*, p. 340; the italics are Wollstonecraft's.

sees her will say, There is a modest and discreet girl; but while you are near her, your eyes and affections wander all over her person, so that you cannot withdraw them; and you would conclude, that every part of her dress, simple as it seems, was only put in its proper order to be taken to pieces by the imagination.'[2] Is this modesty? Is this a preparation for immortality? Again.—What opinion are we to form of a system of education, when the author says of his heroine, 'that with her, doing things well, is but a *secondary* concern; her principal concern is to do them *neatly.*'[3]

Secondary, in fact, are all her virtues and qualities, for, respecting religion, he makes her parents thus address her, accustomed to submission—'Your husband will instruct you in *good time.*'[4]

After thus cramping a woman's mind, if, in order to keep it fair, he have not made it quite a blank, he advises her to reflect, that a reflecting man may not yawn in her company, when he is tired of caressing her.—[5] What has she to reflect about who must obey? and would it not be a refinement on cruelty only to open her mind to make the darkness and misery of her fate *visible*?[6] Yet, these are his sensible remarks; how consistent with what I have already been obliged to quote, to give a fair view of the subject, the reader may determine.

'They who pass their whole lives in working for their daily bread, have no ideas beyond their business or their interest, and all their understanding seems to lie in their fingers' ends. This ignorance is neither prejudicial to their integrity nor their morals; it is often of service to them. Sometimes, by means of reflection, we are led to compound with our duty, and we conclude by substituting a jargon of words, in the room of things. Our own conscience is the most enlightened philosopher. There is no need to be acquainted with Tully's offices,[7] to make a man of probity: and perhaps the most virtuous woman in the world, is the least acquainted with the definition of virtue. But it is no less true, that an improved understanding only can render society agreeable; and it is a melancholy thing for a father of a family, who is fond of home, to be obliged to be always wrapped up in himself, and to have nobody about him to whom he can impart his sentiments.

'Besides, how should a woman void of reflection be capable of educating her children? How should she discern what is proper for them? How should she incline them to those virtues she is unacquainted with, or to that merit of which she has no idea? She can only sooth or chide them; render them insolent or timid; she will make them formal coxcombs, or ignorant blockheads; but will never

2. *Émile*, pp. 356–57.
3. Ibid., p. 358.
4. Ibid., p. 359.
5. Ibid., p. 371.
6. *Paradise Lost* I.63: "No light, but rather darkness visible."
7. "Tully" is Marcus Tullius Cicero (106–43 B.C.) whose philosophical treatise *De officiis* dealt with virtue and morality.

make them sensible or amiable.'[8] How indeed should she, when her husband is not always at hand to lend her his reason?—when they both together make but one moral being. A blind will, 'eyes without hands,'[9] would go a very little way; and perchance his abstract reason, that should concentrate the scattered beams of her practical reason, may be employed in judging of the flavour of wine, descanting on the sauces most proper for turtle; or, more profoundly intent at a card-table, he may be generalizing his ideas as he bets away his fortune, leaving all the *minutiæ* of education to his helpmate, or to chance.

But, granting that woman ought to be beautiful, innocent, and silly, to render her a more alluring and indulgent companion;— what is her understanding sacrificed for? And why is all this preparation necessary only, according to Rousseau's own account, to make her the mistress of her husband, a very short time? For no man ever insisted more on the transient nature of love. Thus speaks the philosopher. 'Sensual pleasures are transient. The habitual state of the affections always loses by their gratification. The imagination, which decks the object of our desires, is lost in fruition. Excepting the Supreme Being, who is self-existent, there is nothing beautiful but what is ideal.'[1]

But he returns to his unintelligible paradoxes again, when he thus addresses Sophia. 'Emilius, in becoming your husband, is become your master; and claims your obedience. Such is the order of nature. When a man is married, however, to such a wife as Sophia, it is proper he should be directed by her: this is also agreeable to the order of nature: it is, therefore, to give you as much authority over his heart as his sex gives him over your person, that I have made you the arbiter of his pleasures. It may cost you, perhaps, some disagreeable self-denial; but you will be certain of maintaining your empire over him, if you can preserve it over yourself—what I have already observed, also, shows me, that this difficult attempt does not surpass your courage.

'Would you have your husband constantly at your feet? keep him at some distance from your person. You will long maintain the authority in love, if you know but how to render your favours rare and valuable. It is thus you may employ even the arts of coquetry in the service of virtue, and those of love in that of reason.'[2]

I shall close my extracts with a just description of a comfortable couple. 'And yet you must not imagine, that even such management will always suffice. Whatever precaution be taken, enjoyment will, by degrees, take off the edge of passion. But when love hath lasted as long as possible, a pleasing habitude supplies its place, and the

8. *Émile*, p. 371.
9. A reference to the quotation from Rousseau, p. 86–87 above: "from their union there results a moral person, of which woman may be termed the eyes, and man the hand."
1. *Émile*, p. 411.
2. Ibid., p. 442–43.

attachment of a mutual confidence succeeds to the transports of passion. Children often form a more agreeable and permanent connection between married people than even love itself. When you cease to be the mistress of Emilius, you will continue to be his wife and friend, you will be the mother of his children.'[3]

Children, he truly observes, form a much more permanent connexion between married people than love. Beauty, he declares, will not be valued, or even seen after a couple have lived six months together; artificial graces and coquetry will likewise pall on the senses: why then does he say that a girl should be educated for her husband with the same care as for an eastern haram?

I now appeal from the reveries of fancy and refined licentiousness to the good sense of mankind, whether, if the object of education be to prepare women to become chaste wives and sensible mothers, the method so plausibly recommended in the foregoing sketch, be the one best calculated to produce those ends? Will it be allowed that the surest way to make a wife chaste, is to teach her to practise the wanton arts of a mistress, termed virtuous coquetry, by the sensualist who can no longer relish the artless charms of sincerity, or taste the pleasure arising from a tender intimacy, when confidence is unchecked by suspicion, and rendered interesting by sense?

The man who can be contented to live with a pretty, useful companion, without a mind, has lost in voluptuous gratifications a taste for more refined enjoyments; he has never felt the calm satisfaction, that refreshes the parched heart, like the silent dew of heaven,—of being beloved by one who could understand him.—In the society of his wife he is still alone, unless when the man is sunk in the brute. 'The charm of life,' says a grave philosophical reasoner, is 'sympathy; nothing pleases us more than to observe in other men a fellow-feeling with all the emotions of our own breast.'[4]

But, according to the tenour of reasoning, by which women are kept from the tree of knowledge, the important years of youth, the usefulness of age, and the rational hopes of futurity, are all to be sacrificed to render women an object of desire for a *short* time. Besides, how could Rousseau expect them to be virtuous and constant when reason is neither allowed to be the foundation of their virtue, nor truth the object of their inquiries?

But all Rousseau's errors in reasoning arose from sensibility, and sensibility to their charms women are very ready to forgive! When he should have reasoned he became impassioned, and reflection inflamed his imagination instead of enlightening his understanding.

---

3. "Rousseau's Emilius" [Wollstonecraft's note]. *Émile*, p. 443.
4. Adam Smith, *The Theory of Moral Sentiments*, op. cit., p. 10: "But whatever may be the cause of sympathy, or however it may be excited, nothing pleases us more than to observe in other men a fellow-feeling with all the emotions of our own breast."

Even his virtues also led him farther astray; for, born with a warm constitution and lively fancy, nature carried him toward the other sex with such eager fondness, that he soon became lascivious. Had he given way to these desires, the fire would have extinguished itself in a natural manner; but virtue, and a romantic kind of delicacy, made him practise self-denial; yet, when fear, delicacy, or virtue, restrained him, he debauched his imagination, and reflecting on the sensations to which fancy gave force, he traced them in the most glowing colours, and sunk them deep into his soul.

He then sought for solitude, not sleep[5] with the man of nature; or calmly investigate the causes of things under the shade where Sir Isaac Newton indulged contemplation,[6] but merely to indulge his feelings. And so warmly has he painted, what he forcibly felt, that, interesting the heart and inflaming the imagination of his readers; in proportion to the strength of their fancy, they imagine that their understanding is convinced when they only sympathize with a poetic writer, who skilfully exhibits the objects of sense, most voluptuously shadowed or gracefully veiled—And thus making us feel whilst dreaming that we reason, erroneous conclusions are left in the mind.

Why was Rousseau's life divided between ecstasy and misery? Can any other answer be given than this, that the effervescence of his imagination produced both; but, had his fancy been allowed to cool, it is possible that he might have acquired more strength of mind. Still, if the purpose of life be to educate the intellectual part of man, all with respect to him was right; yet, had not death led to a nobler scene of action, it is probable that he would have enjoyed more equal happiness on earth, and have felt the calm sensations of the man of nature instead of being prepared for another stage of existence by nourishing the passions which agitate the civilized man.

But peace to his manes![7] I war not with his ashes, but his opinions. I war only with the sensibility that led him to degrade woman by making her the slave of love.

> ————'Curs'd vassalage,
> 'First idoliz'd till love's hot fire be o'er,
> 'Then slaves to those who courted us before.'
>
> *Dryden.* [8]

The pernicious tendency of those books, in which the writers

---

5. The first edition reads "not to sleep," which obviously makes more sense.
6. Tradition has it that as Newton sat under a shade tree in a garden in 1665 and saw an apple fall, he was set to thinking about his theory of gravity.

7. Spirit or "shade" of a departed person.
8. From John Dryden's opera, *The State of Innocence: and Fall of Man* V.i.58–60. The first line, spoken by Eve, should read "Curs'd vassalage of all my future kind."

insidiously degrade the sex whilst they are prostrate before their personal charms, cannot be too often or too severely exposed.

Let us, my dear contemporaries, arise above such narrow prejudices! If wisdom be desirable on its own account, if virtue, to deserve the name, must be founded on knowledge; let us endeavour to strengthen our minds by reflection, till our heads become a balance for our hearts; let us not confine all our thoughts to the petty occurrences of the day, or our knowledge to an acquaintance with our lovers' or husbands' hearts; but let the practice of every duty be subordinate to the grand one of improving our minds, and preparing our affections for a more exalted state!

Beware then, my friends, of suffering the heart to be moved by every trivial incident: the reed is shaken by a breeze, and annually dies, but the oak stands firm, and for ages braves the storm!

Were we, indeed, only created to flutter our hour out and die—why let us then indulge sensibility, and laugh at the severity of reason.—Yet, alas! even then we should want strength of body and mind, and life would be lost in feverish pleasures or wearisome languor.

But the system of education, which I earnestly wish to see exploded, seems to presuppose what ought never to be taken for granted, that virtue shields us from the casualties of life; and that fortune, slipping off her bandage, will smile on a well-educated female, and bring in her hand an Emilius or a Telemachus.[9] Whilst, on the contrary, the reward which virtue promises to her votaries is confined, it seems clear, to their own bosoms; and often must they contend with the most vexatious worldly cares, and bear with the vices and humours of relations for whom they can never feel a friendship.

There have been many women in the world who, instead of being supported by the reason and virtue of their fathers and brothers, have strengthened their own minds by struggling with their vices and follies; yet have never met with a hero, in the shape of a husband; who, paying the debt that mankind owed them, might chance to bring back their reason to its natural dependent state, and restore the usurped prerogative, of rising above opinion, to man.

SECT. II

Dr. Fordyce's sermons have long made a part of a young woman's library; nay, girls at school are allowed to read them; but I should instantly dismiss them from my pupil's, if I wished to strengthen her understanding, by leading her to form sound principles on a

9. Rousseau narrates in *Émile* that Sophy (Émile's intended), languished after having read Fénelon's *Télémaque*, for she had fallen hopelessly in love with its hero.

broad basis; or, were I only anxious to cultivate her taste; though they must be allowed to contain many sensible observations.[1]

Dr. Fordyce may have had a very laudable end in view; but these discourses are written in such an affected style, that were it only on that account, and had I nothing to object against his *mellifluous* precepts, I should not allow girls to peruse them, unless I designed to hunt every spark of nature out of their composition, melting every human quality into female meekness and artificial grace. I say artificial, for true grace arises from some kind of independence of mind.

Children, careless of pleasing, and only anxious to amuse themselves, are often very graceful; and the nobility who have mostly lived with inferiours, and always had the command of money, acquire a graceful ease of deportment, which should rather be termed habitual grace of body, than that superiour gracefulness which is truly the expression of the mind. This mental grace, not noticed by vulgar eyes, often flashes across a rough countenance, and irradiating every feature, shows simplicity and independence of mind.—It is then we read characters of immortality in the eye, and see the soul in every gesture, though when at rest, neither the face nor limbs may have much beauty to recommend them; or the behaviour, any thing peculiar to attract universal attention. The mass of mankind, however, look for more *tangible* beauty; yet simplicity is, in general, admired, when people do not consider what they admire; and can there be simplicity without sincerity? But, to have done with remarks that are in some measure desultory, though naturally excited by the subject—

In declamatory periods Dr. Fordyce spins out Rousseau's eloquence; and in most sentimental rant, details his opinions respecting the female character, and the behaviour which woman ought to assume to render her lovely.

He shall speak for himself, for thus he makes Nature address man. 'Behold these smiling innocents, whom I have graced with my fairest gifts, and committed to your protection; behold them with love and respect; treat them with tenderness and honour. They are timid and want to be defended. They are frail; O do not take advantage of their weakness! Let their fears and blushes endear them. Let their confidence in you never be abused.—But is it possible, that any of you can be such barbarians, so supremely wicked, as to abuse it? Can you find in your hearts[2] to despoil the gentle, trusting creatures of their treasure, or do any thing to strip them of their native robe of virtue? Curst be the impious hand that would dare to violate the unblemished form of Chastity! Thou wretch! thou

---

1. Dr. James Fordyce's *Sermons to Young Women*, first published in 1765, often reprinted in the eighteenth century, was a very popular handbook for young girls' education and deportment.

2. "Can you?—Can you? would be the most emphatical comment, were it drawled out in a whining voice" [Wollstonecraft's note].

ruffian! forbear; nor venture to provoke heaven's fiercest vengeance.'[3] I know not any comment that can be made seriously on this curious passage, and I could produce many similar ones; and some, so very sentimental, that I have heard rational men use the word indecent, when they mentioned them with disgust.

Throughout there is a display of cold artificial feelings, and that parade of sensibility which boys and girls should be taught to despise as the sure mark of a little vain mind. Florid appeals are made to heaven, and to the *beauteous innocents*, the fairest images of heaven here below, whilst sober sense is left far behind.—This is not the language of the heart, nor will it ever reach it, though the ear may be tickled.

I shall be told, perhaps, that the public have been pleased with these volumes.—True—and Hervey's Meditations[4] are still read, though he equally sinned against sense and taste.

I particularly object to the lover-like phrases of pumped up passion, which are every where interspersed. If women be ever allowed to walk without leading-strings,[5] why must they be cajoled into virtue by artful flattery and sexual compliments?—Speak to them the language of truth and soberness, and away with the lullaby strains of condescending endearment! Let them be taught to respect themselves as rational creatures, and not led to have a passion for their own insipid persons. It moves my gall to hear a preacher descanting on dress and needle-work;[6] and still more, to hear him address the *British fair, the fairest of the fair*,[7] as if they had only feelings.

Even recommending piety he uses the following argument. 'Never, perhaps, does a fine woman strike more deeply, than when, composed into pious recollection, and possessed with the noblest considerations, she assumes, without knowing it, superiour dignity and new graces; so that the beauties of holiness seem to radiate about her, and the by-standers are almost induced to fancy her already worshipping amongst her kindred angels!'[8] Why are women to be thus bred up with a desire of conquest? the very word, used in this sense. gives me a sickly qualm! Do religion and virtue offer no stronger motives, no brighter reward? Must they always be debased

---

3. James Fordyce, *Sermons to Young Women* (Philadelphia, 1787), p. 63. Hereafter cited as Fordyce.

4. James Hervey (1714–58) was a devotional writer whose *Meditations and Contemplations*, a highly popular piece of inspirational writing, had reached a twenty-fifth edition by 1791.

5. Strings used to hold up children learning to walk.

6. Fordyce (p. 149 ff.) recommends needlework with "freer patterns" to avoid the eyestrain pursuant

on most close and intricate stitching.

7. This quotation seems unjust, for when Fordyce refers to "ye fair ones of Britain" (p. 30), he is addressing grand ladies, of whom he disapproves, for they "doat on the parade of public assemblies, and sail along in the full-blown pride of fashionable attire. . . ."

8. Fordyce, pp. 275–76. This passage occurs while he is describing behavior appropriate in church— i.e., punctuality, sedateness, etc.

by being made to consider the sex of their companions? Must they be taught always to be pleasing? And when levelling their small artillery at the heart of man, is it necessary to tell them that a little sense is sufficient to render their attention *incredibly soothing*? 'As a small degree of knowledge entertains in a woman, so from a woman, though for a different reason, a small expression of kindness delights, particularly if she have beauty!'[9] I should have supposed for the same reason.

Why are girls to be told that they resemble angels; but to sink them below women? Or, that a gentle innocent female is an object that comes nearer to the idea which we have formed of angels than any other. Yet they are told, at the same time, that they are only like angels when they are young and beautiful; consequently, it is their persons, not their virtues, that procure them this homage.

Idle empty words! What can such delusive flattery lead to, but vanity and folly? The lover, it is true, has a poetic licence to exalt his mistress; his reason is the bubble of his passion, and he does not utter a falsehood when he borrows the language of adoration. His imagination may raise the idol of his heart, unblamed, above humanity; and happy would it be for women, if they were only flattered by the men who loved them; I mean, who love the individual, not the sex; but should a grave preacher interlard his discourses with such fooleries?

In sermons or novels, however, voluptuousness is always true to its text. Men are allowed by moralists to cultivate, as Nature directs, different qualities, and assume the different characters, that the same passions, modified almost to infinity, give to each individual. A virtuous man may have a choleric or a sanguine constitution, be gay or grave, unreproved; be firm till he is almost over-bearing, or, weakly submissive, have no will or opinion of his own; but all women are to be levelled, by meekness and docility, into one character of yielding softness and gentle compliance.

I will use the preacher's own words. 'Let it be observed, that in your sex manly exercises are never graceful; that in them a tone and figure, as well as an air and deportment, of the masculine kind, are always forbidding; and that men of sensibility desire in every woman soft features, and a flowing voice, a form, not robust, and demeanour delicate and gentle.'[1]

Is not the following portrait—the portrait of a house slave? 'I am astonished at the folly of many women, who are still reproaching their husbands for leaving them alone, for preferring this or that company to theirs, for treating them with this and the other mark of disregard or indifference; when, to speak the truth, they have

---

9. Fordyce, p. 324.   1. Ibid., p. 308.

themselves in a great measure to blame. Not that I would justify the men in any thing wrong on their part. But had you behaved to them with more *respectful observance*, and a more *equal tenderness; studying their humours, overlooking their mistakes, submitting to their opinions* in matters indifferent, passing by little instances of unevenness, caprice, or passion, giving *soft* answers to hasty words, complaining as seldom as possible, and making it your daily care to relieve their anxieties and prevent their wishes, to enliven the hour of dulness, and call up the ideas of felicity: had you pursued this conduct, I doubt not but you would have maintained and even increased their esteem, so far as to have secured every degree of influence that could conduce to their virtue, or your mutal satisfaction; and your house might at this day have been the abode of domestic bliss.'[2] Such a woman ought to be an angel—or she is an ass—for I discern not a trace of the human character, neither reason nor passion in this domestic drudge, whose being is absorbed in that of a tyrant's.

Still Dr. Fordyce must have very little acquaintance with the human heart, if he really supposed that such conduct would bring back wandering love, instead of exciting contempt. No, beauty, gentleness, &c. &c. may gain a heart; but esteem, the only lasting affection, can alone be obtained by virtue supported by reason. It is respect for the understanding that keeps alive tenderness for the person.

As these volumes are so frequently put into the hands of young people, I have taken more notice of them than, strictly speaking, they deserve; but as they have contributed to vitiate the taste, and enervate the understanding of many of my fellow-creatures, I could not pass them silently over.

SECT. III

Such paternal solicitude pervades Dr. Gregory's Legacy to his Daughters, that I enter on the task of criticism with affectionate respect;[3] but as this little volume has many attractions to recommend it to the notice of the most respectable part of my sex, I cannot silently pass over arguments that so speciously support opinions which, I think, have had the most baneful effect on the morals and manners of the female world.

His easy familiar style is particularly suited to the tenor of his advice, and the melancholy tenderness which his respect for the memory of a beloved wife, diffuses through the whole work, renders it very interesting; yet there is a degree of concise elegance conspic-

2. Ibid., p. 332; the italics are Wollstonecraft's.
3. Dr. John Gregory's A *Father's Legacy to His Daughters* (1774) is a short book whose avowed purpose is to instruct his daughters after the author's death, since the daughters are motherless and he is in declining health.

uous in many passages that disturbs this sympathy; and we pop on[4] the author, when we only expected to meet the—father.

Besides, having two objects in view, he seldom adhered steadily to either; for wishing to make his daughters amiable, and fearing lest unhappiness should only be the consequence, of instilling sentiments that might draw them out of the track of common life without enabling them to act with consonant independence and dignity, he checks the natural flow of his thoughts, and neither advises one thing nor the other.

In the preface he tells them a mournful truth, 'that they will hear, at least once in their lives, the genuine sentiments of a man who has no interest in deceiving them.'[5]

Hapless woman! what can be expected from thee when the beings on whom thou art said naturally to depend for reason and support, have all an interest in deceiving thee! This is the root of the evil that has shed a corroding mildew on all thy virtues; and blighting in the bud thy opening faculties, has rendered thee the weak thing thou art! It is this separate interest—this insidious state of warfare, that undermines morality, and divides mankind!

If love have made some women wretched—how many more has the cold unmeaning intercourse of gallantry rendered vain and useless! yet this heartless attention to the sex is reckoned so manly, so polite that, till society is very differently organized, I fear, this vestige of gothic[6] manners will not be done away by a more reasonable and affectionate mode of conduct. Besides, to strip it of its imaginary dignity, I must observe, that in the most uncivilized European states this lip-service prevails in a very great degree, accompanied with extreme dissoluteness of morals. In Portugal, the country that I particularly allude to, it takes place of the most serious moral obligations; for a man is seldom assassinated when in the company of a woman. The savage hand of rapine is unnerved by this chivalrous spirit; and, if the stroke of vengeance cannot be stayed—the lady is entreated to pardon the rudeness and depart in peace, though sprinkled, perhaps, with her husband's or brother's blood.[7]

I shall pass over his strictures on religion, because I mean to discuss that subject in a separate chapter.

The remarks relative to behaviour, though many of them very

---

4. Come upon suddenly.

5. Gregory, p. 6.

6. Barbarous or uncouth.

7. This reference probably comes from a book that Wollstonecraft reviewed for the *Analytical Review* (I, 451–57) by Arthur William Costigan called *Sketches of Society and Manners in Portugal* (London, 1787). Costigan relates an anecdote about two Portuguese cousins who entertain a passion for the same woman. One, a widower, meeting the other, an officer, has the officer whipped by a slave, then leaves the country for three years out of fear of retribution. Thinking himself forgiven, he returns but never goes out without his sister, "not supposing any cavalier would be rude enough to attack him in the company of a lady" (p. 402). The officer nonetheless stops the litter, asks his cousin to alight, shoots him dead, and "this being done, he asked a thousand pardons of the lady, for having so far incommoded her, and begged to know, whither she wished to be conducted" (p. 403).

sensible, I entirely disapprove of, because it appears to me to be beginning, as it were, at the wrong end. A cultivated understanding, and an affectionate heart, will never want starched rules of decorum —something more substantial than seemliness will be the result; and, without understanding the behaviour here recommended, would be rank affectation. Decorum, indeed, is the one thing needful!—decorum is to supplant nature, and banish all simplicity and variety of character out of the female world. Yet what good end can all this superficial counsel produce? It is, however, much easier to point out this or that mode of behaviour, than to set the reason to work; but, when the mind has been stored with useful knowledge, and strengthened by being employed, the regulation of the behaviour may safely be left to its guidance.

Why, for instance, should the following caution be given when art of every kind must contaminate the mind; and why entangle the grand motives of action, which reason and religion equally combine to enforce, with pitiful worldly shifts and slight of hand tricks to gain the applause of gaping tasteless fools? 'Be even cautious in displaying your good sense.[8] It will be thought you assume a superiority over the rest of the company—But if you happen to have any learning, keep it a profound secret, especially from the men who generally look with a jealous and malignant eye on a woman of great parts, and a cultivated understanding.'[9] If men of real merit, as he afterwards observes, be superior to this meanness, where is the necessity that the behaviour of the whole sex should be modulated to please fools, or men, who having little claim to respect as individuals, choose to keep close in their phalanx. Men, indeed, who insist on their common superiority, having only this sexual superiority, are certainly very excusable.

There would be no end to rules for behaviour, if it be proper always to adopt the tone of the company; for thus, for ever varying the key, a *flat* would often pass for a *natural* note.

Surely it would have been wiser to have advised women to improve themselves till they rose above the fumes of vanity; and then to let the public opinion come round—for where are rules of accommodation to stop? The narrow path of truth and virtue inclines neither to the right nor left—it is a straightforward business, and they who are earnestly pursuing their road, may bound over many decorous prejudices, without leaving modesty behind. Make the heart clean, and give the head employment, and I will venture to predict that there will be nothing offensive in the behaviour.

8. "Let women once acquire good sense—and if it deserve the name, it will teach them; or, of what use will it be? how to employ it" [Wollstonecraft's note].
9. Gregory, pp. 31–32.

The air of fashion, which many young people are so eager to attain, always strikes me like the studied attitudes of some modern pictures, copied with tasteless servility after the antiques;—the soul is left out, and none of the parts are tied together by what may properly be termed character. This varnish of fashion, which seldom sticks very close to sense, may dazzle the weak; but leave nature to itself, and it will seldom disgust the wise. Besides, when a woman has sufficient sense not to pretend to any thing which she does not understand in some degree, there is no need of determining to hide her talents under a bushel.[1] Let things take their natural course, and all will be well.

It is this system of dissimulation, throughout the volume, that I despise. Women are always to *seem* to be this and that—yet virtue might apostrophize them, in the words of Hamlet—Seems! I know not seems!—Have that within that passeth show!—[2]

Still the same tone occurs; for in another place, after recommending, without sufficiently discriminating delicacy, he adds, 'The men will complain of your reserve. They will assure you that a franker behaviour would make you more amiable. But, trust me, they are not sincere when they tell you so.—I acknowledge that on some occasions it might render you more agreeable as companions, but it would make you less amiable as women: an important distinction, which many of your sex are not aware of.'—[3]

This desire of being always women, is the very consciousness that degrades the sex. Excepting with a lover, I must repeat with emphasis, a former observation,—it would be well if they were only agreeable or rational companions.—But in this respect his advice is even inconsistent with a passage which I mean to quote with the most marked approbation.

'The sentiment, that a woman may allow all innocent freedoms, provided her virtue is secure, is both grossly indelicate and dangerous, and has proved fatal to many of your sex.'[4] With this opinion I perfectly coincide. A man, or a woman, of any feeling, must always wish to convince a beloved object that it is the caresses of the individual, not the sex, that are received and returned with pleasure; and, that the heart, rather than the senses, is moved. Without this natural delicacy, love becomes a selfish personal gratification that soon degrades the character.

I carry this sentiment still further. Affection, when love is out of the question, authorises many personal endearments, that naturally flowing from an innocent heart, give life to the behaviour; but the personal intercourse of appetite, gallantry, or vanity, is despicable.

1. Luke 11:33, Matthew 5:15, and Mark 4:21.
2. Hamlet I.ii.76 and 85: "Seems, Madam! nay it is; I know not 'seems' . . . / But I have that within which passeth show."
3. Gregory, pp. 36–37.
4. Ibid., p. 44.

When a man squeezes the hand of a pretty woman, handing her to a carriage, whom he has never seen before, she will consider such an impertinent freedom in the light of an insult, if she have any true delicacy, instead of being flattered by this unmeaning homage to beauty. These are the privileges of friendship, or the momentary homage which the heart pays to virtue, when it flashes suddenly on the notice—mere animal spirits have no claim to the kindnesses of affection!

Wishing to feed the affections with what is now the food of vanity, I would fain persuade my sex to act from simpler principles. Let them merit love, and they will obtain it, though they may never be told that—'The power of a fine woman over the hearts of men, of men of the finest parts, is even beyond what she conceives.'[5]

I have already noticed the narrow cautions with respect to duplicity, female softness, delicacy of constitution;[6] for these are the changes which he rings round without ceasing—in a more decorous manner, it is true, than Rousseau; but it all comes home to the same point, and whoever is at the trouble to analyze these sentiments, will find the first principles not quite so delicate as the superstructure.

The subject of amusements is treated in too cursory a manner; but with the same spirit.

When I treat of friendship, love, and marriage, it will be found that we materially differ in opinion; I shall not then forestall what I have to observe on these important subjects; but confine my remarks to the general tenor of them, to that cautious family prudence, to those confined views of partial unenlightened affection, which exclude pleasure and improvement, by vainly wishing to ward off sorrow and error—and by thus guarding the heart and mind, destroy also all their energy.—It is far better to be often deceived than never to trust; to be disappointed in love than never to love; to lose a husband's fondness than forfeit his esteem.

Happy would it be for the world, and for individuals, of course, if all this unavailing solicitude to attain worldly happiness, on a confined plan, were turned into an anxious desire to improve the understanding.—'Wisdom is the principal thing: *therefore* get wisdom; and with all thy gettings get understanding.'[7]—'How long, ye simple ones, will ye love simplicity, and hate knowledge?'[8] Saith Wisdom to the daughters of men!—

5. Ibid., p. 42.

6. "We so naturally associate the idea of female softness and delicacy, with a corresponding delicacy of constitution, that when a woman speaks of her great strength, her extraordinary appetite, her ability to bear excessive fatigue, we recoil at the description in a way she is little aware of." Gregory, pp. 50–51.

7. Proverbs 4:7.

8. Proverbs 1:22: "How long, ye simple ones, will ye love simplicity? and the scorners delight in their scorning, and fools hate knowledge?"

SECT. IV

I do not mean to allude to all the writers who have written on the subject of female manners—it would, in fact, be only beating over the old ground, for they have, in general, written in the same strain; but attacking the boasted prerogative of man—the prerogative that may emphatically be called the iron sceptre of tyranny, the original sin of tyrants, I declare against all power built on prejudices, however hoary.

If the submission demanded be founded on justice—there is no appealing to a higher power—for God is Justice itself. Let us then, as children of the same parent, if not bastardized by being the younger born, reason together, and learn to submit to the authority of reason—when her voice is distinctly heard. But, if it be proved, that this throne of prerogative only rests on a chaotic mass of prejudices, that have no inherent principle of order to keep them together, or on an elephant, tortoise, or even the mighty shoulders of a son of the earth,[9] they may escape, who dare to brave the consequence, without any breach of duty, without sinning against the order of things.

Whilst reason raises man above the brutal herd, and death is big with promises, they alone are subject to blind authority who have no reliance on their own strength. 'They are free—who will be free!'—[1]

The being who can govern itself has nothing to fear in life; but if any thing be dearer than its own respect, the price must be paid to the last farthing. Virtue, like every thing valuable, must be loved for herself alone; or she will not take up her abode with us. She will not impart that peace, 'which passeth understanding,'[2] when she is merely made the stilts of reputation; and respected, with pharisaical exactness, because 'honesty is the best policy.'

That the plan of life which enables us to carry some knowledge and virtue into another world, is the one best calculated to ensure content in this, cannot be denied; yet few people act according to this principle, though it be universally allowed that it admits not of dispute. Present pleasure, or present power, carry before it these sober convictions; and it is for the day, not for life, that man bargains with happiness. How few!—how very few! have sufficient foresight, or resolution, to endure a small evil at the moment, to avoid a greater hereafter.

---

9. In ancient Indian cosmogony, the earth was a huge tray supported by three elephants who themselves stood on the back of a giant tortoise. "Son of the earth" is the Titan god Atlas who supported the earth on his shoulders.

1. " 'He is the free man, whom the *truth* makes free!' " [Wollstonecraft's note]. From William Cowper, *The Task*, "The Winter Morning Walk," line 733.

2. Philippians 4:7: "And the peace of God, which passeth all understanding, shall keep your hearts and minds through Christ Jesus."

Woman in particular, whose virtue[3] is built on mutable prejudices, seldom attains to this greatness of mind; so that, becoming
the slave of her own feelings, she is easily subjugated by those of
others. Thus degraded, her reason, her misty reason! is employed
rather to burnish than to snap her chains.

Indignantly have I heard women argue in the same track as men,
and adopt the sentiments that brutalize them, with all the pertinacity of ignorance.

I must illustrate my assertion by a few examples. Mrs. Piozzi,[4]
who often repeated by rote, what she did not understand, comes
forward with Johnsonian periods.

'Seek not for happiness in singularity; and dread a refinement of
wisdom as a deviation into folly.' Thus she dogmatically addresses a
new married man; and to elucidate this pompous exordium, she
adds, 'I said that the person of your lady would not grow more
pleasing to you, but pray let her never suspect that it grows less so:
that a woman will pardon an affront to her understanding much
sooner than one to her person, is well known; nor will any of us
contradict the assertion. All our attainments, all our arts, are
employed to gain and keep the heart of man; and what mortification can exceed the disappointment, if the end be not obtained?
There is no reproof however pointed, no punishment however
severe, that a woman of spirit will not prefer to neglect; and if she
can endure it without complaint, it only proves that she means to
make herself amends by the attention of others for the slights of
her husband!'

These are truly masculine sentiments.— 'All our *arts* are employed to gain and keep the heart of man:'[5]—and what is the
inference?—if her person, and was there ever a person, though
formed with Medicean[6] symmetry, that was not slighted? be
neglected, she will make herself amends by endeavouring to please
other men. Noble morality! But thus is the understanding of the
whole sex affronted, and their virtue deprived of the common basis
of virtue. A woman must know, that her person cannot be as pleasing to her husband as it was to her lover, and if she be offended
with him for being a human creature, she may as well whine about
the loss of his heart as about any other foolish thing.—And this

3. "I mean to use a word that comprehends more
than chastity the sexual virtue" [Wollstonecraft's
note].
4. Hester Lynch Thrale Piozzi (1741–1821), friend
of Dr. Johnson's and woman of letters. She married
Henry Thrale, a prosperous brewer, against her
wishes. After Thrale's death she married Piozzi,
an Italian musician, incurring the wrath both of
Dr. Johnson and her own daughter.
5. All the foregoing Piozzi excerpts are from her
"Letter to a Gentleman newly Married" (see A

Series of Letters on Courtship and Marriage, by
various authors [Trenton, 1813], pp. 144–45).
6. Refers to the Medicean Venus statue in Florence (wrongly) attributed to Cleomenes. It was supposed to have the perfect classical female proportions: "If there be Truth in the Testimony of the
best and fairest judges, no Woman ever equalled
the Delicacy of the Medicean Venus" (James Harris, *Three Treatises* [1744; New York: Garland Publishing Co., 1970], p. 217).

very want of discernment or unreasonable anger, proves that he could not change his fondness for her person into affection for her virtues or respect for her understanding.

Whilst women avow, and act up to such opinions, their understandings, at least, deserve the contempt and obloquy that men, *who never* insult their persons, have pointedly levelled at the female mind. And it is the sentiments of these polite men, who do not wish to be encumbered with mind, that vain women thoughtlessly adopt. Yet they should know, that insulted reason alone can spread that *sacred* reserve about the person, which renders human affections, for human affections have always some base alloy, as permanent as is consistent with the grand end of existence—the attainment of virtue.

The Baroness de Stael[7] speaks the same language as the lady just cited, with more enthusiasm. Her eulogium on Rousseau was accidentally put into my hands, and her sentiments, the sentiments of too many of my sex, may serve as the text for a few comments. 'Though Rousseau,' she observes, 'has endeavoured to prevent women from interfering in public affairs, and acting a brilliant part in the theatre of politics; yet in speaking of them, how much has he done it to their satisfaction! If he wished to deprive them of some rights foreign to their sex, how has he for ever restored to them all those to which it has a claim! And in attempting to diminish their influence over the deliberations of men, how sacredly has he established the empire they have over their happiness! In aiding them to descend from an usurped throne, he has firmly seated them upon that to which they were destined by nature; and though he be full of indignation against them when they endeavour to resemble men, yet when they come before him with all the *charms, weaknesses, virtues* and *errors*, of their sex, his respect for their *persons* amounts almost to adoration.' True!—For never was there a sensualist who paid more fervent adoration at the shrine of beauty. So devout, indeed, was his respect for the person, that excepting the virtue of chastity, for obvious reasons, he only wished to see it embellished by charms, weaknesses, and errors. He was afraid lest the austerity of reason should disturb the soft playfulness of love. The master wished to have a meretricious slave to fondle, entirely dependent on his reason and bounty; he did not want a companion, whom he should be compelled to esteem, or a friend to whom he could confide the care of his children's education, should death deprive them of their father, before he had fulfilled the sacred task. He denies woman reason, shuts her out from knowledge, and turns her aside

7. Madame de Staël (1766–1817) born Anne Louise Germaine Necker, daughter of the finance minister of France, was an essayist and novelist. Citations are all from Mme. La Baronne de Staël, "Letters sur les Écrits et le Caractère de J. J. Rousseau," in *Oeuvres Complètes* (Paris, 1820), I. 20–21.

from truth; yet his pardon is granted, because 'he admits the passion of love.' It would require some ingenuity to shew why women
were to be under such an obligation to him for thus admitting love;
when it is clear that he admits it only for the relaxation of men,
and to perpetuate the species; but he talked with passion, and that
powerful spell worked on the sensibility of a young encomiast.
'What signifies it,' pursues this rhapsodist, 'to women, that his
reason disputes with them the empire, when his heart is devotedly
theirs.' It is not empire,—but equality, that they should contend
for. Yet, if they only wished to lengthen out their sway, they should
not entirely trust to their persons, for though beauty may gain a
heart, it cannot keep it, even while the beauty is in full bloom,
unless the mind lend, at least, some graces.

When women are once sufficiently enlightened to discover their
real interest, on a grand scale, they will, I am persuaded, be very
ready to resign all the prerogatives of love, that are not mutual,
speaking of them as lasting prerogatives, for the calm satisfaction of
friendship, and the tender confidence of habitual esteem. Before
marriage they will not assume any insolent airs, or afterwards
abjectly submit; but endeavouring to act like reasonable creatures,
in both situations, they will not be tumbled from a throne to a
stool.

Madame Genlis has written several entertaining books for children; and her Letters on Education afford many useful hints, that
sensible parents will certainly avail themselves of; but her views are
narrow, and her prejudices as unreasonable as strong.[8]

I shall pass over her vehement argument in favour of the eternity
of future punishments,[9] because I blush to think that a human
being should ever argue vehemently in such a cause, and only make
a few remarks on her absurd manner of making the parental authority supplant reason. For every where does she inculcate not only
blind submission to parents; but to the opinion of the world.[1]

She tells a story of a young man engaged by his father's express
desire to a girl of fortune. Before the marriage could take place, she

8. Stéphanie-Félicité Ducrest de Saint-Albin,
Comtesse de Genlis (1746–1830), French woman
of letters and governess to the Duke of Chartres's
children.
9. In Mme. de Genlis's *Adelaide and Theodore*
(London, 1783), the story of Cecilia, who is forced
by her father to enter a convent and, although in
love with Chevalier de Murville, takes her vows.
So unhappy is she that she wishes to destroy herself. Her father finally realizes his error and near
the end of her short life, understands that he is
"perhaps the cause of her eternal condemnation"
(I, 183), for "Heaven punishes with such severity"
(I, 225).
1. "A person is not to act in this or that way,
though convinced they are right in so doing, because some equivocal circumstances may lead the
world to *suspect* that they acted from different motives.—This is sacrificing the substance for a shadow.
Let people but watch their own hearts, and act
rightly, as far as they can judge, and they may
patiently wait till the opinion of the world comes
round. It is best to be directed by a simple motive—
for justice has too often been sacrificed to propriety;—another word for convenience" [Wollstone-
craft's note].

is deprived of her fortune, and thrown friendless on the world. The father practises the most infamous arts to separate his son from her, and when the son detects his villany, and following the dictates of honour marries the girl, nothing but misery ensues, because forsooth he married *without* his father's consent.[2] On what ground can religion or morality rest when justice is thus set as defiance? With the same view she represents an accomplished young woman, as ready to marry any body that her *mama* pleased to recommend; and, as actually marrying the young man of her own choice, without feeling any emotions of passion, because that a well educated girl had not time to be in love. Is it possible to have much respect for a system of education that thus insults reason and nature?

Many similar opinions occur in her writings, mixed with sentiments that do honour to her head and heart. Yet so much superstition is mixed with her religion, and so much worldly wisdom with her morality, that I should not let a young person read her works, unless I could afterwards converse on the subjects, and point out the contradictions.

Mrs. Chapone's Letters are written with such good sense, and unaffected humility, and contain so many useful observations, that I only mention them to pay the worthy writer this tribute of respect.[3] I cannot, it is true, always coincide in opinion with her; but I always respect her.

The very word respect brings Mrs. Macaulay to my remembrance.[4] The woman of the greatest abilities, undoubtedly, that this country has ever produced.—And yet this woman has been suffered to die without sufficient respect being paid to her memory.

Posterity, however, will be more just; and remember that Catharine Macaulay was an example of intellectual acquirements supposed to be incompatible with the weakness of her sex. In her style of writing, indeed, no sex appears, for it is like the sense it conveys, strong and clear.

I will not call hers a masculine understanding, because I admit not of such an arrogant assumption of reason; but I contend that it was a sound one, and that her judgment, the matured fruit of profound thinking, was a proof that a woman can acquire judgment, in the full extent of the word. Possessing more penetration than sagacity, more understanding than fancy, she writes with sober energy and argumentative closeness; yet sympathy and benevolence give an

2. In *Adelaide and Theodore*, the "Life of St. André" (II, 14–36), conforms generally to Wollstonecraft's summary.
3. Hester Mulso Chapone (1727–1801) was a precocious child, writing her first work at age nine. *Letters on the Improvement of the Mind* (1773), referred to here, is primarily concerned with how to study the Scriptures.
4. Catharine Sawbridge Macaulay Graham (1731–91), historian and intellectual. Her *History of England* in 8 volumes was published beginning in 1763 and the *Letters on Education*, the work Wollstonecraft refers to. in 1790.

interest to her sentiments, and that vital heat to arguments, which forces the reader to weigh them.[5]

When I first thought of writing these strictures I anticipated Mrs. Macaulay's approbation, with a little of that sanguine ardour, which it has been the business of my life to depress; but soon heard with the sickly qualm of disappointed hope; and the still seriousness of regret—that she was no more![6]

SECT. V

Taking a view of the different works which have been written on education, Lord Chesterfield's Letters must not be silently passed over. Not that I mean to analyze his unmanly, immoral system, or even to cull any of the useful, shrewd remarks which occur in his epistles[7]—No, I only mean to make a few reflections on the avowed tendency of them—the art of acquiring an early knowledge of the world. An art, I will venture to assert, that preys secretly, like the worm in the bud, on the expanding powers, and turns to poison the generous juices which should mount with vigour in the youthful frame, inspiring warm affections and great resolves.[8]

For every thing, saith the wise man, there is a season;[9]—and who would look for the fruits of autumn during the genial months of spring? But this is mere declamation, and I mean to reason with those worldly-wise instructors, who, instead of cultivating the judgment, instill prejudices, and render hard the heart that gradual experience would only have cooled. An early acquaintance with human infirmities; or, what is termed knowledge of the world, is the surest way, in my opinion, to contract the heart and damp the natural youthful ardour which produces not only great talents, but great virtues. For the vain attempt to bring forth the fruit of experience, before the sapling has thrown out its leaves, only exhausts its strength, and prevents its assuming a natural form; just as the form and strength of subsiding metals are injured when the attraction of cohesion is disturbed.

Tell me, ye who have studied the human mind, is it not a strange way to fix principles by showing young people that they are seldom

5. "Coinciding in opinion with Mrs. Macaulay relative to many branches of education, I refer to her valuable work, instead of quoting her sentiments to support my own" [Wollstonecraft's note].
6. Catharine Macaulay died June 22, 1791.
7. The first edition reads "frivolous correspondence" for "epistles" and perhaps reflects more honestly Wollstonecraft's attitude towards Lord Chesterfield's *Letters to His Son*.
8. "That children ought to be constantly guarded against the vices and follies of the world, appears, to me, a very mistaken opinion; for in the course of my experience, and my eyes have looked abroad, I never knew a youth educated in this manner, who had early imbibed these chilling suspicions, and repeated by rote the hesitating *if* of age, that did not prove a selfish character" [Wollstonecraft's note].
9. Ecclesiastes 3:1: "To every thing there is a season, and a time to every purpose under the heaven."

stable? And how can they be fortified by habits when they are proved to be fallacious by example? Why is the ardour of youth thus to be damped, and the luxuriancy of fancy cut to the quick? This dry caution may, it is true, guard a character from worldly mischances; but will infallibly preclude excellence in either virtue or knowledge.[1] The stumbling-block thrown across every path by suspicion, will prevent any vigorous exertions of genius or benevolence, and life will be stripped of its most alluring charm long before its calm evening, when man should retire to contemplation for comfort and support.

A young man who has been bred up with domestic friends, and led to store his mind with as much speculative knowledge as can be acquired by reading and the natural reflections which youthful ebullitions of animal spirits and instinctive feelings inspire, will enter the world with warm and erroneous expectations. But this appears to be the course of nature; and in morals, as well as in works of taste, we should be observant of her sacred indications, and not presume to lead when we ought obsequiously to follow.

In the world few people act from principle; present feelings, and early habits, are the grand springs: but how would the former be deadened, and the latter rendered iron corroding fetters, if the world were shewn to young people just as it is; when no knowledge of mankind or their own hearts, slowly obtained by experience, rendered them forbearing? Their fellow creatures would not then be viewed as frail beings; like themselves, condemned to struggle with human infirmities, and sometimes displaying the light, and sometimes the dark side of their character; extorting alternate feelings of love and disgust; but guarded against as beasts of prey, till every enlarged social feeling, in a word,—humanity, was eradicated.

In life, on the contrary, as we gradually discover the imperfections of our nature, we discover virtues, and various circumstances attach us to our fellow creatures, when we mix with them, and view the same objects, that are never thought of in acquiring a hasty unnatural knowledge of the world. We see a folly swell into a vice, by almost imperceptible degrees, and pity while we blame; but, if the hideous monster burst suddenly on our sight, fear and disgust rendering us more severe than man ought to be, might lead us with blind zeal to usurp the character of omnipotence, and denounce damnation on our fellow mortals, forgetting that we cannot read the heart, and that we have seeds of the same vices lurking in our own.

I have already remarked that we expect more from instruction,

---

1. "I have already observed that an early knowledge of the world, obtained in a natural way, by mixing in the world, has the same effect: instancing officers and women" [Wollstonecraft's note].

than mere instruction can produce: for, instead of preparing young people to encounter the evils of life with dignity, and to acquire wisdom and virtue by the exercise of their own faculties, precepts are heaped upon precepts, and blind obedience required, when conviction should be brought home to reason.

Suppose, for instance, that a young person in the first ardour of friendship deifies the beloved object—what harm can arise from this mistaken enthusiastic attachment? Perhaps it is necessary for virtue first to appear in a human form to impress youthful hearts; the ideal model, which a more matured and exalted mind looks up to, and shapes for itself, would elude their sight. He who loves not his brother whom he hath seen, how can he love God? asked the wisest of men.[2]

It is natural for youth to adorn the first object of its affection with every good quality, and the emulation produced by ignorance, or, to speak with more propriety, by inexperience, brings forward the mind capable of forming such an affection, and when, in the lapse of time, perfection is found not to be within the reach of mortals, virtue, abstractedly, is thought beautiful, and wisdom sublime. Admiration then gives place to friendship, properly so called, because it is cemented by esteem; and the being walks alone only dependent on heaven for that emulous panting after perfection which ever glows in a noble mind. But this knowledge a man must gain by the exertion of his own faculties; and this is surely the blessed fruit of disappointed hope! for He who delighteth to diffuse happiness and shew mercy to the weak creatures, who are learning to know him, never implanted a good propensity to be a tormenting ignis fatuus.[3]

Our trees are now allowed to spread with wild luxuriance, nor do we expect by force to combine the majestic marks of time with youthful graces; but wait patiently till they have struck deep their root, and braved many a storm.—Is the mind then, which, in proportion to its dignity, advances more slowly towards perfection, to be treated with less respect? To argue from analogy, every thing around us is in a progressive state; and when an unwelcome knowledge of life produces almost a satiety of life, and we discover by the natural course of things that all that is done under the sun is vanity,[4] we are drawing near the awful close of the drama. The days of activity and hope are over, and the opportunities which the first stage of existence has afforded of advancing in the scale of intelligence, must soon be summed up.—A knowledge at this period of the futility of life, or earlier, if obtained by experience, is very

2. 1 John 4:20: "If a man say, I love God, and hateth his brother, he is a liar: for he that loveth not his brother whom he hath seen, how can he love God whom he hath not seen?"

3. Delusion or an attractive deception.

4. Ecclesiastes 1:2 and 1:9: "all is vanity . . . and there is no new thing under the sun."

useful, because it is natural; but when a frail being is shewn the fol-lies and vices of man, that he may be taught prudently to guard against the common casualties of life by sacrificing his heart—surely it is not speaking harshly to call it the wisdom of this world, con-trasted with the nobler fruit of piety and experience.

I will venture a paradox, and deliver my opinion without reserve; if men were only born to form a circle of life and death, it would be wise to take every step that foresight could suggest to render life happy. Moderation in every pursuit would then be supreme wisdom; and the prudent voluptuary might enjoy a degree of content, though he neither cultivated his understanding nor kept his heart pure. Prudence, supposing we were mortal, would be true wisdom, or, to be more explicit, would procure the greatest portion of happi-ness, considering the whole of life, but knowledge beyond the con-veniences of life would be a curse.

Why should we injure our health by close study? The exalted pleasure which intellectual pursuits afford would scarcely be equiva-lent to the hours of languor that follow; especially, if it be necessary to take into the reckoning the doubts and disappointments that cloud our researches. Vanity and vexation close every inquiry: for the cause which we particularly wished to discover flies like the hori-zon before us as we advance. The ignorant, on the contrary, resem-ble children, and suppose, that if they could walk straight forward they should at last arrive where the earth and clouds meet. Yet, dis-appointed as we are in our researches, the mind gains strength by the exercise, sufficient, perhaps, to comprehend the answers which, in another step of existence, it may receive to the anxious questions it asked, when the understanding with feeble wing was fluttering round the visible effects to dive into the hidden cause.

The passions also, the winds of life, would be useless, if not inju-rious, did the substance which composes our thinking being, after we have thought in vain, only become the support of vegetable life, and invigorate a cabbage, or blush in a rose. The appetites would answer every earthly purpose, and produce more moderate and per-manent happiness. But the powers of the soul that are of little use here, and, probably, disturb our animal enjoyments, even while con-scious dignity makes us glory in possessing them, prove that life is merely an education, a state of infancy, to which the only hopes worth cherishing should not be sacrificed. I mean, therefore, to infer, that we ought to have a precise idea of what we wish to attain by education, for the immortality of the soul is contradicted by the actions of many people who firmly profess the belief.

If you mean to secure ease and prosperity on earth as the first consideration, and leave futurity to provide for itself; you act pru-dently in giving your child an early insight into the weaknesses of his nature. You may not, it is true, make an Inkle[5] of him; but do not imagine that he will stick to more than the letter of the law, who has very early imbibed a mean opinion of human nature; nor will he think it necessary to rise much above the common standard. He may avoid gross vices, because honesty is the best policy; but he will never aim at attaining great virtues. The example of writers and artists will illustrate this remark.

I must therefore venture to doubt whether what has been thought an axiom in morals may not have been a dogmatical assertion made by men who have coolly seen mankind through the medium of books, and say, in direct contradiction to them, that the regulation of the passions is not, always, wisdom.—On the contrary, it should seem, that one reason why men have superiour judgment, and more fortitude than women, is undoubtedly this, that they give a freer scope to the grand passions, and by more frequently going astray enlarge their minds. If then by the exercise of their own[6] reason they fix on some stable principle, they have probably to thank the force of their passions, nourished by *false* views of life, and permitted to overleap the boundary that secures content. But if, in the dawn of life, we could soberly survey the scenes before as in perspective, and see every thing in its true colours, how could the passions gain sufficient strength to unfold the faculties?

Let me now as from an eminence survey the world stripped of all its false delusive charms. The clear atmosphere enables me to see each object in its true point of view, while my heart is still. I am calm as the prospect in a morning when the mists, slowly dispersing, silently unveil the beauties of nature, refreshed by rest.

In what light will the world now appear?—I rub my eyes and think, perchance, that I am just awaking from a lively dream.

I see the sons and daughters of men pursuing shadows, and anxiously wasting their powers to feed passions which have no adequate object—if the very excess of these blind impulses, pampered by that lying, yet constantly trusted guide, the imagination, did not, by preparing them for some other state, render short-sighted mortals wiser without their own concurrence; or, what comes to the same thing, when they were pursuing some imaginary present good.

After viewing objects in this light, it would not be very fanciful to imagine that this world was a stage on which a pantomime is daily performed for the amusement of superiour beings. How would

5. The story of Inkle and Yarico was made popular by Richard Steele's *Spectator* No. 11 (13 March 1711). Thomas Inkle was a handsome young Englishman whose ship on its way to the West Indies was intercepted by hostile Indians. Inkle, however, was rescued and cared for by an Indian maiden, Yarico, who out of love finally flagged down another British ship to rescue herself and her lover. But Inkle, needing money, sold Yarico who brought an even higher price because she was pregnant—by Inkle of course. See *The Spectator*, ed. Donald F. Bond (Oxford, 1965), I, 49–51.

6. " 'I find that all is but lip-wisdom which wants experience,' says Sidney" [Wollstonecraft's note]. Sir Philip Sidney, *Arcadia*, ed. Albert Feuillerat (Cambridge, 1965), I, 113: "I find indeed, that all is but lip-wisdome, which wants experience."

they be diverted to see the ambitious man consuming himself by running after a phantom, and, 'pursuing the bubble fame in the cannon's mouth'[7] that was to blow him to nothing: for when consciousness is lost, it matters not whether we mount in a whirlwind or descend in rain. And should they compassionately invigorate his sight and shew him the thorny path which led to eminence, that like a quicksand sinks as he ascends, disappointing his hopes when almost within his grasp, would he not leave to others the honour of amusing them, and labour to secure the present moment, though from the constitution of his nature he would not find it very easy to catch the flying stream? Such slaves are we to hope and fear!

But, vain as the ambitious man's pursuits would be, he is often striving for something more substantial than fame—that indeed would be the veriest meteor, the wildest fire that could lure a man to ruin.—What! renounce the most trifling gratification to be applauded when he should be no more! Wherefore this struggle, whether man be mortal or immortal, if that noble passion did not really raise the being above his fellows?—

And love! What diverting scenes would it produce—Pantaloon's tricks[8] must yield to more egregious folly. To see a mortal adorn an object with imaginary charms, and then fall down and worship the idol which he had himself set up—how ridiculous! But what serious consequences ensue to rob man of that portion of happiness, which the Deity by calling him into existence has (or, on what can his attributes rest?) indubitably promised: would not all the purposes of life have been much better fulfilled if he had only felt what had been termed physical love? And, would not the sight of the object, not seen through the medium of the imagination, soon reduce the passion to an appetite, if reflection, the noble distinction of man, did not give it force, and make it an instrument to raise him above this earthy dross, by teaching him to love the centre of all perfection; whose wisdom appears clearer and clearer in the works of nature, in proportion as reason is illuminated and exalted by contemplation, and by acquiring that love of order which the struggles of passion produce?

The habit of reflection, and the knowledge attained by fostering any passion, might be shewn to be equally useful, though the object be proved equally fallacious; for they would all appear in the same light, if they were not magnified by the governing passion implanted in us by the Author of all good, to call forth and strengthen the faculties of each individual, and enable it to attain all the experience that an infant can obtain, who does certain things, it cannot tell why.

I descend from my height, and mixing with my fellow-creatures,

---

7. *As You Like It*, II.vii.152–53: "Seeking the bubble reputation / Even in the cannon's mouth."
8. Pantalone, one of the type-characters in the *Commedia dell-Arte*, a comic form full of tricks and dupes played by one character upon another.

feel myself hurried along the common stream; ambition, love, hope, and fear, exert their wonted power, though we be convinced by reason that their present and most attractive promises are only lying dreams; but had the cold hand of circumspection damped each generous feeling before it had left any permanent character, or fixed some habit, what could be expected, but selfish prudence and reason just rising above instinct? Who that has read Dean Swift's disgusting description of the Yahoos, and insipid one of Houyhnhnm[9] with a philosophical eye, can avoid seeing the futility of degrading the passions, or making man rest in contentment?

The youth should *act*; for had he the experience of a grey head he would be fitter for death than life, though his virtues, rather residing in his head than his heart, could produce nothing great, and his understanding, prepared for this world, would not, by its noble flights, prove that it had a title to a better.

Besides, it is not possible to give a young person a just view of life; he must have struggled with his own passions before he can estimate the force of the temptation which betrayed his brother into vice. Those who are entering life, and those who are departing, see the world from such very different points of view, that they can seldom think alike, unless the unfledged reason of the former never attempted a solitary flight.

When we hear of some daring crime—it comes full on us in the deepest shade of turpitude, and raises indignation; but the eye that gradually saw the darkness thicken, must observe it with more compassionate forbearance. The world cannot be seen by an unmoved spectator, we must mix in the throng, and feel as men feel before we can judge of their feelings. If we mean, in short, to live in the world to grow wiser and better, and not merely to enjoy the good things of life, we must attain a knowledge of others at the same time that we become acquainted with ourselves—knowledge acquired any other way only hardens the heart and perplexes the understanding.

I may be told, that the knowledge thus acquired, is sometimes purchased at too dear a rate. I can only answer that I very much doubt whether any knowledge can be attained without labour and sorrow; and those who wish to spare their children both, should not complain, if they are neither wise nor virtuous. They only aimed at making them prudent; and prudence, early in life, is but the cautious craft of ignorant self-love.

I have observed that young people, to whose education particular attention has been paid, have, in general, been very superficial and

---

9. In Jonathan Swift's *Gulliver's Travels*, Book IV, the Yahoos are monkeylike humans with execrable habits and Houyhnhnms are horselike creatures of overly rational perfection.

conceited, and far from pleasing in any respect, because they had
neither the unsuspecting warmth of youth, nor the cool depth of
age. I cannot help imputing this unnatural appearance principally
to that hasty premature instruction, which leads them presumptuously to repeat all the crude notions they have taken upon trust,
so that the careful education which they received, makes them all
their lives the slaves of prejudices.

Mental as well as bodily exertion is, at first, irksome; so much so,
that the many would fain let others both work and think for them.
An observation which I have often made will illustrate my meaning.
When in a circle of strangers, or acquaintances, a person of moderate abilities asserts an opinion with heat, I will venture to affirm, for
I have traced this fact home, very often, that it is a prejudice. These
echoes have a high respect for the understanding of some relation or
friend, and without fully comprehending the opinions, which they
are so eager to retail, they maintain them with a degree of obstinacy, that would surprise even the person who concocted them.

I know that a kind of fashion now prevails of respecting prejudices; and when any one dares to face them, though actuated by
humanity and armed by reason, he is superciliously asked whether
his ancestors were fools. No, I should reply; opinions, at first, of
every description, were all, probably, considered, and therefore were
founded on some reason; yet not unfrequently, of course, it was
rather a local expedient than a fundamental principle, that would
be reasonable at all times. But, moss-covered opinions assume the
disproportioned form of prejudices, when they are indolently
adopted only because age has given them a venerable aspect, though
the reason on which they were built ceases to be a reason, or cannot
be traced. Why are we to love prejudices, merely because they are
prejudices?[1] A prejudice is a fond obstinate persuasion for which we
can give no reason; for the moment a reason can be given for an
opinion, it ceases to be a prejudice, though it may be an error in
judgment: and are we then advised to cherish opinions only to set
reason at defiance? This mode of arguing, if arguing it may be
called, reminds me of what is vulgarly termed a woman's reason.
For women sometimes declare that they love, or believe, certain
things, *because* they love, or believe them.

It is impossible to converse with people to any purpose, who only
use affirmatives and negatives. Before you can bring them to a
point, to start fairly from, you must go back to the simple principles
that were antecedent to the prejudices broached by power; and it is
ten to one but you are stopped by the philosophical assertion, that

1. "Vide Mr. Burke" [Wollstonecraft's note]. Edmund Burke, *Reflections on the Revolution in
France*, ed. Thomas H. D. Mahoney (New York,
1955), pp. 98–102. Burke says, essentially, that we
should cherish social prejudice because it represents the crystallization of all that has been good
in the past.

certain principles are as practically false as they are abstractly true.[2] Nay, it may be inferred, that reason has whispered some doubts, for it generally happens that people assert their opinions with the greatest heat when they begin to waver; striving to drive out their own doubts by convincing their opponent, they grow angry when those gnawing doubts are thrown back to prey on themselves.

The fact is, that men expect from education, what education cannot give. A sagacious parent or tutor may strengthen the body and sharpen the instruments by which the child is to gather knowledge; but the honey must be the reward of the individual's own industry. It is almost as absurd to attempt to make a youth wise by the experience of another, as to expect the body to grow strong by the exercise which is only talked of, or seen.[3] Many of those children whose conduct has been most narrowly watched, become the weakest men, because their instructors only instill certain notions into their minds, that have no other foundation than their authority; and if they be loved or respected, the mind is cramped in its exertions and wavering in its advances. The business of education in this case, is only to conduct the shooting tendrils to a proper pole; yet after laying precept upon precept, without allowing a child to acquire judgment itself, parents expect them to act in the same manner by this borrowed fallacious light, as if they had illuminated it themselves; and be, when they enter life, what their parents are at the close. They do not consider that the tree, and even the human body, does not strengthen its fibres till it has reached its full growth.

There appears to be something analogous in the mind. The senses and the imagination give a form to the character, during childhood and youth; and the understanding, as life advances, gives firmness to the first fair purposes of sensibility—till virtue, arising rather from the clear conviction of reason than the impulse of the heart, morality is made to rest on a rock against which the storms of passion vainly beat.

I hope I shall not be misunderstood when I say, that religion will not have this condensing energy, unless it be founded on reason. If it be merely the refuge of weakness or wild fanaticism, and not a governing principle of conduct, drawn from self-knowledge, and a rational opinion respecting the attributes of God, what can it be expected to produce? The religion which consists in warming the affections, and exalting the imagination, is only the poetical part, and may afford the individual pleasure without rendering it a more

---

2. " 'Convince a man against his will, / He's of the same opinion still' " [Wollstonecraft's note]. Samuel Butler, *Hudibras, Third Part*, Canto III, 547–48: "He that complies against his will, / Is of his own opinion still."

3. " 'One sees nothing when one is content to contemplate only; it is necessary to act oneself to be able to see how others act.' *Rousseau*" [Wollstonecraft's note].

moral being. It may be a substitute for worldly pursuits; yet narrow, instead of enlarging the heart: but virtue must be loved as in itself sublime and excellent, and not for the advantages it procures or the evils it averts, if any great degree of excellence be expected. Men will not become moral when they only build airy castles in a future world to compensate for the disappointments which they meet with in this; if they turn their thoughts from relative duties to religious reveries.

Most prospects in life are marred by the shuffling worldly wisdom of men, who, forgetting that they cannot serve God and mammon, endeavour to blend contradictory things.—If you wish to make your son rich, pursue one course—if you are only anxious to make him virtuous, you must take another; but do not imagine that you can bound from one road to the other without losing your way.[4]

Chap. VI

The Effect Which an Early Association of Ideas Has upon the Character

Educated in the enervating style recommended by the writers on whom I have been animadverting; and not having a chance, from their subordinate state in society, to recover their lost ground, is it surprising that women every where appear a defect in nature? Is it surprising, when we consider what a determinate effect an early association of ideas has on the character, that they neglect their understandings, and turn all their attention to their persons?

The great advantages which naturally result from storing the mind with knowledge, are obvious from the following considerations. The association of our ideas is either habitual or instantaneous; and the latter mode seems rather to depend on the original temperature of the mind than on the will. When the ideas, and matters of fact, are once taken in, they lie by for use, till some fortuitous circumstance makes the information dart into the mind with illustrative force, that has been received at very different periods of our lives.[1] Like the lightning's flash are many recollections;

4. "See an excellent essay on this subject by Mrs. Barbauld, in *Miscellaneous Pieces in Prose*" [Wollstonecraft's note]. The exact essay is Anna Laetitia Barbauld's "Against Inconsistency in our Expectations."
1. Wollstonecraft is talking about one of the epistemological theories of the time generally labeled "associationism." Its chief formulator had been David Hartley (1705–57) whose lengthy *Observations on Man* uses Newton's theory that vibrations moving through aether, a kind of fluid surrounding

matter, produce sensation. Because of Wollstonecraft's deprecating remarks about materialists later in this chapter, however, and because of her reference to "matters of fact," she probably is deriving her information either from Hume's *An Enquiry Concerning Human Understanding* or from his *Enquiry Concerning the Principles of Morals*. Hume was less concerned with the mechanics of how ideas began to associate than with the implications of their accumulation.

one idea assimilating and explaining another, with astonishing rapidity. I do not now allude to that quick perception of truth, which is so intuitive that it baffles research, and makes us at a loss to determine whether it is reminiscence or ratiocination, lost sight of in its celerity, that opens the dark cloud. Over those instantaneous associations we have little power; for when the mind is once enlarged by excursive flights, or profound reflection, the raw materials will, in some degree, arrange themselves. The understanding, it is true, may keep us from going out of drawing when we group our thoughts, or transcribe from the imagination the warm sketches of fancy; but the animal spirits, the indivdual character, give the colouring. Over this subtle electric fluid,[2] how little power do we possess, and over it how little power can reason obtain! These fine intractable spirits appear to be the essence of genius, and beaming in its eagle eye, produce in the most eminent degree the happy energy of associating thoughts that surprise, delight, and instruct. These are the glowing minds that concentrate pictures for their fellow-creatures; forcing them to view with interest the objects reflected from the impassioned imagination, which they passed over in nature.

I must be allowed to explain myself. The generality of people cannot see or feel poetically, they want fancy, and therefore fly from solitude in search of sensible objects; but when an author lends them his eyes they can see as he saw, and be amused by images they could not select, though lying before them.

Education thus only supplies the man of genius with knowledge to give variety and contrast to his associations; but there is an habitual association of ideas, that grows 'with our growth,'[3] which has a great effect on the moral character of mankind; and by which a turn is given to the mind that commonly remains throughout life. So ductile is the understanding, and yet so stubborn, that the associations which depend on adventitious circumstances, during the period that the body takes to arrive at maturity, can seldom be disentangled by reason. One idea calls up another, its old associate, and memory, faithful to the first impressions, particularly when the intellectual powers are not employed to cool our sensations, retraces them with mechanical exactness.

This habitual slavery, to first impressions, has a more baneful effect on the female than the male character, because business and

2. "I have sometimes, when inclined to laugh at materialists, asked whether, as the most powerful effects in nature are apparently produced by fluids, the magnetic, &c. the passions might not be fine volatile fluids that embraced humanity, keeping the more refractory elementary parts together—or whether they were simply a liquid fire that pervaded the more sluggish materials, giving them life and heat?" [Wollstonecraft's note]. The "materi-

alists" like Newton and Hartley, believed that a subtle fluid pervaded everything and that vibrations traveled through this fluid, into the senses, creating knowledge in the perceiver of the object.
3. Alexander Pope, An Essay on Man II.136: "Grows with his growth, and strengthens with his strength"; Pope is speaking of the passions, Wollstonecraft of the seminal ideas which form one's personality.

other dry employments of the understanding, tend to deaden the feelings and break associations that do violence to reason. But females, who are made women of when they are mere children, and brought back to childhood when they ought to leave the go-cart forever, have not sufficient strength of mind to efface the superinductions of art that have smothered nature.

Every thing that they see or hear serves to fix impressions, call forth emotions, and associate ideas, that give a sexual character to the mind. False notions of beauty and delicacy stop the growth of their limbs and produce a sickly soreness, rather than delicacy of organs; and thus weakened by being employed in unfolding instead of examining the first associations, forced on them by every surrounding object, how can they attain the vigour necessary to enable them to throw off their factitious character?—where find strength to recur to reason and rise superiour to a system of oppression, that blasts the fair promises of spring? This cruel[4] association of ideas, which every thing conspires to twist into all their habits of thinking, or, to speak with more precision, of feeling, receives new force when they begin to act a little for themselves; for they then perceive that it is only through their address to excite emotions in men, that pleasure and power are to be obtained. Besides, the books professedly written for their instruction, which make the first impression on their minds, all inculcate the same opinions. Educated then in worse than Egyptian bondage,[5] it is unreasonable, as well as cruel, to upbraid them with faults that can scarcely be avoided, unless a degree of native vigour be supposed, that falls to the lot of very few amongst mankind.

For instance, the severest sarcasms have been levelled against the sex, and they have been ridiculed for repeating 'a set of phrases learnt by rote,'[6] when nothing could be more natural, considering the education they receive, and that their 'highest praise is to obey, unargued'[7]—the will of man. If they be not allowed to have reason sufficient to govern their own conduct—why, all they learn—must be learned by rote! And when all their ingenuity is called forth to adjust their dress, 'a passion for a scarlet coat,'[8] is so natural, that it never surprised me; and, allowing Pope's summary of their character to be just, 'that every woman is at heart a rake,'[9] why should they be bitterly censured for seeking a congenial mind, and preferring a rake to a man of sense?

Rakes know how to work on their sensibility, whilst the modest

---

4. "Cruel" because ideas, once irreversibly set, determine a girl's future mode of thinking and acting.
5. Refers to the years of slavery endured by the Jewish tribes in Egypt before their delivery by Moses.
6. Jonathan Swift, "The Furniture of a Woman's Mind," line 1.
7. *Paradise Lost* IV.636–38: "Unargu'd I obey; so

God ordains, / God is thy law, thou mine: to know no more / Is woman's happiest knowledge and her praise."
8. Swift, "The Furniture of a Woman's Mind," line 2.
9. Pope, *Moral Essays* II.215–16: "Men, some to Bus'ness, some to Pleasure take; / But ev'ry Woman is at heart a Rake."

merit of reasonable men has, of course, less effect on their feelings, and they cannot reach the heart by the way of the understanding, because they have few sentiments in common.

It seems a little absurd to expect women to be more reasonable than men in their *likings*, and still to deny them the uncontrouled use of reason. When do men *fall-in-love* with sense? When do they, with their superiour powers and advantages, turn from the person to the mind? And how can they then expect women, who are only taught to observe behaviour, and acquire manners rather than morals, to despise what they have been all their lives labouring to attain? Where are they suddenly to find judgment enough to weigh patiently the sense of an awkward virtuous man, when his manners, of which they are made critical judges, are rebuffing, and his conversation cold and dull, because it does not consist of pretty repartees, or well turned compliments? In order to admire or esteem any thing for a continuance, we must, at least, have our curiosity excited by knowing, in some degree, what we admire; for we are unable to estimate the value of qualities and virtues above our comprehension. Such a respect, when it is felt, may be very sublime; and the confused consciousness of humility may render the dependent creature an interesting object, in some points of view; but human love must have grosser ingredients; and the person very naturally will come in for its share—and, an ample share it mostly has!

Love is, in a great degree, an arbitrary passion, and will reign, like some other stalking mischiefs, by its own authority, without deigning to reason; and it may also be easily distinguished from esteem, the foundation of friendship, because it is often excited by evanescent beauties and graces, though, to give an energy to the sentiment, something more solid must deepen their impression and set the imagination to work, to make the most fair—the first good.

Common passions are excited by common qualities.—Men look for beauty and the simper of good-humoured docility: women are captivated by easy manners; a gentleman-like man seldom fails to please them, and their thirsty ears eagerly drink the insinuating nothings of politeness, whilst they turn from the unintelligible sounds of the charmer—reason, charm he never so wisely. With respect to superficial accomplishments, the rake certainly has the advantage; and of these females can form an opinion, for it is their own ground. Rendered gay and giddy by the whole tenor of their lives, the very aspect of wisdom, or the severe graces of virtue, must have a lugubrious appearance to them; and produce a kind of restraint from which they and love, sportive child, naturally revolt. Without taste, excepting of the lighter kind, for taste is the offspring of judgment, how can they discover that true beauty and grace must arise from the play of the mind? and how can they be expected to relish in a lover what they do not, or very imperfectly, possess themselves? The sympathy that unites hearts, and invites to confidence, in them is so very faint, that it cannot take fire, and thus mount to passion. No, I repeat it, the love cherished by such minds, must have grosser fewel!

The inference is obvious; till women are led to exercise their understandings, they should not be satirized for their attachment to rakes; or even for being rakes at heart, when it appears to be the inevitable consequence of their education. They who live to please —must find their enjoyments, their happiness, in pleasure! It is a trite, yet true remark, that we never do any thing well, unless we love it for its own sake.

Supposing, however, for a moment, that women were, in some future revolution of time, to become, what I sincerely wish them to be, even love would acquire more serious dignity, and be purified in its own fires; and virtue giving true delicacy to their affections, they would turn with disgust from a rake. Reasoning then, as well as feeling, the only province of woman, at present, they might easily guard against exterior graces, and quickly learn to despise the sensibility that had been excited and hackneyed in the ways of women, whose trade was vice; and allurements, wanton airs. They would recollect that the flame, one must use appropriated expressions, which they wished to light up, had been exhausted by lust, and that the sated appetite, losing all relish for pure and simple pleasures, could only be roused by licentious arts or variety. What satisfaction could a woman of delicacy promise herself in a union with such a man, when the very artlessness of her affection might appear insipid? Thus does Dryden describe the situation,

> ————'Where love is duty, on the female side,
> 'On theirs mere sensual gust, and sought with surly pride.'[1]

But one grand truth women have yet to learn, though much it imports them to act accordingly. In the choice of a husband, they should not be led astray by the qualities of a lover—for a lover the husband, even supposing him to be wise and virtuous, cannot long remain.

Were women more rationally educated, could they take a more comprehensive view of things, they would be contented to love but once in their lives; and after marriage calmly let passion subside into friendship—into that tender intimacy, which is the best refuge from care; yet is built on such pure, still affections, that idle jealousies would not be allowed to disturb the discharge of the sober duties of life, or to engross the thoughts that ought to be otherwise

---

1. John Dryden, *Palamon and Arcite* III.231–32. "Gust" in the second line refers to satisfaction of an appetite.

employed. This is a state in which many men live; but few, very few women. And the difference may easily be accounted for, without recurring to a sexual character. Men, for whom we are told women were made, have too much occupied the thoughts of women; and this association has so entangled love with all their motives of action; and, to harp a little on an old string, having been solely employed either to prepare themselves to excite love, or actually putting their lessons in practice, they cannot live without love. But, when a sense of duty, or fear of shame, obliges them to restrain this pampered desire of pleasing beyond certain lengths, too far for delicacy, it is true, though far from criminality, they obstinately determine to love, I speak of the passion, their husbands to the end of the chapter—and then acting the part which they foolishly exacted from their lovers, they become abject woers, and fond slaves.

Men of wit and fancy are often rakes; and fancy is the food of love. Such men will inspire passion. Half the sex, in its present infantine state, would pine for a Lovelace;[2] a man so witty, so graceful, and so valiant: and can they *deserve* blame for acting according to principles so constantly inculcated? They want a lover, and protector; and behold him kneeling before them—bravery prostrate to beauty! The virtues of a husband are thus thrown by love into the background, and gay hopes, or lively emotions, banish reflection till the day of reckoning comes; and come it surely will, to turn the sprightly lover into a surly suspicious tyrant, who contemptuously insults the very weakness he fostered. Or, supposing the rake reformed, he cannot quickly get rid of old habits.[3] When a man of abilities is first carried away by his passions, it is necessary that sentiment and taste varnish the enormities of vice, and give a zest to brutal indulgences; but when the gloss of novelty is worn off, and pleasure palls upon the sense, lasciviousness becomes barefaced, and enjoyment only the desperate effort of weakness flying from reflection as from a legion of devils. Oh! virtue, thou art not an empty name! All that life can give—thou givest!

If much comfort cannot be expected from the friendship of a reformed rake of superior abilities, what is the consequence when he lacketh sense, as well as principles? Verily misery, in its most hideous shape. When the habits of weak people are consolidated by time, a reformation is barely possible; and actually makes the beings miserable who have not sufficient mind to be amused by innocent pleasure; like the tradesman who retires from the hurry of business, nature presents to them only a universal blank; and the restless

2. Lovelace is the handsome rake in Samuel Richardson's novel of 1747–48, *Clarissa*.
3. "To warn the Inconsiderate and Thoughtless of the one sex . . . upon that dangerous but too commonly received notion, *that a reformed Rake makes the best Husband*" (Samuel Richardson, *Clarissa*, ed. George Sherburn [Boston, 1962], p. xx).

thoughts prey on the damped spirits.[4] Their reformation, as well as his retirement, actually makes them wretched because it deprives them of all employment, by quenching the hopes and fears that set in motion their sluggish minds.

If such be the force of habit; if such be the bondage of folly, how carefully ought we to guard the mind from storing up vicious associations; and equally careful should we be to cultivate the understanding, to save the poor wight[5] from the weak dependent state of even harmless ignorance. For it is the right use of reason alone which makes us independent of every thing—excepting the unclouded Reason—'Whose service is perfect freedom.'[6]

Chap. VII

Modesty.—Comprehensively Considered, and Not as a Sexual Virtue

Modesty! Sacred offspring of sensibility and reason!—true delicacy of mind!—may I unblamed presume to investigate thy nature, and trace to its covert the mild charm, that mellowing each harsh feature of a character, renders what would otherwise only inspire cold admiration—lovely!—Thou that smoothest the wrinkles of wisdom, and softenest the tone of the sublimest virtues till they all melt into humanity;—thou that spreadest the ethereal cloud that, surrounding love, heightens every beauty, it half shades, breathing those coy sweets that steal into the heart, and charm the senses—modulate for me the language of persuasive reason, till I rouse my sex from the flowery bed, on which they supinely sleep life away!

In speaking of the association of our ideas, I have noticed two distinct modes;[1] and in defining modesty, it appears to me equally proper to discriminate that purity of mind, which is the effect of chastity, from a simplicity of character that leads us to form a just opinion of ourselves, equally distant from vanity or presumption, though by no means incompatible with a lofty consciousness of our

4. "I have frequently seen this exemplified in women whose beauty could no longer be repaired. They have retired from the noisy scenes of dissipation; but, unless they became methodists, the solitude of the select society of their family connections or acquaintance, has presented only a fearful void; consequently, nervous complaints, and all the vapourish train of idleness, rendered them quite as useless, and far more unhappy, than when they joined the giddy throng" [Wollstonecraft's note].
5. Person.
6. This phrase was written by Thomas Cranmer

for the Anglican Book of Common Prayer, the Collect from the Morning Prayer, and refers to God, not Reason. It is doubtful that, by using "reason" rather than "God" Wollstonecraft is being either blasphemous or overly rational. More probably she is summarizing an idea from Catharine Macaulay who says, " 'In my service there is perfect freedom,' says the Messiah; and the reason is plain; for the empire of religious sentiment, and the empire of reason, is the same" (Macaulay, *Letters on Education* [London, 1790], pp. 422–23).
1. It "is either habitual or instantaneous," p. 115.

own dignity. Modesty, in the latter signification of the term, is, that soberness of mind which teaches a man not to think more highly of himself than he ought to think, and should be distinguished from humility, because humility is a kind of self-abasement.

A modest man often conceives a great plan, and tenaciously adheres to it, conscious of his own strength, till success gives it a sanction that determines its character. Milton was not arrogant when he suffered a suggestion of judgment to escape him that proved a prophesy;[2] nor was General Washington when he accepted of the command of the American forces. The latter has always been characterized as a modest man; but had he been merely humble, he would probably have shrunk back irresolute, afraid of trusting to himself the direction of an enterprise, on which so much depended.

A modest man is steady, an humble man timid, and a vain one presumptuous:—this is the judgment, which the observation of many characters, has led me to form. Jesus Christ was modest, Moses was humble, and Peter vain.

Thus, discriminating modesty from humility in one case, I do not mean to confound it with bashfulness in the other. Bashfulness, in fact, is so distinct from modesty, that the most bashful lass, or raw country lout, often become the most impudent; for their bashfulness being merely the instinctive timidity of ignorance, custom soon changes it into assurance.[3]

The shameless behaviour of the prostitutes, who infest the streets of this metropolis,[4] raising alternate emotions of pity and disgust, may serve to illustrate this remark. They trample on virgin bashfulness with a sort of bravado, and glorying in their shame, become more audaciously lewd than men, however depraved, to whom this sexual quality has not been gratuitously granted, ever appear to be. But these poor ignorant wretches never had any modesty to lose, when they consigned themselves to infamy; for modesty is a virtue, not a quality. No, they were only bashful, shame-faced innocents; and losing their innocence, their shame-facedness was rudely brushed off; a virtue would have left some vestiges in the mind, had it been sacrificed to passion, to make us respect the grand ruin.

Purity of mind, or that genuine delicacy, which is the only vir-

---

2. Milton, by some contemporaneous biographical accounts, knew quite early in his life that he would someday be famous and did not scruple mentioning the fact.

3. " 'Such is the country-maiden's fright,
   When first a red-coat is in sight;
   Behind the door she hides her face;
   Next time at distance eyes the lace:
   She now can all his terrors stand,
   Nor from his squeeze withdraws her hand.
   She plays familiar in his arms,
   And ev'ry soldier hath his charms;

From tent to tent she spreads her flame;
For custom conquers fear and shame'
Gay" [Wollstonecraft's note]. John Gay, "Fable XIII. The Tame Stag" lines 27–36.

4. It is always difficult to estimate numbers involved in prostitution, but one contemporary observer put the number of prostitutes in London in 1789 at fifty thousand (M. D'Archenholz, *A Picture of England*, [London, 1789], II, 89; cited in Fernando Henriques, *Prostitution in Europe and the New World* [London: MacGibbon & Kee, 1963]).

tuous support of chastity, is near akin to that refinement of humanity, which never resides in any but cultivated minds. It is something nobler than innocence, it is the delicacy of reflections, and not the coyness of ignorance. The reserve of reason, which, like habitual cleanliness, is seldom seen in any great degree, unless the soul is active, may easily be distinguished from rustic shyness or wanton skittishness; and, so far from being incompatible with knowledge, it is its fairest fruit.What a gross idea of modesty had the writer of the following remark! 'The lady who asked the question whether women may be instructed in the modern system of botany, consistently with female delicacy?—was accused of ridiculous prudery: nevertheless, if she had proposed the question to me, I should certainly have answered—They cannot.'⁵ Thus is the fair book of knowledge to be shut with an everlasting seal! On reading similar passages I have reverentially lifted up my eyes and heart to Him who liveth for ever and ever, and said, O my Father, hast Thou by the very constitution of her nature forbid Thy child to seek Thee in the fair forms of truth? And, can her soul be sullied by the knowledge that awfully calls her to Thee?

I have then philosophically pursued these reflections till I inferred that those women who have most improved their reason must have the most modesty—though a dignified sedateness of deportment may have succeeded the playful, bewitching bashfulness of youth.⁶

And thus have I argued. To render chastity the virtue from which unsophisticated modesty will naturally flow, the attention should be called away from employments which only exercise the sensibility; and the heart made to beat time to humanity, rather than to throb with love. The woman who has dedicated a considerable portion of her time to pursuits purely intellectual, and whose affections have been exercised by humane plans of usefulness, must have more purity of mind, as a natural consequence, than the ignorant beings whose time and thoughts have been occupied by gay pleasures or schemes to conquer hearts.⁷ The regulation of the behaviour is not

5. John Berkenhout, *A Volume of Letters to His Son at the University* (Cambridge, 1790), p. 307. Berkenhout (1730?–1801), a physician and naturalist, wrote the *Letters* to instruct young men on a variety of subjects including how to respect the natural reserve of women.
6. "Modesty, is the graceful calm virtue of maturity; bashfulness, the charm of vivacious youth" [Wollstonecraft's note].
7. "I have conversed, as man with man, with medical men, on anatomical subjects; and compared the proportions of the human body with artists— yet such modesty did I meet with, that I was never reminded by word or look of my sex, of the absurd rules which make modesty a pharisaical cloak of weakness. And I am persuaded that in the pursuit of knowledge women would never be insulted by sensible men, and rarely by men of any descrip-

tion, if they did not by mock modesty remind them that they were women: actuated by the same spirit as the Portugueze ladies, who would think their charms insulted, if, when left alone with a man, he did not, at least, attempt to be grossly familiar with their persons. Men are not always men in the company of women, nor would women always remember that they are women, if they were allowed to acquire more understanding" [Wollstonecraft's note]. As a member of the sparkling intellectual circle surrounding publisher Joseph Johnson, Wollstonecraft would routinely have conversed with eminent physicians Dr. George Fordyce and Dr. John Aiken and painters William Blake and Henry Fuseli. As for the Portuguese, Wollstonecraft had been in Portugal in 1785 to visit—then bury—her friend Fanny Blood.

modesty, though those who study rules of decorum are, in general, termed modest women. Make the heart clean, let it expand and feel for all that is human, instead of being narrowed by selfish passions; and let the mind frequently contemplate subjects that exercise the understanding, without heating the imagination, and artless modesty will give the finishing touches to the picture.

She who can discern the dawn of immortality, in the streaks that shoot athwart the misty night of ignorance, promising a clearer day, will respect, as a sacred temple, the body that enshrines such an improvable soul. True love, likewise, spreads this kind of mysterious sanctity round the beloved object, making the lover most modest when in her presence.[8] So reserved is affection that, receiving or returning personal endearments, it wishes, not only to shun the human eye, as a kind of profanation; but to diffuse an encircling cloudy obscurity to shut out even the saucy sparkling sunbeams. Yet, that affection does not deserve the epithet of chaste, which does not receive a sublime gloom of tender melancholy, that allows the mind for a moment to stand still and enjoy the present satisfaction, when a consciousness of the Divine presence is felt—for this must ever be the food of joy!

As I have always been fond of tracing to its source in nature any prevailing custom, I have frequently thought that it was a sentiment of affection for whatever had touched the person of an absent or lost friend, which gave birth to that respect for relicks, so much abused by selfish priests. Devotion, or love, may be allowed to hallow the garments as well as the person; for the lover must want fancy who has not a sort of sacred respect for the glove or slipper of his mistress. He could not confound them with vulgar things of the same kind. This fine sentiment, perhaps, would not bear to be analyzed by the experimental philosopher—but of such stuff is human rapture made up!—A shadowy phantom glides before us, obscuring every other object; yet when the soft cloud is grasped, the form melts into common air, leaving a solitary void, or sweet perfume, stolen from the violet, that memory long holds dear. But, I have tripped unawares on fairy ground, feeling the balmy gale of spring stealing on me, though november frowns.

As a sex, women are more chaste than men, and as modesty is the effect of chastity, they may deserve to have this virtue ascribed to them in rather an appropriated sense; yet, I must be allowed to add an hesitating if:—for I doubt whether chastity will produce modesty, though it may propriety of conduct, when it is merely a respect for the opinion of the world,[9] and when coquetry and the

---

8. "Male or female; for the world contains many modest men" [Wollstonecraft's note].
9. "The immodest behaviour of many married women, who are nevertheless faithful to their husbands' beds, will illustrate this remark" [Wollstonecraft's note].

lovelorn tales of novelists employ the thoughts. Nay, from experience, and reason, I should be led to expect to meet with more modesty amongst men than women, simply because men exercise their understandings more than women.

But, with respect to propriety of behaviour, excepting one class of females, women have evidently the advantage. What can be more disgusting than that impudent dross of gallantry, thought so manly, which makes many men stare insultingly at every female they meet? Can it be termed respect for the sex? No, this loose behaviour shews such habitual depravity, such weakness of mind, that it is vain to expect much public or private virtue, till both men and women grow more modest—till men, curbing a sensual fondness for the sex, or an affectation of manly assurance, more properly speaking, impudence, treat each other with respect—unless appetite or passion give the tone, peculiar to it, to their behaviour. I mean even personal respect—the modest respect of humanity, and fellow-feeling—not the libidinous mockery of gallantry, nor the insolent condescension of protectorship.

To carry the observation still further, modesty must heartily disclaim, and refuse to dwell with that debauchery of mind, which leads a man coolly to bring forward, without a blush, indecent allusions, or obscene witticisms, in the presence of a fellow creature; women are now out of the question, for then it is brutality. Respect for man, as man, is the foundation of every noble sentiment. How much more modest is the libertine who obeys the call of appetite or fancy, than the lewd joker who sets the table in a roar!

This is one of the many instances in which the sexual distinction respecting modesty has proved fatal to virtue and happiness. It is, however, carried still further, and woman, weak woman! made by her education the slave of sensibility, is required, on the most trying occasions, to resist that sensibility. 'Can any thing,' says Knox, 'be more absurd than keeping women in a state of ignorance, and yet so vehemently to insist on their resisting temptation?'—Thus when virtue or honour make it proper to check a passion, the burden is thrown on the weaker shoulders, contrary to reason and true modesty, which, at least, should render the self-denial mutual, to say nothing of the generosity of bravery, supposed to be a manly virtue.

In the same strain runs Rousseau's and Dr. Gregory's advice respecting modesty, strangely miscalled! for they both desire a wife to leave it in doubt whether sensibility or weakness led her to her husband's arms.—The woman is immodest who can let the shadow of such a doubt remain in her husband's mind a moment.

But to state the subject in a different light.—The want of modesty, which I principally deplore as subversive of morality, arises from the state of warfare so strenuously supported by voluptuous men as the very essence of modesty, though, in fact, its bane; because it is a refinement on lust, that men fall into who have not sufficient virtue to relish the innocent pleasures of love. A man of delicacy carries his notions of modesty still further, for neither weakness nor sensibility will gratify him—he looks for affection.

Again; men boast of their triumphs over women, what do they boast of? Truly the creature of sensibility was surprised by her sensibility into folly—into vice;[1] and the dreadful reckoning falls heavily on her own weak head, when reason wakes. For where art thou to find comfort, forlorn and disconsolate one? He who ought to have directed thy reason, and supported thy weakness, has betrayed thee! In a dream of passion thou consented to wander through flowery lawns, and heedlessly stepping over the precipice to which thy guide, instead of guarding, lured thee, thou startest from thy dream only to face a sneering, frowning world, and to find thyself alone in a waste, for he that triumphed in thy weakness is now pursuing new conquests; but for thee—there is no redemption on this side the grave!—And what resource hast thou in an enervated mind to raise a sinking heart?

But, if the sexes be really to live in a state of warfare, if nature have pointed it out, let them act nobly, or let pride whisper to them, that the victory is mean when they merely vanquish sensibility. The real conquest is that over affection not taken by surprise—when, like Heloisa, a woman gives up all the world, deliberately, for love. I do not now consider the wisdom or virtue of such a sacrifice, I only contend that it was a sacrifice to affection, and not merely to sensibility, though she had her share.—And I must be allowed to call her a modest woman, before I dismiss this part of the subject, by saying, that till men are more chaste women will be immodest. Where, indeed, could modest women find husbands from whom they would not continually turn with disgust? Modesty must be equally cultivated by both sexes, or it will ever remain a sickly hothouse plant, whilst the affectation of it, the fig leaf borrowed by wantonness, may give a zest to voluptuous enjoyments.

Men will probably still insist that woman ought to have more modesty than man; but it is not dispassionate reasoners who will most earnestly oppose my opinion. No, they are the men of fancy, the favourites of the sex, who outwardly respect and inwardly despise the weak creatures whom they thus sport with. They cannot submit to resign the highest sensual gratification, nor even to relish the epicurism of virtue—self-denial.

To take another view of the subject, confining my remarks to women.

1. "The poor moth fluttering round a candle, burns its wings" [Wollstonecraft's note].

The ridiculous falsities[2] which are told to children, from mistaken notions of modesty, tend very early to inflame their imaginations and set their little minds to work, respecting subjects, which nature never intended they should think of till the body arrived at some degree of maturity; then the passions naturally begin to take place of the senses, as instruments to unfold the understanding, and form the moral character.

In nurseries, and boarding-schools, I fear, girls are first spoiled; particularly in the latter. A number of girls sleep in the same room, and wash together. And, though I should be sorry to contaminate an innocent creature's mind by instilling false delicacy, or those indecent prudish notions, which early cautions respecting the other sex naturally engender, I should be very anxious to prevent their acquiring nasty, or immodest habits; and as many girls have learned very nasty tricks, from ignorant servants, the mixing them thus indiscriminately together, is very improper.

To say the truth women are, in general, too familiar with each other, which leads to that gross degree of familiarity that so frequently renders the marriage state unhappy. Why in the name of decency are sisters, female intimates, or ladies and their waiting-women, to be so grossly familiar as to forget the respect which one human creature owes to another? That squeamish delicacy which shrinks from the most disgusting offices when affection[3] or humanity lead us to watch at a sick pillow, is despicable. But, why women in health should be more familiar with each other than men are, when they boast of their superiour delicacy, is a solecism in manners which I could never solve.

In order to preserve health and beauty, I should earnestly recommend frequent ablutions, to dignify my advice that it may not offend the fastidious ear; and, by example, girls ought to be taught to wash and dress alone, without any distinction of rank; and if custom should make them require some little assistance, let them not require it till that part of the business is over which ought never to be done before a fellow-creature; because it is an insult to the majesty of human nature. Not on the score of modesty, but decency; for the care which some modest women take, making at

2. "Children very early see cats with their kittens, birds with their young ones, &c. Why then are they not to be told that their mothers carry and nourish them in the same way? As there would then be no appearance of mystery they would never think of the subject more. Truth may always be told to children, if it be told gravely; but it is the immodesty of affected modesty, that does all the mischief; and this smoke heats the imagination by vainly endeavouring to obscure certain objects. If, indeed, children could be kept entirely from improper company, we should never allude to any such subjects; but as this is impossible, it is best to tell them the truth, especially as such information, not interesting them, will make no impression on their imagination" [Wollstonecraft's note].
3. "Affection would rather make one choose to perform these offices, to spare the delicacy of a friend, by still keeping a veil over them, for personal helplessness, produced by sickness, is of an humbling nature" [Wollstonecraft's note].

the same time a display of that care, not to let their legs be seen, is as childish as immodest.[4]

I could proceed still further, till I animadverted on some still more nasty customs, which men never fall into. Secrets are told— where silence ought to reign; and that regard to cleanliness, which some religious sects have, perhaps, carried too far, especially the Essenes,[5] amongst the Jews, by making that an insult to God which is only an insult to humanity, is violated in a beastly manner. How can *delicate* women obtrude on notice that part of the animal oec-onomy, which is so very disgusting?[6] And is it not very rational to conclude, that the women who have not been taught to respect the human nature of their own sex, in these particulars, will not long respect the mere difference of sex in their husbands? After their maidenish bashfulness is once lost, I, in fact, have generally observed, that women fall into old habits; and treat their husbands as they did their sisters or female acquaintance.

Besides, women from necessity, because their minds are not culti-vated, have recourse very often to what I familiarly term bodily wit; and their intimacies are of the same kind. In short, with respect to both mind and body, there are too intimate. That decent personal reserve which is the foundation of dignity of character, must be kept up between woman and woman, or their minds will never gain strength or modesty.

On this account also, I object to many females being shut up together in nurseries, schools, or convents. I cannot recollect with-out indignation, the jokes and hoiden tricks, which knots of young women indulge themselves in, when in my youth accident threw me, an awkward rustic, in their way. They were almost on a par with the double meanings, which shake the convivial table when the glass has circulated freely. But, it is vain to attempt to keep the heart pure, unless the head is furnished with ideas, and set to work to compare them, in order to acquire judgment, by generalizing simple ones; and modesty, by making the understanding damp the sensibility.

It may be thought that I lay too great a stress on personal reserve; but it is ever the handmaid of modesty. So that were I to name the graces that ought to adorn beauty, I should instantly exclaim, cleanliness, neatness, and personal reserve. It is obvious, I suppose, that the reserve I mean, has nothing sexual in it, and that I think it *equally* necessary in both sexes. So necessary, indeed, is

4. "I remember to have met with a sentence, in a book of education, that made me smile. 'It would be needless to caution you against putting your hand, by chance, under your neck-handkerchief; for a modest woman never did so!' " [Wollstone-craft's note].
5. A Jewish communal sect who lived in Palestine from about the 2nd century B.C. to the end of the 1st century A.D. They stressed meticulous adher-ence to laws of purity and practiced ritual washings.
6. "Obtrude" is a strange word here; it means to thrust forward or out. Wollstonecraft is probably trying to find a fastidious way to criticize women who can perform evacuation or urination ("animal oeconomy") in front of others.

that reserve and cleanliness which indolent women too often neglect, that I will venture to affirm that when two or three women live in the same house, the one will be most respected by the male part of the family, who reside with them, leaving love entirely out of the question, who pays this kind of habitual respect to her person.

When domestic friends meet in a morning, there will naturally prevail an affectionate seriousness, especially, if each look forward to the discharge of daily duties; and it may be reckoned fanciful, but this sentiment has frequently risen spontaneously in my mind, I have been pleased after breathing the sweet-bracing morning air, to see the same kind of freshness in the countenances I particularly loved; I was glad to see them braced, as it were, for the day, and ready to run their course with the sun. The greetings of affection in the morning are by these means more respectful than the familiar tenderness which frequently prolongs the evening talk. Nay, I have often felt hurt, not to say disgusted, when a friend has appeared, whom I parted with full dressed the evening before, with her clothes huddled on, because she chose to indulge herself in bed till the last moment.

Domestic affection can only be kept alive by these neglected attentions; yet if men and women took half as much pains to dress habitually neat, as they do to ornament, or rather to disfigure, their persons, much would be done towards the attainment of purity of mind. But women only dress to gratify men of gallantry; for the lover is always best pleased with the simple garb that fits close to the shape. There is an impertinence in ornaments that rebuffs affection; because love always clings round the idea of home.

As a sex, women are habitually indolent; and every thing tends to make them so. I do not forget the spurts of activity which sensibility produces; but as these flights of feelings only increase the evil, they are not to be confounded with the slow, orderly walk of reason. So great in reality is their mental and bodily indolence, that till their body be strengthened and their understanding enlarged by active exertions, there is little reason to expect that modesty will take place of bashfulness. They may find it prudent to assume its semblance; but the fair veil will only be worn on gala days.

Perhaps, there is not a virtue that mixes so kindly with every other as modesty.—It is the pale moon-beam that renders more interesting every virtue it softens, giving mild grandeur to the contracted horizon. Nothing can be more beautiful than the poetical fiction, which makes Diana with her silver crescent, the goddess of chastity.[7] I have sometimes thought, that wandering with sedate step in some lonely recess, a modest dame of antiquity must have

---

7. Roman goddess of the moon, a virgin, huntress, and patron of women in childbirth.

felt a glow of conscious dignity when, after contemplating the soft shadowy landscape, she has invited with placid fervour the mild reflection of her sister's beams to turn to her chaste bosom.

A Christian has still nobler motives to incite her to preserve her chastity and acquire modesty, for her body has been called the Temple of the living God;[8] of that God who requires more than modesty of mien. His eye searcheth the heart; and let her remember, that if she hope to find favour in the sight of purity itself, her chastity must be founded on modesty, and not on worldly prudence; or verily a good reputation will be her only reward; for that awful intercourse, that sacred communication, which virtue establishes between man and his Maker, must give rise to the wish of being pure as he is pure![9]

After the foregoing remarks, it is almost superfluous to add, that I consider all those feminine airs of maturity, which succeed bashfulness, to which truth is sacrificed, to secure the heart of a husband, or rather to force him to be still a lover when nature would, had she not been interrupted in her operations, have made love give place to friendship, as immodest. The tenderness which a man will feel for the mother of his children is an excellent substitute for the ardour of unsatisfied passion; but to prolong that ardour it is indelicate, not to say immodest, for women to feign an unnatural coldness of constitution. Women as well as men ought to have the common appetites and passions of their nature, they are only brutal when unchecked by reason: but the obligation to check them is the duty of mankind, not a sexual duty. Nature, in these respects, may safely be left to herself; let women only acquire knowledge and humanity, and love will teach them modesty.[1] There is no need of falsehoods, disgusting as futile, for studied rules of behaviour only impose on shallow observers; a man of sense soon sees through, and despises the affectation.

The behaviour of young people, to each other, as men and women, is the last thing that should be thought of in education. In fact, behaviour in most circumstances is now so much thought of, that simplicity of character is rarely to be seen: yet, if men were only anxious to cultivate each virtue, and let it take root firmly in the mind, the grace resulting from it, its natural exterior mark, would soon strip affectation of its flaunting plumes; because, fallacious as unstable, is the conduct that is not founded upon truth!

Would ye, O my sisters, really possess modesty, ye must remember that the possession of virtue, of any denomination, is incompati-

8. I Corinthians 3:16: "Know ye not that ye are the temple of God, and that the Spirit of God dwelleth in you?"
9. Matthew 5:48: "Be ye therefore perfect, even as your Father which is in heaven is perfect."
1. "The behaviour of many newly married women has often disgusted me. They seem anxious never to let their husbands forget the privilege of marriage; and to find no pleasure in his society unless he is acting the lover. Short, indeed, must be the reign of love, when the flame is thus constantly blown up, without its receiving any solid fewel!" [Wollstonecraft's note].

ble with ignorance and vanity! ye must acquire that soberness of mind, which the exercise of duties, and the pursuit of knowledge, alone inspire, or ye will still remain in a doubtful dependent situation, and only be loved whilst ye are fair! The downcast eye, the rosy blush, the retiring grace, are all proper in their season; but modesty, being the child of reason, cannot long exist with the sensibility that is not tempered by reflection. Besides, when love, even innocent love, is the whole employ of your lives, your hearts will be too soft to afford modesty that tranquil retreat, where she delights to dwell, in close union with humanity.

Chap. VIII

Morality Undermined by Sexual Notions of the Importance of a
Good Reputation

It has long since occurred to me that advice respecting behaviour, and all the various modes of preserving a good reputation, which have been so strenuously inculcated on the female world, were specious poisons, that incrusting morality eat away the substance. And, that this measuring of shadows produced a false calculation, because their length depends so much on the height of the sun, and other adventitious circumstances.

Whence arises the easy fallacious behaviour of a courtier? From his situation, undoubtedly: for standing in need of dependents, he is obliged to learn the art of denying without giving offence, and, of evasively feeding hope with the chameleon's food:[1] thus does politeness sport with truth, and eating away the sincerity and humanity natural to man, produce the fine gentleman.

Women likewise acquire, from a supposed necessity, an equally artificial mode of behaviour. Yet truth is not with impunity to be sported with, for the practised dissembler, at last, becomes the dupe of his own arts, loses that sagacity, which has been justly termed common sense; namely, a quick perception of common truths: which are constantly received as such by the unsophisticated mind, though it might not have had sufficient energy to discover them itself, when obscured by local prejudices. The greater number of people take their opinions on trust to avoid the trouble of exercising their own minds, and these indolent beings naturally adhere to the letter, rather than the spirit of a law, divine or human. 'Women,' says some author, I cannot recollect who, 'mind not what only heaven sees.' Why, indeed, should they? it is the eye of man that they have been taught to dread—and if they can lull their Argus[2] to sleep, they seldom think of heaven or themselves, because their

---

1. Because this lizard seemed almost inanimate, it was supposed to live on air.
2. According to Greek myth, Zeus fell in love with Io and changed her into a heifer to conceal her from his wife Hera; Hera set Argus, a monster with a hundred eyes, to guard Io.

reputation is safe; and it is reputation, not chastity and all its fair train, that they are employed to keep free from spot, not as a virtue, but to preserve their station in the world.

To prove the truth of this remark, I need only advert to the intrigues of married women, particularly in high life, and in countries where women are suitably married, according to their respective ranks, by their parents. If an innocent girl become a prey to love, she is degraded for ever, though her mind was not polluted by the arts which married women, under the convenient cloke of marriage, practise; nor has she violated any duty—but the duty of respecting herself. The married woman, on the contrary, breaks a most sacred engagement, and becomes a cruel mother when she is a false and faithless wife. If her husband have still an affection for her, the arts which she must practise to deceive him, will render her the most contemptible of human beings; and, at any rate, the contrivances necessary to preserve appearances, will keep her mind in that childish, or vicious, tumult, which destroys all its energy. Besides, in time, like those people who habitually take cordials to raise their spirits, she will want an intrigue to give life to her thoughts, having lost all relish for pleasures that are not highly seasoned by hope or fear.

Sometimes married women act still more audaciously; I will mention an instance.

A woman of quality, notorious for her gallantries, though as she still lived with her husband, nobody chose to place her in the class where she ought to have been placed, made a point of treating with the most insulting contempt a poor timid creature, abashed by a sense of her former weakness, whom a neighbouring gentleman had seduced and afterwards married. This woman had actually confounded virtue with reputation; and, I do believe, valued herself on the propriety of her behaviour before marriage, though when once settled to the satisfaction of her family, she and her lord were equally faithless,—so that the half alive heir to an immense estate came from heaven knows where!

To view this subject in another light.

I have known a number of women who, if they did not love their husbands, loved nobody else, give themselves entirely up to vanity and dissipation, neglecting every domestic duty; nay, even squandering away all the money which should have been saved for their helpless younger children, yet have plumed themselves on their unsullied reputation, as if the whole compass of their duty as wives and mothers was only to preserve it. Whilst other indolent women, neglecting every personal duty, have thought that they deserved their husbands' affection, because, forsooth, they acted in this respect with propriety.

Weak minds are always fond of resting in the ceremonials of duty, but morality offers much simpler motives; and it were to be wished that superficial moralists had said less respecting behaviour, and outward observances, for unless virtue, of any kind, be built on knowledge, it will only produce a kind of insipid decency. Respect for the opinion of the world, has, however, been termed the principal duty of woman in the most express words, for Rousseau declares, 'that reputation is no less indispensable than chastity.' 'A man,' adds he, 'secure in his own good conduct, depends only on himself, and may brave the public opinion: but a woman, in behaving well, performs but half her duty; as what is thought of her, is as important to her as what she really is. It follows hence, that the system of a woman's education should, in this respect, be directly contrary to that of ours. Opinion is the grave of virtue among the men; but its throne among women.'[3] It is strictly logical to infer that the virtue that rests on opinion is merely worldly, and that it is the virtue of a being to whom reason has been denied. But, even with respect to the opinion of the world, I am convinced that this class of reasoners are mistaken.

This regard for reputation, independent of its being one of the natural rewards of virtue, however, took its rise from a cause that I have already deplored as the grand source of female depravity, the impossibility of regaining respectability by a return to virtue, though men preserve theirs during the indulgence of vice. It was natural for women then to endeavour to preserve what once lost— was lost for ever, till this care swallowing up every other care, reputation for chastity, became the one thing needful to the sex. But vain is the scrupulosity of ignorance, for neither religion nor virtue, when they reside in the heart, require such a puerile attention to mere ceremonies, because the behaviour must, upon the whole, be proper, when the motive is pure.

To support my opinion I can produce very respectable authority; and the authority of a cool reasoner ought to have weight to enforce consideration, though not to establish a sentiment. Speaking of the general laws of morality, Dr. Smith observes,—'That by some very extraordinary and unlucky circumstance, a good man may come to be suspected of a crime of which he was altogether incapable, and upon that account be most unjustly exposed for the remaining part of his life to the horror and aversion of mankind. By an accident of this kind he may be said to lose his all, notwithstanding his integrity and justice, in the same manner as a cautious man, notwithstanding his utmost circumspection, may be ruined by an earthquake or an inundation. Accidents of the first kind, however, are perhaps still more rare, and still more contrary to the common

3. *Émile*, p. 328.

course of things than those of the second; and it still remains true, that the practice of truth, justice, and humanity, is a certain and almost infallible method of acquiring what those virtues chiefly aim at, the confidence and love of those we live with. A person may be easily misrepresented with regard to a particular action; but it is scarce possible that he should be so with regard to the general tenor of his conduct. An innocent man may be believed to have done wrong: this, however, will rarely happen. On the contrary, the established opinion of the innocence of his manners will often lead us to absolve him where he has really been in the fault, notwith-standing very strong presumptions.'[4]

I perfectly coincide in opinion with this writer, for I verily believe that few of either sex were ever despised for certain vices without deserving to be despised. I speak not of the calumny of the moment, which hovers over a character, like one of the dense morn-ing fogs of November, over this metropolis, till it gradually subsides before the common light of day, I only contend that the daily con-duct of the majority prevails to stamp their character with the impression of truth. Quietly does the clear light, shining day after day, refute the ignorant surmise, or malicious tale, which has thrown dirt on a pure character. A false light distorted, for a short time, its shadow—reputation; but it seldom fails to become just when the cloud is dispersed that produced the mistake in vision.

Many people, undoubtedly, in several respects obtain a better reputation than, strictly speaking, they deserve; for unremitting industry will mostly reach its goal in all races. They who only strive for this paltry prize, like the Pharisees, who prayed at the cor-ners of streets, to be seen of men,[5] verily obtain the reward they seek; for the heart of man cannot be read by man! Still the fair fame that is naturally reflected by good actions, when the man is only employed to direct his steps aright, regardless of the lookers-on, is, in general, not only more true, but more sure.

There are, it is true, trials when the good man must appeal to God from the injustice of man; and amidst the whining candour or hissings of envy, erect a pavilion in his own mind to retire to till the rumour be overpast; nay, the darts of undeserved censure may pierce an innocent tender bosom through with many sorrows; but these are all exceptions to general rules. And it is according to common laws that human behaviour ought to be regulated. The eccentric orbit of the comet never influences astronomical calculations respecting the invariable order established in the motion of the principal bodies of the solar system.

4. Smith, *Theory of Moral Sentiments*, pp. 227–28.
5. Matthew 6:5: "And when thou prayest, thou shalt not be as the hypocrites are: for they love to pray standing in the synagogues and in the corners of the streets, that they may be seen of men." Pharisees lived by the letter, not the spirit, of the law.

I will then venture to affirm, that after a man is arrived at maturity, the general outline of his character in the world is just, allowing for the before-mentioned exceptions to the rule. I do not say that a prudent, worldly-wise man, with only negative virtues and qualities, may not sometimes obtain a smoother reputation than a wiser or a better man. So far from it, that I am apt to conclude from experience, that where the virtue of two people is nearly equal, the most negative character will be liked best by the world at large, whilst the other may have more friends in private life. But the hills and dales, clouds and sunshine, conspicuous in the virtues of great men, set off each other; and though they afford envious weakness a fairer mark to shoot at, the real character will still work its way to light, though bespattered by weak affection, or ingenious malice.[6]

With respect to that anxiety to preserve a reputation hardly earned, which leads sagacious people to analyze it, I shall not make the obvious comment; but I am afraid that morality is very insidiously undermined, in the female world, by the attention being turned to the shew instead of the substance. A simple thing is thus made strangely complicated; nay, sometimes virtue and its shadow are set at variance. We should never, perhaps, have heard of Lucretia,[7] had she died to preserve her chastity instead of her reputation. If we really deserve our own good opinion we shall commonly be respected in the world; but if we pant after higher improvement and higher attainments, it is not sufficient to view ourselves as we suppose that we are viewed by others, though this has been ingeniously argued, as the foundation of our moral sentiments.[8] Because each by-stander may have his own prejudices, beside the prejudices of his age or country. We should rather endeavour to view ourselves as we suppose that Being views us who seeth each thought ripen into action, and whose judgment never swerves from the eternal rule of right. Righteous are all his judgments—just as merciful!

The humble mind that seeketh to find favour in His sight, and calmly examines its conduct when only His presence is felt, will seldom form a very erroneous opinion of its own virtues. During the still hour of self-collection the angry brow of offended justice will be fearfully deprecated, or the tie which draws man to the Deity will be recognized in the pure sentiment of reverential adoration, that

---

6. "I allude to various biographical writings, but particularly to Boswell's *Life of Johnson*" [Wollstonecraft's note]. James Boswell's *Life of Samuel Johnson* portrays a great man whose life was marred by petty dislikes and human failings.
7. Wife of the Roman Lucius Tarquinius Collatinus, who, having been raped by one of the king's sons, informed her husband and her father of the infamy, exacted their promise of vengeance, then committed suicide.
8. "Smith" [Wollstonecraft's note]. As the subtitle of Adam Smith's work indicates (*Analysis of the Principles by which Men Naturally judge concerning the Conduct and Character, first of their Neighbours, and afterwards of themselves*), he believes that the individual is conditioned by the social factor—sympathy or "fellow-feeling."

swells the heart without exciting any tumultuous emotions. In these solemn moments man discovers the germ of those vices, which like the Java tree[9] shed a pestiferous vapour around—death is in the shade! and he perceives them without abhorrence, because he feels himself drawn by some cord of love to all his fellow-creatures, for whose follies he is anxious to find every extenuation in their nature —in himself. If I, he may thus argue, who exercise my own mind, and have been refined by tribulation, find the serpent's egg[1] in some fold of my heart, and crush it with difficulty, shall not I pity those who have stamped with less vigour, or who have heedlessly nurtured the insidious reptile till it poisoned the vital stream it sucked? Can I, conscious of my secret sins, throw off my fellow-creatures, and calmly see them drop into the chasm of perdition, that yawns to receive them.—No! no! The agonized heart will cry with suffocating impatience—I too am a man! and have vices, hid, perhaps, from human eye, that bend me to the dust before God, and loudly tell me, when all is mute, that we are formed of the same earth, and breathe the same element. Humanity thus rises naturally out of humility, and twists the cords of love that in various convolutions entangle the heart.

This sympathy extends still further, till a man well pleased observes force in arguments that do not carry conviction to his own bosom, and he gladly places in the fairest light, to himself, the shews of reason that have led others astray, rejoiced to find some reason in all the errors of man; though before convinced that he who rules the day makes his sun to shine on all. Yet, shaking hands thus as it were with corruption, one foot on earth, the other with bold stride mounts to heaven, and claims kindred with superiour natures. Virtues, unobserved by man, drop their balmy fragrance at this cool hour, and the thirsty land, refreshed by the pure streams of comfort that suddenly gush out, is crowned with smiling verdure; this is the living green on which that eye may look with complacency that is too pure to behold iniquity!

But my spirits flag; and I must silently indulge the reverie these reflections lead to, unable to describe the sentiments, that have calmed my soul, when watching the rising sun, a soft shower drizzling through the leaves of neighbouring trees, seemed to fall on my languid, yet tranquil spirits, to cool the heart that had been heated by the passions which reason laboured to tame.

The leading principles which run through all my disquisitions,

9. The legend of the Java tree is recounted, tongue-in-cheek, as an afterword to Erasmus Darwin's *Loves of the Plants* (1788). The tree was alleged to cast such poisonous vapors that the land around it was littered with skeletons; to send a doomed criminal to the tree was as sure an execution as the gibbet.
1. *Julius Caesar* II.i.32–33: "Therefore think him as a serpent's egg / Which, hatch'd, would, as his kind, grow mischievous."

would render it unnecessary to enlarge on this subject, if a constant attention to keep the varnish of the character fresh, and in good condition, were not often inculcated as the sum total of female duty; if rules to regulate the behaviour, and to preserve the reputation, did not too frequently supersede moral obligations. But, with respect to reputation, the attention is confined to a single virtue—chastity. If the honour of a woman, as it is absurdly called, be safe, she may neglect every social duty; nay, ruin her family by gaming and extravagance; yet still present a shameless front—for truly she is an honourable woman!

Mrs. Macaulay has justly observed, that 'there is but one fault which a woman of honour may not commit with impunity.'[2] She then justly and humanely adds—'This has given rise to the trite and foolish observation, that the first fault against chastity in woman has a radical power to deprave the character. But no such frail beings come out of the hands of nature. The human mind is built of nobler materials than to be easily corrupted; and with all their disadvantages of situation and education, women seldom become entirely abandoned till they are thrown into a state of desperation, by the venomous rancour of their own sex.'[3]

But, in proportion as this regard for the reputation of chastity is prized by women, it is despised by men: and the two extremes are equally destructive to morality.

Men are certainly more under the influence of their appetites than women; and their appetites are more depraved by unbridled indulgence and the fastidious contrivances of satiety. Luxury has introduced a refinement in eating, that destroys the constitution; and, a degree of gluttony which is so beastly, that a perception of seemliness of behaviour must be worn out before one being could eat immoderately in the presence of another, and afterwards complain of the oppression that his intemperance naturally produced. Some women, particularly French women, have also lost a sense of decency in this respect; for they will talk very calmly of an indigestion. It were to be wished that idleness was not allowed to generate, on the rank soil of wealth, those swarms of summer insects that feed on putrefaction, we should not then be disgusted by the sight of such brutal excesses.

There is one rule relative to behaviour that, I think, ought to regulate every other; and it is simply to cherish such an habitual respect for mankind as may prevent us from disgusting a fellow-creature for the sake of a present indulgence. The shameful indolence

---

2. Macaulay elaborates on the "one fault" as follows: "let her only take care that she is not caught in a love intrigue, and she may lie, she may deceive, she may defame, she may ruin her family with gaming, and the peace of twenty others with her coquettry, and yet preserve both her reputation and her peace" (*Letters on Education*, p. 210).

3. Macaulay, p. 212.

of many married women, and others a little advanced in life, frequently leads them to sin against delicacy. For, though convinced
that the person is the band of union between the sexes, yet, how
often do they from sheer indolence, or, to enjoy some trifling
indulgence, disgust?

The depravity of the appetite which brings the sexes together,
has had a still more fatal effect. Nature must ever be the standard
of taste, the gauge of appetite—yet how grossly is nature insulted
by the voluptuary. Leaving the refinements of love out of the question; nature, by making the gratification of an appetite, in this
respect, as well as every other, a natural and imperious law to preserve the species, exalts the appetite, and mixes a little mind and
affection with a sensual gust.[4] The feelings of a parent mingling
with an instinct merely animal, give it dignity; and the man and
woman often meeting on account of the child, a mutual interest
and affection is excited by the exercise of a common sympathy.
Women then having necessarily some duty to fulfil, more noble
than to adorn their persons, would not contentedly be the slaves of
casual lust; which is now the situation of a very considerable number
who are, literally speaking, standing dishes to which every glutton
may have access.

I may be told that great as this enormity is, it only affects a
devoted part of the sex—devoted for the salvation of the rest. But,
false as every assertion might easily be proved, that recommends the
sanctioning a small evil to produce a greater good; the mischief
does not stop here, for the moral character, and peace of mind, of
the chaster part of the sex, is undermined by the conduct of the
very women to whom they allow no refuge from guilt: whom they
inexorably consign to the exercise of arts that lure their husbands
from them, debauch their sons, and force them, let not modest
women start, to assume, in some degree, the same character themselves. For I will venture to assert, that all the causes of female
weakness, as well as depravity, which I have already enlarged on,
branch out of one grand cause—want of chastity in men.

This intemperance, so prevalent, depraves the appetite to such a
degree, that a wanton stimulus is necessary to rouse it; but the parental design of nature is forgotten, and the mere person, and that
for a moment, alone engrosses the thoughts. So voluptuous, indeed,
often grows the lustful prowler, that he refines on female softness.
Something more soft than woman is then sought for; till, in Italy
and Portugal, men attend the levees of equivocal beings, to sigh for
more than female languor.[5]

To satisfy this genus of men, women are made systematically

4. "Gust" refers to appetite.
5. A levee is a miscellaneous reception of visitors, usually male; "equivocal beings" are probably
homosexuals.

voluptuous, and though they may not all carry their libertinism to the same height, yet this heartless intercourse with the sex, which they allow themselves, depraves both sexes, because the taste of men is vitiated; and women, of all classes, naturally square their behaviour to gratify the taste by which they obtain pleasure and power. Women becoming, consequently, weaker, in mind and body, than they ought to be, were one of the grand ends of their being taken into the account, that of bearing and nursing children, have not sufficient strength to discharge the first duty of a mother; and sacrificing to lasciviousness the parental affection, that ennobles instinct, either destroy the embryo in the womb,[6] or cast it off when born. Nature in every thing demands respect, and those who violate her laws seldom violate them with impunity. The weak ener-vated women who particularly catch the attention of libertines, are unfit to be mothers, though they may conceive; so that the rich sen-sualist, who has rioted among women, spreading depravity and misery, when he wishes to perpetuate his name, receives from his wife only an half-formed being that inherits both its father's and mother's weakness.

Contrasting the humanity of the present age with the barbarism of antiquity, great stress has been laid on the savage custom of exposing the children whom their parents could not maintain;[7] whilst the man of sensibility, who thus, perhaps, complains, by his promiscuous amours produces a most destructive barrenness and contagious flagitiousness[8] of manners. Surely nature never intended that women, by satisfying an appetite, should frustrate the very pur-pose for which it was implanted?

I have before observed, that men ought to maintain the women whom they have seduced; this would be one means of reforming female manners, and stopping an abuse that has an equally fatal effect on population and morals. Another, no less obvious, would be to turn the attention of woman to the real virtue of chastity; for to little respect has that woman a claim, on the score of modesty, though her reputation may be white as the driven snow, who smiles on the libertine whilst she spurns the victims of his lawless appe-tites and their own folly.

Besides, she has a taint of the same folly, pure as she esteems her-self, when she studiously adorns her person only to be seen by men, to excite respectful sighs, and all the idle homage of what is called innocent gallantry. Did women really respect virtue for its own sake, they would not seek for a compensation in vanity, for the self-denial

6. The lascivious father spreads syphilis to his wife, who for her part is so unhealthy and weak that the embryo is naturally aborted or the child is born blind and misshapen by venereal disease.

7. To expose, and allow to die, those infants who had deformities or who were for other reasons un-wanted was common in ancient Greece.

8. Corruption.

which they are obliged to practise to preserve their reputation, nor would they associate with men who set reputation at defiance.

The two sexes mutually corrupt and improve each other. This I believe to be an indisputable truth, extending it to every virtue. Chastity, modesty, public spirit, and all the noble train of virtues, on which social virtue and happiness are built, should be understood and cultivated by all mankind, or they will be cultivated to little effect. And, instead of furnishing the vicious or idle with a pretext for violating some sacred duty, by terming it a sexual one, it would be wiser to shew that nature has not made any difference, for that the unchaste man doubly defeats the purpose of nature, by rendering women barren, and destroying his own constitution, though he avoids the shame that pursues the crime in the other sex. These are the physical consequences, the moral are still more alarming; for virtue is only a nominal distinction when the duties of citizens, husbands, wives, fathers, mothers, and directors of families, become merely the selfish ties of convenience.

Why then do philosophers look for public spirit? Public spirit must be nurtured by private virtue, or it will resemble the factitious sentiment which makes women careful to preserve their reputation, and men their honour. A sentiment that often exists unsupported by virtue, unsupported by that sublime morality which makes the habitual breach of one duty a breach of the whole moral law.

Chap. IX

Of the Pernicious Effects Which Arise from the Unnatural Distinctions Established in Society

From the respect paid to property flow, as from a poisoned fountain, most of the evils and vices which render this world such a dreary scene to the contemplative mind. For it is in the most polished society that noisome reptiles and venomous serpents lurk under the rank herbage; and there is voluptuousness pampered by the still sultry air, which relaxes every good disposition before it ripens into virtue.

One class presses on another; for all are aiming to procure respect on account of their property: and property, once gained, will procure the respect due only to talents and virtue. Men neglect the duties incumbent on man, yet are treated like demi-gods; religion is also separated from morality by a ceremonial veil, yet men wonder that the world is almost, literally speaking, a den of sharpers or oppressors.

There is a homely proverb, which speaks a shrewd truth, that whoever the devil finds idle he will employ. And what but habitual idleness can hereditary wealth and titles produce? For man is so constituted that he can only attain a proper use of his faculties by exercising them, and will not exercise them unless necessity, of some kind, first set the wheels in motion. Virtue likewise can only be acquired by the discharge of relative duties; but the importance of these sacred duties will scarcely be felt by the being who is cajoled out of his humanity by the flattery of sycophants. There must be more equality established in society, or morality will never gain ground, and this virtuous equality will not rest firmly even when founded on a rock, if one half of mankind be chained to its bottom by fate, for they will be continually undermining it through ignorance or pride.

It is vain to expect virtue from women till they are, in some degree, independent of men; nay, it is vain to expect that strength of natural affection, which would make them good wives and mothers. Whilst they are absolutely dependent on their husbands they will be cunning, mean, and selfish, and the men who can be gratified by the fawning fondness of spaniel-like affection, have not much delicacy, for love is not to be bought, in any sense of the words, its silken wings are instantly shrivelled up when any thing beside a return in kind is sought. Yet whilst wealth enervates men; and women live, as it were, by their personal charms, how can we expect them to discharge those ennobling duties which equally require exertion and self-denial. Hereditary property sophisticates[1] the mind, and the unfortunate victims to it, if I may so express myself, swathed from their birth, seldom exert the locomotive faculty of body or mind; and, thus viewing every thing through one medium, and that a false one, they are unable to discern in what true merit and happiness consist. False, indeed, must be the light when the drapery of situation hides the man, and makes him stalk in masquerade, dragging from one scene of dissipation to another the nerveless limbs that hang with stupid listlessness, and rolling round the vacant eye which plainly tells us that there is no mind at home.

I mean, therefore, to infer that the society is not properly organized which does not compel men and women to discharge their respective duties, by making it the only way to acquire that countenance from their fellow-creatures, which every human being wishes some way to attain. The respect, consequently, which is paid to wealth and mere personal charms, is a true north-east blast, that blights the tender blossoms of affection and virtue. Nature has wisely attached affections to duties, to sweeten toil, and to give that vigour to the exertions of reason which only the heart can give. But, the affection which is put on merely because it is the appropriated

1. Corrupts.

insignia of a certain character, when its duties are not fulfilled, is one of the empty compliments which vice and folly are obliged to pay to virtue and the real nature of things.

To illustrate my opinion, I need only observe, that when a woman is admired for her beauty, and suffers herself to be so far intoxicated by the admiration she receives, as to neglect to discharge the indispensable duty of a mother, she sins against herself by neglecting to cultivate an affection that would equally tend to make her useful and happy. True happiness, I mean all the contentment, and virtuous satisfaction, that can be snatched in this imperfect state, must arise from well regulated affections; and an affection includes a duty. Men are not aware of the misery they cause, and the vicious weakness they cherish, by only inciting women to render themselves pleasing; they do not consider that they thus make natural and artificial duties clash, by sacrificing the comfort and respectability of a woman's life to voluptuous notions of beauty, when in nature they all harmonize.

Cold would be the heart of a husband, were he not rendered unnatural by early debauchery, who did not feel more delight at seeing his child suckled by its mother, than the most artful wanton tricks could ever raise; yet this natural way of cementing the matrimonial tie, and twisting esteem with fonder recollections, wealth leads women to spurn. To preserve their beauty, and wear the flowery crown of the day, which gives them a kind of right to reign for a short time over the sex, they neglect to stamp impressions on their husbands' hearts, that would be remembered with more tenderness when the snow on the head began to chill the bosom, than even their virgin charms. The maternal solicitude of a reasonable affectionate woman is very interesting, and the chastened dignity with which a mother returns the caresses that she and her child receive from a father who has been fulfilling the serious duties of his station, is not only a respectable, but a beautiful sight. So singular, indeed, are my feelings, and I have endeavoured not to catch factitious ones, that after having been fatigued with the sight of insipid grandeur and the slavish ceremonies that with cumberous pomp supplied the place of domestic affections, I have turned to some other scene to relieve my eye by resting it on the refreshing green every where scattered by nature. I have then viewed with pleasure a woman nursing her children, and discharging the duties of her station with, perhaps, merely a servant maid to take off her hands the servile part of the household business. I have seen her prepare herself and children, with only the luxury of cleanliness, to receive her husband, who returning weary home in the evening found smiling babes and a clean hearth. My heart has loitered in the midst of the group, and has even throbbed with sympathetic emotion, when the scraping of the well known foot has raised a pleasing tumult.

Whilst my benevolence has been gratified by contemplating this artless picture, I have thought that a couple of this description, equally necessary and independent of each other, because each fulfilled the respective duties of their station, possessed all that life could give.—Raised sufficiently above abject poverty not to be obliged to weigh the consequence of every farthing they spend, and having sufficient to prevent their attending to a frigid system of œconomy, which narrows both heart and mind. I declare, so vulgar are my conceptions, that I know not what is wanted to render this the happiest as well as the most respectable situation in the world, but a taste for literature, to throw a little variety and interest into social converse, and some superfluous money to give to the needy and to buy books. For it is not pleasant when the heart is opened by compassion and the head active in arranging plans of usefulness, to have a prim urchin continually twitching back the elbow to prevent the hand from drawing out an almost empty purse, whispering at the same time some prudential maxim about the priority of justice.

Destructive, however, as riches and inherited honours are to the human character, women are more debased and cramped, if possible, by them, than men, because men may still, in some degree, unfold their faculties by becoming soldiers and statesmen.

As soldiers, I grant, they can now only gather, for the most part, vain glorious laurels, whilst they adjust to a hair the European balance, taking especial care that no bleak northern nook or sound incline the beam. But the days of true heroism are over, when a citizen fought for his country like a Fabricius[2] or a Washington, and then returned to his farm to let his virtuous fervour run in a more placid, but not a less salutary, stream. No, our British heroes are oftener sent from the gaming table than from the plow;[3] and their passions have been rather inflamed by hanging with dumb suspense on the turn of a die, than sublimated by panting after the adventurous march of virtue in the historic page.

The statesman, it is true, might with more propriety quit the Faro Bank,[4] or card-table, to guide the helm, for he has still but to shuffle and trick. The whole system of British politics, if system it may courteously be called, consisting in multiplying dependents and contriving taxes which grind the poor to pamper the rich; thus a war, or any wild goose chace, is, as the vulgar use the phrase, a

---

2. A Roman general (3rd century B.C.) renowned for his incorruptibility; on one occasion when he was sent to ransom prisoners from the enemy, the foe sent back both ransom and the freed prisoners, so impressed were they with Fabricius.
3. Cincinnatus was supposedly called from his plow on his humble farm to defend Rome as com-

mander-in-chief. George Washington is known as the "American Cincinnatus."
4. Faro is a card game in which players bet on which card will chance to appear at the top of the deck; the faro bank is the banker's deposit of money against which players put their stakes.

lucky turn-up of patronage for the minister, whose chief merit is the art of keeping himself in place. It is not necessary then that he should have bowels for[5] the poor, so he can secure for his family the odd trick. Or should some shew of respect, for what is termed with ignorant ostentation an Englishman's birth-right, be expedient to bubble[6] the gruff mastiff that he has to lead by the nose, he can make an empty shew, very safely, by giving his single voice, and suffering his light squadron to file off to the other side. And when a question of humanity is agitated he may dip a sop in the milk of human kindness, to silence Cerberus,[7] and talk of the interest which his heart takes in an attempt to make the earth no longer cry for vengeance as it sucks in its children's blood, though his cold hand may at the very moment rivet their chains, by sanctioning the abominable traffick. A minister is no longer a minister, than while he can carry a point, which he is determined to carry.—Yet it is not necessary that a minister should feel like a man, when a bold push might shake his seat.

But, to have done with these episodical observations, let me return to the more specious slavery which chains the very soul of woman, keeping her for ever under the bondage of ignorance.

The preposterous distinctions of rank, which render civilization a curse, by dividing the world between voluptuous tyrants, and cunning envious dependents, corrupt, almost equally, every class of people, because respectability is not attached to the discharge of the relative duties of life, but to the station, and when the duties are not fulfilled the affections cannot gain sufficient strength to fortify the virtue of which they are the natural reward. Still there are some loop-holes out of which a man may creep, and dare to think and act for himself; but for a woman it is an herculean task, because she has difficulties peculiar to her sex to overcome, which require almost superhuman powers.

A truly benevolent legislator always endeavours to make it the interest of each individual to be virtuous; and thus private virtue becoming the cement of public happiness, an orderly whole is consolidated by the tendency of all the parts towards a common centre. But, the private or public virtue of woman is very problematical; for Rousseau, and a numerous list of male writers, insist that she should all her life be subjected to a severe restraint, that of propriety. Why subject her to propriety—blind propriety, if she be capable of acting from a nobler spring, if she be an heir of immortality? Is sugar always to be produced by vital blood? Is one half of the human species, like the poor African slaves, to be subject to preju-

5. Compassion for.
6. Delude.
7. In Greek myth the dog, usually represented as having three heads, who guarded the entrance to Hades; he could only be silenced by giving a "sop" to all three mouths.

dices that brutalize them, when principles would be a surer guard, only to sweeten the cup of man? Is not this indirectly to deny woman reason? for a gift is a mockery, if it be unfit for use.

Women are, in common with men, rendered weak and luxurious by the relaxing pleasures which wealth procures; but added to this they are made slaves to their persons, and must render them alluring that man may lend them his reason to guide their tottering steps aright. Or should they be ambitious, they must govern their tyrants by sinister tricks, for without rights there cannot be any incumbent duties. The laws respecting woman, which I mean to discuss in a future part, make an absurd unit of a man and his wife;[8] and then, by the easy transition of only considering him as responsible, she is reduced to a mere cypher.

The being who discharges the duties of its station is independent; and, speaking of women at large, their first duty is to themselves as rational creatures, and the next, in point of importance, as citizens, is that, which includes so many, of a mother. The rank in life which dispenses with their fulfilling this duty, necessarily degrades them by making them mere dolls. Or, should they turn to something more important than merely fitting drapery upon a smooth block, their minds are only occupied by some soft platonic attachment; or, the actual management of an intrigue may keep their thoughts in motion; for when they neglect domestic duties, they have it not in their power to take the field and march and countermarch like soldiers, or wrangle in the senate to keep their faculties from rusting.

I know that, as a proof of the inferiority of the sex, Rousseau has exultingly exclaimed, How can they leave the nursery for the camp![9]—And the camp has by some moralists been termed the school of the most heroic virtues; though, I think, it would puzzle a keen casuist to prove the reasonableness of the greater number of wars that have dubbed heroes. I do not mean to consider this question critically; because, having frequently viewed these freaks of ambition as the first natural mode of civilization, when the ground must be torn up, and the woods cleared by fire and sword, I do not choose to call them pests; but surely the present system of war has little connection with virtue of any denomination, being rather the school of *finesse* and effeminacy, than of fortitude.

Yet, if defensive war, the only justifiable war, in the present advanced state of society, where virtue can shew its face and ripen amidst the rigours which purify the air on the mountain's top, were alone to be adopted as just and glorious, the true heroism of antiq-

8. According to the concept of *couverture* in English common law of the period, a husband and wife were one legal unit, and the responsible legal person was the husband.

9. *Émile*, p. 325: "Can [a woman] be a nursing mother today and a soldier tomorrow?"

uity might again animate female bosoms.—But fair and softly, gentle reader, male or female, do not alarm thyself, for though I have compared the character of a modern soldier with that of a civilized woman, I am not going to advise them to turn their distaff into a musket, though I sincerely wish to see the bayonet converted into a pruning-hook.[1] I only recreated an imagination, fatigued by contemplating the vices and follies which all proceed from a feculent stream of wealth that has muddied the pure rills of natural affection, by supposing that society will some time or other be so constituted, that man must necessarily fulfil the duties of a citizen, or be despised, and that while he was employed in any of the departments of civil life, his wife, also an active citizen, should be equally intent to manage her family, educate her children, and assist her neighbours.

But, to render her really virtuous and useful, she must not, if she discharge her civil duties, want, individually, the protection of civil laws; she must not be dependent on her husband's bounty for her subsistence during his life, or support after his death—for how can a being be generous who has nothing of its own? or, virtuous, who is not free? The wife, in the present state of things, who is faithful to her husband, and neither suckles nor educates her children, scarcely deserves the name of a wife, and has no right to that of a citizen. But take away natural rights, and duties become null.

Women then must be considered as only the wanton solace of men, when they become so weak in mind and body, that they cannot exert themselves, unless to pursue some frothy pleasure, or to invent some frivolous fashion. What can be a more melancholy sight to a thinking mind, than to look into the numerous carriages that drive helter-skelter about this metropolis in a morning full of pale-faced creatures who are flying from themselves. I have often wished, with Dr. Johnson, to place some of them in a little shop with half a dozen children looking up to their languid countenances for support.[2] I am much mistaken, if some latent vigour would not soon give health and spirit to their eyes, and some lines drawn by the exercise of reason on the blank cheeks, which before were only undulated by dimples, might restore lost dignity to the character, or rather enable it to attain the true dignity of its nature. Virtue is not to be acquired even by speculation, much less by the negative supineness that wealth naturally generates.

Besides, when poverty is more disgraceful than even vice, is not morality cut to the quick? Still to avoid misconstruction, though I consider that women in the common walks of life are called to fulfil

---

1. Isaiah 2:4: "And they shall beat their swords into plowshares, and their spears into pruning hooks."

2. Wollstonecraft may be referring to the *Rambler* Essay No. 85 (January 8, 1751), "The Mischiefs of Total Idleness."

the duties of wives and mothers, by religion and reason, I cannot help lamenting that women of a superiour cast have not a road open by which they can pursue more extensive plans of usefulness and independence. I may excite laughter, by dropping an hint, which I mean to pursue, some future time, for I really think that women ought to have representatives, instead of being arbitrarily governed without having any direct share allowed them in the deliberations of government.

But, as the whole system of representation is now, in this country, only a convenient handle for despotism, they need not complain, for they are as well represented as a numerous class of hard working mechanics,[3] who pay for the support of royalty when they can scarcely stop their children's mouths with bread. How are they represented whose very sweat supports the splendid stud of an heir apparent, or varnishes the chariot of some female favourite who looks down on shame? Taxes on the very necessaries of life, enable an endless tribe of idle princes and princesses to pass with stupid pomp before a gaping crowd, who almost worship the very parade which costs them so dear. This is mere gothic grandeur, something like the barbarous useless parade of having sentinels on horseback at Whitehall,[4] which I could never view without a mixture of contempt and indignation.

How strangely must the mind be sophisticated when this sort of state impresses it! But, till these monuments of folly are levelled by virtue, similar follies will leaven the whole mass. For the same character, in some degree, will prevail in the aggregate of society: and the refinements of luxury, or the vicious repinings of envious poverty, will equally banish virtue from society, considered as the characteristic of that society, or only allow it to appear as one of the stripes of the harlequin coat, worn by the civilized man.

In the superiour ranks of life, every duty is done by deputies, as if duties could ever be waved, and the vain pleasures which consequent idleness forces the rich to pursue, appear so enticing to the next rank, that the numerous scramblers for wealth sacrifice every thing to tread on their heels. The most sacred trusts are then considered as sinecures, because they were procured by interest, and only sought to enable a man to keep *good company*. Women, in particular, all want to be ladies. Which is simply to have nothing to do, but listlessly to go they scarcely care where, for they cannot tell what.

But what have women to do in society? I may be asked, but to loiter with easy grace; surely you would not condemn them all to

---

3. Men having a manual occupation or working at a trade.

4. The famous Horse Guards who daily post guard on Whitehall, the hub of the British government.

suckle fools and chronicle small beer![5] No. Women might certainly study the art of healing, and be physicians as well as nurses. And midwifery, decency seems to allot to them, though I am afraid the word midwife, in our dictionaries, will soon give place to *accoucheur*,[6] and one proof of the former delicacy of the sex be effaced from the language.

They might, also, study politics, and settle their benevolence on the broadest basis; for the reading of history will scarcely be more useful than the perusal of romances, if read as mere biography; if the character of the times, the political improvements, arts, &c. be not observed. In short, if it be not considered as the history of man; and not of particular men, who filled a niche in the temple of fame, and dropped into the black rolling stream of time, that silently sweeps all before it, into the shapeless void called—eternity.—For shape, can it be called, 'that shape hath none?'[7]

Business of various kinds, they might likewise pursue, if they were educated in a more orderly manner, which might save many from common and legal prostitution. Women would not then marry for a support, as men accept of places under government, and neglect the implied duties; nor would an attempt to earn their own subsistence, a most laudable one! sink them almost to the level of those poor abandoned creatures who live by prostitution. For are not milliners and mantua-makers[8] reckoned the next class? The few employments open to women, so far from being liberal, are menial; and when a superior education enables them to take charge of the education of children as governesses, they are not treated like the tutors of sons, though even clerical tutors are not always treated in a manner calculated to render them respectable in the eyes of their pupils, to say nothing of the private comfort of the individual. But as women educated like gentlewomen, are never designed for the humiliating situation which necessity sometimes forces them to fill; these situations are considered in the light of a degradation; and they know little of the human heart, who need to be told, that nothing so painfully sharpens sensibility as such a fall in life.[9]

Some of these women might be restrained from marrying by a proper spirit or delicacy, and others may not have had it in their power to escape in this pitiful way from servitude; is not that government then very defective, and very unmindful of the happiness of one half of its members, that does not provide for honest, independent women, by encouraging them to fill respectable stations? But in order to render their private virtue a public benefit, they

---

5. *Othello* II.i.160.
6. A male physician who presides at childbirth.
7. *Paradise Lost* II.666–67.
8. Dressmakers.

9. Wollstonecraft had spent one year as governess to the older daughters of the Viscount Kingsborough, County Cork, Ireland.

must have a civil existence in the state, married or single; else we shall continually see some worthy woman, whose sensibility has been rendered painfully acute by undeserved contempt, droop like 'the lily broken down by a plow-share.'[1]

It is a melancholy truth; yet such is the blessed effect of civilization! the most respectable women are the most oppressed; and, unless they have understandings far superiour to the common run of understandings, taking in both sexes, they must, from being treated like contemptible beings, become contemptible. How many women thus waste life away the prey of discontent, who might have practised as physicians, regulated a farm, managed a shop, and stood erect, supported by their own industry, instead of hanging their heads surcharged with the dew of sensibility, that consumes the beauty to which it at first gave lustre; nay, I doubt whether pity and love are so near akin as poets feign, for I have seldom seen much compassion excited by the helplessness of females, unless they were fair; then, perhaps, pity was the soft handmaid of love, or the harbinger of lust.

How much more respectable is the woman who earns her own bread by fulfilling any duty, than the most accomplished beauty!—beauty did I say?—so sensible am I of the beauty of moral loveliness, or the harmonious propriety that attunes the passions of a well-regulated mind, that I blush at making the comparison; yet I sigh to think how few women aim at attaining this respectability by withdrawing from the giddy whirl of pleasure, or the indolent calm that stupifies the good sort of women it sucks in.

Proud of their weakness, however, they must always be protected, guarded from care, and all the rough toils that dignify the mind.— If this be the fiat of fate, if they will make themselves insignificant and contemptible, sweetly to waste 'life away,' let them not expect to be valued when their beauty fades, for it is the fate of the fairest flowers to be admired and pulled to pieces by the careless hand that plucked them. In how many ways do I wish, from the purest benevolence, to impress this truth on my sex; yet I fear that they will not listen to a truth that dear bought experience has brought home to many an agitated bosom, nor willingly resign the privileges of rank and sex for the privileges of humanity, to which those have no claim who do not discharge its duties.

Those writers are particularly useful, in my opinion, who make man feel for man, independent of the station he fills, or the drapery of factitious sentiments. I then would fain convince reasonable men of the importance of some of my remarks, and prevail on them to

1. In Fénelon's *Télémaque*, see the story of Ideomeneus who, to obey the gods, must kill his own son; the lad dies "as a beautiful lily of the fields, that is wounded in its root by the plough-share, droops" (*The Adventures of Telemachus* [Boston, 1797], p. 68). See also Robert Burns's "To a Mountain Daisy," lines 49–54.

weigh dispassionately the whole tenor of my observations.—I appeal to their understandings; and, as a fellow-creature, claim, in the name of my sex, some interest in their hearts. I entreat them to assist to emancipate their companion, to make her a *help meet* for them!

Would men but generously snap our chains, and be content with rational fellowship instead of slavish obedience, they would find us more observant daughters, more affectionate sisters, more faithful wives, more reasonable mothers—in a word, better citizens. We should then love them with true affection, because we should learn to respect ourselves; and the peace of mind of a worthy man would not be interrupted by the idle vanity of his wife, nor the babes sent to nestle in a strange bosom,[2] having never found a home in their mother's.

Chap. X

Parental Affection

Parental affection is, perhaps, the blindest modification of perverse self-love; for we have not, like the French,[1] two terms to distinguish the pursuit of a natural and reasonable desire, from the ignorant calculations of weakness. Parents often love their children in the most brutal manner, and sacrifice every relative duty to promote their advancement in the world.—To promote, such is the perversity of unprincipled prejudices, the future welfare of the very beings whose present existence they imbitter by the most despotic stretch of power. Power, in fact, is ever true to its vital principle, for in every shape it would reign without controul or inquiry. Its throne is built across a dark abyss, which no eye must dare to explore, lest the baseless fabric should totter under investigation. Obedience, unconditional obedience, is the catch-word of tyrants of every description, and to render 'assurance doubly sure,'[2] one kind of despotism supports another. Tyrants would have cause to tremble if reason were to become the rule of duty in any of the relations of life, for the light might spread till perfect day appeared. And when it did appear, how would men smile at the sight of the bugbears at which they started during the night of ignorance, or the twilight of timid inquiry.

Parental affection, indeed, in many minds, is but a pretext to tyr-

2. It was common practice for babies to be suckled by wet-nurses rather than their own mothers.
1. *L'amour propre. L'amour de soi même* [sic]" [Wollstonecraft's note]. This is a distinction made famous by La Rochefoucauld in *Maximes Sup-* *plémentaires*, No. 1, as well as by Rousseau in "A Dissertation on the Origin of Inequality." "L'amour propre" is simple egoism, whereas "l'amour de soi-même" has the overtones of self-respect.
2. *Macbeth* IV.i.83.

annize where it can be done with impunity, for only good and wise men are content with the respect that will bear discussion. Convinced that they have a right to what they insist on, they do not fear reason, or dread the sifting of subjects that recur to natural justice: because they firmly believe that the more enlightened the human mind becomes the deeper root will just and simple principles take. They do not rest in expedients, or grant that what is metaphysically true can be practically false; but disdaining the shifts of the moment they calmly wait till time, sanctioning innovation, silences the hiss of selfishness or envy.

If the power of reflecting on the past, and darting the keen eye of contemplation into futurity, be the grand privilege of man, it must be granted that some people enjoy this prerogative in a very limited degree. Every thing new appears to them wrong; and not able to distinguish the possible from the monstrous, they fear where no fear should find a place, running from the light of reason, as if it were a firebrand; yet the limits of the possible have never been defined to stop the sturdy innovator's hand.

Woman, however, a slave in every situation to prejudice, seldom exerts enlightened maternal affection; for she either neglects her children, or spoils them by improper indulgence. Besides, the affection of some women for their children is, as I have before termed it, frequently very brutish: for it eradicates every spark of humanity. Justice, truth, every thing is sacrificed by these Rebekah's,[3] and for the sake of their *own* children they violate the most sacred duties, forgetting the common relationship that binds the whole family on earth together. Yet, reason seems to say, that they who suffer one duty, or affection, to swallow up the rest, have not sufficient heart or mind to fulfil that one conscientiously. It then loses the venerable aspect of a duty, and assumes the fantastic form of a whim.

As the care of children in their infancy is one of the grand duties annexed to the female character by nature, this duty would afford many forcible arguments for strengthening the female understanding, if it were properly considered.

The formation of the mind must be begun very early, and the temper, in particular, requires the most judicious attention—an attention which women cannot pay who only love their children because they are their children, and seek no further for the foundation of their duty, than in the feelings of the moment. It is this want of reason in their affections which makes women so often run into extremes, and either be the most fond or most careless and unnatural mothers.

---

3. In Genesis 27, Rebekah, wife of Isaac and mother of the twins Jacob and Esau, attempts to gain the blind father's blessing for her favorite son, Jacob, thus earning the reputation of an ambitious and designing mother.

To be a good mother—a woman must have sense, and that independence of mind which few women possess who are taught to depend entirely on their husbands. Meek wives are, in general, foolish mothers; wanting their children to love them best, and take their part, in secret, against the father, who is held up as a scarecrow. When chastisement is necessary, though they have offended the mother, the father must inflict the punishment; he must be the judge in all disputes: but I shall more fully discuss this subject when I treat of private education, I now only mean to insist, that unless the understanding of woman be enlarged, and her character rendered more firm, by being allowed to govern her own conduct, she will never have sufficient sense or command of temper to manage her children properly. Her parental affection, indeed, scarcely deserves the name, when it does not lead her to suckle her children, because the discharge of this duty is equally calculated to inspire maternal and filial affection: and it is the indispensable duty of men and women to fulfil the duties which give birth to affections that are the surest preservatives against vice. Natural affection, as it is termed, I believe to be a very faint tie, affections must grow out of the habitual exercise of a mutual sympathy; and what sympathy does a mother exercise who sends her babe to a nurse, and only takes it from a nurse to send it to a school?

In the exercise of their maternal feelings providence has furnished women with a natural substitute for love, when the lover becomes only a friend, and mutual confidence takes place of overstrained admiration—a child then gently twists the relaxing cord, and a mutual care produces a new mutual sympathy.—But a child, though a pledge of affection, will not enliven it, if both father and mother be content to transfer the charge to hirelings; for they who do their duty by proxy should not murmur if they miss the reward of duty—parental affection produces filial duty.

Chap. XI

Duty to Parents

There seems to be an indolent propensity in man to make prescription always take place of reason, and to place every duty on an arbitrary foundation. The rights of kings are deduced in a direct line from the King of kings; and that of parents from our first parent.

Why do we thus go back for principles that should always rest on the same base, and have the same weight to-day that they had a thousand years ago—and not a jot more? If parents discharge their duty they have a strong hold and sacred claim on the gratitude of their children; but few parents are willing to receive the respectful affection of their offspring on such terms. They demand blind obedience, because they do not merit a reasonable service: and to render these demands of weakness and ignorance more binding, a mysterious sanctity is spread round the most arbitrary principle; for what other name can be given to the blind duty of obeying vicious or weak beings merely because they obeyed a powerful instinct?

The simple definition of the reciprocal duty, which naturally subsists between parent and child, may be given in a few words: The parent who pays proper attention to helpless infancy has a right to require the same attention when the feebleness of age comes upon him. But to subjugate a rational being to the mere will of another, after he is of age to answer to society for his own conduct, is a most cruel and undue stretch of power; and, perhaps, as injurious to morality as those religious systems which do not allow right and wrong to have any existence, but in the Divine will.

I never knew a parent who had paid more than common attention to his children, disregarded;[1] on the contrary, the early habit of relying almost implicitly on the opinion of a respected parent is not easily shook, even when matured reason convinces the child that his father is not the wisest man in the world. This weakness, for a weakness it is, though the epithet amiable may be tacked to it, a reasonable man must steel himself against; for the absurd duty, too often inculcated, of obeying a parent only on account of his being a parent, shackles the mind, and prepares it for a slavish submission to any power but reason.

I distinguish between the natural and accidental duty due to parents.

The parent who sedulously endeavours to form the heart and enlarge the understanding of his child, has given that dignity to the discharge of a duty, common to the whole animal world, that only reason can give. This is the parental affection of humanity, and leaves instinctive natural affection far behind. Such a parent acquires all the rights of the most sacred friendship, and his advice, even when his child is advanced in life, demands serious consideration.

With respect to marriage, though after one and twenty a parent seems to have no right to withhold his consent on any account; yet twenty years of solicitude call for a return, and the son ought, at least, to promise not to marry for two or three years, should the object of his choice not entirely meet with the approbation of his first friend.

1. "Dr. Johnson makes the same observation" [Wollstonecraft's note]. See Johnson's *Rambler* Essay No. 148 (August 17, 1751), "On the Tyranny of Parents."

But, respect for parents is, generally speaking, a much more debasing principle; it is only a selfish respect for property. The father who is blindly obeyed, is obeyed from sheer weakness, or from motives that degrade the human character.

A great proportion of the misery that wanders, in hideous forms, around the world, is allowed to rise from the negligence of parents; and still these are the people who are most tenacious of what they term a natural right, though it be subversive of the birth-right of man, the right of acting according to the direction of his own reason.

I have already very frequently had occasion to observe, that vicious or indolent people are always eager to profit by enforcing arbitrary privileges; and, generally, in the same proportion as they neglect the discharge of the duties which alone render the privileges reasonable. This is at the bottom a dictate of common sense, or the instinct of self-defence, peculiar to ignorant weakness; resembling that instinct, which makes a fish muddy the water it swims in to elude its enemy, instead of boldly facing it in the clear stream.

From the clear stream of argument, indeed, the supporters of prescription, of every denomination, fly; and, taking refuge in the darkness, which, in the language of sublime poetry, has been supposed to surround the throne of Omnipotence, they dare to demand that implicit respect which is only due to His unsearchable ways. But, let me not be thought presumptuous, the darkness which hides our God from us, only respects speculative truths—it never obscures moral ones, they shine clearly, for God is light, and never, by the constitution of our nature, requires the discharge of a duty, the reasonableness of which does not beam on us when we open our eyes.

The indolent parent of high rank may, it is true, extort a shew of respect from his child, and females on the continent are particularly subject to the views of their families, who never think of consulting their inclination, or providing for the comfort of the poor victims of their pride. The consequence is notorious; these dutiful daughters become adulteresses, and neglect the education of their children, from whom they, in their turn, exact the same kind of obedience.

Females, it is true, in all countries, are too much under the dominion of their parents; and few parents think of addressing their children in the following manner, though it is in this reasonable way that Heaven seems to command the whole human race. It is your interest to obey me till you can judge for yourself; and the Almighty Father of all has implanted an affection in me to serve as a guard to you whilst your reason is unfolding; but when your mind arrives at maturity, you must only obey me, or rather respect my opinions, so far as they coincide with the light that is breaking in on your own mind.

A slavish bondage to parents cramps every faculty of the mind; and Mr. Locke very judiciously observes, that 'if the mind be curbed and humbled too much in children; if their spirits be abased and broken much by too strict an hand over them; they lose all their vigour and industry.'[2] This strict hand may in some degree account for the weakness of women; for girls, from various causes, are more kept down by their parents, in every sense of the word, than boys. The duty expected from them is, like all the duties arbitrarily imposed on women, more from a sense of propriety, more out of respect for decorum, than reason; and thus taught slavishly to submit to their parents, they are prepared for the slavery of marriage. I may be told that a number of women are not slaves in the marriage state. True, but they then become tyrants; for it is not rational freedom, but a lawless kind of power resembling the authority exercised by the favourites of absolute monarchs, which they obtain by debasing means. I do not, likewise, dream of insinuating that either boys or girls are always slaves, I only insist that when they are obliged to submit to authority blindly, their faculties are weakened, and their tempers rendered imperious or abject. I also lament that parents, indolently availing themselves of a supposed privilege, damp the first faint glimmering of reason, rendering at the same time the duty, which they are so anxious to enforce, an empty name; because they will not let it rest on the only basis on which a duty can rest securely: for unless it be founded on knowledge, it cannot gain sufficient strength to resist the squalls of passion, or the silent sapping of self-love. But it is not the parents who have given the surest proof of their affection for their children, or, to speak more properly, who by fulfilling their duty, have allowed a natural parental affection to take root in their hearts, the child of exercised sympathy and reason, and not the over-weening offspring of selfish pride, who most vehemently insist on their children submitting to their will merely because it is their will. On the contrary, the parent, who sets a good example, patiently lets that example work; and it seldom fails to produce its natural effect—filial reverence.

Children cannot be taught too early to submit to reason, the true definition of that necessity, which Rousseau insisted on, without defining it; for to submit to reason is to submit to the nature of things, and to that God, who formed them so, to promote our real interest.

Why should the minds of children be warped as they just begin to expand, only to favour the indolence of parents, who insist on a privilege without being willing to pay the price fixed by nature? I have before had occasion to observe, that a right always includes a duty, and I think it may, likewise, fairly be inferred, that they forfeit the right, who do not fulfil the duty.

2. John Locke, *Some Thoughts Concerning Education*, article 46.2.

It is easier, I grant, to command than reason; but it does not follow from hence that children cannot comprehend the reason why they are made to do certain things habitually: for, from a steady adherence to a few simple principles of conduct flows that salutary power which a judicious parent gradually gains over a child's mind. And this power becomes strong indeed, if tempered by an even display of affection brought home to the child's heart. For, I believe, as a general rule, it must be allowed that the affection which we inspire always resembles that we cultivate; so that natural affections, which have been supposed almost distinct from reason, may be found more nearly connected with judgment than is commonly allowed. Nay, as another proof of the necessity of cultivating the female understanding, it is but just to observe, that the affections seem to have a kind of animal capriciousness when they merely reside in the heart.

It is the irregular exercise of parental authority that first injures the mind, and to these irregularities girls are more subject than boys. The will of those who never allow their will to be disputed, unless they happen to be in a good humour, when they relax proportionally, is almost always unreasonable. To elude this arbitrary authority girls very early learn the lessons which they afterwards practise on their husbands; for I have frequently seen a little sharp-faced miss rule a whole family, excepting that now and then mamma's angry will burst out of some accidental cloud;—either her hair was ill dressed,[3] or she had lost more money at cards, the night before, than she was willing to own to her husband; or some such moral cause of anger.

After observing sallies of this kind, I have been led into a melancholy train of reflection respecting females, concluding that when their first affection must lead them astray, or make their duties clash till they rest on mere whims and customs, little can be expected from them as they advance in life. How indeed can an instructor remedy this evil? for to teach them virtue on any solid principle is to teach them to despise their parents. Children cannot, ought not, to be taught to make allowance for the faults of their parents, because every such allowance weakens the force of reason in their minds, and makes them still more indulgent to their own. It is one of the most sublime virtues of maturity that leads us to be severe with respect to ourselves, and forbearing to others; but children should only be taught the simple virtues, for if they begin too early to make allowance for human passions and manners, they wear off the fine edge of the criterion by which they should regulate their

---

3. "I myself heard a little girl once say to a servant, 'My mama has been scolding me finely this morning, because her hair was not dressed to please her.' Though this remark was pert, it was just. And what respect could a girl acquire for such a parent without doing violence to reason?" [Wollstonecraft's note].

own, and become unjust in the same proportion as they grow indulgent.

The affections of children, and weak people, are always selfish; they love their relatives, because they are beloved by them, and not on account of their virtues. Yet, till esteem and love are blended together in the first affection, and reason made the foundation of the first duty, morality will stumble at the threshold. But, till society is very differently constituted, parents, I fear, will still insist on being obeyed, because they will be obeyed, and constantly endeavour to settle that power on a Divine right which will not bear the investigation of reason.

Chap. XII

On National Education [1]

The good effects resulting from attention to private education will ever be very confined, and the parent who really puts his own hand to the plow, will always, in some degree, be disappointed, till education becomes a grand national concern. A man cannot retire into a desert with his child, and if he did he could not bring himself back to childhood, and become the proper friend and play-fellow of an infant or youth. And when children are confined to the society of men and women, they very soon acquire that kind of premature manhood which stops the growth of every vigorous power of mind or body. In order to open their faculties they should be excited to think for themselves; and this can only be done by mixing a number of children together, and making them jointly pursue the same objects.

A child very soon contracts a benumbing indolence of mind, which he has seldom sufficient vigour afterwards to shake off, when he only asks a question instead of seeking for information, and then relies implicitly on the answer he receives. With his equals in age this could never be the case, and the subjects of inquiry, though they might be influenced, would not be entirely under the direction of men, who frequently damp, if not destroy, abilities, by bringing them forward too hastily: and too hastily they will infallibly be brought forward, if the child could be confined to the society of a man, however sagacious that man may be.

Besides, in youth the seeds of every affection should be sown, and the respectful regard, which is felt for a parent, is very different from the social affections that are to constitute the happiness of life as it advances. Of these equality is the basis, and an intercourse of sentiments unclogged by that observant seriousness which prevents

1. The title of the pamphlet outlining Talleyrand's proposal, to which Wollstonecraft refers in her dedication.

disputation, though it may not inforce submission. Let a child have ever such an affection for his parent, he will always languish to play and prattle with children; and the very respect he feels, for filial esteem always has a dash of fear mixed with it, will, if it do not teach him cunning, at least prevent him from pouring out the little secrets which first open the heart to friendship and confidence, gradually leading to more expansive benevolence. Added to this, he will never acquire that frank ingenuousness of behaviour, which young people can only attain by being frequently in society where they dare to speak what they think; neither afraid of being reproved for their presumption, nor laughed at for their folly.

Forcibly impressed by the reflections which the sight of schools, as they are at present conducted, naturally suggested, I have formerly delivered my opinion rather warmly in favour of a private education; but further experience has led me to view the subject in a different light. I still, however, think schools, as they are now regulated, the hot-beds of vice and folly, and the knowledge of human nature, supposed to be attained there, merely cunning selfishness.

At school boys become gluttons and slovens, and, instead of cultivating domestic affections, very early rush into the libertinism which destroys the constitution before it is formed; hardening the heart as it weakens the understanding.

I should, in fact, be averse to boarding-schools, if it were for no other reason than the unsettled state of mind which the expectation of the vacations produce. On these the children's thoughts are fixed with eager anticipating hopes, for, at least, to speak with moderation, half of the time, and when they arrive they are spent in total dissipation and beastly indulgence.

But, on the contrary, when they are brought up at home, though they may pursue a plan of study in a more orderly manner than can be adopted when near a fourth part of the year is actually spent in idleness, and as much more in regret and anticipation; yet they there acquire too high an opinion of their own importance, from being allowed to tyrannize over servants, and from the anxiety expressed by most mothers, on the score of manners, who, eager to teach the accomplishments of a gentleman, stifle, in their birth, the virtues of a man. Thus brought into company when they ought to be seriously employed, and treated like men when they are still boys, they become vain and effeminate.

The only way to avoid two extremes equally injurious to morality, would be to contrive some way of combining a public and private education. Thus to make men citizens two natural steps might be taken, which seem directly to lead to the desired point; for the domestic affections, that first open the heart to the various modifications of humanity, would be cultivated, whilst the children were nevertheless allowed to spend great part of their time, on terms of equality, with other children.

I still recollect, with pleasure, the country day school; where a boy trudged in the morning, wet or dry, carrying his books, and his dinner, if it were at a considerable distance; a servant did not then lead master by the hand, for, when he had once put on coat and breeches, he was allowed to shift for himself, and return alone in the evening to recount the feats of the day close at the parental knee. His father's house was his home, and was ever after fondly remembered; nay, I appeal to many superiour men, who were educated in this manner, whether the recollection of some shady lane where they conned[2] their lesson; or, of some stile, where they sat making a kite, or mending a bat, has not endeared their country to them?

But, what boy ever recollected with pleasure the years he spent in close confinement, at an academy near London? unless, indeed, he should, by chance, remember the poor scare-crow of an usher,[3] whom he tormented; or, the tartman, from whom he caught a cake, to devour it with a cattish appetite of selfishness. At boarding-schools of every description, the relaxation of the junior boys is mischief; and of the senior, vice. Besides, in great schools, what can be more prejudicial to the moral character than the system of tyranny and abject slavery which is established amongst the boys, to say nothing of the slavery to forms, which makes religion worse than a farce? For what good can be expected from the youth who receives the sacrament of the Lord's supper, to avoid forfeiting half a guinea, which he probably afterwards spends in some sensual manner? Half the employment of the youths is to elude the necessity of attending public worship; and well they may, for such a constant repetition of the same thing must be a very irksome restraint on their natural vivacity. As these ceremonies have the most fatal effect on their morals, and as a ritual performed by the lips, when the heart and mind are far away, is not now stored up by our church as a bank to draw on for the fees of the poor souls in purgatory, why should they not be abolished?

But the fear of innovation, in this country, extends to every thing.—This is only a covert fear, the apprehensive timidity of indolent slugs, who guard, by sliming it over, the snug place, which they consider in the light of an hereditary estate; and eat, drink, and enjoy themselves, instead of fulfilling the duties, excepting a few empty forms, for which it was endowed. These are the people who most strenuously insist on the will of the founder being observed, crying out against all reformation, as if it were a violation of justice. I am now alluding particularly to the relicks of popery

---

2. Studied or learned; usually used as a past participle, as in "well-conned."   3. An assistant to a schoolmaster or headmaster.

retained in our colleges, when the protestant members seem to be such sticklers for the established church; but their zeal never makes them lose sight of the spoil of ignorance, which rapacious priests of superstitious memory have scraped together. No, wise in their generation,[4] they venerate the prescriptive right of possession, as a strong hold, and still let the sluggish bell tinkle to prayers, as during the days when the elevation of the host was supposed to atone for the sins of the people, lest one reformation should lead to another, and the spirit kill the letter. These Romish customs[5] have the most baneful effect on the morals of our clergy; for the idle vermin who two or three times a day perform in the most slovenly manner a service which they think useless, but call their duty, soon lose a sense of duty. At college, forced to attend or evade public worship, they acquire an habitual contempt for the very service, the performance of which is to enable them to live in idleness. It is mumbled over as an affair of business, as a stupid boy repeats his task, and frequently the college cant escapes from the preacher the moment after he has left the pulpit, and even whilst he is eating the dinner which he earned in such a dishonest manner.

Nothing, indeed, can be more irreverent than the cathedral service as it is now performed in this country, neither does it contain a set of weaker men than those who are the slaves of this childish routine. A disgusting skeleton of the former state is still exhibited; but all the solemnity that interested the imagination, if it did not purify the heart, is stripped off. The performance of high mass on the continent must impress every mind, where a spark of fancy glows, with that awful melancholy, that sublime tenderness, so near akin to devotion. I do not say that these devotional feelings are of more use, in a moral sense, than any other emotion of taste; but I contend that the theatrical pomp which gratifies our senses, is to be preferred to the cold parade that insults the understanding without reaching the heart.

Amongst remarks on national education, such observations cannot be misplaced, especially as the supporters of these establishments, degenerated into puerilities, affect to be the champions of religion.—Religion, pure source of comfort in this vale of tears! how has thy clear stream been muddied by the dabblers, who have presumptuously endeavoured to confine in one narrow channel, the living waters that ever flow towards God—the sublime ocean of existence! What would life be without that peace which the love of God, when built on humanity, alone can impart? Every earthly affection turns back, at intervals, to prey upon the heart that feeds

4. Luke 16:8: "The children of this world are in their generation wiser than the children of light."
5. Pertaining to the Roman Catholic Church and the "relicks of popery" cited earlier in this paragraph.

it; and the purest effusions of benevolence, often rudely damped by man, must mount as a free-will offering to Him who gave them birth, whose bright image they faintly reflect.

In public schools, however, religion, confounded with irksome ceremonies and unreasonable restraints, assumes the most ungracious aspect: not the sober austere one that commands respect whilst it inspires fear; but a ludicrous cast, that serves to point a pun. For, in fact, most of the good stories and smart things which enliven the spirits that have been concentrated at whist, are manufactured out of the incidents to which the very men labour to give a droll turn who countenance the abuse to live on the spoil.

There is not, perhaps, in the kingdom, a more dogmatical, or luxurious set of men, than the pedantic tyrants who reside in colleges and preside at public schools. The vacations are equally injurious to the morals of the masters and pupils, and the intercourse, which the former keep up with the nobility, introduces the same vanity and extravagance into their families, which banish domestic duties and comforts from the lordly mansion, whose state is awkwardly aped. The boys, who live at a great expence with the masters and assistants, are never domesticated, though placed there for that purpose; for, after a silent dinner, they swallow a hasty glass of wine, and retire to plan some mischievous trick, or to ridicule the person or manners of the very people they have just been cringing to, and whom they ought to consider as the representatives of their parents.

Can it then be a matter of surprise that boys become selfish and vicious who are thus shut out from social converse? or that a mitre often graces the brow of one of these diligent pastors?[6]

The desire of living in the same style, as the rank just above them, infects each individual and every class of people, and meanness is the concomitant of this ignoble ambition; but those professions are most debasing whose ladder is patronage; yet, out of one of these professions the tutors of youth are, in general, chosen. But, can they be expected to inspire independent sentiments, whose conduct must be regulated by the cautious prudence that is ever on the watch for preferment?

So far, however, from thinking of the morals of boys, I have heard several masters of schools argue, that they only undertook to teach Latin and Greek; and that they had fulfilled their duty, by sending some good scholars to college.

A few good scholars, I grant, may have been formed by emulation and discipline; but, to bring forward these clever boys, the health and morals of a number have been sacrificed. The sons of our gentry and wealthy commoners are mostly educated at these

6. The "mitre" is the special bishop's hat; Wollstonecraft asserts that the pastors who curry favor with the local nobility are often promoted in the church.

seminaries, and will any one pretend to assert that the majority, making every allowance, come under the description of tolerable scholars?

It is not for the benefit of society that a few brilliant men should be brought forward at the expence of the multitude. It is true, that great men seem to start up, as great revolutions occur, at proper intervals, to restore order, and to blow aside the clouds that thicken over the face of truth; but let more reason and virtue prevail in society, and these strong winds would not be necessary. Public education, of every denomination, should be directed to form citizens; but if you wish to make good citizens, you must first exercise the affections of a son and a brother. This is the only way to expand the heart; for public affections, as well as public virtues, must ever grow out of the private character, or they are merely meteors that shoot athwart a dark sky, and disappear as they are gazed at and admired.

Few, I believe, have had much affection for mankind, who did not first love their parents, their brothers, sisters, and even the domestic brutes, whom they first played with. The exercise of youthful sympathies forms the moral temperature; and it is the recollection of these first affections and pursuits that gives life to those that are afterwards more under the direction of reason. In youth, the fondest friendships are formed, the genial juices mounting at the same time, kindly mix; or, rather the heart, tempered for the reception of friendship, is accustomed to seek for pleasure in something more noble than the churlish gratification of appetite.

In order then to inspire a love of home and domestic pleasures, children ought to be educated at home, for riotous holidays only make them fond of home for their own sakes. Yet, the vacations, which do not foster domestic affections, continually disturb the course of study, and render any plan of improvement abortive which includes temperance; still, were they abolished, children would be entirely separated from their parents, and I question whether they would become better citizens by sacrificing the preparatory affections, by destroying the force of relationships that render the marriage state as necessary as respectable. But, if a private education produce self-importance, or insulate a man in his family, the evil is only shifted, not remedied.

This train of reasoning brings me back to a subject, on which I mean to dwell, the necessity of establishing proper day-schools.

But, these should be national establishments, for whilst school-masters are dependent on the caprice of parents, little exertion can be expected from them, more than is necessary to please ignorant people. Indeed, the necessity of a master's giving the parents some sample of the boys abilities, which during the vacation is shewn to every visitor,[7] is productive of more mischief than would at first be supposed. For it is seldom done entirely, to speak with moderation, by the child itself; thus the master countenances falsehood, or winds the poor machine up to some extraordinary exertion, that injures the wheels, and stops the progress of gradual improvement. The memory is loaded with unintelligible words, to make a shew of, without the understanding's acquiring any distinct ideas; but only that education deserves emphatically to be termed cultivation of mind, which teaches young people how to begin to think. The imagination should not be allowed to debauch the understanding before it gained strength, or vanity will become the forerunner of vice: for every way of exhibiting the acquirements of a child is injurious to its moral character.

How much time is lost in teaching them to recite what they do not understand? whilst, seated on benches, all in their best array, the mammas listen with astonishment to the parrot-like prattle, uttered in solemn cadences, with all the pomp of ignorance and folly. Such exhibitions only serve to strike the spreading fibres of vanity through the whole mind; for they neither teach children to speak fluently, nor behave gracefully. So far from it, that these frivolous pursuits might comprehensively be termed the study of affectation; for we now rarely see a simple, bashful boy, though few people of taste were ever disgusted by that awkward sheepishness so natural to the age, which schools and an early introduction into society, have changed into impudence and apish grimace.

Yet, how can these things be remedied whilst school-masters depend entirely on parents for a subsistence; and, when so many rival schools hang out their lures, to catch the attention of vain fathers and mothers, whose parental affection only leads them to wish that their children should outshine those of their neighbours?

Without great good luck, a sensible, conscientious man, would starve before he could raise a school, if he disdained to bubble weak parents by practising the secret tricks of the craft.

In the best regulated schools, however, where swarms are not crammed together, many bad habits must be acquired; but, at common schools, the body, heart, and understanding, are equally stunted, for parents are often only in quest of the cheapest school, and the master could not live, if he did not take a much greater number than he could manage himself; nor will the scanty pittance, allowed for each child, permit him to hire ushers sufficient to assist in the discharge of the mechanical part of the business. Besides, whatever appearance the house and garden may make, the children

---

7. "I now particularly allude to the numerous academies in and about London, and to the behaviour of the trading part of this great city" [Wollstonecraft's note].

do not enjoy the comfort of either, for they are continually reminded by irksome restrictions that they are not at home, and the state-rooms, garden, &c. must be kept in order for the recreation of the parents; who, of a Sunday, visit the school, and are impressed by the very parade that renders the situation of their children uncomfortable.

With what disgust have I heard sensible women, for girls are more restrained and cowed than boys, speak of the wearisome confinement, which they endured at school. Not allowed, perhaps, to step out of one broad walk in a superb garden, and obliged to pace with steady deportment stupidly backwards and forwards, holding up their heads and turning out their toes, with shoulders braced back, instead of bounding, as nature directs to complete her own design, in the various attitudes so conducive to health.[8] The pure animal spirits, which make both mind and body shoot out, and unfold the tender blossoms of hope, are turned sour, and vented in vain wishes or pert repinings, that contract the faculties and spoil the temper; else they mount to the brain, and sharpening the understanding before it gains proportionable strength, produce that pitiful cunning which disgracefully characterizes the female mind—and I fear will ever characterize it whilst women remain the slaves of power!

The little respect paid to chastity in the male world is, I am persuaded, the grand source of many of the physical and moral evils that torment mankind, as well as of the vices and follies that degrade and destroy women; yet at school, boys infallibly lose that decent bashfulness, which might have ripened into modesty, at home.

And what nasty indecent tricks do they not also learn from each other, when a number of them pig together in the same bedchamber, not to speak of the vices, which render the body weak, whilst they effectually prevent the acquisition of any delicacy of mind.[9] The little attention paid to the cultivation of modesty, amongst men, produces great depravity in all the relationships of society; for, not only love—love that ought to purify the heart, and first call forth all the youthful powers, to prepare the man to discharge the

8. "I remember a circumstance that once came under my own observation, and raised my indignation. I went to visit a little boy at a school where young children were prepared for a larger one. The master took me into the school-room, &c. but whilst I walked down a broad gravel walk, I could not help observing that the grass grew very luxuriantly on each side of me. I immediately asked the child some questions, and found that the poor boys were not allowed to stir off the walk, and that the master sometimes permitted sheep to be turned in to crop the untrodden grass. The tyrant of this domain used to sit by a window that overlooked the prison yard, and one nook turning from it, where the unfortunate babes could sport freely, he enclosed, and planted it with potatoes. The wife likewise was equally anxious to keep the children in order, lest they should dirty or tear their clothes" [Wollstonecraft's note].
9. Masturbation has erroneously been thought to weaken the body and brain.

benevolent duties of life, is sacrificed to premature lust; but, all the social affections are deadened by the selfish gratifications, which very early pollute the mind, and dry up the generous juices of the heart. In what an unnatural manner is innocence often violated; and what serious consequences ensue to render private vices a public pest. Besides, an habit of personal order, which has more effect on the moral character, than is, in general, supposed, can only be acquired at home, where that respectable reserve is kept up which checks the familiarity, that sinking into beastliness, undermines the affection it insults.

I have already animadverted on the bad habits which females acquire when they are shut up together; and, I think, that the observation may fairly be extended to the other sex, till the natural inference is drawn which I have had in view throughout—that to improve both sexes they ought, not only in private families, but in public schools, to be educated together. If marriage be the cement of society, mankind should all be educated after the same model, or the intercourse of the sexes will never deserve the name of fellowship, nor will women ever fulfil the peculiar duties of their sex, till they become enlightened citizens, till they become free by being enabled to earn their own subsistence, independent of men; in the same manner, I mean, to prevent misconstruction, as one man is independent of another. Nay, marriage will never be held sacred till women, by being brought up with men, are prepared to be their companions rather than their mistresses; for the mean doublings of cunning will ever render them contemptible, whilst oppression renders them timid. So convinced am I of this truth, that I will venture to predict that virtue will never prevail in society till the virtues of both sexes are founded on reason; and, till the affections common to both are allowed to gain their due strength by the discharge of mutual duties.

Were boys and girls permitted to pursue the same studies together, those graceful decencies might early be inculcated which produce modesty without those sexual distinctions that taint the mind. Lessons of politeness, and that formulary of decorum, which treads on the heels of falsehood, would be rendered useless by habitual propriety of behaviour. Not, indeed, put on for visitors like the courtly robe of politeness, but the sober effect of cleanliness of mind. Would not this simple elegance of sincerity be a chaste homage paid to domestic affections, far surpassing the meretricious compliments that shine with false lustre in the heartless intercourse of fashionable life? But, till more understanding preponderates in society, there will ever be a want of heart and taste, and the harlot's *rouge* will supply the place of that celestial suffusion which only virtuous affections can give to the face. Gallantry, and what is called love, may subsist without simplicity of character; but the main pillars of friendship, are respect and confidence—esteem is never founded on it cannot tell what!

A taste for the fine arts requires great cultivation; but not more than a taste for the virtuous affections; and both suppose that enlargement of mind which opens so many sources of mental pleasure. Why do people hurry to noisy scenes, and crowded circles? I should answer, because they want activity of mind, because they have not cherished the virtues of the heart. They only, therefore, see and feel in the gross, and continually pine after variety, finding every thing that is simple insipid.

This argument may be carried further than philosophers are aware of, for if nature destined woman, in particular, for the discharge of domestic duties, she made her susceptible of the attached affections in a great degree. Now women are notoriously fond of pleasure; and, naturally must be so according to my definition, because they cannot enter into the minutiae of domestic taste; lacking judgment, the foundation of all taste. For the understanding, in spite of sensual cavillers, reserves to itself the privilege of conveying pure joy to the heart.

With what a languid yawn have I seen an admirable poem thrown down, that a man of true taste returns to, again and again with rapture; and, whilst melody has almost suspended respiration, a lady has asked me where I bought my gown. I have seen also an eye glanced coldly over a most exquisite picture, rest, sparkling with pleasure, on a caricature rudely sketched; and whilst some terrific feature in nature has spread a sublime stillness through my soul, I have been desired to observe the pretty tricks of a lap-dog, that my perverse fate forced me to travel with. Is it surprising that such a tasteless being should rather caress this dog than her children? Or, that she should prefer the rant of flattery to the simple accents of sincerity?

To illustrate this remark I must be allowed to observe, that men of the first genius, and most cultivated minds, have appeared to have the highest relish for the simple beauties of nature; and they must have forcibly felt, what they have so well described, the charm which natural affections, and unsophisticated feelings spread round the human character. It is this power of looking into the heart, and responsively vibrating with each emotion, that enables the poet to personify each passion, and the painter to sketch with a pencil of fire.

True taste is ever the work of the understanding employed in observing natural effects; and till women have more understanding, it is vain to expect them to possess domestic taste. Their lively senses will ever be at work to harden their hearts, and the emotions struck out of them will continue to be vivid and transitory, unless a proper education store their mind with knowledge.

It is the want of domestic taste, and not the acquirement of knowledge, that takes women out of their families, and tears the smiling babe from the breast that ought to afford it nourishment. Women have been allowed to remain in ignorance, and slavish dependence, many, very many years, and still we hear of nothing but their fondness of pleasure and sway, their preference of rakes and soldiers, their childish attachment to toys, and the vanity that makes them value accomplishments more than virtues.

History brings forward a fearful catalogue of the crimes which their cunning has produced, when the weak slaves have had sufficient address to over-reach their masters. In France, and in how many other countries, have men been the luxurious despots, and women the crafty ministers?—Does this prove that ignorance and dependence domesticate them? Is not their folly the by-word of the libertines, who relax in their society; and do not men of sense continually lament that an immoderate fondness for dress and dissipation carries the mother of a family for ever from home? Their hearts have not been debauched by knowledge, or their minds led astray by scientific pursuits; yet, they do not fulfil the peculiar duties which as women they are called upon by nature to fulfil. On the contrary, the state of warfare which subsists between the sexes, makes them employ those wiles, that often frustrate the more open designs of force.

When, therefore, I call women slaves, I mean in a political and civil sense; for, indirectly they obtain too much power, and are debased by their exertions to obtain illicit sway.

Let an enlightened nation[1] then try what effect reason would have to bring them back to nature, and their duty; and allowing them to share the advantages of education and government with man, see whether they will become better, as they grow wiser and become free. They cannot be injured by the experiment; for it is not in the power of man to render them more insignificant than they are at present.

To render this practicable, day schools, for particular ages, should be established by government, in which boys and girls might be educated together. The school for the younger children, from five to nine years of age, ought to be absolutely free and open to all classes.[2] A sufficient number of masters should also be chosen by a select committee, in each parish, to whom any complaint of negligence, &c. might be made, if signed by six of the children's parents.

1. "France" [Wollstonecraft's note].
2. "Treating this part of the subject, I have borrowed some hints from a very sensible pamphlet, written by the late bishop of Autun on Public Education" [Wollstonecraft's note]. The reference is to Talleyrand's *Rapport sur L' Instruction Publique* (Paris, 1791).

Ushers would then be unnecessary; for I believe experience will ever prove that this kind of subordinate authority is particularly injurious to the morals of youth. What, indeed, can tend to deprave the character more than outward submission and inward contempt? Yet how can boys be expected to treat an usher with respect, when the master seems to consider him in the light of a servant, and almost to countenance the ridicule which becomes the chief amusement of the boys during the play hours?

But nothing of this kind could occur in an elementary day-school, where boys and girls, the rich and poor, should meet together. And to prevent any of the distinctions of vanity, they should be dressed alike, and all obliged to submit to the same discipline, or leave the school. The school-room ought to be surrounded by a large piece of ground, in which the children might be usefully exercised, for at this age they should not be confined to any sedentary employment for more than an hour at a time. But these relaxations might all be rendered a part of elementary education, for many things improve and amuse the senses, when introduced as a kind of show, to the principles of which, dryly laid down, children would turn a deaf ear. For instance, botany, mechanics, and astronomy. Reading, writing, arithmetic, natural history, and some simple experiments in natural philosophy, might fill up the day; but these pursuits should never encroach on gymnastic plays in the open air. The elements of religion, history, the history of man, and politics, might also be taught by conversations, in the socratic form.

After the age of nine, girls and boys, intended for domestic employments, or mechanical trades, ought to be removed to other schools, and receive instruction, in some measure appropriated to the destination of each individual, the two sexes being still together in the morning; but in the afternoon, the girls should attend a school, where plain-work, mantua-making, millinery, &c. would be their employment.

The young people of superior abilities, or fortune, might now be taught, in another school, the dead and living languages, the elements of science, and continue the study of history and politics, on a more extensive scale, which would not exclude polite literature.

Girls and boys still together? I hear some readers ask: yes. And I should not fear any other consequence than that some early attachment might take place; which, whilst it had the best effect on the moral character of the young people, might not perfectly agree with the views of the parents, for it will be a long time, I fear, before the world will be so far enlightened that parents, only anxious to render their children virtuous, shall allow them to choose companions for life themselves.

Besides, this would be a sure way to promote early marriages, and from early marriages the most salutary physical and moral effects naturally flow. What a different character does a married citizen assume from the selfish coxcomb, who lives, but for himself, and who is often afraid to marry lest he should not be able to live in a certain style. Great emergencies excepted, which would rarely occur in a society of which equality was the basis, a man can only be prepared to discharge the duties of public life, by the habitual practice of those inferiour ones which form the man.

In this plan of education the constitution of boys would not be ruined by the early debaucheries, which now make men so selfish, or girls rendered weak and vain, by indolence, and frivolous pursuits. But, I presuppose, that such a degree of equality should be established between the sexes as would shut out gallantry and coquetry, yet allow friendship and love to temper the heart for the discharge of higher duties.

These would be schools of morality—and the happiness of man, allowed to flow from the pure springs of duty and affection, what advances might not the human mind make? Society can only be happy and free in proportion as it is virtuous; but the present distinctions, established in society, corrode all private, and blast all public virtue.

I have already inveighed against the custom of confining girls to their needle, and shutting them out from all political and civil employments; for by thus narrowing their minds they are rendered unfit to fulfil the peculiar duties which nature has assigned them.

Only employed about the little incidents of the day, they necessarily grow up cunning. My very soul has often sickened at observing the sly tricks practised by women to gain some foolish thing on which their silly hearts were set. Not allowed to dispose of money, or call any thing their own, they learn to turn the market penny; or, should a husband offend, by staying from home, or give rise to some emotions of jealousy—a new gown, or any pretty bawble, smooths Juno's angry brow. [3]

But these *littlenesses* would not degrade their character, if women were led to respect themselves, if political and moral subjects were opened to them; and, I will venture to affirm, that this is the only way to make them properly attentive to their domestic duties.—An active mind embraces the whole circle of its duties, and finds time enough for all. It is not, I assert, a bold attempt to emulate masculine virtues; it is not the enchantment of literary pursuits, or the steady investigation of scientific subjects, that leads women astray from duty. No, it is indolence and vanity—the love of pleasure and the love of sway, that will reign paramount in an empty

3. Juno, wife of Jupiter (or Zeus) is the prototypical demanding, nagging wife in mythology.

mind. I say empty emphatically, because the education which women now receive scarcely deserves the name. For the little knowledge that they are led to acquire, during the important years of youth, is merely relative to accomplishments; and accomplishments without a bottom, for unless the understanding be cultivated, superficial and monotonous is every grace. Like the charms of a made up face, they only strike the senses in a crowd; but at home, wanting mind, they want variety. The consequence is obvious; in gay scenes of dissipation we meet the artificial mind and face, for those who fly from solitude dread, next to solitude, the domestic circle; not having it in their power to amuse or interest, they feel their own insignificance, or find nothing to amuse or interest themselves.

Besides, what can be more indelicate than a girl's *coming out*[4] in the fashionable world? Which, in other words, is to bring to market a marriageable miss, whose person is taken from one public place to another, richly caparisoned. Yet, mixing in the giddy circle under restraint, these butterflies long to flutter at large, for the first affection of their souls is their own persons, to which their attention has been called with the most sedulous care whilst they were preparing for the period that decides their fate for life. Instead of pursuing this idle routine, sighing for tasteless shew, and heartless state, with what dignity would the youths of both sexes form attachments in the schools that I have cursorily pointed out; in which, as life advanced, dancing, music, and drawing, might be admitted as relaxations, for at these schools young people of fortune ought to remain, more or less, till they were of age. Those, who were designed for particular professions, might attend, three or four mornings in the week, the schools appropriated for their immediate instruction.

I only drop these observations at present, as hints; rather, indeed, as an outline of the plan I mean, than a digested one; but I must add, that I highly approve of one regulation mentioned in the pamphlet[5] already alluded to, that of making the children and youths independent of the masters respecting punishments. They should be tried by their peers, which would be an admirable method of fixing sound principles of justice in the mind, and might have the happiest effect on the temper, which is very early soured or irritated by tyranny, till it becomes peevishly cunning, or ferociously overbearing.

My imagination darts forward with benevolent fervour to greet these amiable and respectable groups, in spite of the sneering of cold hearts, who are at liberty to utter, with frigid self-importance,

4. "Coming out" meant in the eighteenth century what it does now: a young girl's debut into the social world.

5. "The Bishop of Autun's" [Wollstonecraft's note]. I.e., Talleyrand's *Rapport sur L' Instruction Publique*.

the damning epithet—romantic; the force of which I shall endeavour to blunt by repeating the words of an eloquent moralist.—'I
know not whether the allusions of a truly humane heart, whose zeal
renders every thing easy, be not preferable to that rough and repuls-
ing reason, which always finds in indifference for the public good,
the first obstacle to whatever would promote it.'

I know that libertines will also exclaim, that woman would be
unsexed by acquiring strength of body and mind, and that beauty,
soft bewitching beauty! would no longer adorn the daughters of
men. I am of a very different opinion, for I think that, on the contrary, we should then see dignified beauty, and true grace; to produce which, many powerful physical and moral causes would concur.—Not relaxed beauty, it is true, or the graces of helplessness;
but such as appears to make us respect the human body as a majestic pile fit to receive a noble inhabitant, in the relics of antiquity.

I do not forget the popular opinion that the Grecian statues were
not modelled after nature. I mean, not according to the proportions
of a particular man; but that beautiful limbs and features were
selected from various bodies to form an harmonious whole. This
might, in some degree, be true. The fine ideal picture of an exalted
imagination might be superiour to the materials which the statuary
found in nature, and thus it might with propriety be termed rather
the model of mankind than of a man. It was not, however, the
mechanical selection of limbs and features; but the ebullition of an
heated fancy that burst forth, and the fine senses and enlarged
understanding of the artist selected the solid matter, which he drew
into this glowing focus.

I observed that it was not mechanical, because a whole was produced—a model of that grand simplicity, of those concurring energies, which arrest our attention and command our reverence. For
only insipid lifeless beauty is produced by a servile copy of even
beautiful nature. Yet, independent of these observations, I believe
that the human form must have been far more beautiful than it is
at present, because extreme indolence, barbarous ligatures, and
many causes, which forcibly act on it, in our luxurious state of
society, did not retard its expansion, or render it deformed. Exercise
and cleanliness appear to be not only the surest means of preserving
health, but of promoting beauty, the physical causes only considered; yet, this is not sufficient, moral ones must concur, or beauty
will be merely of that rustic kind which blooms on the innocent,
wholesome, countenances of some country people, whose minds
have not been exercised. To render the person perfect, physical and
moral beauty ought to be attained at the same time; each lending
and receiving force by the combination. Judgment must reside on
the brow, affection and fancy beam in the eye, and humanity curve

the cheek, or vain is the sparkling of the finest eye or the elegantly turned finish of the fairest features: whilst in every motion that displays the active limbs and well-knit joints, grace and modesty should appear. But this fair assemblage is not to be brought together by chance; it is the reward of exertions calculated to support each other; for judgment can only be acquired by reflection, affection by the discharge of duties, and humanity by the exercise of compassion to every living creature.

Humanity to animals should be particularly inculcated as a part of national education, for it is not at present one of our national virtues. Tenderness for their humble dumb domestics, amongst the lower class, is oftener to be found in a savage than a civilized state. For civilization prevents that intercourse which creates affection in the rude hut, or mud hovel, and leads uncultivated minds who are only depraved by the refinements which prevail in the society, where they are trodden under foot by the rich, to domineer over them to revenge the insults that they are obliged to bear from their superiors.

This habitual cruelty is first caught at school, where it is one of the rare sports of the boys to torment the miserable brutes that fall in their way. The transition, as they grow up, from barbarity to brutes to domestic tyranny over wives, children, and servants, is very easy. Justice, or even benevolence, will not be a powerful spring of action unless it extend to the whole creation; nay, I believe that it may be delivered as an axiom, that those who can see pain, unmoved, will soon learn to inflict it.

The vulgar are swayed by present feelings, and the habits which they have accidentally acquired; but on partial feelings much dependence cannot be placed, though they be just; for, when they are not invigorated by reflection, custom weakens them, till they are scarcely perceptible. The sympathies of our nature are strengthened by pondering cogitations, and deadened by thoughtless use. Macbeth's heart smote him more for one murder, the first, than for a hundred subsequent ones, which were necessary to back it. But, when I used the epithet vulgar, I did not mean to confine my remark to the poor, for partial humanity, founded on present sensations, or whim, is quite as conspicuous, if not more so, amongst the rich.

The lady who sheds tears for the bird starved in a snare, and execrates the devils in the shape of men, who goad to madness the poor ox, or whip the patient ass, tottering under a burden above its strength, will, nevertheless, keep her coachman and horses whole hours waiting for her, when the sharp frost bites, or the rain beats against the well-closed windows which do not admit a breath of air to tell her how roughly the wind blows without. And she who takes her dogs to bed, and nurses them with a parade of sensibility, when sick, will suffer her babes to grow up crooked in a nursery. This illustration of my argument is drawn from a matter of fact. The woman whom I allude to was handsome, reckoned very handsome, by those who do not miss the mind when the face is plump and fair; but her understanding had not been led from female duties by literature, nor her innocence debauched by knowledge. No, she was quite feminine, according to the masculine acceptation of the word; and, so far from loving these spoiled brutes that filled the place which her children ought to have occupied, she only lisped out a pretty mixture of French and English nonsense, to please the men who flocked round her.[6] The wife, mother, and human creature, were all swallowed up by the factitious character which an improper education and the selfish vanity of beauty had produced.

I do not like to make a distinction without a difference, and I own that I have been as much disgusted by the fine lady who took her lap-dog to her bosom instead of her child; as by the ferocity of a man, who, beating his horse, declared, that he knew as well when he did wrong, as a Christian.

This brood of folly shews how mistaken they are who, if they allow women to leave their harams, do not cultivate their understandings, in order to plant virtues in their hearts. For had they sense, they might acquire that domestic taste which would lead them to love with reasonable subordination their whole family, from their husband to the house-dog; nor would they ever insult humanity in the person of the most menial servant by paying more attention to the comfort of a brute, than to that of a fellow-creature.

My observations on national education are obviously hints; but I principally wish to enforce the necessity of educating the sexes together to perfect both, and of making children sleep at home that they may learn to love home; yet to make private support, instead of smothering, public affections, they should be sent to school to mix with a number of equals, for only by the jostlings of equality can we form a just opinion of ourselves.

To render mankind more virtuous, and happier of course, both sexes must act from the same principle; but how can that be expected when only one is allowed to see the reasonableness of it? To render also the social compact truly equitable, and in order to spread those enlightening principles, which alone can meliorate the fate of man, women must be allowed to found their virtue on knowledge, which is scarcely possible unless they be educated by the same pursuits as men. For they are now made so inferiour by ignorance and low desires, as not to deserve to be ranked with them; or, by the serpentine wrigglings of cunning they mount the tree of knowledge, and only acquire sufficient to lead men astray.

6. A possible reference to Lady Kingsborough, Wollstonecraft's employer from 1786 to 1787.

It is plain from the history of all nations, that women cannot be confined to merely domestic pursuits, for they will not fulfil family duties, unless their minds take a wider range, and whilst they are kept in ignorance they become in the same proportion the slaves of pleasure as they are the slaves of man. Nor can they be shut out if great enterprises, though the narrowness of their minds often make them mar, what they are unable to comprehend.

The libertinism, and even the virtues of superiour men, will always give women, of some description, great power over them; and these weak women, under the influence of childish passions and selfish vanity, will throw a false light over the objects which the very men view with their eyes, who ought to enlighten their judgment. Men of fancy, and those sanguine characters who mostly hold the helm of human affairs, in general, relax in the society of women; and surely I need not cite to the most superficial reader of history the numerous examples of vice and oppression which the private intrigues of female favourites have produced; not to dwell on the mischief that naturally arises from the blundering interposition of well-meaning folly. For in the transactions of business it is much better to have to deal with a knave than a fool, because a knave adheres to some plan; and any plan of reason may be seen through much sooner than a sudden flight of folly. The power which vile and foolish women have had over wise men, who possessed sensibility, is notorious; I shall only mention one instance.

Who ever drew a more exalted female character than Rousseau?[7] though in the lump he constantly endeavoured to degrade the sex. And why was he thus anxious? Truly to justify to himself the affection which weakness and virtue had made him cherish for that fool Theresa. He could not raise her to the common level of her sex; and therefore he laboured to bring woman down to her's. He found her a convenient humble companion, and pride made him determine to find some superiour virtues in the being whom he chose to live with; but did not her conduct during his life, and after his death, clearly shew how grossly he was mistaken who called her a celestial innocent.[8] Nay, in the bitterness of his heart, he himself laments, that when his bodily infirmities made him no longer treat her like a woman, she ceased to have an affection for him.[9] And it was very natural that she should, for having so few sentiments in common, when the sexual tie was broken, what was to hold her? To hold her affection whose sensibility was confined to one sex, nay, to one

7. A reference to the heroine of Rousseau's novel, *Julie, ou La Nouvelle Héloïse.*
8. Rousseau says, "Le coeur de ma Thérèse était celui d'un ange" (Rousseau, *Oeuvres Complètes,* ed. Marcel Raymond et Bernard Gangnebin [Paris, 1959], I, 353.) Thérèse Le Vasseur was Rousseau's lifelong mistress; he never called her "innocent,"

though she had "la simplicité d'ésprit" (Ibid., p. 355).
9. Rousseau was plagued with a congenital defect of the urinary tract, a very painful malady which in later years must have affected his sexual performance.

man, it requires sense to turn sensibility into the broad channel of humanity; many women have not mind enough to have an affection for a woman, or a friendship for a man. But the sexual weakness that makes woman depend on man for a subsistence, produces a kind of cattish affection which leads a wife to purr about her husband as she would about any man who fed and caressed her.

Men are, however, often gratified by this kind of fondness, which is confined in a beastly manner to themselves; but should they ever become more virtuous, they will wish to converse at their fire-side with a friend, after they cease to play with a mistress.

Besides, understanding is necessary to give variety and interest to sensual enjoyments, for low, indeed, in the intellectual scale, is the mind that can continue to love when neither virtue nor sense give a human appearance to an animal appetite. But sense will always preponderate; and if women be not, in general, brought more on a level with men, some superiour woman, like the Greek courtezans,[1] will assemble the men of abilities around them, and draw from their families many citizens, who would have stayed at home had their wives had more sense, or the graces which result from the exercise of the understanding and fancy, the legitimate parents of taste. A woman of talents, if she be not absolutely ugly, will always obtain great power, raised by the weakness of her sex; and in proportion as men acquire virtue and delicacy, by the exertion of reason, they will look for both in women, but they can only acquire them in the same way that men do.

In France or Italy, have the women confined themselves to domestic life? though they have not hitherto had a political existence, yet, have they not illicitly had great sway? corrupting themselves and the men with whose passions they played. In short, in whatever light I view the subject, reason and experience convince me that the only method of leading women to fulfil their peculiar duties, is to free them from all restraint by allowing them to participate in the inherent rights of mankind.

Make them free, and they will quickly become wise and virtuous, as men become more so; for the improvement must be mutual, or the injustice which one half of the human race are obliged to submit to, retorting on their oppressors, the virtue of men will be worm-eaten by the insect whom he keeps under his feet.

Let men take their choice, man and woman were made for each other, though not to become one being; and if they will not improve women, they will deprave them!

I speak of the improvement and emancipation of the whole sex, for I know that the behaviour of a few women, who, by accident, or following a strong bent of nature, have acquired a portion of knowl-

1. The Greek *hetaerae* were educated and often brilliant courtesans who exerted political influence behind the scenes.

edge superiour to that of the rest of their sex, has often been over-bearing; but there have been instances of women who, attaining knowledge, have not discarded modesty, nor have they always pedantically appeared to despise the ignorance which they laboured to disperse in their own minds. The exclamations then which any advice respecting female learning, commonly produces, especially from pretty women, often arise from envy. When they chance to see that even the lustre of their eyes, and the flippant sportiveness of refined coquetry will not always secure them attention, during a whole evening, should a woman of a more cultivated understanding endeavour to give a rational turn to the conversation, the common source of consolation is, that such women seldom get husbands. What arts have I not seen silly women use to interrupt by *flirtation*, a very significant word to describe such a manoeuvre, a rational conversation which made the men forget that they were pretty women.

But, allowing what is very natural to man, that the possession of rare abilities is really calculated to excite over-weening pride, disgusting in both men and women—in what a state of inferiority must the female faculties have rusted when such a small portion of knowledge as those women attained, who have sneeringly been termed learned women, could be singular?—Sufficiently so to puff up the possessor, and excite envy in her contemporaries, and some of the other sex. Nay, has not a little rationality exposed many women to the severest censure? I advert to well known facts, for I have frequently heard women ridiculed, and every little weakness exposed, only because they adopted the advice of some medical men, and deviated from the beaten track in their mode of treating their infants.[2] I have actually heard this barbarous aversion to innovation carried still further, and a sensible woman stigmatized as an unnatural mother, who has thus been wisely solicitous to preserve the health of her children, when in the midst of her care she has lost one by some of the casualties of infancy, which no prudence can ward off. Her acquaintance have observed, that this was the consequence of new-fangled notions—the new-fangled notions of ease and cleanliness. And those who pretending to experience, though they have long adhered to prejudices that have, according to the opinion of the most sagacious physicians, thinned the human race, almost rejoiced at the disaster that gave a kind of sanction to prescription.

Indeed, if it were only on this account, the national education of women is of the utmost consequence, for what a number of human sacrifices are made to that moloch[3] prejudice! And in how many ways are children destroyed by the lasciviousness of man? The want

2. That is, in suckling their own children rather than giving them to peasant women to nurse.
3. Moloch was the Canaanite idol to whom children were supposedly sacrificed and therefore signifies any idolatrous object to which great sacrifice is paid.

of natural affection, in many women, who are drawn from their duty by the admiration of men, and the ignorance of others, render the infancy of man a much more perilous state than that of brutes; yet men are unwilling to place women in situations proper to enable them to acquire sufficient understanding to know how even to nurse their babes.

So forcibly does this truth strike me, that I would rest the whole tendency of my reasoning upon it, for whatever tends to incapacitate the maternal character, takes woman out of her sphere.

But it is vain to expect the present race of weak mothers either to take that reasonable care of a child's body, which is necessary to lay the foundation of a good constitution, supposing that it do not suffer for the sins of its fathers;[4] or, to manage its temper so judiciously that the child will not have, as it grows up, to throw off all that its mother, its first instructor, directly or indirectly taught; and unless the mind have uncommon vigour, womanish follies will stick to the character throughout life. The weakness of the mother will be visited on the children! And whilst women are educated to rely on their husbands for judgment, this must ever be the consequence, for there is no improving an understanding by halves, nor can any being act wisely from imitation, because in every circumstance of life there is a kind of individuality, which requires an exertion of judgment to modify general rules. The being who can think justly in one track, will soon extend its intellectual empire; and she who has sufficient judgment to manage her children, will not submit, right or wrong, to her husband, or patiently to the social laws which make a nonentity of a wife.

In public schools women, to guard against the errors of ignorance, should be taught the elements of anatomy and medicine, not only to enable them to take proper care of their own health, but to make them rational nurses of their infants, parents, and husbands; for the bills of mortality[5] are swelled by the blunders of self-willed old women, who give nostrums of their own without knowing any thing of the human frame. It is likewise proper only in a domestic view, to make women acquainted with the anatomy of the mind, by allowing the sexes to associate together in every pursuit; and by leading them to observe the progress of the human understanding in the improvement of the sciences and arts; never forgetting the science of morality, or the study of the political history of mankind.

A man has been termed a microcosm; and every family might also be called a state. States, it is true, have mostly been governed by arts that disgrace the character of man; and the want of a just constitution, and equal laws, have so perplexed the notions of the

---

4. Venereal disease can affect unborn children.
5. Weekly publications of deaths, and, later, births, in each parish of London and its environs.

worldly wise, that they more than question the reasonableness of contending for the rights of humanity. Thus morality, polluted in the national reservoir, sends off streams of vice to corrupt the constituent parts of the body politic; but should more noble, or rather, more just principles regulate the laws, which ought to be the government of society, and not those who execute them, duty might become the rule of private conduct.

Besides, by the exercise of their bodies and minds women would acquire that mental activity so necessary in the maternal character, united with the fortitude that distinguishes steadiness of conduct from the obstinate perverseness of weakness. For it is dangerous to advise the indolent to be steady, because they instantly become rigorous, and to save themselves trouble, punish with severity faults that the patient fortitude of reason might have prevented.

But fortitude presupposes strength of mind; and is strength of mind to be acquired by indolent acquiescence? by asking advice instead of exerting the judgment? by obeying through fear, instead of practising the forbearance, which we all stand in need of ourselves?—The conclusion which I wish to draw, is obvious; make women rational creatures, and free citizens, and they will quickly become good wives, and mothers; that is—if men do not neglect the duties of husbands and fathers.

Discussing the advantages which a public and private education combined, as I have sketched, might rationally be expected to produce, I have dwelt most on such as are particularly relative to the female world, because I think the female world oppressed; yet the gangrene, which the vices engendered by oppression have produced, is not confined to the morbid part, but pervades society at large: so that when I wish to see my sex become more like moral agents, my heart bounds with the anticipation of the general diffusion of that sublime contentment which only morality can diffuse.

Chap. XIII

Some Instances of the Folly Which the Ignorance of Women Generates; with Concluding Reflections on the Moral Improvement That a Revolution in Female Manners Might Naturally Be Expected to Produce

There are many follies, in some degree, peculiar to women: sins against reason of commission as well as of omission; but all flowing from ignorance or prejudice, I shall only point out such as appear to be particularly injurious to their moral character. And in animadverting on them, I wish especially to prove, that the weakness of mind and body, which men have endeavoured, impelled by various motives, to perpetuate, prevents their discharging the peculiar duty of their sex: for when weakness of body will not permit them to suckle their children, and weakness of mind makes them spoil their tempers—is woman in a natural state?

SECT. I

One glaring instance of the weakness which proceeds from ignorance, first claims attention, and calls for severe reproof.

In this metropolis a number of lurking leeches infamously gain a subsistence by practising on the credulity of women, pretending to cast nativities,[1] to use the technical phrase; and many females who, proud of their rank and fortune, look down on the vulgar with sovereign contempt, shew by this credulity, that the distinction is arbitrary, and that they have not sufficiently cultivated their minds to rise above vulgar prejudices. Women, because they have not been led to consider the knowledge of their duty as the one thing necessary to know, or, to live in the present moment by the discharge of it, are very anxious to peep into futurity, to learn what they have to expect to render life interesting, and to break the vacuum of ignorance.

I must be allowed to expostulate seriously with the ladies who follow these idle inventions; for ladies, mistresses of families, are not ashamed to drive in their own carriages to the door of the cunning man.[2] And if any of them should peruse this work, I entreat them to answer to their own hearts the following questions, not forgetting that they are in the presence of God.

Do you believe that there is but one God, and that he is powerful, wise, and good?

Do you believe that all things were created by him, and that all beings are dependent on him?

Do you rely on his wisdom, so conspicuous in his works, and in your own frame, and are you convinced that he has ordered all things which do not come under the cognizance of your senses, in the same perfect harmony, to fulfil his designs?

Do you acknowledge that the power of looking into futurity, and seeing things that are not, as if they were, is an attribute of the Creator? And should he, by an impression on the minds of his creatures, think fit to impart to them some event hid in the shades of time yet unborn, to whom would the secret be revealed by immediate inspiration? The opinion of ages will answer this question—to reverend old men, to people distinguished for eminent piety.

The oracles of old were thus delivered by priests dedicated to the

---

1. To predict the future by astrological calculations.
2. "I once lived in the neighbourhood of one of these men, a *handsome* man, and saw with surprise and indignation, women, whose appearance and attendance bespoke that rank in which females are supposed to receive a superiour education, flock to his door" [Wollstonecraft's note].

service of the God who was supposed to inspire them. The glare of worldly pomp which surrounded these impostors, and the respect paid to them by artful politicians, who knew how to avail themselves of this useful engine to bend the necks of the strong under the dominion of the cunning, spread a sacred mysterious veil of sanctity over their lies and abominations. Impressed by such solemn devotional parade, a Greek, or Roman lady might be excused, if she inquired of the oracle, when she was anxious to pry into futurity, or inquire about some dubious event: and her inquiries, however contrary to reason, could not be reckoned impious.—But, can the professors of Christianity ward off that imputation? Can a Christian suppose that the favourites of the most High, the highly favoured, would be obliged to lurk in disguise, and practise the most dishonest tricks to cheat silly women out of the money—which the poor cry for in vain?

Say not that such questions are an insult to common sense—for it is your own conduct, O ye foolish women! which throws an odium on your sex! And these reflections should make you shudder at your thoughtlessness, and irrational devotion.—For I do not suppose that all of you laid aside your religion, such as it is, when you entered those mysterious dwellings. Yet, as I have throughout supposed myself talking to ignorant women, for ignorant ye are in the most emphatical sense of the word, it would be absurd to reason with you on the egregious folly of desiring to know what the Supreme Wisdom has concealed.

Probably you would not understand me, were I to attempt to shew you that it would be absolutely inconsistent with the grand purpose of life, that of rendering human creatures wise and virtuous: and that, were it sanctioned by God, it would disturb the order established in creation; and if it be not sanctioned by God, do you expect to hear truth? Can events be foretold, events which have not yet assumed a body to become subject to mortal inspection, can they be foreseen by a vicious worldling, who pampers his appetites by preying on the foolish ones?

Perhaps, however, you devoutly believe in the devil, and imagine, to shift the question, that he may assist his votaries; but, if really respecting the power of such a being, an enemy to goodness and to God, can you go to church after having been under such an obligation to him?

From these delusions to those still more fashionable deceptions, practised by the whole tribe of magnetisers,[3] the transition is very natural. With respect to them, it is equally proper to ask women a few questions.

Do you know any thing of the construction of the human frame?

3. Mesmerists or hypnotists who attempt to treat bodily or spiritual infirmity.

If not, it is proper that you should be told what every child ought to know, that when its admirable œconomy has been disturbed by intemperance or indolence, I speak not of violent disorders, but of chronical diseases, it must be brought into a healthy state again, by slow degrees, and if the functions of life have not been materially injured, regimen, another word for temperance, air, exercise, and a few medicines, prescribed by persons who have studied the human body, are the only human means, yet discovered, of recovering that inestimable blessing health, that will bear investigation.

Do you then believe that these magnetisers, who, by hocus pocus tricks, pretend to work a miracle, are delegated by God, or assisted by the solver of all these kind of difficulties—the devil?

Do they, when they put to flight, as it is said, disorders that have baffled the powers of medicine, work in conformity to the light of reason? or, do they effect these wonderful cures by supernatural aid?

By a communication, an adept may answer, with the world of spirits. A noble privilege, it must be allowed. Some of the ancients mention familiar daemons, who guarded them from danger by kindly intimating, we cannot guess in what manner, when any danger was nigh; or, pointed out what they ought to undertake. Yet the men who laid claim to this privilege, out of the order of nature, insisted that it was the reward, or consequence, of superiour temperance and piety. But the present workers of wonders are not raised above their fellows by superiour temperance or sanctity. They do not cure for the love of God, but money. These are the priests of quackery, though it is true they have not the convenient expedient of selling masses for souls in purgatory,[4] or churches where they can display crutches, and models of limbs made sound by a touch or a word.

I am not conversant with the technical terms, or initiated into the arcana, therefore, I may speak improperly; but it is clear that men who will not conform to the law of reason, and earn a subsistence in an honest way, by degrees, are very fortunate in becoming acquainted with such obliging spirits. We cannot, indeed, give them credit for either great sagacity or goodness, else they would have chosen more noble instruments, when they wished to shew themselves the benevolent friends of man.

It is, however, little short of blasphemy to pretend to such powers!

From the whole tenour of the dispensations of Providence, it appears evident to sober reason, that certain vices produce certain effects; and can any one so grossly insult the wisdom of God, as to

---

4. In the Roman Catholic church one could purchase a Mass to be said to release a deceased person's soul from purgatory.

suppose that a miracle will be allowed to disturb his general laws, to restore to health the intemperate and vicious, merely to enable them to pursue the same course with impunity? Be whole, and sin no more, said Jesus.[5] And, are greater miracles to be performed by those who do not follow his footsteps, who healed the body to reach the mind?

The mentioning of the name of Christ, after such vile impostors, may displease some of my readers—I respect their warmth; but let them not forget that the followers of these delusions bear his name, and profess to be the disciples of him, who said, by their works we should know who were the children of God or the servants of sin. I allow that it is easier to touch the body of a saint, or to be magnetised, than to restrain our appetites or govern our passions; but health of body or mind can only be recovered by these means, or we make the Supreme Judge partial and revengeful.

Is he a man that he should change, or punish out of resentment? He—the common father, wounds but to heal, says reason, and our irregularities producing certain consequences, we are forcibly shewn the nature of vice; that thus learning to know good from evil, by experience, we may hate one and love the other, in proportion to the wisdom which we attain. The poison contains the antidote; and we either reform our evil habits and cease to sin against our own bodies, to use the forcible language of scripture, or a premature death, the punishment of sin, snaps the thread of life.

Here an awful stop is put to our inquiries.—But, why should I conceal my sentiments? Considering the attributes of God, I believe that whatever punishment may follow, will tend, like the anguish of disease, to shew the malignity of vice, for the purpose of reformation. Positive punishment appears so contrary to the nature of God, discoverable in all his works, and in our own reason, that I could sooner believe that the Deity paid no attention to the conduct of men, than that he punished without the benevolent design of reforming.

To suppose only that an all-wise and powerful Being, as good as he is great, should create a being foreseeing, that after fifty or sixty years of feverish existence, it would be plunged into never ending woe—is blasphemy. On what will the worm feed that is never to die? On folly, on ignorance, say ye—I should blush indignantly at drawing the natural conclusion could I insert it, and wish to withdraw myself from the wing of my God! On such a supposition, I speak with reverence, he would be a consuming fire.[6] We should wish, though vainly, to fly from his presence when fear absorbed love, and darkness involved all his counsels!

5. John 5:14: "Behold, thou art made whole: sin no more, lest a worse thing come unto thee."

6. Isaiah 66:24: "For their worm shall not die, neither shall their fire be quenched."

I know that many devout people boast of submitting to the Will of God blindly, as to an arbitrary sceptre or rod, on the same principle as the Indians worship the devil. In other words, like people in the common concerns of life, they do homage to power, and cringe under the foot that can crush them. Rational religion, on the contrary, is a submission to the will of a being so perfectly wise, that all he wills must be directed by the proper motive—must be reasonable.

And, if thus we respect God, can we give credit to the mysterious insinuations, which insult his laws? can we believe, though it should stare us in the face, that he would work a miracle to authorize confusion by sanctioning an error? Yet we must either allow these impious conclusions, or treat with contempt every promise to restore health to a diseased body by supernatural means, or to foretell the incidents that can only be foreseen by God.

SECT. II

Another instance of that feminine weakness of character, often produced by a confined education, is a romantic twist of the mind, which has been very properly termed *sentimental*.

Women subjected by ignorance to their sensations, and only taught to look for happiness in love, refine on sensual feelings, and adopt metaphysical notions respecting that passion, which lead them shamefully to neglect the duties of life, and frequently in the midst of these sublime refinements they plump into actual vice.

These are the women who are amused by the reveries of the stupid novelists, who, knowing little of human nature, work up stale tales, and describe meretricious scenes, all retailed in a sentimental jargon, which equally tend to corrupt the taste, and draw the heart aside from its daily duties. I do not mention the understanding, because never having been exercised, its slumbering energies rest inactive, like the lurking particles of fire which are supposed universally to pervade matter.

Females, in fact, denied all political privileges, and not allowed, as married women, excepting in criminal cases, a civil existence, have their attention naturally drawn from the interest of the whole community to that of the minute parts, though the private duty of any member of society must be very imperfectly performed when not connected with the general good. The mighty business of female life is to please, and restrained from entering into more important concerns by political and civil oppression, sentiments become events, and reflection deepens what it should, and would have effaced, if the understanding had been allowed to take a wider range.

But, confined to trifling employments, they naturally imbibe opinions which the only kind of reading calculated to interest an innocent frivolous mind, inspires. Unable to grasp any thing great, is it surprising that they find the reading of history a very dry task, and disquisitions addressed to the understanding intolerably tedious, and almost unintelligible? Thus are they necessarily dependent on the novelist for amusement. Yet, when I exclaim against novels, I mean when contrasted with those works which exercise the understanding and regulate the imagination.—For any kind of reading I think better than leaving a blank still a blank, because the mind must receive a degree of enlargement and obtain a little strength by a slight exertion of its thinking powers; besides, even the productions that are only addressed to the imagination, raise the reader a little above the gross gratification of appetites, to which the mind has not given a shade of delicacy.

This observation is the result of experience; for I have known several notable women, and one in particular, who was a very good woman—as good as such a narrow mind would allow her to be, who took care that her daughters (three in number) should never see a novel. As she was a woman of fortune and fashion, they had various masters to attend them, and a sort of menial governess to watch their footsteps. From their masters they learned how tables, chairs, &c. were called in French and Italian; but as the few books thrown in their way were far above their capacities, or devotional, they neither acquired ideas nor sentiments, and passed their time, when not compelled to repeat *words*, in dressing, quarrelling with each other, or conversing with their maids by stealth, till they were brought into company as marriageable.

Their mother, a widow, was busy in the mean time in keeping up her connections, as she termed a numerous acquaintance, lest her girls should want a proper introduction into the great world. And these young ladies, with minds vulgar in every sense of the word, and spoiled tempers, entered life puffed up with notions of their own consequence, and looking down with contempt on those who could not vie with them in dress and parade.

With respect to love, nature, or their nurses, had taken care to teach them the physical meaning of the word; and, as they had few topics of conversation, and fewer refinements of sentiment, they expressed their gross wishes not in very delicate phrases, when they spoke freely, talking of matrimony.

Could these girls have been injured by the perusal of novels? I almost forgot a shade in the character of one of them; she affected a simplicity bordering on folly, and with a simper would utter the most immodest remarks and questions, the full meaning of which she had learned whilst secluded from the world, and afraid to speak in her mother's presence, who governed with a high hand: they were all educated, as she prided herself, in a most exemplary manner; and read their chapters and psalms before breakfast, never touching a silly novel.

This is only one instance; but I recollect many other women who, not led by degrees to proper studies, and not permitted to choose for themselves, have indeed been overgrown children; or have obtained, by mixing in the world, a little of what is termed common sense: that is, a distinct manner of seeing common occurrences, as they stand detached: but what deserves the name of intellect, the power of gaining general or abstract ideas, or even intermediate ones, was out of the question. Their minds were quiescent, and when they were not roused by sensible objects and employments of that kind, they were low-spirited, would cry, or go to sleep.

When, therefore, I advise my sex not to read such flimsy works, it is to induce them to read something superiour; for I coincide in opinion with a sagacious man, who, having a daughter and niece under his care, pursued a very different plan with each.

The niece, who had considerable abilities, had, before she was left to his guardianship, been indulged in desultory reading. Her he endeavoured to lead, and did lead to history and moral essays; but his daughter, whom a fond weak mother had indulged, and who consequently was averse to every thing like application, he allowed to read novels: and used to justify his conduct by saying, that if she ever attained a relish for reading them, he should have some foundation to work upon; and that erroneous opinions were better than none at all.

In fact the female mind has been so totally neglected, that knowledge was only to be acquired from this muddy source, till from reading novels some women of superiour talents learned to despise them.

The best method, I believe, that can be adopted to correct a fondness for novels is to ridicule them: not indiscriminately, for then it would have little effect; but, if a judicious person, with some turn for humour, would read several to a young girl, and point out both by tones, and apt comparisons with pathetic incidents and heroic characters in history, how foolishly and ridiculously they caricatured human nature, just opinions might be substituted instead of romantic sentiments.

In one respect, however, the majority of both sexes resemble, and equally shew a want of taste and modesty. Ignorant women, forced to be chaste to preserve their reputation, allow their imagination to revel in the unnatural and meretricious scenes sketched by the novel writers of the day, slighting as insipid the sober dignity and matron graces of history,[7] whilst men carry the same vitiated taste into life, and fly for amusement to the wanton, from the unsophisticated charms of virtue, and the grave respectability of sense.

Besides, the reading of novels makes women, and particularly ladies of fashion, very fond of using strong expressions and superlatives in conversation; and, though the dissipated artificial life which they lead prevents their cherishing any strong legitimate passion, the language of passion in affected tones slips for ever from their glib tongues, and every trifle produces those phosphoric bursts which only mimick in the dark the flame of passion.

SECT. III

Ignorance and the mistaken cunning that nature sharpens in weak heads as a principle of self-preservation, render women very fond of dress, and produce all the vanity which such a fondness may naturally be expected to generate, to the exclusion of emulation and magnanimity.

I agree with Rousseau that the physical part of the art of pleasing consists in ornaments, and for that very reason I should guard girls against the contagious fondness for dress so common to weak women, that they may not rest in the physical part. Yet, weak are the women who imagine that they can long please without the aid of the mind, or, in other words, without the moral art of pleasing. But the moral art, if it be not a profanation to use the word art, when alluding to the grace which is an effect of virtue, and not the motive of action, is never to be found with ignorance; the sportiveness of innocence, so pleasing to refined libertines of both sexes, is widely different in its essence from this superiour gracefulness.

A strong inclination for external ornaments ever appears in barbarous states, only the men not the women adorn themselves; for where women are allowed to be so far on a level with men, society has advanced, at least, one step in civilization.

The attention to dress, therefore, which has been thought a sexual propensity, I think natural to mankind. But I ought to express myself with more precision. When the mind is not sufficiently opened to take pleasure in reflection, the body will be adorned with sedulous care; and ambition will appear in tattooing or painting it.

So far is this first inclination carried, that even the hellish yoke of slavery cannot stifle the savage desire of admiration which the black heroes inherit from both their parents, for all the hardly earned sav-

7. "I am not now alluding to that superiority of mind which leads to the creation of ideal beauty, when he, surveyed with a penetrating eye, appears a tragicomedy, in which little can be seen to satisfy the heart without the help of fancy" [Wollstonecraft's note].

ings of a slave are commonly expended in a little tawdry finery. And I have seldom known a good male or female servant that was not particularly fond of dress. Their clothes were their riches; and, I argue from analogy, that the fondness for dress, so extravagant in females, arises from the same cause—want of cultivation of mind. When men meet they converse about business, politics, or literature; but, says Swift, 'how naturally do women apply their hands to each others lappets and ruffles.'[8] And very natural is it—for they have not any business to interest them, have not a taste for literature, and they find politics dry, because they have not acquired a love for mankind by turning their thoughts to the grand pursuits that exalt the human race, and promote general happiness.

Besides, various are the paths to power and fame which by accident or choice men pursue, and though they jostle against each other, for men of the same profession are seldom friends, yet there is a much greater number of their fellow-creatures with whom they never clash. But women are very differently situated with respect to each other—for they are all rivals.

Before marriage it is their business to please men; and after, with a few exceptions, they follow the same scent with all the persevering pertinacity of instinct. Even virtuous women never forget their sex in company, for they are for ever trying to make themselves *agreeable*. A female beauty, and a male wit, appear to be equally anxious to draw the attention of the company to themselves; and the animosity of contemporary wits is proverbial.

Is it then surprising that when the sole ambition of woman centres in beauty, and interest gives vanity additional force, perpetual rivalships should ensue? They are all running the same race, and would rise above the virtue of mortals, if they did not view each other with a suspicious and even envious eye.

An immoderate fondness for dress, for pleasure, and for sway, are the passions of savages; the passions that occupy those uncivilized beings who have not yet extended the dominion of the mind, or even learned to think with the energy necessary to concatenate that abstract train of thought which produces principles. And that women from their education and the present state of civilized life, are in the same condition, cannot, I think, be controverted. To laugh at them then, or satirize the follies of a being who is never to be allowed to act freely from the light of her own reason, is as absurd as cruel; for, that they who are taught blindly to obey authority, will endeavour cunningly to elude it, is most natural and certain.

8. Jonathan Swift, "A Letter to a Young Lady on Her Marriage," written in 1727 (*Satires and Personal Writings by Jonathan Swift*, ed. William Alfred Eddy [New York, 1932], p. 67).

Yet let it be proved that they ought to obey man implicitly, and I shall immediately agree that it is woman's duty to cultivate a fondness for dress, in order to please, and a propensity to cunning for her own preservation.

The virtues, however, which are supported by ignorance must ever be wavering—the house built on sand could not endure a storm.[9] It is almost unnecessary to draw the inference.—If women are to be made virtuous by authority, which is a contradiction in terms, let them be immured in seraglios and watched with a jealous eye.—Fear not that the iron will enter into their souls—for the souls that can bear such treatment are made of yielding materials, just animated enough to give life to the body.

> 'Matter too soft a lasting mark to bear,
> 'And best distinguish'd by black, brown, or fair.'[1]

The most cruel wounds will of course soon heal, and they may still people the world, and dress to please man—all the purposes which certain celebrated writers have allowed that they were created to fulfil.

SECT. IV

Women are supposed to possess more sensibility, and even humanity, than men, and their strong attachments and instantaneous emotions of compassion are given as proofs; but the clinging affection of ignorance has seldom any thing noble in it, and may mostly be resolved into selfishness, as well as the affection of children and brutes. I have known many weak women whose sensibility was entirely engrossed by their husbands; and as for their humanity, it was very faint indeed, or rather it was only a transient emotion of compassion. Humanity does not consist 'in a squeamish ear,' says an eminent orator. 'It belongs to the mind as well as the nerves.'

But this kind of exclusive affection, though it degrades the individual, should not be brought forward as a proof of the inferiority of the sex, because it is the natural consequence of confined views: for even women of superior sense, having their attention turned to little employments, and private plans, rarely rise to heroism, unless when spurred on by love! and love, as an heroic passion, like genius, appears but once in an age. I therefore agree with the moralist who asserts, 'that women have seldom so much generosity as men;'[2] and that their narrow affections, to which justice and humanity are often sacrificed, render the sex apparently inferior, especially, as

---

9. Matthew 7:26–27: "A foolish man, which built his house upon the sand: And the rain descended, and the floods came, and the winds blew, and beat upon that house; and it fell."

1. Pope, Moral Essays II.3–4.

2. Adam Smith, Theory of Moral Sentiments, p. 274: "Humanity is the virtue of a woman, generosity of a man. The fair sex, who have commonly much more tenderness than ours, have seldom so much generosity."

they are commonly inspired by men; but I contend that the heart would expand as the understanding gained strength, if women were not depressed from their cradles.

I know that a little sensibility, and great weakness, will produce a strong sexual attachment, and that reason must cement friendship; consequently, I allow that more friendship is to be found in the male than the female world, and that men have a higher sense of justice. The exclusive affections of women seem indeed to resemble Cato's most unjust love for his country.[3] He wished to crush Carthage, not to save Rome, but to promote its vain-glory; and, in general, it is to similar principles that humanity is sacrificed, for genuine duties support each other.

Besides, how can women be just or generous, when they are the slaves of injustice?

SECT. V

As the rearing of children, that is, the laying a foundation of sound health both of body and mind in the rising generation, has justly been insisted on as the peculiar destination of woman, the ignorance that incapacitates them must be contrary to the order of things. And I contend that their minds can take in much more, and ought to do so, or they will never become sensible mothers. Many men attend to the breeding of horses, and overlook the management of the stable, who would, strange want of sense and feeling! think themselves degraded by paying any attention to the nursery; yet, how many children are absolutely murdered by the ignorance of women! But when they escape, and are destroyed neither by unnatural negligence nor blind fondness, how few are managed properly with respect to the infant mind! So that to break the spirit, allowed to become vicious at home, a child is sent to school; and the methods taken there, which must be taken to keep a number of children in order, scatter the seeds of almost every vice in the soil thus forcibly torn up.

I have sometimes compared the struggles of these poor children, who ought never to have felt restraint, nor would, had they been always held in with an even hand, to the despairing plunges of a spirited filly, which I have seen breaking on a strand: its feet sinking deeper and deeper in the sand every time it endeavoured to throw its rider, till at last it sullenly submitted.

I have always found horses, animals I am attached to, very tractable when treated with humanity and steadiness, so that I doubt whether the violent methods taken to break them, do not essen-

3. Marcus Porcius Cato (234–149 B.C), once he learned of the civilization of Carthage, felt it must be razed if Rome were to survive. His unceasing message was "Delenda est Carthago"—"Carthage must be destroyed."

tially injure them; I am, however, certain that a child should never be thus forcibly tamed after it has injudiciously been allowed to run wild; for every violation of justice and reason, in the treatment of children, weakens their reason. And, so early do they catch a character, that the base of the moral character, experience leads me to infer, is fixed before their seventh year, the period during which women are allowed the sole management of children. Afterwards it too often happens that half the business of education is to correct, and very imperfectly is it done, if done hastily, the faults, which they would never have acquired if their mothers had had more understanding.

One striking instance of the folly of women must not be omitted. —The manner in which they treat servants in the presence of children, permitting them to suppose that they ought to wait on them, and bear their humours. A child should always be made to receive assistance from a man or woman as a favour; and, as the first lesson of independence, they should practically be taught, by the example of their mother, not to require that personal attendance, which it is an insult to humanity to require, when in health; and instead of being led to assume airs of consequence, a sense of their own weakness should first make them feel the natural equality of man. Yet, how frequently have I indignantly heard servants imperiously called to put children to bed, and sent away again and again, because master or miss hung about mamma, to stay a little longer. Thus made slavishly to attend the little idol, all those most disgusting humours were exhibited which characterize a spoiled child.

In short, speaking of the majority of mothers, they leave their children entirely to the care of servants; or, because they are their children, treat them as if they were little demi-gods, though I have always observed, that the women who thus idolize their children, seldom shew common humanity to servants, or feel the least tenderness for any children but their own.

It is, however, these exclusive affections, and an individual manner of seeing things, produced by ignorance, which keep women for ever at a stand, with respect to improvement, and make many of them dedicate their lives to their children only to weaken their bodies and spoil their tempers, frustrating also any plan of education that a more rational father may adopt; for unless a mother concur, the father who restrains will ever be considered as a tyrant.

But, fulfilling the duties of a mother, a woman with a sound constitution, may still keep her person scrupulously neat, and assist to maintain her family, if necessary, or by reading and conversations with both sexes, indiscriminately, improve her mind. For nature has so wisely ordered things, that did women suckle their children, they would preserve their own health, and there would be such an interval between the birth of each child, that we should seldom see a houseful of babes.[4] And did they pursue a plan of conduct, and not waste their time in following the fashionable vagaries of dress, the management of their household and children need not shut them out from literature, or prevent their attaching themselves to a science, with that steady eye which strengthens the mind, or practising one of the fine arts that cultivate the taste.

But, visiting to display finery, card-playing, and balls, not to mention the idle bustle of morning trifling, draw women from their duty to render them insignificant, to render them pleasing, according to the present acceptation of the word, to every man, but their husband. For a round of pleasures in which the affections are not exercised, cannot be said to improve the understanding, though it be erroneously called seeing the world; yet the heart is rendered cold and averse to duty, by such a senseless intercourse, which becomes necessary from habit even when it has ceased to amuse.

But, we shall not see women affectionate till more equality be established in society, till ranks are confounded and women freed, neither shall we see that dignified domestic happiness, the simple grandeur of which cannot be relished by ignorant or vitiated minds; nor will the important task of education ever be properly begun till the person of a woman is no longer preferred to her mind. For it would be as wise to expect corn from tares, or figs from thistles, as that a foolish ignorant woman should be a good mother.

SECT. VI

It is not necessary to inform the sagacious reader, now I enter on my concluding reflections, that the discussion of this subject merely consists in opening a few simple principles, and clearing away the rubbish which obscured them. But, as all readers are not sagacious, I must be allowed to add some explanatory remarks to bring the subject home to reason—to that sluggish reason, which supinely takes opinions on trust, and obstinately supports them to spare itself the labour of thinking.

Moralists have unanimously agreed, that unless virtue be nursed by liberty, it will never attain due strength—and what they say of man I extend to mankind, insisting that in all cases morals must be fixed on immutable principles; and, that the being cannot be termed rational or virtuous, who obeys any authority, but that of reason.

To render women truly useful members of society, I argue that they should be led, by having their understandings cultivated on a

4. Although it is not a very reliable modern form of birth control, nursing a baby can keep a mother from conceiving another. The historian Dorothy McLaren has investigated the relation between fertility and lactation and concludes that women who nursed their own babies produced fewer and more survived. See Dorothy McLaren, "Marital Fertility and Lactation, 1570–1720," in *Women in English Society 1500–1800*, ed. Mary Prior (New York: Methuen, 1985), pp. 22–53.

large scale, to acquire a rational affection for their country, founded on knowledge, because it is obvious that we are little interested about what we do not understand. And to render this general knowledge of due importance, I have endeavoured to shew that private duties are never properly fulfilled unless the understanding enlarges the heart; and that public virtue is only an aggregate of private. But, the distinctions established in society undermine both, by beating out the solid gold of virtue, till it becomes only the tinsel-covering of vice; for whilst wealth renders a man more respectable than virtue, wealth will be sought before virtue; and, whilst women's persons are caressed, when a childish simper shews an absence of mind—the mind will lie fallow. Yet, true voluptuousness must proceed from the mind—for what can equal the sensations produced by mutual affection, supported by mutual respect? What are the cold, or feverish caresses of appetite, but sin embracing death, compared with the modest overflowings of a pure heart and exalted imagination? Yes, let me tell the libertine of fancy when he despises understanding in woman—that the mind, which he disregards, gives life to the enthusiastic affection from which rapture, short-lived as it is, alone can flow! And, that, without virtue, a sexual attachment must expire, like a tallow candle in the socket, creating intolerable disgust. To prove this, I need only observe, that men who have wasted great part of their lives with women, and with whom they have sought for pleasure with eager thirst, entertain the meanest opinion of the sex.—Virtue, true refiner of joy!—if foolish men were to fright thee from earth, in order to give loose to all their appetites without a check—some sensual wight of taste would scale the heavens to invite thee back, to give a zest to pleasure!

That women at present are by ignorance rendered foolish or vicious, is, I think, not to be disputed; and, that the most salutary effects tending to improve mankind might be expected from a REVOLUTION in female manners, appears, at least, with a face of probability, to rise out of the observation. For as marriage has been termed the parent of those endearing charities which draw man from the brutal herd, the corrupting intercourse that wealth, idleness, and folly, produce between the sexes, is more universally injurious to morality than all the other vices of mankind collectively considered. To adulterous lust the most sacred duties are sacrificed, because before marriage, men, by a promiscuous intimacy with women, learned to consider love as a selfish gratification—learned to separate it not only from esteem, but from the affection merely built on habit, which mixes a little humanity with it. Justice and friendship are also set at defiance, and that purity of taste is vitiated which would naturally lead a man to relish an artless display of affection rather than affected airs. But that noble simplicity of affection, which dares to appear unadorned, has few attractions for the libertine, though it be the charm, which by cementing the matrimonial tie, secures to the pledges of a warmer passion the necessary parental attention; for children will never be properly educated till friendship subsists between parents. Virtue flies from a house divided against itself—and a whole legion of devils take up their residence there.

The affection of husbands and wives cannot be pure when they have so few sentiments in common, and when so little confidence is established at home, as must be the case when their pursuits are so different. That intimacy from which tenderness should flow, will not, cannot subsist between the vicious.

Contending, therefore, that the sexual distinction which men have so warmly insisted upon, is arbitrary, I have dwelt on an observation, that several sensible men, with whom I have conversed on the subject, allowed to be well founded; and it is simply this, that the little chastity to be found amongst men, and consequent disregard of modesty, tend to degrade both sexes; and further, that the modesty of women, characterized as such, will often be only the artful veil of wantonness instead of being the natural reflection of purity, till modesty be universally respected.

From the tyranny of man, I firmly believe, the greater number of female follies proceed; and the cunning, which I allow makes at present a part of their character, I likewise have repeatedly endeavoured to prove, is produced by oppression.

Were not dissenters,[5] for instance, a class of people, with strict truth, characterized as cunning? And may I not lay some stress on this fact to prove, that when any power but reason curbs the free spirit of man, dissimulation is practised, and the various shifts of art are naturally called forth? Great attention to decorum, which was carried to a degree of scrupulosity, and all that puerile bustle about trifles and consequential solemnity, which Butler's caricature of a dissenter, brings before the imagination, shaped their persons as well as their minds in the mould of prim littleness.[6] I speak collectively, for I know how many ornaments to human nature have been enrolled amongst sectaries; yet, I assert, that the same narrow prejudice for their sect, which women have for their families, prevailed in the dissenting part of the community, however worthy in other respects; and also that the same timid prudence, or headstrong efforts, often disgraced the exertions of both. Oppression thus

---

5. Those who separated themselves from the Established Church in England.
6. In Samuel Butler's *Hudibras* the hero, Hudibras, is the pompous, pseudo-intellectual Puritan knight who harangues and misadventures with his squire Ralpho in a travesty of heroic themes. This may also refer to Butler's "A Hypocritical Nonconformist," one of his nearly two hundred characters (or short depictions of human types).

formed many of the features of their character perfectly to coincide with that of the oppressed half of mankind; or is it not notorious that dissenters were, like women, fond of deliberating together, and asking advice of each other, till by a complication of little contrivances, some little end was brought about? A similar attention to preserve their reputation was conspicuous in the dissenting and female world, and was produced by a similar cause.

Asserting the rights which women in common with men ought to contend for, I have not attempted to extenuate their faults; but to prove them to be the natural consequence of their education and station in society. If so, it is reasonable to suppose that they will change their character, and correct their vices and follies, when they are allowed to be free in a physical, moral, and civil sense.[7]

Let woman share the rights and she will emulate the virtues of man; for she must grow more perfect when emancipated, or justify the authority that chains such a weak being to her duty.—If the latter, it will be expedient to open a fresh trade with Russia for whips; a present which a father should always make to his son-in-law on his wedding day, that a husband may keep his whole family in order by the same means; and without any violation of justice reign, wielding this sceptre, sole master of his house, because he is the only being in it who has reason:—the divine, indefeasible earthly sovereignty breathed into man by the Master of the universe. Allowing this position, women have not any inherent rights to claim; and, by the same rule, their duties vanish, for rights and duties are inseparable.

Be just then, O ye men of understanding! and mark not more severely what women do amiss, than the vicious tricks of the horse or the ass for whom ye provide provender—and allow her the privileges of ignorance, to whom ye deny the rights of reason, or ye will be worse than Egyptian task-masters, expecting virtue where nature has not given understanding!

7. "I had further enlarged on the advantages which might reasonably be expected to result from an improvement in female manners, towards the general reformation of society; but it appeared to me that such reflections would more properly close the last volume" [Wollstonecraft's note].

Backgrounds

JOHN LOCKE

From Some Thoughts Concerning Education†

[*Clothes*]

One thing the Mention of the Girls brings into my Mind, which must not be forgot; and that is, that your Son's *Cloths* be *never* made *strait*, especially about the Breast. Let Nature have scope to fashion the Body as she thinks best; she works of her self a great deal better, and exacter, than we can direct her: And if Women were themselves to frame the Bodies of their Children in their Wombs, as they often endeavour to mend their Shapes when they are out, we should as certainly have no perfect children born, as we have few well-shaped that are *strait-laced*[1] or much tamper'd with. This Consideration should, me-thinks, keep busie People (I will not say ignorant Nurses and Bodice-makers) from medling in a Matter they understand not; and they should be afraid to put Nature out of her Way in fashioning the Parts, when they know now how the least and meanest is made, and yet I have seen so many Instances of Children receiving great harm from *strait-lacing*, that I cannot but conclude, there are other Creatures as well as Monkeys, who little wiser than they destroy their young Ones by senseless fondness, and too much embracing.

Narrow Breasts, short and stinking Breath, ill Lungs, and Crookedness, are the Natural and almost constant Effects of *hard Bodice*, and *Cloths that pinch*. That way of making slender Wastes and fine Shapes, serves but the more effectually to spoil them. Nor can there indeed but be disproportion in the Parts, when the nourishment prepared in the several Offices of the Body, cannot be distributed as Nature designs; and therefore what wonder is it, if it being laid where it can on some part not so *braced*, it often makes a Shoulder or a Hip higher or bigger than its just proportion. 'Tis generally known, that the women of *China*

† John Locke (1632–1704) received a medical degree from Oxford and in 1666 became the physician for Anthony Ashley Cooper, later Earl of Shaftesbury; he was also given direction over the education of the fifteen-year-old son of the family. Locke is best known for his philosophical work, *The Second Treatise of Civil Government*, an inspiration to the Founding Fathers and the work from which Thomas Jefferson took the phrase "all men are created equal." *Some Thoughts Concerning Education* was published in 1693 and is a practical and lucid manual not just on education but on diet, punishment, and even "going to stool." Locke never directly addresses the education of women specifically except to say in Article 6: "I have said *he* here, because the principal aim of my Discourse is, how a young Gentleman should be brought up from his Infancy, which, in all things, will not so perfectly suit the Education of *Daughters*, though where the difference of Sex requires different treatment, 'twill be no hard matter to distinguish." Wollstonecraft had read Locke and cites him in the *Vindication*. Our selections consist of articles 11, 12, and 110.

1. "Straight-laced" has come to mean proper and correct, but it originally meant to be fitted inside a tightly laced bodice or corset, a torment to which not just women but also children were subjected [Editor].

(imagining I know not what kind of beauty in it) by bracing and binding them hard from their infancy, have very little Feet. I saw a pair of *China* Shooes lately, exceedingly disproportioned to the Feet of one of the same Age amongst us; their Womens Shooes would scarce be big enough for one of our little Girls.[2] Besides this, 'tis observed, That their women are also very little and short lived, whereas the Men are of the ordinary Stature of other Men, and live to a proportionable Age. These Defects in the Female Sex in that Country, are by some, imputed to the unreasonable binding of their Feet, whereby the free Circulation of the Blood is hindred, and the Growth and Health of the whole Body suffers. And how often do we see, that some small part of the Foot being injured by a Wrench or a Blow, the whole Leg and thigh thereby lose their Strength and Nourishment, and dwindle away? How much greater Inconveniences may we expect, when the *Thorax*, wherein is placed the Heart and Seat of Life, is unnaturally *compressed*, and hindred from its due Expansion?

[*Cruelty*]

One thing I have frequently observed in Children, that when they have got possession of any poor Creature, they are apt to use it ill: They often torment, and treat very roughly young Birds, Butterflies, and such other poor Animals, which fall into their Hands, and that with a seeming kind of Pleasure. This I think should be watched in them, and if they incline to any such *Cruelty*, they should be taught the contrary Usage. For the custom of tormenting and killing of Beasts will, by degrees, harden their Minds even towards Men; and they who delight in the suffering and destruction of inferiour Creatures, will not be apt to be very compassionate or benigne to those of their own kind. Our Practice takes notice of this in the exclusion of *Butchers* from Juries of Life and Death. Children should from the beginning be bred up in an abhorrence of killing, or tormenting any living Creature; and be taught not to spoil or destroy any thing, unless it be for the preservation or advantage of some other that is Nobler. And truly, if the preservation of all Mankind, as much as in him lies, were every one's persuasion, as indeed it is every one's Duty, and the true Principle to regulate our Religion, Politicks and Morality by, the World would be much quieter, and better natur'd than it is. But to return to our present Business, I cannot but commend both the Kindness and Prudence of a Mother I knew, who was wont always to indulge her Daughters, when any of them desired Dogs, Squirils, Birds, or any such things, as young Girls use to be delighted with. But then, when they had them, they must be sure to keep them well, and look diligently after them, that they wanted nothing, or were not

2. Wollstonecraft refers to the practice of foot-binding on p. 41 of the present text [*Editor*].

ill used: For if they were negligent in their Care of them, it was counted a great Fault, which often forfeited their Possession, or at least they fail'd not to be rebuked for it; whereby they were early taught Diligence and good Nature. And indeed, I think People should be accustomed, from their Cradles, to be tender to all sensible Creatures, and to spoil or waste nothing at all.

MARY ASTELL

From A Serious Proposal to the Ladies†

* * *

For since GOD has given Women as well as Men intelligent Souls, why should they be forbidden to improve them? Since he has not denied us the faculty of Thinking, why shou'd we not (at least in gratitude to him) employ our Thoughts on himself their noblest Object, and not unworthily bestow them on Trifles and Gaities and secular Affairs? Being the Soul was created for the contemplation of Truth as well as for the fruition of Good, is it not as cruel and unjust to exclude Women from the knowledge of the one as from the enjoyment of the other? Especially since the Will is blind, and cannot chuse but by the direction of the Understanding; or to speak more properly, since the Soul always *Wills* according as she *Understands*, so that if she Understands amiss, she Wills amiss. And as Exercise enlarges and exalts any Faculty, so thro' want of using it becomes crampt and lessened; if therefore we make little or no use of our Understandings, we shall shortly have none to use; and the more contracted and unemploy'd the deliberating and directive Power is, the more liable is the elective to unworthy and mischievous choices. What is it but the want of an ingenious[1] Education, that renders the generality of Feminine Conversations so insipid and foolish and their solitude so insupportable? Learning is therefore necessary to render them more agreeable and useful in company, and to furnish them with becoming entertainments when alone, that so they may not be driven to those miserable shifts, which too many make use of to put off their Time, that precious Talent that never lies on the hands of a judicious Person. And since our Happiness in the next World, depends so far on those dispositions which we carry along with us out of this, that without

† From Mary Astell, A *Serious Proposal to the Ladies* (London, 1701; New York: Source Book Press, 1970), pp. 18–20 and 129–31. Mary Astell (1668–1731), born in Newcastle-upon-Tyne, had been highly educated by her clergyman uncle. At age twenty she moved to London to continue her studies and in 1697 published A *Serious Proposal . . .* She then invented a scheme for a ladies college, which had the support of Queen Anne but was squelched by Bishop Burnet. Jonathan Swift in *The Tatler* satirized her as "Madonella" and her education scheme as a "Protestant nunnery." Footnotes for this selection are by the editor.

1. In its original sense "ingenious" meant "high intellectual capacity," so Astell is saying that because they lack solid learning, women often have trivial conversations, and their time alone is boring and unimaginative.

a right habitude and temper of mind we are not capable of Felicity; and seeing our Beatitude consists in the contemplation of the divine Truth and Beauty, as well as in the fruition of his Goodness, can Ignorance be a fit preparative for heaven? Is't likely that she whose Understanding has been busied about nothing but froth and trifles, shou'd be capable of delighting her self in noble and sublime Truths? Let such therefore as deny us the improvement of our Intellectuals, either take up *his* Paradox, who said that *Women have no Souls*, which at a time when the most contend to have them allow'd to Brutes, wou'd be as unphilosophical as it is unmannerly, or else let them permit us to cultivate and improve them. There is a sort of Learning indeed which is worse than the greatest Ignorance: A Woman may study Plays and Romances all her days, and be a great deal more knowing but never a jot the wiser. Such a knowledge as this serves only to instruct and put her forward in the practice of the greatest Follies, yet how can they justly blame her who forbid, or at least won't afford opportunity of better? A rational mind *will* be employ'd, it will never be satisfy'd in doing nothing, and if you neglect to furnish it with good materials, 'tis like to take up with such as come to hand.

We pretend not that Women shou'd teach in the Church, or usurp Authority where it is not allow'd them; permit us only to understand our *own* duty, and not be forc'd to take it upon trust from others; to be at least so far learned, as to be able to form in our minds a true Idea of Christianity, it being so very necessary to fence us against the danger of these *last* and *perilous days*, in which Deceivers a part of whose Character is to *lead captive silly Women*, need not *creep into Houses* since they have Authority to proclaim their Errors on the *House top*. And let us also acquire a true Practical knowledge, such as will convince us of the absolute necessity of *Holy Living* as well as of *Right Believing*, and that no Heresy is more dangerous than that of an ungodly and wicked Life. And since the *French Tongue* is understood by most Ladies, methinks they may much better improve it by the study of Philosophy (as I hear the *French Ladies* do) *des Cartes, Malebranche*[2] and others, than by reading idle *Novels* and *Romances*. 'Tis strange we shou'd be so forward to imitate their Fashions and Fopperies, and have no regard to what really deserves our Imitation. And why shall it not be thought as genteel to understand *French Philosophy*, as to be accoutred in a *French Mode*? Let therefore the famous Madam *D'acier, Scudery*, &c, and our own imcomparable *Orinda*, excite the Emulation of the English Ladies.[3]

2. Author of the famous formula "I think, therefore I am," French philosopher and mathematician René Descartes (1596–1650) is generally credited with moving modern philosophy toward rationalism. Nicolas Malebranche (1638–1715), a French theologian and philosopher, was an early follower of Descartes who later concentrated on reconciling faith and reason, matter and spirit.
3. Madame Dacier (1654–1720) was a learned stu-dent of Greek and Latin who translated Homer's *Iliad* and *Odyssey*, among other projects. Madeleine de Scudéry (1607–1701), sister of the dramatist Georges de Scudéry, was a French novelist who introduced arguments about women's education into the mouths of her characters. She was also famous for her "samedis," Saturday afternoon literary gatherings at her home. Katherine Philips was the "Matchless Orinda," (1631–64), a poet

The Ladies, I'm sure, have no reason to dislike this Proposal, but I know not how the Men will resent it to have their enclosure broke down, and Women invited to taste of that Tree of knowledge they have so long unjustly *Monopoliz'd*. But they must excuse me, if I be as partial to my own Sex as they are to theirs, and think Women as capable of Learning as Men are, and that it becomes them as well. For I cannot imagine wherein the hurt lies, if instead of doing mischief to one another, by an uncharitable and vain Conversation, Women be enabled to inform and instruct those of their own Sex at least; the Holy Ghost having left it on record, that *Priscilla* as well as her Husband, catechiz'd the eloquent *Apollos* and the great Apostle found no fault with her.[4] It will therefore be very proper for our Ladies to spend part of their time in this Retirement, in adorning their minds with useful Knowledge.

* * *

And indeed as unnecessary as it is thought for Women to have Knowledge, she who is truly good finds very great use of it, not only in the Conduct of her own Soul but in the managment of her Family, in the Conversation of her Neighbours and in all the Concerns of Life. Education of Children is a most necessary Employment, perhaps the chief of those who have any; But it is as Difficult as it is Excellent when well perform'd; and I question not but that the mistakes which are made in it, are a principal Cause of that Folly and Vice, which is so much complain'd of and so little mended. Now this, at least the foundation of it, on which in a great measure the success of all depends, shou'd be laid by the Mother, for Fathers find other Business, they will not be confin'd to such laborious work, they have not such opportunities of observing a Childs Temper, nor are the greatest part of 'em like to do much good, since Precepts contradicted by Example seldom prove effectual. Neither are Strangers so proper for it, because hardly any thing besides Paternal Affection can sufficiently quicken the Care of performing, and sweeten the labour of such a task. But Tenderness alone will never discharge it well, she who wou'd do it to purpose must throughly understand Human nature, know how to manage different Tempers Prudently, be Mistress of her own, and able to bear with all the little humours and follies of Youth, neither Severeity nor Lenity[5] are to be always us'd, it wou'd ruin some to be treated in that manner which is fit for others. As Mildness makes some ungovernable, and as there is a stupor in many from which nothing but Terrors can rouse them, so sharp Reproofs and Solemn Lectures serve to no purpose but to harden

---

much admired in her own day, befriended by famous men and women alike, and mourned by many at her early death from smallpox.

4. Priscilla (or Prisca) is mentioned six times in the New Testament, always in conjunction with her husband Aquila, a Jew who had been expelled from Rome. Prominent in the early church, they accompanied Paul to Ephesus where they taught Apollos, "an eloquent man, well-versed in the faith." Their house was often used for Christian worship, and Paul always speaks of them with affection.

5. Mildness or gentleness.

others, in faults from which they might be won by an agreeable Address and tender application. GOD himself waits to be gracious and administers his Medicines in the most proper season, and Parents shou'd imitate him in this, for the want of observing it, and of accommodating their Methods to the several Dispositions they have to deal with, is perhaps the reason that many Pious Persons lose the fruit of their Pains and Care.

Nor will Knowledge lie dead upon their hands who have no Children to Instruct; the whole World is a single Ladys Family, her opportunities of doing good are not lessen'd but encreas'd by her being unconfin'd. Particular Obligations do not contract her Mind, but her Beneficence moves in the largest Sphere. And perhaps the Glory of Reforming this Prophane and Profligate Age is reserv'd for you Ladies, and that the natural and unprejudic'd Sentiments of your Minds being handsomly express'd, may carry a more strong conviction than the Elaborate Arguments of the Learned. Such as fence themselves against the Cannon they bring down, may lie open to an Ambuscade[6] from you. And whilst the strong arguings of the Schools like the Wind in the Fable, seems but to harden these Sturdy Sinners, your Persuasions like the Suns mild and powerful rays, may oblige them to cast off that Cloak of Maliciousness in which they are so much intangled. And surely it is worth your while to fit your selves for this: Tis a Godlike thing to relieve even the Temporal wants of our Fellow Creatures, to keep a *Body* from perishing, but it is much more Divine, to *Save a Soul from Death!* A Soul which in his estimate who best knows the value of it, is worth more than all the World. They who are thus *wise shall shine as the brightness of the Firmament, and they who turn many to Righteousness as the Stars for ever;* which is a Glory we may honestly Contend for, a Beauty we may lawfully Covet; O that we had but Ambition enough to aspire after it! O that we had but so much at least as we see daily thrown away on a poor transitory Earthly Diadem, which sets uneasy on his head who wears it, and which a longer arm may wrest from his Brows! But alas it was in our fore-fathers days that the Kingdom of Heav'n was took by violence; they thought nothing, and we think every thing too much to Do or Suffer to obtain it! Not but that it is still as bright and glorious, as truly attractive, but we are dull and stupid we shut our eyes and won't behold its Charms. Were we but duly sensible of this we shou'd think no Posterity so desireable as the Offspring of our Minds, nor any state so great as the carrying a large Train of Followers with us to the Court of Heaven! So much Knowledge therefore as is necessary to engage and keep us firm in our Christian Course, to fit us to help others in theirs, to stir us up to pursue, and direct us in our endeavours after one of the brightest Crowns of Glory, does very well become us; and more than

---

6. "Ambuscade" means "ambush"; a woman's strong and clear reasoning might be effective against a man who has defended himself by sophistical arguments.

this I do not contend for, being far from desiring that any one shou'd neglect her Necessary Affairs to amuse her self with nice Speculations. No; She who has a Family is discharging part of her Christian Calling whilst She's taking care for it's Support and Government, and wou'd be very much out, if she lock'd her self in her Study, when her Domesticks had need of her direction. But there are few of those to whom I write, who have not a good deal of time to spare, if you reckon whats thrown away on fantastic Impertinencies, and tis this I wou'd have better employ'd: Were not a Morning more advantageously spent at a Book than at a Looking-Glass, and an Evening in Meditation than in Gaming? Were not Pertinent and Ingenious Discourse more becoming in a visit, than Idle twattle and uncharitable Remarks? than a Nauseous repetition of a set of fine words which no body believes or cares for? And is not the fitting our selves to do Real Services to our Neighbours, a better expression of our Civility than the formal performance of a thousand ridiculous Ceremonies, which every one condemns and yet none has the Courage to break thro?

* * *

JAMES BURGH

Of the Peculiar Management of Daughters†

Female children being as much by nature rational creatures, as males, it seems pretty obvious, that, in bringing them up to maturity, there is some regard to be had to the cultivation of their reason, as well as the adorning of their persons. As to the forming of their tempers, the directions above given will, with some small variation, suit them. As girls are more apt to run into vanity, on account of their beauty or dress, than the other sex; it will be necessary to guard against this folly, which, else, will grow with years, till it becomes unsufferable. And after all, there is no doubt, but a foolish head is always contemptible, whether it be covered with a cap or a wig. And a creature, that values itself only upon its form, and has no other ambition but to make that agreeable, must be sunk to a very low pitch of understanding, and has little pretence to rank itself with rational beings.

The proper education of a daughter, if a parent has a mind she should ever be fit for filling a place in society, and being a suitable companion

† From James Burgh, *The Dignity of Human Nature* (London, 1767), pp. 126–28. Burgh (1714–75), a Scottish political economist, had lived in Newington Green before Wollstonecraft set up her school there in 1784. Befriended by his widow, she probably read and was influenced by the deceased man's works, notably *Political Disquisitions* and the book on education from which this excerpt is taken. Burgh was a liberal in politics and education, and his can be considered an enlightened attitude toward women for the period.

and help meet for a man of sense, is, first, Reading with propriety and life; readiness at her needle, especially for people in middling stations; a free command of her pen, and complete knowledge of numbers, as far as the rule called *Practice*.[1] A woman cannot with certainty keep, or examine, the accounts of her own family, without these accomplishments. The knowledge of *English* grammar or orthography is absolutely necessary to any person, who would write to be read. Without some acquaintance with geography and history, a woman's conversation must be confined within a very narrow compass, and she will enjoy much less pleasure in that of her husband and his friends; and his entertainment from her conversation must likewise be very much abridged, if she can bear no part on any but the subjects of fashion or scandal.

Plays, romances, love-verses, and cards, are utter ruin to young women. For, if they find any entertainment in them, they must unavoidably give their minds a cast, which can never be suitable to the useful part of a female character, which is wholly domestic. For, whatever the fine ladies of our age may think of the matter, it is certain, that the only rational ambition they can have, must be to make obedient daughters, loving wives, faithful friends, and good christians; characters much more valuable than those of skilful gamesters, fine dancers, or dressers, or than even of wits and critics.

* * *

CATHARINE MACAULAY†

From Letters on Education

Letter IV.
Amusement and Instruction of Boys and Girls to Be the Same

* * *

I could say a great deal, Hortensia,[1] on those personal advantages, which the strength of the mother gives to her offspring, and the ill effects which must accrue both to the male and female issue from her feebleness. I could expatiate on the mental advantages which accompany a firm constitution, and on that evenness and complacency of temper, which commonly attends the blessing of health. I could turn the other side of the argument, and show you, that most of the caprices, the teasing follies, and often the vices of women, proceed from weakness,

---

1. *Practica Italica*, a kind of computation used in everyday business [*Editor*].
† From Catharine Macaulay, *Letters on Education* (London, 1790), from Letter IV (pp. 48–50), Letter XXI (201–2), and all of Letters XXII–XXIII (pp. 203–15). Macaulay (1731–91) was an historian whose eight-volume history of England was respected. Wollstonecraft admired Macaulay and mentions her passing in the *Vindication* (p. 106), but the two never met or corresponded. Footnotes for this selection are by the editor, except when noted otherwise.
1. The *Letters* are addressed to this fictitious recipient.

or some other defect in their corporeal frame; but when I have sifted the subject to the bottom, and taken every necessary trouble to illustrate and enforce my opinion, I shall, perhaps, still continue singular in it. My arguments may serve only to strengthen my ideas, and my sex will continue to lisp with their tongues, to totter in their walk, and to counterfeit more weakness and sickness than they really have, in order to attract the notice of the male; for, says a very elegant author, perfection is not the proper object of love: we admire excellence, but we are more enclined to love those we despise. [2]

There is another prejudice, Hortensia, which affects yet more deeply female happiness, and female importance; a prejudice, which ought ever to have been confined to the regions of the east, [a] state of slavery to which female nature in that part of the world has been ever subjected, and can only suit with the notion of a positive inferiority in the intellectual powers of the female mind. You will soon perceive, that the prejudice which I mean, is that degrading difference in the culture of the understanding, which has prevailed for several centuries in all European societies. Our ancestors, on the first revival of letters, dispensed with an equal hand the advantages of a classical education to all their offspring; but as pedantry was the fault of that age, a female student might not at that time be a very agreeable character. True philosophy in those ages was rarely an attendant on learning, even in the male sex; but it must be obvious to all those who are not blinded by the mist of prejudice, that there is no cultivation which yields so promising a harvest as the cultivation of the understanding; and that a mind, irradiated by the clear light of wisdom, must be equal to every talk which reason imposes on it. The social duties in the interesting characters of daughter, wife, and mother, will be but ill performed by ignorance and levity; and in the domestic converse of husband and wife; the alternative of an enlightened, or an unenlightened companion, cannot be indifferent to any man of taste and true knowledge. Be no longer niggards, then, O ye parents, in bestowing on your offspring, every blessing which nature and fortune renders them capable of enjoying! Confine not the education of your daughters to what is regarded as the ornamental parts of it, nor deny the graces to your sons. Suffer no prejudices to prevail on you to weaken Nature, in order to render her more beautiful; take measures for the virtue and the harmony of your family, by uniting their young minds early in the soft bonds of friendship. Let your children be brought up together; let their sports and studies be the same; let them enjoy, in the constant presence of those who are set over them, all that freedom which innocence renders harmless, and in which Nature rejoices. By the uninterrupted intercourse which you will thus establish, both sexes

2. See Mr. Burke on the Sublime and Beautiful [Macaulay's note]. The reference is to Edmund Burke's essay on aesthetics, *On the Sublime and the Beautiful*, Part III, Section IX, where he argues that perfection cannot cause beauty because in the female sex, where beauty is highest, it "almost always carries with it an idea of weakness and imperfection."

will find, that friendship may be enjoyed between them without passion. The wisdom of your daughters will preserve them from the bane of coquetry, and even at the age of desire, objects of temptation will lose somewhat of their stimuli, by losing their novelty. Your sons will look for something more solid in women, than a mere outside; and be no longer the dupes to the meanest, the weakest, and the most profligate of the sex. They will become the constant benefactors of that part of their family who stand in need of their assistance; and in regard to all matters of domestic concern, the unjust distinction of primogeniture will be deprived of its sting.

Letter XXI.
Morals Must Be Taught on Immutable Principles
* * *

* * * Know then, good Hortensia, that I have given similar rules for male and female education, on the following grounds of reasoning.

First, That there is but one rule of right for the conduct of all rational beings; consequently that true virtue in one sex must be equally so in the other, whenever a proper opportunity calls for its exertion; and, *vice versa*, what is vice in one sex, cannot have a different property when found in the other.

Secondly, That true wisdom, which is never found at variance with rectitude, is as useful to women as to men; because it is necessary to the highest degree of happiness, which can never exist with ignorance.

Lastly, That as on our first entrance into another world, our state of happiness may possibly depend on the degree of perfection we have attained in this, we cannot justly lessen, in one sex or the other, the means by which perfection, that is another word for wisdom, is acquired.

It would be paying you a bad compliment, Hortensia, were I to answer all the frivolous objections which prejudice has framed against the giving a learned education to women; for I know of no learning, worth having, that does not tend to free the mind from error, and enlarge our stock of useful knowledge. Thus much it may be proper to observe, that those hours which are spent in studious retirement by learned women, will not in all probability intrude so much on the time for useful avocation, as the wild and spreading dissipation of the present day; that levity and ignorance will always be found in opposition to what is useful and graceful in life; and that the contrary may be expected from a truly enlightened understanding. However, Hortensia, to throw some illustration on what I have advanced on this subject, it may be necessary to shew you, that all those vices and imperfections which have been generally regarded as inseparable from the female character, do not in any manner proceed from sexual causes, but are entirely the effects of situation and education. But these observations must be left to farther discussion.

Letter XXII.
No Characteristic Difference in Sex

The great difference that is observable in the characters of the sexes, Hortensia, as they display themselves in the scenes of social life, has given rise to much false speculation on the natural qualities of the female mind.—For though the doctrine of innate ideas, and innate affections, are in a great measure exploded by the learned, yet few persons reason so closely and so accurately on abstract subjects as, through a long chain of deductions, to bring forth a conclusion which in no respect militates with their premises.

It is a long time before the crowd give up opinions they have been taught to look upon with respect; and I know many persons who will follow you willingly through the course of your argument, till they perceive it tends to the overthrow of some fond prejudice; and then they will either sound a retreat, or begin a contest in which the contender for truth, though he cannot be overcome, is effectually silenced, from the mere weariness of answering positive assertions, reiterated without end. It is from such causes that the notion of a sexual difference in the human character has, with a very few exceptions, universally prevailed from the earliest times, and the pride of one sex, and the ignorance and vanity of the other, have helped to support an opinion which a close observation of Nature, and a more accurate way of reasoning, would disprove.

It must be confessed, that the virtues of the males among the human species, though mixed and blended with a variety of vices and errors, have displayed a bolder and a more consistent picture of excellence than female nature has hitherto done. It is on these reasons that, when we compliment the appearance of a more than ordinary energy in the female mind, we call it masculine; and hence it is, that Pope has elegantly said *a perfect woman's but a softer man.*[3] And if we take in the consideration, that there can be but one rule of moral excellence for beings made of the same materials, organized after the same manner, and subjected to similar laws of Nature, we must either agree with Mr. Pope, or we must reverse the proportion, and say, that *a perfect man is a woman formed after a coarser mold.* The difference that actually does subsist between the sexes, is too flattering for men to be willingly imputed to accident; for what accident occasions, wisdom might correct; and it is better, says Pride, to give up the advantages we might derive from the perfection of our fellow associates, than to own that Nature has been just in the equal distribution of her favours. These are the sentiments of the men; but mark how readily they are yielded to by the women; not from humility I assure you, but merely to preserve with character those fond vanities on which they set their hearts. No; suffer them to idolize their persons,

3. Alexander Pope, *Moral Essays* II.272.

to throw away their life in the pursuit of trifles, and to indulge in the gratification of the meaner passions, and they will heartily join in the sentence of their degradation.

Among the most strenuous asserters of a sexual difference in character, Rousseau is the most conspicuous, both on account of that warmth of sentiment which distinguishes all his writings, and the eloquence of his compositions: but never did enthusiasms and the love of paradox, those enemies to philosophical disquisition, appear in more strong opposition to plain sense than in Rousseau's definition of this difference. He sets out with a supposition, that Nature intended the subjection of the one sex to the other; that consequently there must be an inferiority of intellect in the subjected party; but as man is a very imperfect being, and apt to play the capricious tyrant, Nature, to bring things nearer to an equality, bestowed on the woman such attractive graces, and such an insinuating address, as to turn the balance on the other scale. Thus Nature, in a giddy mood, recedes from her purposes, and subjects prerogative to an influence which must produce confusion and disorder in the system of human affairs. Rousseau saw this objection; and in order to obviate it, he has made up a moral person of the union of the two sexes, which, for contradiction and absurdity, outdoes every metaphysical riddle that was ever formed in the schools.[4] In short, it is not reason, it is not wit; it is pride and sensuality that speak in Rousseau, and, in this instance, has lowered the man of genius to the licentious pedant.

But whatever might be the wise purpose intended by Providence in such a disposition of things, certain it is, that some degree of inferiority, in point of corporal strength, seems always to have existed between the two sexes;[5] and this advantage, in the barbarous ages of mankind, was abused to such a degree, as to destroy all the natural rights of the female species, and reduce them to a state of abject slavery. What accidents have contributed in Europe to better their condition, would not be to my purpose to relate; for I do not intend to give you a history of women; I mean only to trace the sources of their peculiar foibles and vices; and these I firmly believe to originate in situation and education only: for so little did a wise and just Providence intend to make the condition of slavery an unalterable law of female nature, that in the same proportion as the male sex have consulted the interest of their own happiness, they have relaxed in their tyranny over women; and such is their use in the system of mundane[6] creation, and such their natural influence over the male mind, that were these advantages properly exerted, they might carry every point of any importance to their honour and happiness.

4. Mary Wollstonecraft also attacks this idea in Rousseau (p. 89), when he says that "from their union there results a moral person, of which woman may be termed the eyes, and man the hand." A woman cannot make a moral decision without a man.

5. Compare the wording here to Wollstonecraft's on p. 8: "In the government of the physical world it is observable that the female in point of strength is, in general, inferior to the male."

6. Having to do with worldly things.

However, till that period arrives in which women will act wisely, we will amuse ourselves in talking of their follies. The situation and education of women, Hortensia, is precisely that which must necessarily tend to corrupt and debilitate both the powers of mind and body. From a false notion of beauty and delicacy, their system of nerves is depraved before they come out of their nursery; and this kind of depravity has more influence over the mind, and consequently over morals, than is commonly apprehended. But it would be well if such causes only acted towards the debasement of the sex; their moral education is, if possible, more absurd than their physical. The principles and nature of virtue, which is never properly explained to boys, is kept quite a mystery to girls. They are told indeed, that they must abstain from those vices which are contrary to their personal happiness, or they will be regarded as criminals, both by God and man; but all the higher parts of rectitude, every thing that ennobles our being, and that renders us both innoxious[7] and useful, is either not taught, or is taught in such a manner as to leave no proper impression on the mind. This is so obvious a truth, that the defects of female education have ever been a fruitful topic of declamation for the moralist; but not one of this class of writers have laid down any judicious rules for amendment. Whilst we still retain the absurd notion of a sexual excellence, it will militate against the perfecting a plan of education for either sex. The judicious Addison animadverts on the absurdity of bringing a young lady up with no higher idea of the end of education than to make her agreeable to a husband, and confining the necessary excellence for this happy acquisition to the mere graces of person.[8]

Every parent and tutor may not express himself in the same manner as is marked out by Addison; yet certain it is, that the admiration of the other sex is held out to women as the highest honour they can attain; and whilst this is considered as their *summum bonum*, and the beauty of their persons the chief *desideratum*[9] of men, Vanity, and its companion Envy, must taint, in their characters, every native and every acquired excellence. Nor can you, Hortensia, deny, that these qualities, when united to ignorance, are fully equal to the engendering and rivetting all those vices and foibles which are peculiar to the female sex; vices and foibles which have caused them to be considered, in ancient times, as beneath cultivation, and in modern days have subjected them to the censure and ridicule of writers of all descriptions, from the deep thinking philosopher to the man of ton[1] and gallantry, who, by the bye,

7. Literally, "harmless"; that is, making women capable of doing good, not harm.
8. The most likely reference here is to *The Spectator*, No. 66, on the education of girls, which remarks that "the Management of a young Lady's Person is not to be overlooked, but the Erudition of her Mind is much more to be regarded." The essay is not by Addison, but by his cohort Richard Steele, a fact that may not have been known to Macaulay since the original essays were not signed. Joseph Addison was a popular essayist in the early eighteenth century who commented freely on morals.
9. *Summon bonum* means "the highest good"; "desideratum" is that which is most needed and desired.
1. The French *ton* means "style" or "fashion."

sometimes distinguishes himself by qualities which are not greatly superior to those he despises in women. Nor can I better illustrate the truth of this observation than by the following picture, to be found in the polite and gallant Chesterfield. "Women," says his Lordship, "are only children of a larger growth. They have an entertaining tattle, sometimes wit; but for solid reasoning, and good sense, I never in my life knew one that had it, or who acted or reasoned in consequence of it for four and twenty hours together. A man of sense only trifles with them, plays with them, humours and flatters them, as he does an engaging child; but he neither consults them, nor trusts them in serious matters."[2]

Letter XXIII.
Coquetry

Though the situation of women in modern Europe, Hortensia, when compared with that condition of abject slavery in which they have always been held in the east, may be considered as brilliant; yet if we withhold comparison, and take the matter in a positive sense, we shall have no great reason to boast of our privileges, or of the candour and indulgence of the men towards us. For with a total and absolute exclusion of every political right to the sex in general, married women, whose situation demand a particular indulgence, have hardly a civil right to save them from the grossest injuries;[3] and though the gallantry of some of the European societies have necessarily produced indulgence, yet in others the faults of women are treated with a severity and rancour which militates against every principle of religion and common sense. Faults, my friend, I hear you say; you take the matter in too general a sense; you know there is but one fault which a woman of honour may not commit with impunity; let her only take care that she is not caught in a love intrigue, and she may lie, she may deceive, she may defame, she may ruin her own family with gaming, and the peace of twenty others with her coquetry, and yet preserve both her reputation and her peace. These are glorious privileges indeed, Hortensia; but whilst plays and novels are the favourite study of the fair, whilst the admiration of men continues to be set forth as the chief honour of woman, whilst power is only acquired by personal charms, whilst continual dissipation banishes the hour of reflection, Nature and flattery will too often prevail; and when this is the case, self preservation will sugggest to the conscious weakness those methods which are the most likely to conceal the ruinous trespass, however base and criminal they may be in nature. The crimes that women have committed, both to conceal and to indulge their natural failings, shock the feelings of moral sense; but indeed every love intrigue,

2. From Lord Chesterfield's *Letters to His Son*, Letter CCXCIV (November 16, 1752), also cited by Wollstonecraft on p. 00 in the *Vindication*. Chesterfield's letters were written to his illegitimate son from the age of five to his death, a kind of long-distance child rearing. They were criticized for their advice on sexual licentiousness.

3. At the time Macaulay was writing, married women had virtually no rights: their property became their husband's at marriage and their children were given to the father's custody after a separation—divorce being almost unheard of.

though it does not terminate in such horrid catastrophes, must naturally tend to debase the female mind, from its violence to educational impressions, from the secrecy with which it must be conducted, and the debasing dependancy to which the intriguer, if she is a woman of reputation, is subjected. Lying, flattery, hypocrisy, bribery, and a long catalogue of the meanest of the human vices, must all be employed to preserve necessary appearances. Hence delicacy of sentiment gradually decreases; the warnings of virtue are no longer felt; the mind becomes corrupted, and lies open to every solicitation which appetite or passion prevents. This must be the natural course of things in every being formed after the human plan; but it gives rise to the trite and foolish observation, that the first fault against chastity in woman has a radical power to deprave the character. But no such frail beings come out of the hands of Nature. The human mind is built of nobler materials than to be so easily corrupted; and with all the disadvantages of situation and education, women seldom become entirely abandoned till they are thrown into a state of desperation by the venomous rancour of their own sex.

The superiority of address peculiar to the female sex, says Rousseau, is a very equitable indemnification for their inferiority in point of strength. Without this, woman would not be the companion of man, but his slave; it is by her superior art and ingenuity that she preserves her equality, and governs him, whilst she affects to obey. Woman has every thing against her; as well our faults, as her own timidity and weakness. She has nothing in her favor but her subtlety and her beauty; is it not very reasonable therefore that she should cultivate both?

I am persuaded that Rousseau's understanding was too good to have led him into this error, had he not been blinded by his pride and his sensuality. The first was soothed by the opinion of superiority, lulled into acquiescence by cajolement; and the second was attracted by the idea of women playing off all the arts of coquetry to raise the passions of the sex. Indeed the author fully avows his sentiments, by acknowledging that he would have a young French woman cultivate her agreeable talents, in order to please her future husband, with as much care and assiduity as a young Circassion cultivates her's to fit her for the harem of an eastern bashaw.[4]

These agreeable talents, as the author expresses it, are played off to great advantage by women in all the courts of Europe; who, for the arts of female allurement, do not give place to the Circassian. But it is the practice of these very arts, directed to enthral the men, which act in a peculiar manner to corrupting the female mind. Envy, malice, jealousy, a cruel delight in inspiring sentiments which at first perhaps were never intended to be reciprocal, are leading features in the character of the coquet, whose aim is to subject the whole world to her own humour;

---

4. *Émile*, p. 337. Wollstonecraft cites the same passage on p. 86. "Bashaw" is a pasha or a high Turkish official.

but in this vain attempt she commonly sacrifices both her decency and her virtue.

By the intrigues of women, and their rage for personal power and importance, the whole world has been filled with violence and injury; and their levity and influence have proved so hostile to the existence or permanence of rational manners, that it fully justifies the keeness of Mr. Pope's satire on the sex.[5]

But I hear my Hortensia say, whither will this fit of moral anger carry you? I expected an apology, instead of a libel, on women; according to your description of the sex, the philosopher has more reason to regret the indulgence, than what you have sometimes termed the injustice of the men; and to look with greater complacency on the surly manners of the ancient Greeks, and the selfishness of Asiatic luxury, than on the gallantry of modern Europe.

Though you have often heard me express myself with warmth in the vindication of female nature, Hortensia, yet I never was an apologist for the conduct of women. But I cannot think the surliness of the Greek manners, or the selfishness of Asiatic luxury, a proper remedy to apply to the evil. If we could inspect narrowly into the domestic concerns of ancient and modern Asia, I dare say we should perceive that the first springs of the vast machine of society were set a going by women; and as to the Greeks, though it might be supposed that the peculiarity of their manners would have rendered them indifferent to the sex, yet they were avowedly governed by them. They only transferred that confidence which they ought to have given their wives, to their courtezans, in the same manner as our English husbands do their tenderness and their complaisance.[6] They will sacrifice a wife of fortune and family to resentment, or the love of change, provided she give them opportunity, and bear with much Christian patience to be supplanted by their footman in the person of their mistress.

No; as Rousseau observes, it was ordained by Providence that women should govern some way or another; and all that reformation can do, is to take power out of the hands of vice and folly, and place it where it will not be liable to be abused.

To do the sex justice, it must be confessed that history does not set forth more instances of positive power abused by women, than by men; and when the sex have been taught wisdom by education, they will be glad to give up indirect influence for rational privileges; and the precarious sovereignty of an hour enjoyed with the meanest and most infamous of the species, for those established rights which, independent of accidental circumstances, may afford protection to the whole sex.

---

5. Alexander Pope's satiric "Of the Characters of Women," *Moral Essay* II, is frequently cited by Wollstonecraft.

6. Wollstonecraft makes the same point about Greek courtesans on p. 175.

MARY WOLLSTONECRAFT

Letter to Henry Gabell†

Dublin April 16th [1787]

My dear friend

The evening I received your letter I intended answering it; but was prevented; and since that vexations which I cannot banish, have not allowed me leisure to consider abstruse speculations. I am of opinion that much may be said on both sides of the question—and yet cannot entirely coincide with you. It appears to me self-evident, that an All-wise and good Being created nothing in vain. He cannot be mistaken, or cause *needless* pain.[1] Ignorance would be desirable if all our attainments had a reference only to our present mode of existence. Man would then disquiet himself in vain—and enlarge his mind, for no other purpose; but to extend the dominion of sorrow, and sharpen the arrows of affliction. A *good* understanding prevents a person's enjoying the common pleasures of this life—if it does not prepare him for a better it is a *curse*. Why have we implanted in us an irresistible desire to think—if thinking is not in some measure necessary to make us wise unto salvation. Indeed intellectual and moral improvement seem to me so connected—I cannot, even in thought separate them. Employing the understanding purifies the heart, gives dignity to the affections, by allowing the mind to analyze them—and they who can assign a reason for loving their fellow-creatures—will endeavor to serve The Great Spirit *rationally*—they will see the *beauty* of holiness, and be drawn by the cords of love. How can the mind govern the body if it is not exercised—Dr. Johnson, has said, that the most trivial occupations such as collecting shells, &c &c are of use, and even, promote the cause of virtue, as some time is stolen from sensual pursuits.[2] I agree with him—and think that if we were more perfect the *single* desire of pleasing the Author of all good might be sufficient to make us virtuous—but we are so framed that we want continual variety—and the appetites will rule if the mind is *vacant*.[3] It is true our reasonings are often fallacious—and our knowledge mostly conjectural—yet these flights into an obscure region open the faculties of the soul. St. Paul says, "we *see* through a glass *darkly*"[4]—but he does

† From *Shelley and His Circle: 1773–1822*, ed. Kenneth Cameron (1961), IV, 857–58. © 1970 by the Carl and Lily Pforzheimer Foundation. Reprinted by permission of the Harvard University Press. Mary Wollstonecraft met Henry Gabell on the boat transporting her to Ireland where she was to become governess to Lord Kingsborough's daughters. Gabell was at the same time on his way to become a tutor, probably to a family named O'Neill. The two corresponded after their arrival in Ireland. Some biographers have suggested a brief infatuation between the two, but in any case Gabell soon married and in later years became headmaster at Winchester College. Footnotes for this selection are by the editor.

1. In Chapter I of the *Vindication* (p. 14), this observation is expanded into a discussion of why God cannot cause evil. He is omniscient and therefore knows about the evil choices man will make, but he cannot, because He is all-good, cause the evil to occur.
2. Possibly a reference to Johnson's *Idler*, No. 56 (May 12, 1759).
3. That a vacant mind is ruled solely be sensual appetites becomes a powerful argument for educating the minds of women in the *Vindication*.
4. 1 Corinthians 13:12.

not assert that we are *blind*. Besides if animals have souls, I should not suppose that when they leave the body they will be on a par with man— on the contrary, I *imagine* they must be an inferior link in the great chain[5]—in which man, I should *conjecture*, does not hold a very high place. In short the more I reflect, the less apt am I to concur with you— if I did, I should envy *comfortable* folly—"Fat contented ignorance"! Well are you almost tired—I promised you a sermon, and behold I have written one—yet I have not done with the subject. The main hinge on which my argument turns is this, refinement genius—and those charming talents which my soul instinctively loves, produce misery in this world—abundantly more pain than pleasure. Why then do they at all unfold themselves *here*? if useless, would not the Searcher of hearts, the tender Father, have shut them up 'till they could bloom in a more favorable climate; where no keen blasts could blight the opening flower. Besides sensibility renders the path of duty more intricate—and the warfare *much* more severe—Surely *peculiar* wretchedness has something to balance it! I was pleased with you[r] manner of treating the subject— and beg you to continue to write to me in this way. We generally conclude from ou[r] own partial experience. My reason has been too far stretched, and tottered almost on the brink of madness—no wonder then, if I humbly hope, that the ordeal trial answered some end, and that I have not suffered in vain. Pray write soon under cover of Lord K.[6] you are enjoying the sweets of spring—while I scarcely know how vegetation advances.

Adieu, your affectionate

Sister[7]

Mary

RALPH M. WARDLE

[The Intellectual and Historical Background of A *Vindication of the Rights of Woman*][†]

* * * The overwhelming majority of Englishwomen of [Wollstone-craft's] time had known [little economic and intellectual] freedom. Most of the advantages which their sex had gained during the late Middle Ages and the Renaissance, largely because of worship of the Virgin, had been swept away in England with the triumph of Puritanism. Devout

5. The view of the universe that, in general, implies an ascending order of creation, with God at the top and the inanimate world at the bottom.
6. Lord Kingsborough, Wollstonecraft's employer. The family was residing in Dublin at the time.
7. This closing probably suggests that Wollstone-

craft's affection for Gabell was no longer (if it ever had been) amorous but was genial and sisterly.
† From *Mary Wollstonecraft*, by Ralph Wardle, pp. 135–36, 139–42, 143–45. Copyright © 1951 by the University of Kansas Press. Reprinted by permission of the University Press of Kansas. The author's footnotes have been renumbered.

Christian gentlemen could find good Biblical precedent for their disdainful attitude toward women: St. Paul had enjoined on the sex the
virtues of silence and submission as a means of atoning for their share
in man's fall from grace.[1] Actually the gentlemen may have been a bit
afraid of women and their subtle powers. So at least one would gather
from the statute which Parliament passed in the year 1770, declaring
that "all women of whatever age, rank, profession, or degree, whether
virgin maid or widow, that shall from and after such Act impose upon,
seduce, and betray into matrimony any of His Majesty's subjects by
means of scent, paints, cosmetics, washes, artificial teeth, false hair,
Spanish wool, iron stays, hoops, high-heeled shoes, or bolstered hips,
shall incur the penalty of the law now in force against witchcraft and
like misdemeanours, and that the marriage upon conviction shall stand
null and void." Moreover, the common law of England ruled that
whatever property a woman owned before marriage or might receive
thereafter became automatically her husband's. Sir William Blackstone,[2]
in the chapter "Of Husband and Wife" in his *Commentaries on the
Laws of England*, explained the ruling by maintaining that when women
became one with their husbands they lost their legal identity; and he
claimed that the law was designed for women's protection and benefit.
Dr. Johnson, however, had a different explanation: "Nature has given
women so much power," he declared, "that the law has wisely given
them little."[3] But whatever the reason, the fact remained that English
common law allowed women little real freedom—and, incidentally, left
wealthy girls a prey to unscrupulous fortune-hunters seeking to settle
themselves in life by means of an advantageous marriage.

* * *

The majority of women of the eighteenth century accepted their
inferior status without complaint. Even the Bluestockings,[4] who had
managed to gain a sort of equality with men, were careful not to press
the point. Probably they were more eager to retain their own position
than to extend it to other women—at the risk of stirring up a dissension
which might rob them of their privileges. At least they made no attempt
to proselytize for their sex. Mrs. Barbauld, in a dainty poem "To a Lady,
with Some Painted Flowers," assured the recipient: "Your BEST, your
SWEETEST empire is—to PLEASE."[5] And when she was asked to
head a projected girls' school where foreign languages were to be taught,

1. See Ephesians 5:22–24 and I Timothy 2:11–
14.
2. Eighteenth-century English legal commentator
and jurist whose *Commentaries* for a long time was
considered an authoritative handbook of English
common law. [*Editor*].
3. James Boswell, *The Life of Samuel Johnson*, ed.
G. Birbeck Hill (Oxford and New York, 1887),
V. 226n.

4. Originally eighteenth-century literary and intellectual clubs where the attire was informal and
the conversation literary; named for the blue or
worsted stockings invariably worn by a male atten-
der, Mr. Benjamin Stillingfleet. The term generalized to mean literary or intellectual women.
[*Editor*].
5. Wollstonecraft quotes this Barbauld poem in
the *Vindication*, p. 53 above [*Editor*].

she declined immediately and made it emphatically clear that she disapproved of any scheme of general education for women. Hannah More, to be sure, wrote a book entitled *Strictures on the Modern System of Female Education*; yet she confined herself largely to the suggestion that women be taught propriety, convinced that if they were truly moral, there would be no need for a reform in their status. Certainly she did not want anything like freedom for her sex. "I am sure I have as much liberty as I can make use of, now I am an old maid," she wrote to Horace Walpole in 1792; "and when I was a young one, I had, I dare say, more than was good for me."[6] Most intelligent women would probably have agreed with Lady Mary Wortley Montagu, who insisted that "learning is necessary to the happiness of women, and ignorance the common foundation of their errors," but who advised that a young girl conceal what learning she had "with as much solicitude as she would hide crookedness or lameness."[7] Women were so used to being treated with condescension or disdain that they had grown servile. They accepted subjection as their lot in life and stifled whatever rebellion they felt. To be feminine was to be docile.

The conventional attitude toward women was summed up in two very popular books of the day: Dr. James Fordyce's *Sermons to Young Women* (1765) and Dr. John Gregory's *Father's Legacy to His Daughters* (1774). They sold by the thousands; and no wonder, for in them girls could learn specifically what two Christian gentlemen of unquestionable moral standards believed to be the duties of women—that is to say, how they could render themselves pleasing to men.

Dr. Fordyce, the brother of Mary's friend Dr. George Fordyce, recommended "the retiring graces." He urged his readers to be meek, timid, yielding, complacent, sweet, benign, and tender, modeling themselves on Milton's Eve (before the Temptation, of course). "With the character of a Christian woman," he declared, "nothing, methinks, can better correspond than a propensity to melt into affectionate sorrow."[8] He warned girls against indulging in any sort of strenuous exercise because it might deprive them of their valued softness. And to enhance the values of piety he remarked:

> Never perhaps does a fine woman strike more deeply, than when composed into a pious recollection, and possessed with the noblest considerations, she assumes, without knowing it, superior dignity and new graces; so that the beauties of holiness seem to radiate about her, and the by-standers are almost induced to fancy her already worshipping amongst her kindred angels.[9]

6. Quoted in [W. Clark] Durant's Supplement to [William Godwin's] *Memoirs*, p. 216. [Author More's conservative views on women were probably still more liberal than those of Walpole, who castigated Wollstonecraft as "a hyena in petticoats."]
7. Lady Mary Wortley Montagu, *Letters*, 1709–

1762, Everyman's Library, London and New York, pp. 414 and 454 [Montague was a well-known poet, essayist, and letter writer of the eighteenth century.]
8. James Fordyce, *Sermons for Young Women*, 11th ed., London, 1792, I, 185.
9. The same, II, 163.

To be sure, Fordyce suggested that young ladies study history, travels, geography, astronomy, noble fiction (such as the *Spectator*), and "the most obvious branches both of Natural and Moral Philosophy." But he added:

> You yourselves, I think, will allow that war, commerce, politics, exercises of strength and dexterity, abstract philosophy, and all the abstruser sciences, are most properly the province of men. I am sure those masculine women, that would plead for your sharing any part of this province equally with us, do not understand your true interests. [1]

Obviously Fordyce considered women who wanted to study abstract philosophy to be as "masculine" as those who wanted to serve in the army.

Sometimes Dr. Gregory seems more enlightened than Fordyce. He urges that women be men's companions and equals—though he adds: "to soften our hearts and polish our manners." By and large he seems to give women credit for good sense; yet he advises them to conceal it. In fact his *Legacy to His Daughters* cautions young women to conceal not only their good sense but whatever wit or learning they may possess; and it warns them that they must resist the temptation to fall in love until they are sure of being loved in return. Obviously dissimulation plays a strong part in the Gregory code of etiquette; in fact, he goes so far as to say that if women are truly wise, they will never reveal the full extent of their love. He virtually admits, in short, that, though women (at least his daughters) may not be so flighty as most men assume, they will do well to cultivate an appearance of flightiness. To be sure, he seems often to be trying to aid intelligent women to reconcile themselves to the position which society has accorded them. Yet though he perhaps deserves some credit for his realistic approach to the subject, his realism is fundamentally cynical: most men are deceivers, he says in effect, and women cannot afford to be too honest.

The women for whom such books were written were certainly not slaves. They had their little liberties and their little triumphs, but always they were obliged to confine themselves to such liberties and triumphs as were approved in the code by which they lived. They were bound, as Mary said, in "silken fetters." They were reminded constantly of what was expected of them as daughters and wives, and nobody thought to inquire what they expected of their fathers and husbands. It was a pleasant state of affairs for the woman who had no ambition or self-respect; but for a Mary Wollstonecraft it was downright humiliating.

* * *

Mary was not alone in deploring the position of women or in blaming their faulty education for it. For over a hundred years alert Englishmen had been arguing that women should be given a better education to

1. I, 272.

render them more rational beings. As early as 1673 Mrs. Makin had published *An Essay to Revive the Ancient Education of Gentlewomen*, and in 1694 Mary Astell had advocated, in her *Serious Proposal to Ladies*, a sort of convent where serious-minded women might retire for study and contemplation. Three years later Daniel Defoe had included in his *Essay on Projects* a suggestion for an academy for women, where they might study whatever subjects they chose. And he observed: "We reproach the sex every day with folly and impertinence, while I am confident, had they the advantages of education equal to us, they would be guilty of less than ourselves." Then Sir Richard Steele took up the cause; and in the *Tatler* and the *Spectator* he urged that women be treated more respectfully, and pleaded for a better education for them. "The general mistake among us in the educating our children," he wrote in *Spectator* No. 66, "is, that in our daughters we take care of their persons and neglect their minds; in our sons, we are so intent upon adorning their minds that we wholly neglect their bodies."[2] Even men like Addison and Swift, who were often disdainful of contemporary women, advocated that they be given a better education to render them more tolerable companions.[3]

By far the most vigorous champion of women's rights in the first half of the eighteenth century was a woman who signed herself "Sophia" and who is sometimes identified with Lady Mary Wortley Montagu. In her first book, *Woman Not Inferior to Man* (1739), Sophia argued not only for a better education for women but also for an independent position in society. She maintained that women had achieved less than men only because they had been given less education—and went so far as to refer to her sex as slaves. But she believed that women were inherently more "responsible" than men and that, if relieved of their bondage to household duties, they would make good teachers, physicians, lawyers (because they are good talkers!), even soldiers—and more sensible philosophers. And when "A Gentleman" replied with arch condescension in *Man Superior to Woman*, Sophia countered boldly with *Woman's Superior Excellence to Man* (1740), acknowledging the faults of women but blaming them directly on inadequate education and the tyranny of men.

Among Mary's contemporaries there were several in France who had written in behalf of women. Antoine Léonard Thomas's *Essay on the Character, Customs, and Minds of Women in Different Centuries* (1772) had shown sympathy with the sex without offering any really constructive criticism.[4] But Olympe de Gouges had spoken boldly in defense of her

2. See also the *Tatler*, No. 61, 141, and 248, and the *Spectator*, No. 53 and 66.
3. See Swift's "Letter to a Very Young Lady on Her Marriage," his fragmentary essay "Of the Education of Ladies," and Addison's *Spectator*, No. 10. Note also that in Bk. I, Ch. 6, and Bk. IV, Ch. 8, of *Gulliver's Travels* Swift implies that he approves of the same education for both sexes.

4. An expanded translation of the introduction to this essay was published as "An Occasional Letter on the Female Sex" in the *Pennsylvania Magazine* in 1775 and has often been attributed to Tom Paine. Concerning the real authorship of the piece, see Frank Smith, "The Authorship of 'An Occasional Letter on the Female Sex,'" *American Literature*, II (1930–31), 277–80.

sex in her various publications (one of which was called A *Declaration of the Rights of Woman*).[5] And Condorcet had advocated better education for women in the first of his *Memoirs on Public Instruction* (1790).[6] But Mary was probably familiar with none of these works. She was certainly familiar, however, with another treatment of the subject, Catharine Macaulay's *Letters on Education*; in fact she had reviewed the book for the *Analytical* with enthusiastic approval. And there can be no doubt that she was considerably indebted to it for the formation of her own thesis.[7] For though *Letters on Education* was not primarily concerned with the education of women, Mrs. Macaulay had a good deal to say on the subject: she denied that there was any fundamental difference in character between the sexes and maintained that they should be given the same education. She also attributed women's weaknesses to their faulty education and social position, advocated that they be taught not only light accomplishments but solid virtues, and urged that they develop more strength so that they might be better mothers. Mrs. Macaulay deplored the common practice of training girls only to please their husbands; and she demonstrated that, because they had been denied their rights, they had contrived by ignoble means to achieve a kind of sovereignty by utilizing their powers of pleasing. Yet she did not despair of her sex; she believed that they would gladly sacrifice their privileges if they were granted their rights. And she warned men that, if they wished women to improve, they must improve themselves; specifically she demanded that men be modest as the first step toward improvement in women.—Obviously Mrs. Macaulay was far ahead of her generation in her thinking on this subject. Obviously, too, Mary had studied her book attentively, for in *The Rights of Woman* she was to repeat and develop almost every point which Mrs. Macaulay had made. Unfortunately for the author, *Letters on Education* appeared only after Mrs. Macaulay had sacrificed her extraordinary popularity by her second marriage. And it remained for Mary Wollstonecraft to circulate many of the ideas advanced in the *Letters*.

5. Olympe de Gouges (1748–93), fiery French playwright and pamphleteer, published *Déclaration des Droits de la femme et de la Citoyenne* in 1791, but apparently Wollstonecraft had not read it before she wrote the *Vindication*. De Gouges was guillotined during the Reign of Terror [*Editor*]. 6. Condorcet (1743–94), French philosopher and early sociologist, believed that the human race developed in stages, from barbaric to civilized. An early architect of the French Revolution, he was forced into hiding during the Terror and, when finally captured, poisoned himself in prison [*Editor*]. 7. After Mary's death her friend Mary Hays wrote: "It is but justice to add, that the principles of [*The Rights of Woman*] are to be found in Catharine *Rights of Woman*] are to be found in Catharine Macauley's [sic] Treatise on Education" (*Annual Necrology, 1797–8*, London, 1800, p. 422). Miss Hays's claim was repeated in George G. Cunningham's *Lives of Eminent and Illustrious Englishmen* (Glasgow, 1835–37, VI, 248), but since then it seems never to have been noticed.

The
Wollstonecraft
Debate

Caricature of Mary Wollstonecraft

Drawing by David Levine. Reprinted with permission from *The New York Review of Books*. Copyright © 1972, Nyrev, Inc.

Probably most figures in the history of ideas have their detractors and their proponents: that is the nature of the history of ideas. But Mary Wollstonecraft seems almost a special case. Since she first issued the clarion challenge of *A Vindication of the Rights of Woman* in 1792, then died a poignant early death in childbirth five years later, she seems to have elicited extreme responses from both defenders and attackers, and the sensational aspects of her life have been allowed to color the validity of her work. "Debate" seems a fitting word for the critical exchange, since people have rarely been neutral about her.

It is instructive to look at Mary Wollstonecraft's reputation over the nearly two centuries since she first issued her challenge. That is what this gathering of materials is about: what has been written and said about her from her death in 1797 onward to the present. To trace the fortunes of a great idea is always a telling exercise, but it is even more so in this case, because it is also to trace the painful vicissitudes of what used to be called "the woman question."

People have gone to great lengths to ridicule ideas about equality; it is interesting to study the scurrilous prose in which they do that. But it is also interesting to watch other minds engage with Wollstonecraft's and take courage themselves, whether it be a George Eliot comparing Margaret Fuller and Mary Wollstonecraft—and measuring her own mental status at the same time—or an Emma Goldman lauding the passion and pluck of a woman who faced down formidable odds much like Goldman's own. Recent scholars[1] point out that the *Vindication of the Rights of Woman* was generally well received when it first appeared, for it was seen as the latest "treatise on female education," to use the phrasing of Mary Hays, Wollstonecraft's friend and protégé, who reviewed it favorably for the *Analytical Review*. We should remember the revolutionary social and intellectual milieu in which it appeared in 1792. There had been an uprising in the American colonies that had led to independence, a revolution was exploding in France, and controversial radical ideas were afoot in England. Even a call for equality for all social classes was receiving a respectful hearing, so how much more respectable might seem a thoughtful request that women be educated equally. People had been pleading for women's education for at least a century, so the *Vindication* with its renewed plea brought rather more respect than criticism.

Not in all quarters, of course. The formerly respectful Mary Hays took the occasion right after Wollstonecraft's death to deprecate her "high masculine tone, sometimes degenerating into coarseness." Perhaps the most extreme view is voiced by Thomas Taylor, who derided Wollstonecraft in his *Vindication of the Rights of Brutes* (1792) by pruriently suggesting that elephants might be satisfactory lovers for ladies because from their "great and unexampled gallantries" would emerge "a mixt kind of species . . . in which the enchanting elegance of woman would be united with the prodigious strength and terrific bulk of elephant." Taylor also chides Wollstonecraft's long-held idea that sex education ought to be dealt with straightforwardly: in the *Rights of Woman* she says, "truth may always be told to children, if it be told gravely; but it is the immodesty of affected modesty, that does all the mischief" (p. 127). Taylor hoots at the idea, and his *reductio ad absurdum* is the proposal to use dogs to instruct children in the facts of life.

1. See especially the R. M. Janes article, pp. 297–307, in the Criticism section of this volume.

Several scholars have pointed out that it was only after her death, and then only after publication of a book that was meant to exonerate and explain her, that Wollstonecraft's reputation became an issue. Her grieving husband, William Godwin, wrote an apologia for his dead wife's life and work, A *Memoir of the Author of the Vindication of the Rights of Woman*. Thus were disseminated details about her life, such as her infatuation with the painter Henry Fuseli, her liaison with Gilbert Imlay in Paris, and her suicide attempts—facts that had not perhaps been widely known or cared about. This proved to be the incendiary material that future critics would use against her, and from which future defenders would try to exonerate her. Her personality had become an issue, and she a *cause célèbre*.

Godwin had lauded his wife's fairness, patience with children, and consideration to servants. From his book critics seized evidence of what they saw to be a scandalous and immoral life. Her irregular life evoked the snide, self-righteous couplets of the Reverend Richard Polwhele. As we read *The Unsex'd Females* today, we wonder what exactly could have so enraged Polwhele about a woman he had never met. Polwhele and his compatriot across the Atlantic, Benjamin Silliman, say as much about the mind of a misogynist as they do about anything Mary Wollstonecraft said or did. Silliman's is the more shocking attack in some ways, because it comes from America, the new land of freedom, a place to which Mary Wollstonecraft herself had dreamed of immigrating one day.

But other men were adulatory, an attitude that can be found with variations into our own day. William Blake probably saw and perhaps conversed with Wollstonecraft when they were both members of the informal literary circle that had gathered around the publisher Joseph Johnson in London. Blake had illustrated Wollstonecraft's earlier book, *Original Stories*, and while it can never be proven with certainty, it is fair to assume that "To Mary" is directed to her memory in some way.

The poet Robert Southey was another admirer. After meeting her in London in 1797, he had written to his publisher Joseph Cottle, "Of all the lions or literati I have seen here, Mary Imlay's countenance is the best, infinitely the best . . . her eyes are light brown, and although the lid of one of them is affected by a little paralysis, they are the most meaning [sic] I ever saw."[2] His prefatory note to the longer poem "The Triumph of Woman" continues the note of admiration.

After a lull during the first part of the nineteenth century, Mary Wollstonecraft's ideas about equality were again taken up, this time by the rising women's movement in America. The catalyst had proven to be the abolitionist movement, and more particularly the World Anti-Slavery meeting in London in 1840. Two staunch abolitionists, Lucretia Mott and Elizabeth Cady Stanton, had attended with their husbands and been forced to watch the proceedings from the galleries because it had been voted that only male delegates could participate. As women they were neither free nor equal when it came to discussing racial equality.

Out of that shocking realization came the Seneca Falls convention on women's rights of 1848, organized by Stanton and Mott and three other women. A Declaration of Principles emanated from that meeting and initiated the struggle that in many ways has not yet ended. Years after the brave start, when political

2. C. Kegan Paul, *William Godwin* (Boston, 1876) I.234.

infighting came to dominate the movement and the suffrage cause faltered, the foremothers of American feminism decided to compile the history of that struggle. In the *History of Woman Suffrage* (1881–1922), Mary Wollstonecraft's influence is given a nod in a passage surprisingly full of errors. The title of her book is spelled incorrectly ("women" for "woman"), the date of publication is wrong, and even the ideas are awry:

> In 1790, Mary Wollstonecraft's *"Vindication of the Rights of Women,"* published in London, attracted much attention from liberal minds. She examined the position of women in the light of existing civilizations, and demanded for her the widest opportunities of education, industry, political knowledge, and the right of representation. Although her work is filled with maxims of the highest morality and purest wisdom, it called forth such a violent abuse, that her husband appealed for her from the judgement of her contemporaries to that of mankind. So exalted were her ideas of woman, so comprehensive her view of life, that Margaret Fuller, in referring to her, said: 'Mary Wollstonecraft—a woman whose existence proved the need of some new interpretation of woman's rights, belonging to that class who by birth find themselves in places so narrow that, by breaking bonds, they become outlaws.'[3]

"The light of existing civilizations" suggests an ambitious cross-cultural look at the status of women: Wollstonecraft confines herself to criticisms of French women and to some references to Chinese foot-binding, "Mahometan" ideas about women's souls, and ancient Greek courtesans. While Wollstonecraft certainly demands opportunity for education, she brings up the idea of the franchise only to dismiss it.[4] And we know now that the "violent abuse" to which the authors of the *History* allude was in part occasioned by her husband's appeal and that, in fact, the *Vindication* itself had been fairly well received.

The authors of the *History of Woman Suffrage* were not careless or ill-intentioned women. What had happened by this time was that the *Vindication* had become a monument and its author a pioneer and martyr. The American women found in her work what they wanted, a broad agenda for the pressing social and political concerns that the women's rights movement in England and America had articulated. They were interested in more than mere accuracy.

But their linkage of Mary Wollstonecraft with Margaret Fuller is important. It had already been made by the great English novelist George Eliot, who had meditated on the two in an essay in 1855. Like Wollstonecraft, Fuller was a member of a noted intellectual circle of her day, the Boston Transcendentalists. She had edited their literary magazine, *The Dial*; Wollstonecraft had written voluminously for Joseph Johnson's *Analytical Review*, a repository of radical ideas in the 1780's and 1790's. Both led something of an irregular life at the end of their days: Margaret Fuller had gone to Italy, where she met and married a younger husband, not of her class. They and their child perished tragically at sea. Wollstonecraft perished early in her life by childbirth. The stories begged to be compared: two gifted, intellectual women brought down by the struggle of what it was to be a woman in society not altogether ready for them.

The second century of critical responses to Wollstonecraft has been much like the first, with new forms of female heroism and new twists in misogyny. The

3. Elizabeth Cady Stanton, Susan B. Anthony, and Matilda Joslyn Gage, *History of Woman Suf-* *frage* (New York: Fowler & Wells, 1881) 1:34.
4. See p. 147 in this edition.

critical assaults came as reactions, first from the bastion of Freudian psychiatry after World War II in Ferdinand Lundberg and Marynia Farnham's *Modern Woman: The Lost Sex*, where Wollstonecraft is used as the case study of woman gone wrong. Freudian psychiatry has provided a debating ground for the modern "woman question." The period after World War II, the cultural epoch so energetically described in Betty Friedan's *The Feminine Mystique*, brought about the 1960's and 1970's, revolutionary times for the women's movement. That period, in turn, brought the vituperative backlash of Richard Cobb, professor of modern history at Oxford University, who, in a front-page review for the *Times Literary Supplement*, of Claire Tomalin's biography of Wollstonecraft, excoriated Wollstonecraft for being "always silly: she was almost always egotistical; and she was generally envious, rancorous, and meddlescme."[5] He suggests that the cause of justice was set back considerably by such an advocate: "She undertook, in sudden spurts of enthusiasm, many projects, and finished few of them; this was no great loss, as what she did finish was mediocre and ill-written, or appallingly gushing, polemical, and hysterical."

Cobb spends little time discussing the *Rights of Woman* and prefers to focus on her stay in Paris during the Revolution, her liaison with Imlay, and her death—the last four years of her life. To Tomalin's suggestion that Wollstonecraft's contribution to education be recognized by dedicating a school or college in her name, Cobb replied:

> As it has always been customary thus to commemorate those who did the most harm to education, or those who, understanding the least about it, wrote the most about it, someone in high places should certainly take heed of her plea. Mary's very surname has about it an unmistakable ring of crankiness, ungainliness, and discomfort, a promise of puritanism and serious intent.

Cobb's narrow focus and belittling language prove—if proof were needed—that misogyny is alive and well and appearing in print.

It is telling that the occasion for Cobb's attack comes in a review of biography: accounts of her life have been by far the most common kind of writing about Wollstonecraft since 1950. She is, if anything, "over-biographed." The reason may be that she is irresistible; she attracts the biographer anxious to figure out what life events can explain such revolutionary work. Although some of the authors are occasionally critical of their subject, Wollstonecraft seems by and large to invoke sympathetic treatments, never hatchet jobs.

But there is a new voice in the twentieth century: the woman writer who has experienced the emancipation made possible not just by Mary Wollstonecraft, but by a whole succession of women who provide a foundation on which to stand. That new woman cogitates in print about her foremother of long ago.

Virginia Woolf, the English novelist who could make a whole novel around a dinner party (*Mrs. Dalloway*) or the promise of a trip (*To the Lighthouse*), is caught up in wondering about the relationships in Mary Wollstonecraft's life. She chuckles over Godwin's big head and Gilbert Imlay's limited intelligence.

Emma Goldman, the anarchist and radical speaker and thinker, who not only preached free love but lived it, is fascinated by the passion she finds in Wollstonecraft's life. The commentator Alice Wexler describes the personal events

5. *The Times Literary Supplement* (Sept. 6, 1974), 941–44.

in Goldman's life at the time the essay was composed, and it is clear that Goldman is looking for a mentor, as well as for the assurance that a passionate, intelligent, intellectual woman could survive.

Wexler mentions along with Goldman the anthropologist Ruth Benedict, whose essay on Wollstonecraft was not published until her protégé Margaret Mead collected her unpublished papers in *An Anthropologist at Work*. At the time she wrote the essay, Ruth Benedict had not yet discovered her career in anthropology. She was an unhappy social worker, a young wife who longed for (and was unable to have) a child, and a brilliant thinker who had not yet invented her life. Benedict's journal essay reveals how inspiring had been the picture of Wollstonecraft in the National Portrait Gallery that she had first seen as a child: "I wanted so desperately to know how other women had saved their souls alive. . . . She *had* saved her soul alive; it looked out from her steady eyes unafraid."

And so it is that men and women alike have looked for over two hundred years at Mary Wollstonecraft, her life and work, and often seen a part of themselves. Some have identified with what they saw and made Mary Wollstonecraft into a heroine. Others hated what they saw, excoriated her, and took her to task for not being perfect. But before them all the time was a real person, of course, with her foibles and her gifts, her brilliance and her human limitations. Adrienne Rich speaks of that Wollstonecraft in her poem "Snapshots of a Daughter-in-Law":

> "To have in this uncertain world some stay
> which cannot be undermined, is
> of the utmost consequence."[6]
>
>   Thus wrote
> a woman, partly brave and partly good,
> who fought with what she partly understood.
> Few men about her would or could do more,
> hence she was labeled harpy, shrew and whore.

---

6. From Mary Wollstonecraft, *Thoughts on the Education of Daughters*, London, 1787 [Rich's note].

MARY HAYS

Memoirs of Mary Wollstonecraft†

* * *

A just confidence in her own talents, increased probably by the success of this publication [A *Vindication of the Rights of Men*][1] now induced [Wollstonecraft] to essay her strength on a subject that affected her still more; a subject which she had keenly felt, on which she had deeply meditated, which her sex, her situation, all the circumstances of her life, irresistibly led her to consider,—*A Vindication of the Rights of Woman*.—There are few situations in which a woman of cultivated understanding has not occasion to observe and deplore, the systematic vassalage, the peculiar disadvantages, civil and social, to which she is subjected, even in the most polished societies, on the account of her sex. It might be difficult to convince such a woman, conscious of superiority to the majority of men with whom she converses, that nature has placed between them, in what respects intellectual attainments, an insuperable barrier: she would be tempted to remind such partial reasoners of the reply given to the philosopher who disputed the existence of motion, when his adversary gravely rose up and walked before him.

It is little wonderful that the magnanimous advocate of freedom, and the opponent of Burke, should throw down the gauntlet, challenge her arrogant oppressors, and, hurried away by a noble enthusiasm, deny the existence of a sexual character.

In the cause of half the human race she stood forth, deprecating and exposing, in a tone of impassioned eloquence, the various means and arts by which woman had been forcibly subjugated, flattered into imbecility, and invariably held in bondage. Dissecting the opinions, and commenting upon the precepts of those writers who, having expressly considered the condition of the female sex, had suggested means for its improvement, she endeavours, with force and acuteness, to convict them of narrow views, voluptuous prejudices, contradictory principles, and selfish, though impolitic ends. It is but justice to add, that the principles of this celebrated work are to be found in Catharine Macauley's [*sic*] *Treatise on Education*.[2] It may also be here observed, that in the intellectual advancement of women, and their consequent privileges in society, is to be traced the progress of civilization, or knowledge gradually superseding the dominion of *brute-force*.

† From *The Annual Necrology for 1797–8* (London, 1800), pp. 422–23. Mary Hays (1759 or 1760–1843), feminist and novelist who wrote *The Memoirs of Emma Courtney*, was befriended by Wollstonecraft and came to admire her extravagantly; she was at Wollstonecraft's bedside in the last days of her life.

1. Wollstonecraft's A *Vindication of the Rights of Men* (1790) was written as an answer to Edmund Burke's *Reflections on the Revolution in France* [Editor].
2. See the selection in this volume from Catharine Macaulay's *Letters on Education*, pp. 204–12 [Editor].

A production thus bold and spirited, excited attention and provoked discussion; prejudices were shocked, vanity wounded, interest alarmed, and indolence roused: yet, amidst the virulence of opposition, the clamours of ignorance, the cavils of superstition, and the misrepresentation of wilful perversion, seeds were scattered that promised, when the ferment had subsided, a rich and abundant harvest. The high masculine tone, sometimes degenerating into coarseness, that characterizes this performance, is in a variety of parts softened and blended with a tenderness of sentiment, an exquisite delicacy of feeling, that touches the heart, and takes captive the imagination. As a composition it discovers considerable power and energy of thought; but in perspicuity and arrangement it must be confessed to be defective: its style, though frequently rich and glowing, is sometimes inflated, and generally incorrect. It is to be regretted, that the author's intention of revising and remedying these defects in a future edition, was protracted, and ultimately defeated. Its faults are perhaps to be attributed to the rapidity with which it was composed and committed to the press; being, we are informed, begun and completed within a period of six weeks. It would be unnecessary to comment on the imprudence and impolicy manifested (whatever be the talents of the writer) by such precipitation. A second part was promised to the public, for which but scanty materials were found, after her decease, among the papers of the author.

* * *

THOMAS TAYLOR

From A Vindication of the Rights of Brutes†

* * *

And that I may first of all please the ladies, I shall begin with the elephant, a beast by nature very amorous; and from his prodigious size, very well calculated to become the darling of our modern virgins, who having wisely laid aside the foolish veils of antiquity, and have assumed greater boldness, are seldom intimidated at any thing uncommonly large. Plutarch then, in that treatise of his, in which he contrasts the sagacity of land animals, with that of the aquatic species, observes, concerning the amours of brutes, that some are furious and mad; but that others observe a kind of human decency, united with a very courtly kind of conversation.

† Thomas Taylor (1758–1835), generally called "the Platonist," was a philosophical writer and translator of the classics. His parody of Wollstonecraft also appeared in 1792. This selection is taken from the modern reprint with introduction by Louise Schutz Boas (Gainesville: Scholars' Facsimiles and Reprints, 1966), pp. 77–83.

"Such," says he, "was the amour of the elephant at Alexandria, that rivalled Aristophanes the grammarian. For they were both in love with a virgin that sold garlands: nor was the elephant's courtship less conspicuous than the grammarian's. For as he passed through the fruit-market, he always bought her apples, and stayed with her for some time: and besides this, thrusting his proboscis within her waistcoat, as a substitute for a hand, took great delight in gently feeling her breasts."

From this instance, it may be fairly concluded, that if elephants were to associate with ladies in common (each at the same time understanding the other's language) great and unexampled gallantries would take place on each side, and a mixt kind of species would be produced, in which the enchanting elegance of woman would be united with the prodigious strength and terrific bulk of the elephant.

No less charming, likewise, would be the advantages arising from an association of the fair sex with dragons, as is evident from the History of the Dragon, who was in love with an Etolian woman. For he used (says Plutarch)[1] to visit her in the night, and creeping under her garments to her very skin, embraced her naked body; and never, either voluntarily or involuntarily, injured her, but always departed very gallantly about break of day, but the relations of the woman observing that this was the custom of the dragon, removed her to a considerable distance from this amorous spot. After this the dragon was not seen for the space of three or four days; being all this time, as it seemed, wandering in search of her. But at length having with great difficulty found out the place of her abode, he accosted her somewhat less gallant and gentle than before; and with the folds of his body, having first bound her hands and arms, he lashed the calves of her legs, with the end of his tail; expressing by this means a gentle and loving anger, which contained more of indulgent expostulation than punishment.

Plutarch adds, that he shall say nothing respecting a goose in Egypt in love with a boy; nor of the ram in love with Glauce that played on the harp, because, (says he) the story is well known to every one. Indeed the instances already adduced are sufficient to convince the sagacious reader, that prodigious benefits must arise from the mutual converse and copulation of species, which have hitherto been considered as un-allied and inimical to each other.

And here I cannot refrain from mentioning a most singular advantage, which would arise from an association with dogs, when their language is perfectly understood by us; the advantage I allude to, respects a thing of no less importance than the instruction of youth in one of the most interesting particulars belonging to juvenile tuition. Every one knows how universally prevalent the practice of self-pollution is become amongst children; and how dreadful its consequences are in debilitating the constitution, and corrupting the morals of the unhappy youths who are the votaries of this detestable vice. Now that extraordinary genius, Mrs.

1. Greek biographer and moralist [*Editor*].

Wollstonecraft, proposes the following remedy for this pernicious practice, in that great work of hers, called, *Elements of Morality for Children*[2]:— "I am thoroughly persuaded," says she, "that the most efficacious method to root out this dreadful evil, which poisons the source of human happiness, would be to speak to children of the organs of generation as freely as we speak of the other parts of the body, and explain to them the noble use, which they were designed for, and how they may be injured." She adds, "I have conversed with the most sensible schoolmasters on this subject, and they have confirmed me in my opinion." This plan is beyond all doubt a most striking proof of her uncommon capacity, and the truth of her grand theory, *the equality of the female nature with the male*; for whoever considers this affair with the attention it deserves, must be convinced, that if children were but told how the genital parts may be injured, and how they are to be employed in a natural way, they would not have the least curiosity to make any experiments, which might tend to frustrate the benevolent intention of nature.

But however great and original this thought may be, yet it would certainly be very much improved, by committing the instruction of youth in this particular to dogs; for these sagacious animals, all of whom appear to be Cynic philosophers,[3] would not only be very well calculated to explain the noble use for which the parts were designed, but would be very willing, at any time, and in any place, to give them specimens of the operation of the parts in the natural way. Not to mention, that they would likewise teach them how to get above those foolish habits, decency and shame, which false opinion first introduced [to mankind].

* * *

WILLIAM GODWIN

From Memoirs of the Author of A *Vindication of the Rights of Woman*†

* * *

No person was ever better formed for the business of education; if it be not a sort of absurdity to speak of a person as formed for an inferior object, who is in possession of talents, in the fullest degree adequate to

---

2. Page 14 of the Introductory Address. [Mary Wollstonecraft published her translation of Christian Salzmann's *Elements of Morality* in 1790. Although the book is a translation, the introduction is Wollstonecraft's writing—*Editor*.]
3. There was in fact a school of "cynic" (originally stoic) philosophers in ancient Athens; our word "cynic" comes from the Greek word for "dog" [*Editor*].

† From William Godwin, *Memoirs of the Author of A Vindication of the Rights of Woman* (London, 1798; rpt. with intro. by Gina Luria, New York: Garland Publishing Co., 1974), pp. 41–44 and 79–85. A well-known philosopher and novelist, Godwin had married Mary Wollstonecraft on March 29, 1797. Inconsolable at her death, he wrote the *Memoirs*. Footnotes for this selection are by the editor.

something on a more important and comprehensive scale. Mary had a quickness of temper, not apt to take offence with inadvertencies, but which led her to imagine that she saw the mind of the person with whom she had any transaction, and to refer the principle of her approbation or displeasure to the cordiality or injustice of their sentiments. She was occasionally severe and imperious in her resentments; and, when she strongly disapproved, was apt to express her censure in terms that gave a very humiliating sensation to the person against whom it was directed. Her displeasure however never assumed its severest form, but when it was barbed by disappointment. Where she expected little, she was not very rigid in her censure of error.

But, to whatever the defects of her temper might amount, they were never exercised upon her inferiors in station or age. She scorned to make use of an ungenerous advantage, or to wound the defenceless. To her servants there never was a mistress more considerate or more kind. With children she was the mirror of patience. Perhaps, in all her extensive experience upon the subject of education, she never betrayed one symptom of irascibility. Her heart was the seat of every benevolent feeling; and accordingly, in all her intercourse with children, it was kindness and sympathy alone that prompted her conduct. Sympathy, when it mounts to a certain height, inevitably begets affection in the person towards whom it is exercised; and I have heard her say, that she never was concerned in the education of one child, who was not personally attached to her, and earnestly concerned not to incur her displeasure. Another eminent advantage she possessed in the business of education, was that she was little troubled with scepticism and uncertainty. She saw, as it were by intuition, the path which her mind determined to pursue, and had a firm confidence in her own power to effect what she desired. Yet, with all this, she had scarcely a tincture of obstinacy. She carefully watched symptoms as they rose, and the success of her experiments; and governed herself accordingly. While I thus enumerate her more than maternal qualities, it is impossible not to feel a pang at the recollection of her orphan children![1]

* * *

Never did any author enter into a cause, with a more ardent desire to be found, not a flourishing and empty declaimer, but an effectual champion. She considered herself as standing forth in defence of one half of the human species, labouring under a yoke which, through all the records of time, had degraded them from the station of rational beings, and almost sunk them to the level of the brutes. She saw indeed, that they were often attempted to be held in silken fetters, and bribed

---

1. Mary Wollstonecraft died ten days after the birth of her second daughter, Mary; her first child, Fanny, was three years old at the time.

into the love of slavery; but the disguise and the treachery served only the more fully to confirm her opposition. She regarded her sex, in the language of Calista, as

"In every state of life the slaves of men:"[2]

the rich as alternately under the despotism of a father, a brother, and a husband; and the middling and the poorer classes shut out from the acquisition of bread with independence, when they are not shut out from the very means of an industrious subsistence. Such were the views she entertained of the subject; and such the feelings with which she warmed her mind.

The work is certainly a very bold and original production. The strength and firmness with which the author repels the opinion of Rousseau, Dr. Gregory, and Dr. James Fordyce, respecting the condition of women, cannot but make a strong impression upon every ingenuous[3] reader. The public at large formed very different opinions respecting the character of the performance. Many of the sentiments are undoubtedly of a rather masculine description. The spirited and decisive way in which the author explodes the system of gallantry, and the species of homage with which the sex is usually treated, shocked the majority. Novelty produced a sentiment in their mind, which they mistook for a sense of injustice. The pretty, soft creatures that are so often to be found in the female sex, and that class of men who believe they could not exist without such pretty, soft creatures to resort to, were in arms against the author of so heretical and blasphemous a doctrine. There are also, it must be confessed, occasional passages of a stern and rugged feature, incompatible with the true stamina of the writer's character. But, if they did not belong to her fixed and permanent character, they belonged to her character *pro tempore*;[4] and what she thought, she scorned to qualify.

Yet, along with this rigid, and somewhat amazonian temper, which characterised some parts of the book, it is impossible not to remark a luxuriance of imagination, and a trembling delicacy of sentiment, which would have done honour to a poet, bursting with all the visions of an Armida and a Dido.[5]

The contradiction, to the public apprehension, was equally great, as to the person of the author, as it was when they considered the temper of the book. In the champion of her sex, who was described as endeavouring to invest them with all the rights of man, those whom curiosity prompted to seek the occasion of beholding her, expected to find a sturdy,

2. From Nicholas Rowe's *The Fair Penitent* (1703) 3.1.40–41. The play's heroine is Calista and her lover is "the gay Lothario."
3. Frank, open, or candid.
4. For the time being; temporarily.
5. Armida appears in Tasso's *Jerusalem Delivered* (1581); niece of the king of Damascus, she lures the Christian knights into an enchanted and aromatic garden during the siege of Jerusalem, and there they lose all desire to go back to the fight. Dido is the queen of Carthage, who, in Virgil's *Aeneid*, falls in love with Aeneas; when he must leave, she erects a funeral pyre and kills herself as he sails away.

muscular, raw-boned virago; and they were not a little surprised, when, instead of all this, they found a woman, lovely in her person, and, in the best and most engaging sense, feminine in her manners.

The Vindication of the Rights of Woman is undoubtedly a very unequal performance, and eminently deficient in method and arrangement. When tried by the hoary and long-established laws of literary composition, it can scarcely maintain its claim to be placed in the first class of human productions. But when we consider the importance of its doctrines, and the eminence of genius it displays, it seems not very improbable that it will be read as long as the English language endures. The publication of this book forms an epocha[6] in the subject to which it belongs; and Mary Wollstonecraft will perhaps hereafter be found to have performed more substantial service for the cause of her sex, than all the other writers, male or female, that ever felt themselves animated in the behalf of oppressed and injured beauty.

The censure of the liberal critic as to the defects of this performance, will be changed into astonishment, when I tell him, that a work of this inestimable moment, was begun, carried on, and finished in the state in which it now appears, in a period of no more than six weeks.

* * *

I think I may venture to say, that no two persons ever found in each other's society, a satisfaction more pure and refined. What it was in itself, can now only be known, in its full extent, to the survivor. But, I believe, the serenity of her countenance, the increasing sweetness of her manners, and that consciousness of enjoyment that seemed ambitious that every one she saw should be happy as well as herself, were matters of general observation to all her acquaintance. She had always possessed, in an unparalleled degree, the art of communicating happiness, and she was now in the constant and unlimited exercise of it. She seemed to have attained that situation, which her dispostion and character imperiously demanded, but which she had never before attained; and her understanding and her heart felt the benefit of it.

While we lived as near neighbours only, and before our last removal, her mind had attained considerable tranquillity, and was visited but seldom with those emotions of anguish, which had been but too familiar to her. But the improvement in this respect, which accrued upon our removal and establishment, was extremely obvious. She was a worshipper of domestic life. She loved to observe the growth of affection between me and her daughter, then three years of age, as well as my anxiety respecting the child not yet born. Pregnancy itself, unequal as the decree of nature seems to be in this respect, is the source of a thousand en-

6. A common variant usage of the period for "epoch," or a point in time defined by a particular event or moment in the history of anything.

dearments. No one knew better than Mary how to extract sentiments of exquisite delight, from trifles, which a suspicious and formal wisdom would scarcely deign to remark. A little ride into the country with myself and the child, has sometimes produced a sort of opening of the heart, a general expression of confidence and affectionate soul, a sort of infantine, yet dignified endearment, which those who have felt may understand, but which I should in vain attempt to pourtray.

* * *

RICHARD POLWHELE

From The Unsex'd Females†

* * *

I shudder at the new unpictur'd scene,   15
Where unsex'd woman vaunts the imperious mien;
Where girls, affecting to dismiss the heart,
Invoke the Proteus of petrific art;[1]
With equal ease, in body or in mind,
To Gallic freaks or Gallic faith resign'd,[2]   20
The crane-like neck, as Fashion bids, lay bare,
Or frizzle, bold in front, their borrow'd hair;
Scarce by a gossamery film carest,
Sport,[3] in full view, the meretricious breast;
Loose the chaste cincture,[4] where the graces shone,   25
And languish'd all the Loves, the ambrosial zone;
As lordly domes inspire dramatic rage,
Court prurient Fancy to the private stage;
With bliss botanic[5] as their bosoms heave,

---

† Reverend Richard Polwhele (1760–1838) was a poet, theologian, and literary writer who also served as a curate and vicar in the Anglican church. Prolific in his writing career, he contributed to magazines and also wrote topographical histories of Devon and Cornwall. He never managed to make himself distinguished in any of his callings; however, his poem about Wollstonecraft has the distinction of being the most critical and vociferous known.
1. Proteus is the Old Man of the Sea in Homer's *Odyssey*, who has the power to assume many different forms. "Petrific" means having the quality of changing something into stone, as Perseus's shield, for example. Polwhele is suggesting that a sculptor of these "unsex'd females" would need the qualities of a Proteus, so changeable are women [*Editor*].
2. "Gallic" has to do with French customs, thought, or language [*Editor*].

3. To "sport a face," is a cant phrase in one of our Universities, by which is meant an impudent obtrusion of a man's person in company. It is not inapplicable, perhaps, to the open bosom—a fashion which we have never invited or sanctioned.
4. Loose the girdle, or wide belt surrounding the waist and upper torso [*Editor*].
5. Botany has lately become a fashionable amusement with the ladies. But how the study of the sexual system of plants can accord with female modesty, I am not able to comprehend.

> * * * I had, at first written:
> More eager for illicit knowlege pant,
> With lustful boys anatomize a plant;
> The virtues of its dust prolific speak,
> Or point its pistill with unblushing cheek.

I have, several times, seen boys and girls botanizing together.

Still pluck forbidden fruit, with mother Eve,   30
For puberty in sighing florets pant,
Or point the prostitution of a plant;
Dissect[6] its organ of unhallow'd lust,
And fondly gaze the titillating dust;
With liberty's sublimer views expand,   35
And o'er the wreck of kingdoms ‖ sternly stand;
And, frantic midst the democratic storm,
Pursue, Philosophy! thy phantom-form.
    Far other is the female shape and mind,
By modest luxury heighten'd and refin'd;   40
Those limbs, that figure, tho' by Fashion grac'd,
By Beauty polish'd, and adorn'd by Taste;
That soul, whose harmony perennial flows,
In Music trembles, and in Color glows;
Which bids sweet Poesy reclaim the praise   45
With faery light to gild fastidious days,
From sullen clouds relieve domestic care,
And melt in smiles the withering frown of war.
Ah! once the female Muse, to NATURE true,
The unvalued store from FANCY, FEELING drew;   50
Won, from the grasp of woe, the roseate hours,
Cheer'd life's dim vale, and strew'd the grave with flowers.
    But lo! where, pale amidst the wild, she draws
Each precept cold from sceptic Reason's vase;
Pours with rash arm the turbid stream along,   55
And in the foaming torrent whelms the throng.
    Alas! her pride sophistic flings a gloom,
To chase, sweet Innocence! thy vernal bloom,
Of each light joy to damp the genial glow,
And with new terrors clothe the groupe of woe,   60
Quench the pure daystar in oblivion deep,
And, Death! restore thy "long, unbroken sleep."
    See Wollstonecraft, whom no decorum checks,
Arise, the intrepid champion of her sex;
O'er humbled man assert the sovereign claim,   65
And slight the timid blush[7] of virgin fame.
    "Go, go," she cries, "ye tribes of melting maids,
Go, screen your softness in sequester'd shades;
With plaintive whispers woo the unconscious grove,

6. Miss Wollstonecraft does not blush to say, in an introduction to a book designed for the use of young ladies, that, "in order to lay the axe at the root of corruption, it would be proper to familiarize the sexes to an unreserved discussion of those topics, which are generally avoided in conversation from a principle of false delicacy; and that it would be right to speak of the organs of generation as freely as we mention our eyes or our hands." To such language our botanizing girls are doubtless familiarized: and, they are in a fair way of becoming worthy disciples of Miss W. If they do not take heed to their ways, they will soon exchange the blush of modesty for the bronze of impudence.

7. That Miss Wollstonecraft was a sworn enemy to blushes, I need not remark. But many of my readers, perhaps, will be astonished to hear, that at several of our boarding-schools for young ladies, a blush incurs a penalty.

And feebly perish, as depis'd ye love. 70
What tho' the fine Romances of Rousseau
Bid the frame flutter, and the bosom glow;
Tho' the rapt Bard, your empire fond to own,
Fall prostrate and adore your living throne,
The living throne his hands presum'd to rear, 75
Its seat a simper, and its base a tear;[8]
Soon shall the sex disdain the illusive sway,
And wield the sceptre in yon blaze of day;
Ere long, each little artifice discard,
No more by weakness[9] winning fond regard; 80
Nor eyes, that sparkle from their blushes, roll,
Nor catch the languors of the sick'ning soul,
Nor the quick flutter, nor the coy reserve,
But nobly boast the firm gymnastic nerve;[1]
Nor more affect with Delicacy's fan 85
To hide the emotion from congenial man;
To the bold heights where glory beams, aspire,
Blend mental energy with Passion's fire,
Surpass their rivals in the powers of mind
And vindicate *the Rights of womankind.*" 90

* * *

BENJAMIN SILLIMAN

From The Letters of Shahcoolen†

[*Second Letter*]

False philosophy, striving to impress upon mankind the conviction, that it soars above common pleasures, and common ideas, has ever affected to despise and to degrade that sex, which the great Brumma has given us to alleviate, by their delightful tenderness, all the pains, and to animate all the joys of this life. Knowing, as thou dost, my warm partiality for this lovliest, best part of creation, thou canst not be surprised, that in all the countries through which I have passed, their happiness has been among the earliest subjects of my investigation.

8. According to Rousseau, the empire of women is the empire of softness—of address: their commands, are caresses; their menaces, are tears.

9. "Like monarchs, we have been flattered into imbecillity, by those who wish to take advantage of our weakness;" says Mary Hays (Essays and Letters, p. 92.) But, whether flattered or not, women were always weak: and female weakness hath accomplished, what the force of arms could not effect.

1. Miss Wollstonecraft seriously laments the neglect of all muscular exercises, at our female Boarding-schools.

† Benjamin Silliman (1779–1864) was a prominent American scientist and professor of Yale University. He wrote *The Letters of Shahcoolen* when he was twenty-two. They are addressed to a fictional Hindu recipient, El Hassan, and use other imaginary Oriental terms. Silliman's aim was to explain American mores and character.

Know then, that a total renovation of the female character, and a destination in society, totally new, is one grand object contemplated by that new philosophy, of which, in my last epistle, I gave some small account.

Mary Woolstonecraft, [*sic*] a female philosopher of the *new school*, has written, within these few years past, a book, which she named "A *vindication of the Rights of Woman;*" composed, for the express purpose of rousing her sex from their inglorious repose, and of stimulating them to a vigorous exertion of their native *energies*.

She discards all that sexual tenderness, delicacy and modesty, which constitute the female loveliness; boldly pronounces them equal to the rougher sex in every thing but bodily strength; and even imputes their deficiency, in this particular, principally to a falsely refined education. She asserts that a husband is a *paltry* bauble, compared with *the attainments of reason*; that the female should be subject, or superior to the male, just in proportion to those attainments; and that the want of them constitutes the only obligation for the submission of the wife to the husband. This female philosopher indignantly rejects the idea of a sex in the soul, pronouncing the sensibility, timidity and tenderness of women, to be merely artificial refinements of character, introduced and fostered by men, to render sensual pleasure more voluptuous. She indeed professes a high regard for chastity; but unfortunately the practice of her life was at war with her precepts. She admitted one *sentimental lover* after another, to the full fruition of her charms, and proved the *attainments of reason*, to be, in her view, sources of pleasure, far inferior, in value, to the pleasures of sense.

In short, polluted as she was by the *last crime of woman*, MARY stepped forth as the champion and reformer of her sex; she wished to strip them of every thing feminine, and to assimilate them, as fast as possible, to the masculine character.

O, my dear El Hassan, how opposite her views to every thing, which *we* deem lovely in the sex! O, lovely ALAGRA, the brightest gem that sparkles on the beauteous plains of AGIMERE, how would thy virgin soul shrink back at the contemplation of a female soul *unsexed* a man in female form!

A complete exhibition of the regenerating system of this female lunatic, would fatigue thy patience, and occupy too large a portion of these epistles.

So singular, however, is her system and so directly opposed to the received opinions of mankind, that I cannot refrain from tracing an imperfect outline. Not satisfied with masculine ideas, and masculine habits, Mary Wollstonecraft wished, as the consummation of female independence, to introduce the sex into the Camp, the Rostrum and the Cabinet; and although she does not recommend a total dereliction of *the household good*, still she would not cramp the female energies by an occupation so much beneath their dignity, except so far, as stern necessity commands.

She seriously advocates the right of female representation—for in this country, and in some parts of Europe, the right of representation, which in an epistle from England, I have already explained, is fully established.[1]

Suppose, my dear friend, that a band of female representatives, beautiful as the thirty RAGINIS,[2] who, crowned with flowery wreaths, dance to the muse of NARED, among the spicy groves of MALDOOVAN, should mix with a Legislative band; would not the cares of Legislation be excluded by the witchcraft of love! The charms of the fair Orator would plead more powerfully than her tongue, and gallantry would induce compliance, where reason would have simulated to strenuous opposition.

In the Cabinet, their sway would be still more complete. Smiles, tears and sighs would decide the fate of nations; and beauty would direct the march of armies on the frontiers, and the course of navies upon the ocean.

It is true that in *defensive* war *only*, Miss Woolstonecraft [sic] indulges the idea, which even *she* allows to be an enthusiastic one, of seeing the exploits of ancient heroines renewed, and the deadly weapon directed by the hand of Beauty.

This idea of hers is undoubtedly a most ingenious one. At the sight of a band of heroines, beautiful as the morning, marching forward to the combat, what warrior's sword would not drop from his hand?—what soldier would not surrender himself a prisoner!

Had the God RAMA, when he led forth his army of APES, and spread destruction among his enemies, only exchanged his apes for beautiful virgins, his victory would have been less bloody, and his conquest more complete.

As a necessary preparative for the support of bodily fatigue, the female philosopher recommends an early initation of females into the athletic sports, and gymastic exercises of boys and young men.

She would have them run, leap, box, wrestle, fence and fight, that the united exertion of bodily and mental energy may produce, by mysterious cooperation, that amazing force of character, of which she supposes her sex to be capable.

She even recommends that these sports should be mutually shared between girls and boys, that the distinction of sex may remain concealed, until the physical progress of the body, calling into operation the latent passions, shall discover the wonderful secret.

This strange philosopher, my dear El Hassan, has detained me, by

1. Technically speaking, women had the right to vote in America until they were constitutionally forbidden it in the Fourteenth Amendment, which mentioned only "male citizens." Their right to do so had been a state matter—and in some states they had voted—until after the Civil War [Editor].
2. Female Passions.

the novelty of her doctrines, longer than I intended. Perhaps in some future communication, I may notice some of her remaining tenets; and I intend particularly to delineate the practical influence, which they have already acquired over the female sex in this country.

Keep this philosophy a profound secret from the fair daughters of Hindustan, for, thou canst not divine what influence its novelty, and the idea of independence on man may have over the heart even of the modest, unassuming Hindu.

ROBERT SOUTHEY

To Mary Wollstonecraft†

The lily cheek, the 'purple light of love,'
The liquid lustre of the melting eye, . . .
Mary! of these the Poet sung, for these
Did Woman triumph; . . . turn not thou away
Contemptuous from the theme. No Maid of Arc[1]
Had, in those ages, for her country's cause
Wielded the sword of freedom; no Roland[2]
Had borne the palm of female fortitude;
No Cordé[3] with self-sacrificing zeal
Had glorified again the Avenger's name,
As erst when Caesar perish'd: haply too
Some strains may hence be drawn, befitting me
To offer, nor unworthy thy regard.

WILLIAM BLAKE†

Mary

Sweet Mary, the first time she ever was there,
Came into the Ball room among the Fair;
The young Men & Maidens around her throng,
And these are the words upon every tongue:

† Robert Southey (1774–1843) was an English poet and man of letters. An early friend of Coleridge, Southey had worked out with him a scheme for social utopia called "pantisocracy." He was enthusiastic about the French Revolution and had written a poem about Joan of Arc. This brief poem is prefatory to the longer "Triumph of Woman," written in Bristol in 1795.
1. I.e., Joan of Arc, the maiden saint of Orleans who led the French army [*Editor*].

2. Madame Manon Roland, who was executed at the guillotine in 1793 during the Reign of Terror [*Editor*].
3. Charlotte Corday had stabbed Marat to death in his bath in 1793, hoping that by assassinating the radical leader she could forward the Girondists, the moderates, during the Revolution. She was executed immediately [*Editor*].
† This poem comes from Blake's small collection of poems known as "The Pickering Manuscript,"

"An Angel is here from the heavenly Climes,   5
Or again does return the Golden times.
Her eyes outshine every brilliant ray,
She opens her lips—'tis the Month of May."

Mary moves in soft beauty & conscious delight
To augment with sweet smiles all the joys of the Night,   10
Nor once blushes to own to the rest of the Fair
That sweet Love & Beauty are worthy our care.

In the Morning the Villagers rose with delight
And repeated with pleasure the joys of the night;
And Mary rose among Friends to be free,   15
But no Friend from henceforward thou, Mary, shalt see.

Some said she was proud, some calld her a whore,
And some when she passed by shut to the door;
A damp cold o'er her, her blushes all fled;
Her lillies & roses are blighted & shed.   20

"O, why was I born with a different Face?
Why was I not born like this Envious race?
Why did Heaven adorn me with bountiful hand,
And then set me down in an envious Land?

"To be weak as a Lamb & smooth as a dove,   25
And not to raise Envy, is calld Christian Love;
But if you raise Envy your Merit's to blame
For planting such spite in the weak & the tame.

"I will humble my Beauty, I will not dress fine,
I will keep from the Ball, & my Eyes shall not shine;   30
And if any Girl's Lover forsakes her for me,
I'll refuse him my hand & from Envy be free."

She went out in Morning attird plain & neat;
"Proud Mary's gone Mad," said the Child in the Street;
She went out in Morning in plain neat attire,   35
And came home in Evening bespatterd with mire.

---

probably written between 1801 and 1805. William
Gaunt's biography of Blake, *Arrows of Desire* (London: Museum Press, 1956), argues that Wollstonecraft is Blake's "ideal woman." Gaunt's view may
be extreme, but most Blake scholars acknowledge
some influence on Blake by Wollstonecraft, and
it is fair to assume that this poem is directed in
some way to her memory.

She trembled & wept, sitting on the Bed side;
She forgot it was Night & she trembled & cried;
She forgot it was Night, she forgot it was Morn;
Her soft Memory imprinted with Faces of Scorn,   40

With Faces of Scorn & with Eyes of disdain
Like foul Fiends inhabiting Mary's mild Brain;
She remembers no Face like the Human Divine.
All Faces have Envy, sweet Mary, but thine:

And thine is a Face of sweet Love in despair,   45
And thine is a Face of mild sorrow & care,
And thine is a Face of wild terror & fear
That shall never be quiet till laid on its bier.

GEORGE SAINTSBURY

[Mary Wollstonecraft in Literary History]†

* * *

Even if fate and metaphysical aid had not conjoined Godwin and
Mary Wollstonecraft in the closest bond possible between man and
woman, it would have been proper to mention their names together as
authors. For as Godwin's "New Philosphy" was the boldest attempt made
by any man of the time in print to overthrow received conventions of
the relations of man to man, and incidentally of man to woman, so was
his wife's *Vindication of the Rights of Woman* a complement of it in
relation to the status of the other sex as such. She was rather hardly
treated in her own time; Horace Walpole calling her, it is said (I have
not verified the quotation), a "hyena in petticoats": it would be at least
as just to call Lord Orford a baboon in breeches.[1] And though of late
years she has been made something of a heroine, it is to be feared that
admiration has been directed rather to her crotchets than to her character. This last appears to have been as lovable as her hap was ill. The
daughter of an Irishman of means, who squandered them and became
a burden on his children; the sister of an attorney who was selfishly
indifferent to his sisters—she had to fend for herself almost entirely. At
one time she and her sisters kept school; then she was, thanks to the

---

† George Saintsbury (1845–1933) was a prolific
literary critic, editor, and journalist whose *History
of the Nineteenth Century*, from which this selection is taken, was highly respected. He gave his
name to a kind of personal criticism that focused
on the reader's reaction to literary style.
1. Horace (or Horatio) Walpole (1717–97) was the

fourth earl of Orford. The often repeated comment
about Wollstonecraft occurs in a letter that he wrote
to Hannah More. Walpole uttered it not in reference to women's rights, however, but because
he thought she had been harsh on the French
queen in her *Vindication of the Rights of Men*
(1790) [*Editor*].

recommendation of Mr. Prior, a master at Eton, introduced as governess to the family of Lord Kingsborough; then, after doing hack-work for Johnson, the chief Liberal publisher of the period, she went to Paris, and unluckily fell in with a handsome scoundrel, Gilbert Imlay, an American soldier. She lived with him, he deserted her, and she nearly committed the suicide which was actually the fate of her unfortunate daughter by him, Fanny Imlay or Godwin. Only at the last had she a glimpse of happiness. Godwin, who had some weaknesses, but who was not a scoundrel, met her, and fell in love with her, and as both had independently demonstrated that marriage was a failure, they naturally married; but she died a week after giving birth to a daughter—the future Mrs. Shelley. The *Vindication of the Rights of Woman*, on which Mary Wollstonecraft's fame as an author almost wholly rests, is in some ways a book nearly as faulty as it can be. It is not well written; it is full of prejudices quite as wrong-headed as those it combats; it shows very little knowledge either of human nature or of good society; and its "niceness," to use the word in what was then its proper sense, often goes near to the nasty. But its protest on the one hand against the "proper" sentimentality of such English guides of female youth as Drs. Fordyce and Gregory, on the other against the "improper" sentimentality of Rousseeau, is genuine and generous. Many of its positions and contentions may be accepted unhesitatingly to-day by those who are by no means enamoured of advanced womanhood; and Mary, as contrasted with most of her rights-of-women followers, is curiously free from bumptiousness and the general qualities of the virago. She had but ill luck in life, and perhaps showed no very good judgment in letters, but she had neither bad brains nor bad blood; and the references to her, long after her death, by such men as Southey, show the charm which she exercised.

* * *

GEORGE ELIOT

Margaret Fuller and Mary Wollstonecraft†

The dearth of new books just now gives us time to recur to less recent ones which we have hitherto noticed but slightly; and among these we choose the late edition of Margaret Fuller's *Woman in the Nineteenth Century*, because we think it has been unduly thrust into the background

---

† The great English novelist George Eliot (a pen-name; her real name was Mary Ann Evans) began her career as a translator and an assistant editor at *The Westminister Review* in London. This essay appeared in another journal, called *The Leader*, on October 13, 1855, as a book review comparing Wollstonecraft's *Vindication of the Rights of Woman* and Margaret Fuller's *Woman in the Nineteenth Century* (1855). Footnotes for this selection are by the editor.

by less comprehensive and candid productions on the same subject. Notwithstanding certain defects of taste and a sort of vague spiritualism and grandiloquence which belong to all but the very best American writers, the book is a valuable one: it has the enthusiasm of a noble and sympathetic nature, with the moderation and breadth and large allowance of a vigorous and cultivated understanding. There is no exaggeration of woman's moral excellence or intellectual capabilities; no injudicious insistance on her fitness for this or that function hitherto engrossed by men; but a calm plea for the removal of unjust laws and artificial restrictions, so that the possibilities of her nature may have room for full development, a wisely stated demand to disencumber her of the

> Parasitic forms
> That seem to keep her up, but drag her down—
> And leave her field to burgeon and to bloom
> From all within her, make herself her own
> To give or keep, to live and learn and be
> All that not harms distinctive womanhood[1].

It is interesting to compare this essay of Margaret Fuller's published in its earliest form in 1843,[2] with a work on the position of woman, written between sixty and seventy years ago—we mean Mary Wollstonecraft's *Rights of Woman*. The latter work was not continued beyond the first volume; but so far as this carries the subject, the comparison, at least in relation to strong sense and loftiness of moral tone, is not at all disadvantageous to the woman of the last century. There is in some quarters a vague prejudice against the *Rights of Woman* as in some way or other a reprehensible book, but readers who go to it with this impression will be surprised to find it eminently serious, severely moral, and withal rather heavy—the true reason, perhaps, that no edition has been published since 1796, and that it is now rather scarce. There are several points of resemblance, as well as of striking difference, between the two books. A strong understanding is present in both; but Margaret Fuller's mind was like some regions of her own American continent, where you are constantly stepping from the sunny 'clearings' into the mysterious twilight of the tangled forest—she often passes in one breath from forcible reasoning to dreamy vagueness; moreover, her unusually varied culture gives her great command of illustration. Mary Wollstonecraft, on the other hand, is nothing if not rational; she has no erudition, and her grave pages are lit up by no ray of fancy. In both writers we discern, under the brave bearing of a strong and truthful nature, the beating of a loving woman's heart, which teaches them not to undervalue the

---

1. Tennyson, *The Princess* 7.253–58. Editor Thomas Pinney notes that Eliot is using the early, 1847, edition of the poem and is misquoting slightly.

2. The essay was originally published in 1843 as *The Great Lawsuit*.

smallest offices of domestic care or kindliness. But Margaret Fuller, with all her passionate sensibility, is more of the literary woman, who would not have been satisfied without intellectual production; Mary Wollstonecraft, we imagine, wrote not at all for writing's sake, but from the pressure of other motives. So far as the difference of date allows, there is a striking coincidence in their trains of thought; indeed, every important idea in the *Rights of Woman*, except the combination of home education with a common day-school for boys and girls, reappears in Margaret Fuller's essay.

One point on which they both write forcibly is the fact that, while men have a horror of such faculty or culture in the other sex as tends to place it on a level with their own, they are really in a state of subjection to ignorant and feeble-minded women. Margaret Fuller says:

> Wherever man is sufficiently raised above extreme poverty or brutal stupidity, to care for the comforts of the fireside, or the bloom and ornament of life, woman has always power enough, if she choose to exert it, and is usually disposed to do so, in proportion to her ignorance and childish vanity. Unacquainted with the importance of life and its purposes, trained to a selfish coquetry and love of petty power, she does not look beyond the pleasure of making herself felt at the moment, and governments are shaken and commerce broken up to gratify the pique of a female favourite. The English shopkeeper's wife does not vote, but it is for her interest that the politician canvasses by the coarsest flattery.

Again:

> All wives, bad or good, loved or unloved, inevitably influence their husbands from the power their position not merely gives, but necessitates of colouring evidence and infusing feelings in hours when the— patient, shall I call him?—is off his guard.

Hear now what Mary Wollstonecraft says on the same subject:

> Women have been allowed to remain in ignorance and slavish dependence many, very many years, and still we hear of nothing but their fondness of pleasure and sway, their preference of rakes and soldiers, their childish attachment to toys, and the vanity that makes them value accomplishments more than virtues. History brings forward a fearful catalogue of the crimes which their cunning has produced, when the weak slaves have had sufficient address to overreach their masters. . . . When, therefore, I call women slaves, I mean in a political and civil sense; for indirectly they obtain too much power, and are debased by their exertions to obtain illicit sway. . . . The libertinism, and even the virtues of superior men, will always give women of some description great power over them; and these weak women, under the influence of childish passions and selfish vanity,

will throw a false light over the objects which the very men view with their eyes who ought to enlighten their judgment. Men of fancy, and those sanguine characters who mostly hold the helm of human affairs in general, relax in the society of women; and surely I need not cite to the most superficial reader of history the numerous examples of vice and oppression which the private intrigues of female favourites have produced; not to dwell on the mischief that naturally arises from the blundering interposition of well-meaning folly. *For in the transactions of business it is much better to have to deal with a knave than a fool, because a knave adheres to some plan, and any plan of reason may be seen through sooner than a sudden flight of folly.* The power which vile and foolish women have had over wise men who possessed sensibility is notorious.[3]

There is a notion commonly entertained among men that an instructed woman, capable of having opinions, is likely to prove an impracticable yoke-fellow, always pulling one way when her husband wants to go the other, oracular in tone, and prone to give curtain lectures on metaphysics. But surely, so far as obstinacy is concerned, your unreasoning animal is the most unmanageable of creatures, where you are not allowed to settle the question by a cudgel, a whip and bridle, or even a string to the leg. For our own parts, we see no consistent or commodious medium between the old plan of corporal discipline and that thorough education of women which will make them rational beings in the highest sense of the word. Wherever weakness is not harshly controlled it must *govern*, as you may see when a strong man holds a little child by the hand, how he is pulled hither and thither, and wearied in his walk by his submission to the whims and feeble movements of his companion. A really cultured woman, like a really cultured man, will be ready to yield in trifles. So far as we see, there is no indissoluble connexion between infirmity of logic and infirmity of will, and a woman quite innocent of an opinion in philosophy, is as likely as not to have an indomitable opinion about the kitchen. As to airs of superiority, no woman ever had them in consequences of true culture, but only because her culture was shallow or unreal, only as a result of what Mrs. Malaprop well calls 'the ineffectual qualities in a woman'[4]—mere acquisitions carried about, and not knowledge thoroughly assimilated so as to enter into the growth of the character.

To return to Margaret Fuller, some of the best things she says are on the folly of absolute definitions of woman's nature and absolute demarcations of woman's mission. 'Nature,' she says, 'seems to delight in varying the arrangements, as if to show that she will be fettered by no rule; and we must admit the same varieties that she admits.' Again: 'If

3. A *Vindication of the Rights of Woman*, pp. 167 and 174 in this edition. The italics are Eliot's.
4. Mrs. Malaprop in Richard Brinsley Sheridan's *The Rivals* continually misuses words, thus giving rise to the word "malapropism." This quotation comes from *The Rivals* 3.3.

nature is never bound down, nor the voice of inspiration stifled, that is enough. We are pleased that women should write and speak, if they feel need of it, from having something to tell; but silence for ages would be no misfortune, if that silence be from divine command, and not from man's tradition.' And here is a passage, the beginning of which has been often quoted:

> If you ask me what offices they (women) may fill, I reply—any. I do not care what case you put; let them be sea-captains if you will. I do not doubt there are women well fitted for such an office, and, if so, I should be as glad as to welcome the Maid of Saragossa, or the Maid of Missolonghi, or the Suliote heroine, or Emily Plater.[5] I think women need, especially at this juncture, a much greater range of occupation than they have, to rouse their latent powers. . . . In families that I know, some little girls like to saw wood, others to use carpenter's tools. Where these tastes are indulged, cheerfulness and good-humour are promoted. Where they are forbidden, because 'such things are not proper for girls,' they grow sullen and mischievous. Fourier[6] had observed these wants of women, as no one can fail to do who watches the desires of little girls, or knows the *ennui* that haunts grown women, except where they make to themselves a serene little world by art of some kind. He, therefore, in proposing a great variety of employments, in manufactures or the care of plants and animals, allows for one-third of women as likely to have a taste for masculine pursuits, one-third of men for feminine. . . . I have no doubt, however, that a large proportion of women would give themselves to the same employments as now, because there are circumstances that must lead them. Mothers will delight to make the nest soft and warm. Nature would take care of that; no need to clip the wings of any bird that wants to soar and sing, or finds in itself the strength of pinion for a migratory flight unusual to its kind. The difference would be that *all* need not be constrained to employments for which *some* are unfit.

A propos of the same subject, we find Mary Wollstonecraft offering a suggestion which the women of the United States have already begun to carry out. She says:

> Women, in particular, all want to be ladies. Which is simply to have nothing to do, but listlessly to go they scarcely care where, for they cannot tell what. But what have women to do in society? I may be asked, but to loiter with easy grace; surely you would not condemn

5. The Maid of Saragossa was Maria Agustin, who fought against the French at the siege of Saragossa, in Spain, in 1808 (see Byron's *Childe Harold's Pilgrimage* 1.54–56); the maid of Missolonghi, an unidentified Greek, must have made some heroic exploit during the Turkish sieges of that town in 1822 or 1826; the Suliote heroine was probably Moscha, who led a band of three hundred women to rout the Turks during the siege of Souli, in Albania, in 1803; Emily Plater, a Polish patriot, became a captain in command of a company in the insurgent army fighting the Russians in 1831 [Sandra M. Gilbert and Susan Gubar's note].
6. Charles Fourier (1772–1837), in his utopian treatise *The New Industrial World* (1829–30), develops these theories in his discussion of "The Little Hordes." [Sandra M. Gilbert and Susan Gubar's note].

them all to suckle fools and chronicle small beer. No. *Women might certainly study the art of healing, and be physicians as well as nurses. . . .* Business of various kinds they might likewise pursue, if they were educated in a more orderly manner. . . . Women would not then marry for a support, as men accept of places under government, and neglect the implied duties. [7]

Men pay a heavy price for their reluctance to encourage self-help and independent resources in women. The precious meridian years of many a man of genius have to be spent in the toil of routine, that an 'establishment' may be kept up for a woman who can understand none of his secret yearnings, who is fit for nothing but to sit in her drawing-room like a doll-Madonna in her shrine. No matter. Anything is more endurable than to change our established formulæ about women, or to run the risk of looking up to our wives instead of looking down on them. *Sit divus, dummodo non sit vivus* (let him be a god, provided he be not living), said the Roman magnates of Romulus; and so men say of women, let them be idols, useless absorbents of precious things, provided we are not obliged to admit them to be strictly fellow-beings, to be treated, one and all, with justice and sober reverence.

On one side we hear that woman's position can never be improved until women themselves are better; and, on the other, that women can never become better until their position is improved—until the laws are made more just, and a wider field opened to feminine activity. But we constantly hear the same difficulty stated about the human race in general. There is a perpetual action and reaction between individuals and institutions; we must try and mend both by little and little—the only way in which human things can be mended. Unfortunately, many over-zealous champions of women assert their actual equality with men— nay, even their moral superiority to men—as a ground for their release from oppressive laws and restrictions. They lose strength immensely by this false position. If it were true, then there would be a case in which slavery and ignorance nourished virtue, and so far we should have an argument for the continuance of bondage. But we want freedom and culture for woman, because subjection and ignorance have debased her, and with her, Man; for—

> If she be small, slight-natured, miserable,
> How shall men grow? [8]

Both Margaret Fuller and Mary Wollstonecraft have too much sagacity to fall into this sentimental exaggeration. Their ardent hopes of what women may become do not prevent them from seeing and painting women as they are. On the relative moral excellence of men and women Mary Wollstonecraft speaks with the most decision:

7. A *Vindication of the Rights of Woman*, pp. 147–48 in this edition.   8. Tennyson, *The Princess* 7.249–50.

Women are supposed to possess more sensibility, and even humanity, than men, and their strong attachments and instantaneous emotions of compassion are given as proofs; but the clinging affection of ignorance has seldom anything noble in it, and may mostly be resolved into selfishness, as well as the affection of children and brutes. I have known many weak women whose sensibility was entirely engrossed by their husbands; and as for their humanity, it was very faint indeed, or rather it was only a transient emotion of compassion. Humanity does not consist 'in a squeamish ear,' says an eminent orator. 'It belongs to the mind as well as to the nerves.' But this kind of exclusive affection, though it degrades the individual, should not be brought forward as a proof of the inferiority of the sex, because it is the natural consequence of confined views; for even women of superior sense, having their attention turned to little employments and private plans, rarely rise to heroism, unless when spurred on by love! and love, as an heroic passion, like genius, appears but once in an age. I therefore agree with the moralist who asserts 'that women have seldom so much generosity as men;' and that their narrow affections, to which justice and humanity are often sacrificed, render the sex apparently inferior, especially as they are commonly inspired by men; but I contend that the heart would expand as the understanding gained strength, if women were not depressed from their cradles.[9]

We had marked several other passages of Margaret Fuller's for extract, but as we do not aim at an exhaustive treatment of our subject, and are only touching a few of its points, we have, perhaps, already claimed as much of the reader's attention as he will be willing to give to such desultory material.

EMMA GOLDMAN

Mary Wollstonecraft: Her Tragic Life and Her Passionate Struggle for Freedom†

The Pioneers of human progress are like the Seagulls, they behold new coasts, new spheres of daring thought, when their co-voyagers see only the endless stretch of water. They send joyous greetings to the distant lands. Intense, yearning, burning faith pierces the clouds of doubt, because the sharp ears of the harbingers of life discern from the

9. *A Vindication of the Rights of Woman*, pp. 188–89 in this edition.
† Emma Goldman (1869–1940), the fiery speaker and radical organizer known as "Red Emma," early in her life espoused the anarchist cause and was sent to prison in 1893 for inciting a riot. She and her lifelong friend Alexander Berkman were deported from the U.S. in 1919. Disappointed with the communism she found in the Soviet Union, she finally moved to Canada, where she died. She is buried in Chicago. Footnotes for this selection are by the editor. This article is reprinted from *Feminist Studies*, Volume 7, no. 1 (1981): 114–21, by permission of the publisher *Feminist Studies*, Inc., c/o Women's Studies Program, University of Maryland, College Park, MD 20742.

maddening roar of the waves, the new message, the new symbol for humanity.

The latter does not grasp the new, dull, and inert, it meets the pioneer of truth with misgivings and resentment, as the disturber of its peace, as the annihilator of all stable habits and traditions.

Thus the pathfinders are heard only by the few, because they will not tread the beaten tracks, and the mass lacks the strength to follow into the unknown.

In conflict with every institution of their time since they will not compromise, it is inevitable that the advance guards should become aliens to the very one[s] they wish to serve; that they should be isolated, shunned, and repudiated by the nearest and dearest of kin. Yet the tragedy every pioneer must experience is not the lack of understanding— it arises from the fact that having seen new possibilities for human advancement, the pioneers can not take root in the old, and with the new still far off they become outcast roamers of the earth, restless seekers for the things they will never find.

They are consumed by the fires of compassion and sympathy for all suffering and with all their fellows, yet they are compelled to stand apart from their surroundings. Nor need they ever hope to receive the love their great souls crave, for such is the penalty of a great spirit, that what he receives is but nothing compared to what he gives.

Such was the fate and tragedy of Mary Wollstonecraft. What she gave the World, to those she loved, towered high above the average possibility to receive, nor could her burning, yearning soul content itself with the miserly crumbs that fall from the barren table of the average life.

Mary Wollstonecraft came into the World at a time when her sex was in chattel slavery: owned by the father while at home and passed on as a commodity to her husband when married. It was indeed a strange World that Mary entered into on the twenty-seventh of April 1759, yet not very much stranger than our own. For while the human race has no doubt progressed since that memorable moment, Mary Wollstone-craft is still very much the pioneer, far ahead of our own time.

She was one of many children of a middle-class family, the head of which lived up to his rights as master by tyrannizing his wife and children and squandering his capital in idle living and feasting. Who could stay him, the creator of the universe? As in many other things, so have his rights changed little, since Mary's father's time. The family soon found itself in dire want, but how were middle-class girls to earn their own living with every avenue closed to them? They had but one calling, that was marriage. Mary's sister probably realized that. She married a man she did not love in order to escape the misery of the parents' home. But Mary was made of different material, a material so finely woven it could not fit into coarse surroundings. Her intellect saw the degradation of her sex, and her soul—always at white heat against every wrong—rebelled against the slavery of half of the human race. She determined to stand on her own feet. In that determination she was strengthened by her friendship with Fannie Blood,[1] who herself had made the first step towards emancipation by working for her own support. But even without Fannie Blood as a great spiritual force in Mary's life, nor yet even without the economic factor, she was destined by her very nature to become the Iconoclast of the false Gods whose standards the World demanded her to obey. Mary was a born rebel, one who would have created rather than submit to any form set up for her.

It has been said that nature uses a vast amount of human material to create one genius. The same holds good of the true rebel, the true pioneer. Mary was born and not made through this or that individual incident in her surroundings. The treasure of her soul, the wisdom of her life's philosophy, the depth of her World of thought, the intensity of her battle for human emancipation and especially her indomitable struggle for the liberation of her own sex, are even today so far ahead of the average grasp that we may indeed claim for her the rare exception which nature has created but once in a century. Like the Falcon who soared through space in order to behold the Sun and then paid for it with his life, Mary drained the cup of tragedy, for such is the price of wisdom.

Much has been written and said about this wonderful champion of the eighteenth century, but the subject is too vast and still very far from being exhausted. The woman's movement of today and especially the suffrage movement will find in the life and struggle of Mary Wollstonecraft much that would show them the inadequacy of mere external gain as a means of freeing their sex. No doubt much has been accomplished since Mary thundered against women's economic and political enslavement, but has that made her free? Has it added to the depth of her being? Has it brought joy and cheer in her life? Mary's own tragic life proves that economic and social rights for women alone are not enough to fill her life, nor yet enough to fill any deep life, man or woman. It is not true that the deep and fine man—I do not mean the mere male—differs very largely from the deep and fine woman. He too seeks for beauty and love, for harmony and understanding. Mary realized that, because she did not limit herself to her own sex, she demanded freedom for the whole human race.

To make herself economically independent, Mary first taught school and then accepted a position as Governess to the pampered children of a pampered lady,[2] but she soon realized that she was unfit to be a servant and that she must turn to something that would enable her to live, yet

---

1. Fanny Blood was Wollstonecraft's closest friend in her youth. Wollstonecraft had lived with the Blood family, had taught with Fanny in the school they established in Newington Green, and had traveled to Lisbon to be with her during what proved to be her fatal childbirth in 1785.
2. In 1786–87, Wollstonecraft had been a governess in the Irish family of Viscount and Lady Kingsborough.

at the same time would not drag her down. She learned the bitterness and humiliation of the economic struggle. It was not so much the lack of external comforts, that galled Mary's soul, but it was the lack of inner freedom which results from poverty and dependence which made her cry out, "How can anyone profess to be a friend to freedom yet not see that poverty is the greatest evil."

Fortunately for Mary and posterity, there existed a rare specimen of humanity, which we of the twentieth century still lack, the daring and liberal Publisher Johnson. He was the first to publish the works of Blake, of Thomas Paine, of Godwin and of all the rebels of his time without any regard to material gain. He also saw Mary's great possibilities and engaged her as proofreader, translator, and contributor to his paper, the *Analytical Review*. He did more. He became her most devoted friend and advisor. In fact, no other man in Mary's life was so staunch and understood her difficult nature, as did that rare man. Nor did she ever open up her soul as unreservedly to any one as she did to him. Thus she writes in one of her analytical moments:

> Life is but a jest. I am a strange compound of weakness and resolution. There is certainly a great defect in my mind, my wayward heart creates its own misery. Why I have been made thus I do not know and until I can form some idea of the whole of my existence, I must be content to weep and dance like a child, long for a toy and be tired of it as soon as I get it. We must each of us wear a fool's cap, but mine alas has lost its bells and is grown so heavy, I find it intolerably trouble-some.[3]

That Mary should write thus of herself to Johnson shows that there must have been a beautiful comradeship between them. At any rate, thanks to her friend she found relief from the terrible struggle. She found also intellectual food. Johnson's rooms were the rendezvous of the intellectual elite of London. Thomas Paine, Godwin, Dr. Fordyce, the Painter Fuseli, and many others gathered there to discuss all the great subjects of their time.

Mary came into their sphere and became the very center of that intellectual bustle. Godwin relates how he came to hear Tom Paine at an evening arranged for him, but instead he had to listen to Mary Wollstonecraft, her conversational powers like everything else about her inevitably stood in the center of the stage.

Thus Mary could soar through space, her spirit reaching out to great heights. The opportunity soon offered itself. The erstwhile champion of English liberalism, the great Edmund Burke, delivered himself of a sentimental sermon against the French Revolution. He had met the fair Marie Antoinette and bewailed her lot at the hands of the infuriated people of Paris. His middle-class sentimentality saw in the greatest of

---

3. The complete letter can be found in Ralph M. Wardle, ed., *Collected Letters of Mary Wollstonecraft* (Ithaca: Cornell UP, 1979), pp. 220–21.

all uprisings only the surface and not the terrible wrongs the French people endured before they were driven to their acts. But Mary Wollstonecraft saw and her reply to the mighty Burke, *The Vindication of the Rights of Man,* is one of the most powerful pleas for the oppressed and disinherited ever made.

It was written at white heat, for Mary had followed the revolution intently. Her force, her enthusiasm, and, above all, her logic and clarity of vision proved this erstwhile schoolmistress to be possessed of a tremendous brain and of a deep and passionately throbbing heart. That such should emanate from a woman was like a bomb explosion, unheard of before. It shocked the World at large, but gained for Mary the respect and affection of her male contemporaries. They felt no doubt, that she was not only their equal, but in many respects, superior to most of them.

> When you call yourself a friend of liberty, ask your own heart whether it would not be more consistent to style yourself the champion of Property, the adorer of the golden image which power has set up?
>
> Security of Property! behold in a few words the definition of English liberty. But softly, it is only the property of the rich that is secure, the man who lives by the sweat of his brow has no asylum from oppression. [4]

Think of the wonderful penetration in a woman more than one hundred years ago. Even today there are few among our so-called reformers, certainly very few among the women reformers, who see as clearly as this giant of the eighteenth Century. She understood only too well that mere political changes are not enough and do not strike deep into the evils of Society.

Mary Wollstonecraft on Passion:

> The regulating of passion is not always wise. On the contrary, it should seem that one reason why men have a superior judgment and more fortitude than women is undoubtedly this, that they give a freer scope to the grand passion and by more frequently going astray enlarge their minds.
>
> Drunkenness is due to lack of better amusement rather than to innate viciousness, crime is often the outcome of a superabundant life.
>
> The same energy which renders a man a daring villain would have rendered him useful to society had that society been well organized.

Mary was not only an intellectual, she was, as she says herself, possessed of a wayward heart. That is she craved love and affection. It was therefore but natural for her to be carried away by the beauty and passion of the Painter Fuseli, but whether he did not reciprocate her love, or because he lacked courage at the critical moment, Mary was forced to go through her first experience of love and pain. She certainly was not

4. Mary Wollstonecraft, A *Vindication of the Rights of Men* (1790; New York: Scholars Facsimiles & Reprints, 1975), pp. 20 and 24.

the kind of a woman to throw herself on any man's neck. Fuseli was an easy-go-lucky sort and easily carried away by Mary's beauty. But he had a wife, and the pressure of public opinion was too much for him. Be it as it may, Mary suffered keenly and fled to France to escape the charms of the artist.

Biographers are the last to understand their subject or else they would not have made so much ado of the Fuseli episode, for it was nothing else. Had the loud-mouthed Fuseli been as free as Mary to gratify their sex attraction, Mary would probably have settled down to her normal life. But he lacked courage and Mary, having been sexually starved, could not easily quench the aroused senses.

However, it required but a strong intellectual interest to bring her back to herself. And that interest she found in the stirring events of the French Revolution.

However, it was before the Fuseli incident that Mary added to her *Vindication of the Rights of Man* the *Vindication of the Rights of Woman*, a plea for the emancipation of her sex. It is not that she held man responsible for the enslavement of woman. Mary was too big and too universal to place the blame on one sex. She emphasized the fact that woman herself is a hindrance to human progress because she persists in being a sex object rather than a personality, a creative force in life. Naturally, she maintained that man has been the tyrant so long that he resents any encroachment upon his domain, but she pleaded that it was as much for his as for woman's sake that she demanded economic, political, and sexual freedom for women as the only solution to the problem of human emancipation. "The laws respecting women made an absurd unit of a man and his wife and then by the easy transition of only considering him as responsible, she is reduced to a mere cypher."[5]

Nature has certainly been very lavish when she fashioned Mary Wollstonecraft. Not only has she endowed her with a tremendous brain, but she gave her great beauty and charm. She also gave her a deep soul, deep both in joy and sorrow. Mary was therefore doomed to become the prey of more than one infatuation. Her love for Fuseli soon made way for a more terrible, more intense love, the greatest force in her life, one that tossed her about as a willess, helpless toy in the hands of fate.

Life without love for a character like Mary is inconceivable, and it was her search and yearning for love which hurled her against the rock of inconsistency and despair.

While in Paris, Mary met in the house of T[homas] Paine where she had been welcomed as a friend, the vivacious, handsome, and elemental American, [Gilbert] Imlay. If not for Mary's love for him the World might never have known of this Gentleman. Not that he was ordinary, Mary could not have loved him with that mad passion which nearly wrecked her life. He had distinguished himself in the American War

5. A *Vindication of the Rights of Woman*, p. 145 in this edition.

and had written a thing or two, but on the whole he would never have set the World on fire. But he set Mary on fire and held her in a trance for a considerable time.

The very force of her infatuation for him excluded harmony, but is it a matter of blame as far as Imlay is concerned? He gave her all he could, but her insatiable hunger for love could never be content with little, hence the tragedy. Then too, he was a roamer, an adventurer, an explorer into the territory of female hearts. He was possessed by the Wanderlust, could not rest at peace long anywhere. Mary needed peace, she also needed what she had never had in her family, the quiet and warmth of a home. But more than anything else she needed love, unreserved, passionate love. Imlay could give her nothing and the struggle began shortly after the mad dream had passed.

Imlay was much away from Mary at first under the pretext of business. He would not be an American to neglect his love for business. His travels brought him, as the Germans say, to other cities and other loves. As a man that was his right, equally so was it his right to deceive Mary. What she must have endured only those can appreciate who have themselves known the tempest.

All through her pregnancy with Imlay's child, Mary pined for the man, begged and called, but he was busy. The poor chap did not know that all the wealth in the world could not make up for the wealth of Mary's love. The only consolation she found was in her work. She wrote *The French Revolution* right under the very influence of that tremendous drama. Keen as she was in her observation, she saw deeper than Burke, beneath all the terrible loss of life, she saw the still more terrible contrast between poverty and riches and [that] all the bloodshed was in vain so long as that contrast continued. Thus she wrote: "if the aristocracy of birth is leveled with the ground only to make room for that of riches, I am afraid that the morale of the people will not be much improved by the change. Everything whispers to me that names not principles are changed." She realized while in Paris what she had predicted in her attack on Burke, that the demon of property has ever been at hand to encroach on the sacred rights of man.

With all her work Mary could not forget her love. It was after a vain and bitter struggle to bring Imlay to her that she attempted suicide. She failed, and to get back her strength she went to Norway on a mission for Imlay. She recuperated physically, but her soul was bruised and scarred. Mary and Imlay came together several times, but it was only dragging out the inevitable. Then came the final blow. Mary learned that Imlay had other affairs and that he had been deceiving her, not so much out of mischief as out of cowardice.

She then took the most terrible and desperate step, she threw herself into the Thames after walking for hours to get her clothing wet [so] that she may surely drown. Oh, the inconsistencies, cry the superficial critics. But was it?

In the struggle between her intellect and her passion Mary had suffered a defeat. She was too proud and too strong to survive such a terrible blow. What else was there for her but to die?

Fate that had played so many pranks with Mary Wollstonecraft willed it otherwise. It brought her back to life and hope, only to kill her at their very doors.

She found in Godwin the first representative of Anarchist Communism, a sweet and tender camaraderie, not of the wild, primitive kind but the quiet, mature, warm sort, that soothes one like a cold hand upon a burning forehead. With him she lived consistently with her ideas in freedom, each apart from the other, sharing what they could of each other.

Again Mary was about to become a mother, not in stress and pain as the first time, but in peace and surrounded by kindness. Yet so strange is fate, that Mary had to pay with her life for the life of her little girl, Mary Godwin. She died on September tenth, 1797, barely thirty-eight years of age. Her confinement with the first child, though under the most trying of circumstances, was mere play, or as she wrote to her sister, "an excuse for staying in bed." Yet that tragic time demanded its victim. Fannie Imlay died of the death her mother failed to find. She committed suicide by drowning, while Mary Wollstonecraft Godwin became the wife of the sweetest lark of liberty, Shelley.

Mary Wollstonecraft, the intellectual genius, the daring fighter of the eighteenth, nineteenth, and twentieth Centuries, Mary Wollstonecraft, the woman and lover, was doomed to pain because of the very wealth of her being: With all her affairs she yet was pretty much alone, as every great soul must be alone—no doubt, that is the penalty for greatness.

Her indomitable courage in behalf of the disinherited of the earth has alienated her from her own time and created the discord in her being which alone accounts for her terrible tragedy with Imlay. Mary Wollstonecraft aimed for the highest summit of human possibilities. She was too wise and too worldly not to see the discrepancy between her world of ideals and her world of love that caused the break of the string of her delicate, complicated soul.

Perhaps it was best for her to die at that particular moment. For he who has ever tasted the madness of life can never again adjust himself to an even tenor. But we have lost much and can only be reconciled by what she has left, and that is much. Had Mary Wollstonecraft not written a line, her life would have furnished food for thought. But she has given both, she therefore stands among the world's greatest, a life so deep, so rich, so exquisitely beautiful in her complete humanity.

ALICE WEXLER

Afterword [Emma Goldman, Mary Wollstonecraft, and Ruth Benedict]†

"The most notable fact that culture imprints on women," writes Adrienne Rich, "is the sense of our limits. The most important thing one woman can do for another is to illuminate and expand her sense of actual possibilities."[1] Although Rich was writing about biological mothers and daughters, her insight also applies to their historical counterparts. For early nineteenth-century feminists such as Frances Wright, Lucretia Mott, and Elizabeth Cady Stanton, Mary Wollstonecraft's *Vindication of the Rights of Woman* was an important source of inspiration. The revival of Wollstonecraft's personal reputation in the late nineteenth century stimulated renewed interest in her life, as well as her ideas. By the early twentieth century, a number of rebellious women were finding in that life a major statement of female potentiality. Despite, or perhaps because of, her complex and ambivalent legacy, the attempt to assess that legacy was for some women, at least, a way of clarifying their own identities and options. To confront Mary Wollstonecraft was also a way of confronting oneself.

That Emma Goldman should identify with Mary Wollstonecraft is not surprising. As a leading figure in the international anarchist movement between 1889 and 1940, Goldman looked to Wollstonecraft as a precursor of her own revolt against the constraints of authority, particularly against the economic, intellectual, and social restrictions on women. Like Wollstonecraft, Goldman also called for a transformation of consciousness, the overcoming of inhibitions and fears that would make it more possible for women "to be human in the truest sense."[2] Both stressed inner freedom, independence of mind and judgment, as essential elements of liberation. "Independence," wrote Wollstonecraft, "I have long considered as the grand blessing of life, the basis of every virtue. . . ."[3] "Until woman has learned . . . to stand firmly on her own ground and to insist upon her own unrestricted freedom . . . she cannot call herself emancipated," echoed Goldman.[4]

Parallels between the lives of Wollstonecraft and Goldman are also striking, despite the fact that one grew up in eighteenth-century England, the other in nineteenth-century Russia, Germany, and America. Both came from middle-class families of declining fortunes. Both women

† This article is reprinted from *Feminist Studies*, Volume 7, no. 1 (1981): 113–33, by permission of the publisher, *Feminist Studies*, Inc., % Women's Studies Program, University of Maryland, College Park, MD 20742.

1. Adrienne Rich, *Of Woman Born* (New York: Norton, 1976), p. 246.

2. Emma Goldman, "The Tragedy of Woman's Emancipation," *Mother Earth* 1 (March 1906): 10.
3. Mary Wollstonecraft, A *Vindication of the Rights of Woman* (1792; reprint ed., New York: Norton, 1987).
4. Goldman, "Tragedy," p. 3.

perceived their mothers as downtrodden, but rejecting. Both recalled childhoods dominated by fathers who were harsh, authoritarian, and unloving, but at the same time somewhat ineffective in their dealings with the world outside the family. Both Wollstonecraft and Goldman had been rebellious from an early age, intense in their desires for education and independence, as well as love. They both directly confronted the enormous gap between their own soaring ambitions and the few alternatives available to young women who sought economic independence. Both women were angry, energetic, passionate, and intellectual, yet also subject to periods of depression. Unlike Wollstonecraft, who was primarily a writer, Goldman was predominantly an activist, whose multiple talents made her one of the most respected figures in the anarchist movement during her lifetime. Yet while Goldman often described herself as an agitator and propagandist (as well as publisher of *Mother Earth*), she ultimately came to think of herself as an educator, like Wollstonecraft.

Goldman evidently became interested in Wollstonecraft in 1911, when she first presented this lecture. She indicated that she had read about Wollstonecraft before that year and had also attended a lecture in 1893 given by another anarchist, Voltairine de Cleyre, on the eighteenth-century feminist. Yet Goldman's own comments and the fact that neither Wollstonecraft nor the *Vindication of the Rights of Woman* are mentioned in any of her feminist essays (most of which were written prior to 1911) suggest that her disapproval of Wollstonecraft's love life had blocked her appreciations for any strengths or insights to be gained, either from the life or the work. If Wollstonecraft did influence Goldman's thinking about women, that influence was unacknowledged.[5]

By 1911, changes in Goldman's life, and the publication of a new biography, revived her interest. That same year, G. R. Stirling Taylor published *Mary Wollstonecraft: A Study in Economics and Romance.* The similarities in content, emphasis, and quotations between this study and Goldman's essay indicates that it was almost certainly Goldman's main source of information. Yet it is not Goldman's reading of Taylor, but rather her "misreading," her modification of Taylor's interpretation, that provides the most revealing glimpse, not only of Goldman's understanding of Wollstonecraft, but also of herself.

For Taylor, Wollstonecraft's blend of powerful intellect and passionate temperament was indicative of her greatness. Goldman agreed. For Taylor, Wollstonecraft's intellectual and sexual struggles culminated in a successful resolution. If her life and ideas shocked the sensibilities of most of her contemporaries and earned her a scandalous reputation, she also earned the admiration and respect, during her lifetime, of some of

---

5. Goldman to Ben Reitman, 26 July 1911. Ben Reitman Papers, University of Illinois at Chicago. I am grateful to Candace Falk for first calling my attention to this reference.

the most brilliant radical minds in London. Despite the agony of her affair with Imlay—which drove her twice to attempt suicide—she ultimately recovered from this affair. Her capacity to form a more mutual, less obsessive, and more satisfying relationship with William Godwin was evidence of her ability to learn from experience, and to really live in accordance with her ideal of combining intimacy and independence. As Taylor described it:

> She had in her famous book taught what she held to be the true theory of the sex relation. She now had an opportunity of putting her theories into practice in at least a partially complete form. For a year she lived a life of comparative quiet and content. She saw enough of Godwin to soothe her restless desire for personal affection; she had the freedom which satisfied her great sense of independence; and together they gave her peace.[6]

Goldman's interpretation was quite different. While admitting that Wollstonecraft had been admired by many brilliant London intellectuals, Goldman emphasized the rejection and repudiation by the general public which attended such daring nonconformity. Yet this "lack of understanding" was not the deepest "tragedy" of her life, in Goldman's view. Rather, it was her own inner conflict, "the fact that having seen new possibilities for human advancement, the pioneers can not take root in the old, and with the new still far off they become outcast roamers of the earth, restless seekers for the things they will never find."

In Goldman's interpretation, Wollstonecraft's unhappy passion for Gilbert Imlay was the great turning point and tragic climax of her life, and one from which she never really recovered. Goldman observed elsewhere that she thought Wollstonecraft's life had been "wrecked through that one great passion." The subsequent relationship with Godwin, from Goldman's perspective, was pallid by comparison, "a sweet and tender comaraderie, not of the wild primitive kind but the quiet mature warm sort, that soothes one like a cold hand upon a burning forehead." Goldman suggested that her death may have come at an appropriate moment. "For he who has ever tasted the madness of life can never again adjust himself to an even tenor." She came close to suggesting that Wollstonecraft's early death in childbirth was somehow just retribution for her daring intellectual and social revolt, as well as being the inevitable price of wisdom. "Mary Wollstonecraft aimed for the highest summit of human possibilities," Goldman wrote. And like the falcon "who soared through space in order to behold the sun and then paid for it with his life, Mary drained the cup of tragedy, for such is the price of wisdom."

Taylor, however, had not intimated that Wollstonecraft's life was tragic. In his interpretation, she had triumphed. He had mentioned "the

6. G. R. Stirling Taylor, *Mary Wollstonecraft: A Study in Economics and Romance* (1911; reprint ed., New York: Haskell House Publishers, 1969), p. 193.

tragedy of the prophet crying in the wilderness" only in passing, in relation to the *Vindication*.[7] Goldman made this idea a central theme. Indeed, Taylor had suggested a final integration between her love life and her intellectual life in the relationship with Godwin. Goldman emphasized instead "the discrepancy between her world of ideals and her world of love" which caused her to attempt suicide. Instead of growth and achievement, Goldman emphasized anguish and pain. Instead of respect, she emphasized repudiation. Given the evidence in Taylor's biography, why did Goldman see Wollstonecraft's life as somehow doomed and unsuccessful? Why, in short, did she see it as "tragic"?

In fact, Goldman really presented two conflicting images of Wollstonecraft: the "pioneer of modern womanhood" and the tragic romantic heroine. The positive Wollstonecraft was a woman who triumphed over her circumstances by virtue of her intelligence and determination. She was a "daring fighter," a "path-finder," a "pioneer" who would "not tread the beaten tracks," would not compromise, who "aimed for the highest summit of human possibilities." The tragic Wollstonecraft was a "born" rebel whose life seemed continually bound by the exigencies of "fate," "destiny," and "inevitability." So, for example, it was "inevitable" that the advance guards should be "isolated, shunned, and repudiated by the nearest and dearest of kin." Wollstonecraft was "destined by her very nature" to become a great rebel. She was "doomed to suffering by the very wealth of her being." She was also "doomed" to become the helpless prey of love, but "so strange is fate" that she had to "pay with her life" for the life of her child.

These two images, the positive and the tragic, reflect a contradiction that informs the entire essay, and that corresponds to a conflict in Goldman's thought. On the one hand, she believed in free will, the human power to make choices and to act, the possibility of freedom. On the other hand, she seemed also to believe, perhaps at a less conscious level, that many aspects of human behavior were determined by heredity, by destiny, by conditions beyond human control. Rather than attempting to assess the weight of specific factors in any given situation, Goldman tended to alternate between determinist and voluntarist modes of explanation, without any real attempt at integration.

Thus, Goldman's anarchism was based on a belief in the power of the individual to act, the power of "the ideal" to motivate economic and social revolt. "I do not believe in this theory 'what has to be must be.' It is an excuse for cowards and weaklings," she once wrote.[8] And in her own life, Goldman translated this belief into action. Her tremendous energy as an agitator, propagandist, nurse, publisher, author, organizer, theatrical manager, and drama critic testifies to her success in shaping her life according to her own will.

7. Ibid., p. 110.
8. Goldman to Ben Reitman, June 22, no year, Ben Reitman Papers.

Yet in her private correspondence, Goldman often alluded to fate, heredity, destiny, and inevitability, particularly in describing or explaining her own behavior. She once described her psychology as that of a gambler, "driven by an irresistible force, until he has lost his last shirt."[9] She "could no more help crying out [against injustice] than I could if I were drowning. I am an anarchist of the Topsy variety—I was just born so."[1] Thus, her ambivalent portrait of Wollstonecraft—as both architect and victim of her own life—suggests Goldman's similarly conflicting images of herself.

Goldman's tendency to appeal to "fate" also suggests a certain self-dramatizing quality characteristic of her personality. The inflated, sentimental, grandiose tone of the Wollstonecraft essay, particularly at the beginning, conveys Goldman's tendency to imagine herself, like Wollstonecraft, as a great prophet whose vision placed her far beyond the capacity of her contemporaries to appreciate or understand her. There was, of course, considerable truth in this idea. Still, Goldman's narcissism often led her to downplay the efforts of other radicals who shared her struggle, and at times to regard the very people she was trying to reach with a kind of Nietzschean contempt. Her observation that Wollstonecraft was "pretty much alone as every great soul must be alone—no doubt, that is the penalty for greatness" suggests the way Goldman often thought about herself.[2]

Goldman may have emphasized the negative or "tragic" aspects of Wollstonecraft's life because she was feeling depressed about her own life around the time she wrote the essay. Early in 1911, in a particularly low mood, Goldman wrote a poignant letter to her friend, Hutchins Hapgood, describing feelings of sadness and resignation that contrast dramatically with her determined and optimistic public persona:

I must be getting old, Hutchie dear. I see nothing but clouds most times, or is it my own fancy? I can not tell. I only know I have grown so damnably sensitive to all kinds of impressions, as if my soul were covered with tissue paper. Fate or the devil must have entered into some sort of a conspiracy when I was thrust into the public arena. I realize more and more how deficient I am for that. And yet I am not much fit for a private life. Truth is, I am pretty much of an abortion, Hutchie boy. I find life hard to endure under all circumstances. You see, I am not as lucky as you. I too do not like myself, still less do I like life, or that which we call life. . . . Contrary to my reputation, I never could enter into a momentary relationship.

Every experience meant more to me than the birth of a child. I have always paid much more than I got out, which is no one's fault but my own, possibly I am too insatiable, I don't know. . . . I am a

9. Goldman to "friend," 20 February 1909, Ben Reitman Papers.

1. Quoted in Richard Drinnon, *Rebel in Paradise* (1961: reprint ed., New York: Bantam, 1973), p.

22.

2. See Emma Goldman, *Living My Life* (1931; reprint ed., New York: Dover, 1970), p. 343.

queer specimen, Hutchie darling. It's only fortunate my friends do not know me, or I would be lonelier than I am now.[3]

The mood evoked in this letter may well have led Goldman to emphasize the anguish, the loneliness, the feelings of inner conflict and unsatisfied longing in Wollstonecraft's life, because these feelings seem to have characterized her own life while she was thinking and writing about Wollstonecraft. There was an additional reason for Goldman to emphasize at this moment in her life both the "tragic" and the "inevitable" in the life of Wollstonecraft. At the time she wrote the essay, Goldman had been involved for three years in a love affair which she regarded as similar in certain ways to Wollstonecraft's passionate involvement with Imlay. Goldman's lover was Ben Reitman, a flamboyant and irascible doctor from Chicago, ten years younger than she. Like Imlay, Reitman was an American who symbolized for the immigrant Goldman the brashness, exuberance, and "primitive" quality of American life. Just as Imlay was always leaving Wollstonecraft on "business," Reitman too was a restless wanderer (and former hobo) who could not stay peacefully with Goldman for long. Reitman left his medical practice in Chicago in 1908 and for nearly ten years traveled with Goldman for several months each year as manager during her lecture tours. He was very effective in this role, being a talented publicist and promoter (although not an anarchist). Yet their times together were stormy and full of conflict. Although their sexual relationship was intense and satisfying, Goldman felt tormented, not only by Reitman's long absences (he continued to maintain a home in Chicago), but also by his continual infidelities, which he seemed unable or unwilling to control. Despite her perception of him as shallow, narcissistic, and callous, she was obsessed by him with an intensity she occasionally described as "not a healthy thing by any means."[4]

Committed to freedom and independence in love as well as in politics, Goldman found herself feeling bound and enslaved by her passion for Reitman. Unable to explain this obsession with a man of whom her reason disapproved, she generally attributed it to "destiny" or to "ironies of fate." Her erotic dependence on Reitman, and consequent unhappiness, was "inevitable."[5]

Emphasizing the element of fate and destiny in Wollstonecraft's life, Goldman was also describing her own feelings of helplessness before emotional forces she could neither understand nor control. Emphasizing Wollstonecraft's need for love, and the importance of sexuality in her life, Goldman also described her own intense hunger for love, and the pervasive feelings of unsatisfied longing that persisted throughout her

3. Goldman to Hutchins Hapgood, 23 February 1911. Hutchins Hapgood Papers, Beinecke Rare Book and Manuscript Library, Yale University, New Haven, Conn.

4. Goldman to Ben Reitman, 9 July 1912 and 26 September 1912. Ben Reitman Papers.

5. Goldman to Ben Reitman, 30 December 1909, Ben Reitman Papers.

life. Her vision of Wollstonecraft's life as "tragic" suggests her sense of her own relationship with Reitman as "a great painful tragedy," but one which she felt powerless to change.

In a larger context, Goldman's emphasis on the "tragic" in Wollstonecraft's life reflects her conception of the "tragedy" of the "emancipated" or "modern" woman which she retained throughout her life. In her essay, "The Tragedy of Woman's Emancipation," first published in 1906, Goldman had criticized the American feminist movement for focusing too narrowly on the "external tyrants" while neglecting the power of the "internal tyrannies" which "seem to get along as beautifully in the heads and hearts cf the most active exponents of woman's emancipation, as in the heads and hearts of our grandmothers."[6] Goldman wrote that the narrowness of the modern ideal of emancipation induced women "to make a dignified, proper appearance, while the inner life is growing empty and dead." It had made of her "a compulsory vestal," fearful of love and sexual intimacy. "The tragedy of the self-supporting or economically free woman does not lie in too many, but in too few experiences." Only by "emancipating herself from emancipation," that is, by beginning with her "inner regeneration," and cutting loose "from the weight of prejudices, traditions and customs" that stifled her sexual and emotional life, would she really liberate herself from the chains of the past.

Later in her life, Goldman described this conflict somewhat differently. "The tragedy of all emancipated women, myself included," she wrote in 1925 to her comrade, Alexander Berkman, is that "we are still rooted in the old soil, though our visions are of the future and our desire is to be free and independent."[7] Most of Goldman's activist and radical women contemporaries would probably have rejected her implied assessment of their lives as tragic. For the autobiographies and correspondence of women such as Charlotte Perkins Gilman, Elizabeth Gurley Flynn, Jane Addams, Crystal Eastman, and Lillian Wald convey their authors' sense of purpose and deep satisfaction with their lives. Nevertheless, it is Goldman's awareness, not only of the external, objective barriers to emancipation, but also the internal, subjective ones—the power of irrational emotions to persist even in the face of clear intellectual awareness of their irrationability—that gives her feminism its significance today. If her sensitivity to the power of sexuality and emotion in her own life caused her to exaggerate—at times—its power in other lives, that same sensitivity also formed the basis of her most compelling feminist insights.

In this light, it is instructive to compare Goldman's portrait of Wollstonecraft with that of Ruth Benedict, written only a few years later,

6. Goldman, "Tragedy," pp. 9–18.
7. Goldman to Alexander Berkman, 4 September 1925, in *Nowhere at Home: Letters from Exile of* *Emma Goldman and Alexander Berkman*, ed. Richard Drinnon and Anna Maria Drinnon (New York: Schocken, 1975), p. 128.

between 1914 and 1917.[8] For Benedict, Wollstonecraft's story was "that most precious of human documents: the story of a life that achieved an idea." The idea, however, was not an abstraction learned in a study. It was grasped from experience. "She attained to her idea by the rich processes of living; and the faith which she had laid hold on, she brought again stoutly to its testing in her own experience." Her life was a series of passionate experiments, lived "with all the alertness of her brain focused upon the abrupt experiences of her life. . . ." For Wollstonecraft,

> life had no axioms; its geometry was all experimental. She was forever testing, probing; forever dominated by an utter unwillingness to accept the pretense, the convention in place of the reality. She reasoned because she must; because a passionately intellectual attitude toward living was her essential tool.

Benedict regarded the *Vindication of the Rights of Woman* as "the main statement of her life idea," an idea which "has become one of the great forces that is shaping our modern world." Yet despite Wollstonecraft's "startling way of 'raising all the questions at once'—religious, economic, sexual and philosophic," Benedict also emphasized the limits of her challenge: her love of domesticity, her approval of marriage, her affection for family life. She "never feared that she was upsetting the balance of society by asking a little elbowroom for women; those unheard-of changes she demanded . . . promised no terrors for her. She knew the world was not so insecurely poised."

In the *Vindications of the Rights of Woman*, Wollstonecraft had regarded love as an "unwelcome intruder." Yet her own life had been profoundly shaped by its vicissitudes. Unlike Goldman, Benedict saw the relationship with Godwin as the culmination of her search for happiness. Wollstonecraft died "in the prime of her maturity, a woman with whom life had gone hard, upon whom fate had loved to play the full gamut of its ironies, but—let us say it in all honor—one who had come to her last resting bed, 'weary and content and undishonored.' "

In the conclusion of her essay, Benedict spelled out the personal meaning of Wollstonecraft to her own life. The contrast between this conclusion and Emma Goldman's reflects more than the difference between the two individual sensibilities. It also illuminates the distance between women of Goldman's generation, culture, and class background, and those of Benedict's. The pessimism of Goldman's essay reflects the constraints imposed upon the female imagination by the conservatism of East European Jewish culture, anti-Semitism, the shock of immigration to America, and the descent from petit-bourgeois to proletarian class status.

" 'Girls do not have to learn much!' " Goldman recalled her father

8. Ruth Benedict, "Mary Wollstonecraft," in *An Anthropologist at Work: Writings of Ruth Benedict*, ed. Margaret Mead (Boston: Houghton Mifflin, 1959), pp. 491–519.

telling her as a child. " 'All a Jewish daughter needs to know is how to prepare a gefüllte fish, cut noodles fine, and give the man plenty of children!' "[9] From her father's perspective, her wishes "to study, to know life, to travel," to marry only for love (or to love and not marry) were simply expressions of disobedience. In his eyes, she became "a loose character" and a "disgrace" to the family. In the context of this world, the revolt of a woman like Wollstonecraft, even to a rebellious daughter like Goldman, appeared an ambivalent challenge: to freedom, intellectual growth, and self-expression, on the one hand; to rejection, inner conflict, and anguish on the other.

Goldman, like Wollstonecraft, was successful in escaping the claustrophobic world represented to her by her parents. She even managed eventually to win their respect and admiration. Still, one senses that she never wholly forgot (or forgave) those early paternal curses, which represented the judgment not simply of one father, but of an entire class and culture. Her ironic sense of herself as the devil's "own child," as someone whose head was "made for a rope, not for a hat," was one legacy of that familial conflict.[1] Her portrayal of Wollstonecraft reflects her confidence that her own revolt had been necessary and legitimate, but also her fear that such audacity and ambition must inevitably be accompanied by tragedy.

The greater optimism of Benedict's essay reflects the expanded sense of possbilities available to women born seventeen years later into the educated American middle class. Benedict's widowed mother was a teacher and librarian who encouraged her daughter's intellectual interests. Benedict attended college and worked as a teacher and social worker, both before and after her marriage, prior to beginning a career as an anthropologist when she was in her thirties. At the time she wrote on Wollstonecraft, Benedict was struggling with the question of how, as a woman married to a man she loved, she could also engage in challenging work. (Neither teaching nor social work satisfied her.) Struggling with the problem of vocation, she wrote in her diary of 1914 of her plan

> to steep myself in the lives of restless and highly enslaved women of past generations and write a series of biographical papers from the standpoint of the "new woman." My conclusion so far as I see it now is that there is nothing "new" about the whole thing except the phraseology and the more independent economic standing of recent times— that the restlessness and groping are inherent in the nature of women and this generation can outdo the others long since past only in the frankness with which it acts upon these. . . .[2]

9. Goldman, *Living My Life*, p. 12.
1. See Frank Harris, "A Biographical Sketch of Emma Goldman," in *Contemporary Portraits*, 4th ser. (New York: Brentano's, 1923); reprinted in Emma Goldman, *My Disillusionment in Russia* (New York: Thomas Y. Crowell, 1970), p. xi; and

Goldman to Lillian Mendelsohn, 9 September 1938, William Mendelsohn Papers, Laguna Hills, California.
2. Ruth Benedict, "Journals," *An Anthropologist at Work*, p. 132.

Three years later, in 1917, she wrote that she longed "to speak out the intense inspiration that comes to me from the lives of strong women. They have made of their lives a great adventure; they have proved that out of much bewilderment of soul, steadfast aims may . . . [emerge]."[3]

The world in which Benedict had grown up was one in which the lessons of the *Vindication of the Rights of Woman* had begun to be felt, in the form of increased educational and professional opportunities for at least some women. Hopes such as those cherished by Goldman as a child no longer appeared as outrageous assaults on parental authority. The normality of female sexual desire was more openly asserted, as was the legitimacy of women's intellectual and political aspirations.

Within the context of this world, Mary Wollstonecraft was neither as heroic nor as tragic as she had appeared to Goldman. Neither, however, was she as radical. If Goldman had romanticized Wollstonecraft, she nevertheless grasped the radicalism of Wollstonecraft's project, both in life and in thought. In presenting a less heroic, less romantic Wollstonecraft, Benedict also domesticated her. Her goals were more possible because they were more limited. In contrast to Goldman's contradictory portrait, Benedict's more integrated portrayal suggests both the narrowing of vision and the widening of actual possibilities available to her generation and class. To Goldman, Wollstonecraft's challenge had been both personal and political. To Benedict, her challenge was almost entirely personal. Reacting against the conservatism of the middle-class American suffrage movement in the years before World War I, Goldman saw Wollstonecraft as a great historical heroine whose vision was far more radical than that of the suffragists. Identifying herself with that same movement, Benedict saw Wollstonecraft as a contemporary. Goldman's feminism was one aspect of a total ideology of anarchist revolution. The liberation of women involved the transformation of all aspects of society.

For Benedict, feminism seemed to mean liberalizing the structures of marriage, family life, and work. Her comments on Wollstonecraft suggest the boundaries of her own beliefs: "She had more faith in the love of husband and home and children than those have had since then who have feared to shift an ornament or open a window in the house of love, lest it should tumble in ruins." Goldman's feminism was romantic, radical, and revolutionary. Benedict's feminism was practical, liberal, and reformist. Goldman projected into her portrait of Wollstonecraft both her greatest hopes and her worst fears about the possibilities of love and freedom. Benedict saw her hopes confirmed. Her Wollstonecraft was less tormented, in part because Benedict's world was closer to accepting the life of such a woman, but also because the feminist expectations shaped by that world were more limited:

3. Benedict, "Journals," Ibid., p. 140.

In the National Portrait Gallery hangs a picture of Mary Wollstone-craft, a picture of her as she was a few scant months before her death. I remember the child I was when I saw it first, haunted by the terror of youth before experience. I wanted so desperately to know how other women had saved their souls alive. And the woman in the little frame arrested me, this woman with the auburn hair, and the sad, steady, light-brown eyes, and the gallant poise of the head. She *had* saved her soul alive; it looked out from her steady eyes unafraid. The price, too, that life had demanded of her was written ineradicably there. But to me, then, standing before her picture, even that costly payment was a guarantee, a promise. For I knew that in those days when she sat for that picture, she was content. And in the light of that content, I still spell out her life.[4]

That two women as different as Emma Goldman and Ruth Benedict could both look to Mary Wollstonecraft for inspiration suggest, not only the richness of Wollstonecraft's legacy, but also the process by which each generation both discovers and creates its own predecessors. In recreating Wollstonecraft, Goldman inadvertently drew the outlines of her own idealized self-image. Similarly, Benedict portrayed a Woll-stonecraft with striking similarities to herself, or to what she hoped to become. It is difficult to know whether or not Benedict or Goldman recognized themselves in these portraits, or whether they were changed by the encounter with Wollstonecraft. In any case, in the attempt to delineate Wollstonecraft for themselves, both women revealed some of their own deepest values, hopes, and fears. In reinventing Wollstone-craft, both Goldman and Benedict were also inventing themselves.

VIRGINIA WOOLF

Mary Wollstonecraft†

Great wars are strangely intermittent in their effects. The French Revolution took some people and tore them asunder; others it passed over without disturbing a hair of their heads. Jane Austen, it is said, never mentioned it; Charles Lamb ignored it; Beau Brummell[1] never gave the matter a thought. But to Wordsworth and to Godwin it was the dawn; unmistakably they saw

> France standing on the top of golden hours,
> And human nature seeming born again.[2]

4. Benedict, "Mary Wollstonecraft," Ibid., p. 519.
† From *The Second Common Reader*, by Virginia Woolf, pp. 168–76. Copyright, 1932, by Harcourt Brace Jovanovich, Inc.; copyright, 1960, by Leonard Woolf. Reprinted by permission of the Literary Estate of Virginia Woolf, the Hogarth Press and Harcourt Brace Jovanovich, Inc. Footnotes for this selection are by the editor.
1. Charles Lamb (1775–1834), essayist; George Bryan ("Beau") Brummel (1778–1840), known for his sartorial elegance, witty conversation, and elegant bachelor establishment on Chesterfield Street.
2. William Wordsworth, *The Prelude* VI. 340–41.

Thus it would be easy for a picturesque historian to lay side by side the most glaring contrasts—here in Chesterfield Street was Beau Brummell letting his chin fall carefully upon his cravat and discussing in a tone studiously free from vulgar emphasis the proper cut of the lapel of a coat; and here in Somers Town was a party of ill-dressed, excited young men, one with a head too big for his body and a nose too long for his face, holding forth day by day over the tea-cups upon human perfectibility, ideal unity, and the rights of man.[3] There was also a woman present with very bright eyes and a very eager tongue, and the young men, who had middle-class names, like Barlow and Holcroft[4] and Godwin, called her simply "Wollstonecraft", as if it did not matter whether she were married or unmarried, as if she were a young man like themselves.

Such glaring discords among intelligent people—for Charles Lamb and Godwin, Jane Austen and Mary Wollstonecraft were all highly intelligent—suggest how much influence circumstances have upon opinions. If Godwin had been brought up in the precincts of the Temple and had drunk deep of antiquity and old letters at Christ's Hospital,[5] he might never have cared a straw for the future of man and his rights in general. If Jane Austen had lain as a child on the landing to prevent her father from thrashing her mother, her soul might have burnt with such a passion against tyranny that all her novels might have been consumed in one cry for justice.

Such had been Mary Wollstonecraft's first experience of the joys of married life. And then her sister Everina[6] had been married miserably and had bitten her wedding ring to pieces in the coach. Her brother had been a burden on her; her father's farm had failed, and in order to start that disreputable man with the red face and the violent temper and the dirty hair in life again she had gone into bondage among the aristocracy as a governess—in short, she had never known what happiness was, and, in its default, had fabricated a creed fitted to meet the sordid misery of real human life. The staple of her doctrine was that nothing mattered save independence. "Every obligation we receive from our fellow-creatures is a new shackle, takes from our native freedom, and debases the mind."[7] Independence was the first necessity for a woman; not grace or charm, but energy and courage and the power to put her

3. William Godwin (1756–1836), future husband of Wollstonecraft, is being described here. Somers Town was the Georgian suburban development where first Godwin, then Godwin and Wollstonecraft, lived.
4. Joel Barlow (1754–1812), American poet and statesman who also for a time lived in London; Thomas Holcroft (1745–1809), dramatist and translator of, among other things, Beaumarchais's *Le Mariage de Figaro*.
5. Charles Lamb was raised near the Temple, the historical section of London around the Inns of Court; he, as well as Coleridge and Leigh Hunt, were educated at Christ's Hospital, originally founded as a charitable school for poor boys.
6. It was Wollstonecraft's sister Elizabeth ("Eliza") Bishop who purportedly bit her ring to pieces as she fled her husband's home for protection in the secret lodging Mary had arranged beforehand.
7. Quoted in Durant's Supplement to William Godwin's *Memoirs of Mary Wollstonecraft* (New York, 1927), p. 172.

will into effect were her necessary qualities. It was her highest boast to be able to say, "I never yet resolved to do anything of consequence that I did not adhere readily to it". Certainly Mary could say this with truth. When she was a little more than thirty she could look back upon a series of actions which she had carried out in the teeth of opposition. She had taken a house by prodigious efforts for her friend Fanny, only to find that Fanny's mind was changed and she did not want a house after all. She had started a school. She had persuaded Fanny into marrying Mr. Skeys. She had thrown up her school and gone to Lisbon alone to nurse Fanny when she died. On the voyage back she had forced the captain of the ship to rescue a wrecked French vessel by threatening to expose him if he refused. And when, overcome by passion for Fuseli,[8] she declared her wish to live with him and was refused flatly by his wife, she had put her principle of decisive action instantly into effect, and had gone to Paris determined to make her living by her pen.

The Revolution thus was not merely an event that had happened outside her; it was an active agent in her own blood. She had been in revolt all her life—against tyranny, against law, against convention. The reformer's love of humanity, which has so much of hatred in it as well as love, fermented within her. The outbreak of revolution in France expressed some of her deepest theories and convictions, and she dashed off in the heat of that extraordinary moment those two eloquent and daring books—the *Reply to Burke*[9] and the *Vindication of the Rights of Woman*, which are so true that they seem now to contain nothing new in them—their originality has become our commonplace. But when she was in Paris lodging by herself in a great house, and saw with her own eyes the King whom she despised driving past surrounded by National Guards and holding himself with greater dignity than she expected, then, "I can scarcely tell you why", the tears came to her eyes. "I am going to bed," the letter ended, "and, for the first time in my life, I cannot put out the candle."[1] Things were not so simple after all. She could not understand even her own feelings. She saw the most cherished of her convictions put into practice—and her eyes filled with tears. She had won fame and independence and the right to live her own life—and she wanted something different. "I do not want to be loved like a goddess," she wrote, "but I wish to be necessary to you." For Imlay,[2] the fascinating

8. Henry Fuseli (1741–1825), English painter and writer of Swiss origin. Coming to painting late in his life, Fuseli is especially known for his imaginative and often grotesque interpretations of scenes in Shakespeare and Milton.
9. I.e., *A Vindication of the Rights of Men* (1790), written as a reply to Edmund Burke's *Reflections on the Revolution in France*.
1. Wollstonecraft's letter to Joseph Johnson, cited in Durant's Supplement to Godwin's *Memoirs*, p. 223.
2. Gilbert Imlay, American explorer, writer and entrepreneur, became Wollstonecraft's lover in France in 1793; their daughter Fanny was born in 1794. Although Gilbert and Mary were registered as man and wife at the American embassy in Paris, they were not married and were only trying to obtain protection for Wollstonecraft in the revolution-torn city where to be British was to be in danger. The complete letter is no. 113 (Paris, December 26, 1792) in Ralph M. Wardle, ed., *Collected Letters of Mary Wollstonecraft* (Ithaca: Cornell UP, 1979).

American to whom her letter was addressed, had been very good to her. Indeed, she had fallen passionately in love with him. But it was one of her theories that love should be free—"that mutual affection was marriage and that the marriage tie should not bind after the death of love, if love should die."[3] And yet at the same time that she wanted freedom she wanted certainty. "I like the word affection," she wrote, "because it signifies something habitual."[4]

The conflict of all these contradictions shows itself in her face, at once so resolute and so dreamy, so sensual and so intelligent, and beautiful into the bargain with its great coils of hair and the large bright eyes that Southey thought the most expressive he had ever seen. The life of such a woman was bound to be tempestuous. Every day she made theories by which life should be lived; and every day she came smack against the rock of other people's prejudices. Every day too—for she was no pedant, no cold-blooded theorist—something was born in her that thrust aside her theories and forced her to model them afresh. She acted upon her theory that she had no legal claim upon Imlay; she refused to marry him; but when he left her alone week after week with the child she had borne him her agony was unendurable.

Thus distracted, thus puzzling even to herself, the plausible and treacherous Imlay cannot be altogether blamed for failing to follow the rapidity of her changes and the alternate reason and unreason of her moods. * * * Tickling minnows he had hooked a dolphin, and the creature rushed him through the waters till he was dizzy and only wanted to escape. After all, though he had played at theory-making too, he was a business man, he depended upon soap and alum; "the secondary pleasures of life", he had to admit, "are very necessary to my comfort".[5] And among them was one that for ever evaded Mary's jealous scrutiny. Was it business, was it politics, was it a woman that perpetually took him away from her? He shillied and shallied; he was very charming when they met; then he disappeared again. Exasperated at last, and half insane with suspicion, she forced the truth from the cook. A little actress in a strolling company was his mistress, she learnt. True to her own creed of decisive action, Mary at once soaked her skirts so that she might sink unfailingly, and threw herself from Putney Bridge. But she was rescued; after unspeakable agony she recovered, and then her "unconquerable greatness of mind",[6] her girlish creed of independence, asserted itself again, and she determined to make another bid for happiness and to earn her living without taking a penny from Imlay for herself or their child.

It was in this crisis that she again saw Godwin, the little man with the big head, whom she had met when the French Revolution was

3. C. Kegan Paul, *William Godwin: His Friends and Contemporaries*, 2 vols. (Boston, 1876), I, 214.
4. Wardle, *Collected Letters*, p. 233 (no. 119).
5. Imlay was involved in the importing business at the time. See complete letter in *Letters to Imlay*, ed. Paul, pp. 58, 95.
6. Godwin, *Memoirs of Mary Wollstonecraft*, p. 30.

making the young men in Somers Town think that a new world was being born. She met him—but that is a euphemism, for in fact Mary Wollstonecraft actually visited him in his own house. Was it the effect of the French Revolution? Was it the blood she had seen spilt on the pavement and the cries of the furious crowd that had rung in her ears that made it seem a matter of no importance whether she put on her cloak and went to visit Godwin in Somers Town, or waited in Judd Street West for Godwin to come to her? And what strange upheaval of human life was it that inspired that curious man, who was so queer a mixture of meanness and magnanimity, of coldness and deep feeling— for the memoir of his wife could not have been written without unusual depth of heart—to hold the view that she did right—that he respected Mary for trampling upon the idiotic convention by which women's lives were tied down? He held the most extraordinary views on many subjects, and upon the relations of the sexes in particular. He thought that reason should influence even the love between men and women. He thought that there was something spiritual in their relationship. He had written that "marriage is a law, and the worst of all laws . . . marriage is an affair of property, and the worst of all properties".[7] He held the belief that if two people of the opposite sex like each other, they should live together without any ceremony, or, for living together is apt to blunt love, twenty doors off, say, in the same street. And he went further; he said that if another man liked your wife "this will create no difficulty. We may all enjoy her conversation, and we shall all be wise enough to consider the sensual intercourse a very trivial object."[8] True, when he wrote those words he had never been in love; now for the first time he was to experience that sensation. It came very quietly and naturally, growing "with equal advances in the mind of each" from those talks in Somers Town, from those discussions upon everything under the sun which they held so improperly alone in his rooms. "It was a friendship melting into love . . .", he wrote. "When, in the course of things, the disclosure came, there was nothing in a manner for either party to disclose to the other."[9] Certainly they were in agreement upon the most essential points; they were both of opinion, for instance, that marriage was unnecessary. They would continue to live apart. Only when Nature again intervened, and Mary found herself with child, was it worth while to lose valued friends, she asked, for the sake of a theory? She thought not, and they were married. And then that other theory—that it is best for husband and wife to live apart—was not that also incompatible with other feelings that were coming to birth in her? "A husband is a convenient part of the furniture of the house",[1] she wrote. Indeed, she discovered that she was passionately domestic. Why not, then, revise

7. William Godwin, *An Enquiry concerning Political Justice* (London, 1793) II. 850.
8. Godwin, *Political Justice* II. 853.
9. The three preceding quotations are from Durant's Supplement to Godwin, *Memoirs*, pp. 99–100.
1. From a letter fromWollstonecraft to Godwin, cited in Paul, *William Godwin* I. 251.

that theory too, and share the same roof? Godwin should have a room some doors off to work in; and they should dine out separately if they liked—their work, their friends, should be separate. Thus they settled it, and the plan worked admirably. The arrangement combined "the novelty and lively sensation of a visit with the more delicious and heart-felt pleasures of domestic life".[2] Mary admitted that she was happy; Godwin confessed that, after all one's philosophy, it was "extremely gratifying" to find that "there is some one who takes an interest in one's happiness."[3] All sorts of powers and emotions were liberated in Mary by her new satisfaction. Trifles gave her an exquisite pleasure—the sight of Godwin and Imlay's child playing together; the thought of their own child who was to be born; a day's jaunt into the country. One day, meeting Imlay in the New Road, she greeted him without bitterness. But, as Godwin wrote, "Ours is not an idle happiness, a paradise of selfish and transitory pleasures".[4] No, it too was an experiment, as Mary's life had been an experiment from the start, an attempt to make human conventions conform more closely to human needs. And their marriage was only a beginning; all sorts of things were to follow after. Mary was going to have a child. She was going to write a book to be called *The Wrongs of Women*. She was going to reform education. She was going to come down to dinner the day after her child was born. She was going to employ a midwife and not a doctor at her confinement—but that experiment was her last. She died in child-birth. She whose sense of her own existence was so intense, who had cried out even in her misery, "I cannot bear to think of being no more—of losing myself—nay, it appears to me impossible that I should cease to exist",[5] died at the age of thirty-six.[6] But she has her revenge. Many millions have died and been forgotten in the hundred and thirty years that have passed since she was buried; and yet as we read her letters and listen to her arguments and consider her experiments, above all that most fruitful experiment, her relation with Godwin, and realise the high-handed and hot-blooded manner in which she cut her way to the quick of life, one form of immortality is hers undoubtedly: she is alive and active, she argues and experiments, we hear her voice and trace her influence even now among the living.

---

2. Godwin, *Memoirs*, p. 110.
3. From a letter form Godwin to Wollstonecraft, cited in Paul, *William Godwin* I. 255.
4. Godwin, *Memoirs*, p. 109.
5. Wollstonecraft says this in her *Letters Written*

during a Short Residence in Sweden, Norway and Denmark (London, 1796), p. 97.
6. Mary Wollstonecraft actually died in 1797 at the age of thirty-*eight*.

FERDINAND LUNDBERG and MARYNIA FARNHAM

[Mary Wollstonecraft and the Psychopathology of Feminism]†

* * *

The tenets of feminism, which have undergone no change to our day, may be traced to a single fateful book, A *Vindication of the Rights of Women*,[1] by Mary Wollstonecraft, published in London in 1792.

Mary Wollstonecraft stated or implied the entire feminist philosophy. She expressed virtually all of the conscious demands of the feminists to follow her (what their far more significant unconscious demands were we leave until later), and laid down all the factually erroneous major assumptions on which the later feminists were to wage their formally victorious social and political struggle.

Briefly summarized, A *Vindication* held:

That women are identical with men (that is, they are equal, as 1 is to 1 and 2 is to 2).

That women, therefore, should be subject to exactly the same social, political and personal treatment as men.

That women should receive the same educations as men.

That women should be governed by the same moral standards.

That women should have the same political rights and obligations.

That women should have the same work opportunities and the same work as men.

And, in general, that women should behave as nearly as possible like men.

The conception was extremely narrow and highly individualistic. It took little heed of anything except of women as individuals, and as individuals with extremely narrow needs.

One of the many unconscious implications in this book, which was composed hurriedly and under great emotional stress, was that men are exceptionally wonderful creatures, capable of practically anything, and that women can do nothing better than emulate them in every possible way.

Mary Wollstonecraft hated men. She had every personal reason possible known to psychiatry for hating them. Hers was hatred of creatures she greatly admired and feared, creatures that seemed to her capable of doing everything while women to her seemed capable of doing nothing whatever, in their own nature being pitifully weak in comparison with the strong, lordly male.

† From *Modern Woman: The Lost Sex*, by Ferdinand Lundberg and Marynia F. Farnham, pp. 144–45, 159–63. Copyright, 1947, by Ferdinand Lundberg and Marynia F. Farnham. Reprinted by permission of Harper & Row, Publishers, Inc. Footnotes for this selection are by the editor.

1. The correct title, of course, reads "Woman," not "Women."

She wrote with the fires of the French Revolution raging across the Channel. Only the year before Thomas Paine had published his highly incendiary (for his day) *The Rights of Man*, and Mary was a friend of Paine's who came forward to his defense when he was put on trial for treason.[2]

Much of the ideology of the French Revolution was embraced in *A Vindication*. The revolutionary slogans were a heady draught to the intellectuals of the day, as were those of the Russian Revolution more than a century later. The central slogan of the Revolution was "liberty, equality and fraternity," which in the feminist scheme was adopted as "Freedom, equality and companionship." These three words are encountered constantly in the vast bulk of feminist literature that has accumulated.

As William Godwin later wrote, Mary "considered herself as standing forth in defense of one half of the human species, labouring under a yoke which through all the records of time had degraded them from the station of rational beings and almost sunk them to the level of the brutes."[3]

This factually erroneous and socially mischievous conception, arising from a tortured woman's soul, was ever after to lie at the heart of the feminist movement; it does to this day. The all-powerful, all-evil male had contrived for long ages to enslave and degrade the delicate, weak, all-good female. Only now was she finally to be liberated—by Mary Wollstonecraft!

* * *

That Mary Wollstonecraft was an extreme neurotic of a compulsive type there can be no doubt. Out of her illness arose the ideology of feminism, which was to express the feelings of so many women in years to come.

Consciously, as a strictly moral character, Mary was out to do only good. Feminism, too, was dedicated—on the surface—only to good works, to bringing the lives of women somewhat nearer to ideal perfection. Unconsciously, however, Mary and the feminists wanted to do injury. Mary had a real grievance, but it was against her parents; the same was true of later feminists. These parents had been the agents of a vicious society (as exemplified by the childhood household) vis-a-vis the growing child. To Mary, all men were oppressors of women. All women were long-suffering, all the cards in the deck stacked against them—they were muscularly weaker and smaller than the male, inflicted with menstruation, pregnancy, childbirth, child tending and were denied the marvelous sphere of carefree action of the male (as for sober example, on the battlefield, an enlarged playing field).[4] All men had always,

2. Paine was indicted but never tried for treason in England, and there is no evidence of a "defense" by Wollstonecraft.
3. Godwin, *Memoirs of Mary Wollstonecraft*, ed. W. Clark Durant (New York, 1927), pp. 53–54.
4. Actually, from her letters it is clear that Woll-

stonecraft found the birth of her daughter Fanny very easy and breast-fed her for nearly a year with great joy; also the *Vindication* makes it evident that she rather scorns than admires soldiers and thinks only defensive wars are justifiable.

without exception, beaten women black and blue, humiliated them, degraded them, as her father had done to her and her mother. And all women had, like her mother, accepted such humiliation without a whimper. It was a notion that the feminists never tired of elaborating upon. The first line, for example, in the *History of Woman Suffrage* (1889), by Susan B. Anthony, Elizabeth Cady Stanton and Matilda Gage, militant American feminists, reads: "The prolonged slavery of woman is the darkest page in human history."

In retaliation Mary wanted women to turn on men and injure them. The worst humiliation she could think of for them, however, the crowning ignominy, was to make them acknowledge the "equality" of women, their identity with men. Mary could visualize nothing worse, for while hating and condemning them she had too much need of them. Men, in her distorted view, could never be regarded as inferior to women. Men were never, in her view, overcome by women. It was women who were overcome by men. Underneath her aggressive writings, Mary was a masochist like her mother, as indeed all the leading feminist theorists were in fact. Aggressively Mary flung herself at men, only to be repeatedly repulsed. For her actions invited repulse. Overeager for what she desired—a man the precise opposite of her father, but measured against his remembered silhouette—Mary discerned what she sought where it did not exist and then took the initiative, committing the unpardonable sexual blunder of depriving the male of the initiative. The feminists were always doing this, thereby either driving men away from them or capturing psychologically impaired males.

By behaving as she did Mary indicated, as we know from clinical practice, that she was unconsciously seeking to deprive the male of his power, to castrate him. Unconsciously she probably wished to emulate the heroine of Greek drama, Electra,[5] and kill her father, but this desire, although powerful, was powerfully deflected as untenable. It came out only in her round scolding of all men. The feminists have ever since symbolically slain their fathers by verbally consigning all men to perdition as monsters.

What Mary wanted, underneath all the confusion of her mind, was brought out in the stress of her tortured pursuit of Imlay when in a letter she expressed the desire to go with him to America, settle on a farm, and bear six children. She was ready, in emotional extremity, to repeat her mother's role, and unquestionably she would even have endured Imlay's blows—gladly—if only he had married her.[6] Mary was ready to settle for anything, and therein further revealed her neuroticism. Women down through history have, as a rule, not bowed so low before the male as the archfeminist, Mary Wollstonecraft, bowed before Imlay.

5. In Greek legend Electra, with the aid of her brother Orestes, killed their *mother*, Clytemnestra; the Electra complex in psychology refers to a girl's latent hostility toward her mother and favoritism for her father.

6. While her letters to Imlay reveal that they had planned to emigrate to America to buy a farm and that, because she loved children, Wollstonecraft wanted a large family, there is no indication of physical cruelty on Imlay's part or willingness of Wollstonecraft to bear it, had there been.

276 · Lundberg and Farnham

Mary was emotionally forced to strive for power (until capitulating on any terms) vis-a-vis Imlay or any other man. This striving came out in her rushing talk and her professed familiarity with every idea that might be broached. It also came out in the way she forced herself on men and in the way she sought to hold Imlay to a bargain that had not been made. Not to strive for power, for mastery, made Mary feel helpless, then afraid and anxious, then utterly hostile and unhappy. Mastery made her feel less helpless; it was a defense against anxiety that, actually, revolved about her deep doubt of her power as a woman. This power was hopelessly compromised by her male strivings. The happiness she felt during the first stage of her affair with Imlay undoubtedly derived in large measure from the feelings of mastery it gave her. She had suddenly, we may surmise, glimpsed the possibility of establishing mastery as a woman. We can only guess at the state of her libidinal organization, but Imlay was unquestionably a versatile lover, had enchanted her sexually. Very probably he had been the instrument for lifting her sexual inhibitions.

Feminism did not select its underlying ideas from Mary's letters to Imlay. If it had done so it would have been the opposite of what it was. In either event, it would have been drawing from a poisoned source. Only deeply disturbed women—disturbed by the nature of their childhood upbringing in the shattered home and the constricted circumstances they encountered in adult life—could have drawn what they supposed was pure wisdom from A *Vindication*.

As we have seen, A *Vindication* prescribed "equality" in all things between the sexes. Equality was the political catchword of the day; it would resolve everything, especially if joined with Reason and Liberty. In sober fact, however, whatever else men and women may be in relation to each other, they are not equal, identical. They are similar in species, different individually, and always complementary. *In relation to each other what is crucial is not their similarity but their difference.* Havelock Ellis,[7] himself not a little infected with the feminist virus, tried to resolve the confusion caused by the easy use of word "equality" by substituting for it the term "equivalence," meaning equality of value. But Ellis' well-intentioned efforts were hardly appreciated, and Ellis entirely missed the point of what the feminists were actually aiming for, which was definitely not justice. It was, as Mary Wollstonecraft flatly said (and as many repeated after her), simply *masculinity*. And a female who attempts to achieve masculinity is psychically ill in the same way as a male who attempts to achieve femininity.

* * *

---

7. Ellis (1859–1939), English psychologist, author of many works, the best known being the series called *Studies in the Psychology of Sex* (1897–1910).

Criticism

EMMA RAUSCHENBUSCH-CLOUGH

[Mary Wollstonecraft's Demands for the Education of Woman]†

* * *

Mary Wollstonecraft deals with the actual facts in the economic conditions of her times, that made it desirable, that the nation should carry on the work of education. Her course is in the direction of socialism. Her criticism of the system of education prevalent in England at the time, was all levelled against the interference of property with pedagogical principles. Two kinds of schools were in vogue, boarding schools and day schools, and both were private enterprises. The evils, which follow in the train of private property, foremost of which is competition, were of peculiar effect here. Mary Wollstonecraft spoke from experience; for she too had conducted a day-school, and had found herself dependent on the caprice of parents. She describes, how the master finds himself under necessity of giving the parents some sample of the boy's abilities, which during vacation is shown to every visitor; how he loads the memory of the pupil with unintelligible words, of which to make a show; and winds the poor machine up to some extraordinary exertion, that injures the wheels and stops the progress of gradual improvement. "Yet how can these things be remedied," she says, "whilst schoolmasters depend entirely on parents for a subsistence; and, when so many rival schools hang out their lures to catch the attention of vain fathers and mothers, whose parental affection only leads them to wish that their children should outshine those of their neighbours?"[1] This evil must have had unusual scope at that time in England; for she adds: "Without great good luck, a sensible, conscientious man would starve before he could raise a school, if he disdained to bubble weak parents by practising the secret tricks of the craft."

In boarding schools the strain was apparent in another direction. The parents were often in quest of the cheapest schools, and the master could not live, if he did not take a much greater number than he could manage. Many crammed together, the body, heart and understanding were equally stunted. Boys, who, at great expense, lived with the masters and assistants, were never domesticated; for the former kept up an intercourse with the nobility, which introduced vanity and extravagance into their families. Those professions, says Mary Wollstonecraft, are most debasing, whose ladder is patronage; yet out of one of these professions the

† From Emma Rauschenbusch-Clough, *A Study of Mary Wollstonecraft and the Rights of Woman* (London, 1898), pp. 152–63. Since all the footnotes in the original work refer to *A Vindication* of the Rights of Woman, Rauschenbusch-Clough's notes have been corrected to refer to the present edition simply by page number.
1. P. 163.

tutors of the boys were chosen. "But, can they be expected to inspire independent sentiments, whose conduct must be regulated by the cautious prudence that is ever on the watch for preferment?" She continues: "So far, however, from thinking of the morals of boys, I have heard several masters of schools argue, that they only undertook to teach Latin and Greek; and that they had fulfilled their duty, by sending some good scholars to college."[2]

Her remarks in this connection show how closely she occasionally touches the doctrines of socialism. She admits, that a few good scholars may have been formed by emulation and discipline, but she regrets the health and morals of the large number, who have been sacrificed to bring forward these few clever boys. "It is not for the benefit of society," she says, "that a few brilliant men should be brought forward at the expense of the multitude. It is true that great men seem to start up, as great revolutions occur, at proper intervals, to restore order, and to blow aside the clouds that thicken over the face of truth; but let more reason and virtue prevail in society, and these strong winds would not be necessary."[3] Her contention is against an aristocracy of learning; though she perceives, that where there is equality of opportunity, and the survival of the fittest does not imply so much of stress, exceptionally great men will no longer arise, but the average will rise to a higher level. She is in favour of a high average.

The restraint and wearisome confinement, in boarding schools for girls, was even greater than that endured by boys. Even in their hours of recreation, as Mary Wollstonecraft had seen in some institutions, they were not allowed to play in the garden, in healthful exercise, but were obliged to pace with steady deportment, stupidly backwards and forwards, in the one broad walk; holding up their heads and turning out their toes, with shoulders braced back. "The pure animal spirits, which make both mind and body shoot out, and unfold the tender blossoms of hope, were turned sour, and were vented in vain wishes or pert repinings, that contract the faculties and spoil the temper."[4] Some of the characteristics of the female mind, that Mary Wollstonecraft deplores, she traces to the influences that stunted the development of girls in these boarding schools.

The author draws a pleasing picture of the country day-school, where a boy trudged in the morning, wet or dry, carrying his books, and returned in the evening to recount the feats of the day close at the parental knee. She appeals to many superior men, who were educated in this manner, whether their father's home was not ever after fondly remembered; and whether the recollection of some shady lane, where they conned[5] their lesson, or of some stile, where they sat making a kite, did not endear their country to them. Those day-schools, she

2. P. 161.
3. P. 162.

4. P. 164.
5. Learned by repeating [Editor].

believed, contained the most important elements of a sound education; for they gave opportunity for that blending of home influences and school discipline, that tends to mould the citizen. "Public education, of every denomination," she says, "should be directed to form citizens; but if you wish to make good citizens, you must first exercise the affections of a son and a brother. This is the only way to expand the heart; for public affections as well as public virtues must ever grow out of the private character."[6]

This is a beautiful vindication of home life and family ties. In the State, the individual finds his highest development; yet this cannot be attained without the nurture of the heart, and that exercise of youthful sympathies, to which family life gives play. Affection for mankind is seldom found in those, "who did not first love their parents, their brothers, sisters, and even the domestic brutes, their first play-mates."[7] If children were separated from their parents for educational purposes, Mary Wollstonecraft doubts, whether they would become better citizens, by sacrificing the preparatory affections and thus "destroying the force of relationships that render the marriage state as necessary as it is respectable."[8]

Those who, judging from the title, expected to find that the *Vindication of the Rights of Woman* attacked the sanctity of the family, had here the strongest evidence, that this was not the case. The claims, which children have upon that permanent union of their parents, that forms the foundation of the influences, that have the most powerful bearing upon their lives, is here respected and insisted upon. Moreover, since the immediate care of the children devolves upon the mother, Mary Wollstonecraft marked out to a majority of women their chief employment, for at least a term of years. She expresses this in another connection in the following words: "Speaking of women at large, their first duty is to themselves as rational creatures, and the next in point of importance, as citizens, is that, which includes so many, of a mother."[9] The duties of motherhood do not, according to her opinion, take the first place. Woman owes it to herself and to the family, which she may rear, to strive in the direction of a rich intellectual and moral maturity, that shall fit her to choose the kind of work, to which she would give herself, whether this work is dictated by the claims of maternity, or by fitness for other pursuits.

Mary Wollstonecraft is in advance of her time, in her demand, that mothers should represent personality in themselves. They are not to sink into the daily routine of caring for their children's wants, generally the material wants only; for the mother, who is reduced to the drudge, has lost the elasticity of mind, that keeps step with the mental growth of her children. "If children are to be educated to understand the true principle

6. P. 162.
7. Ibid.

8. Ibid.
9. P. 145.

of patriotism, their mother must be a patriot," Mary Wollstonecraft rightly says. The *Vindication of the Rights of Woman* has the aim of making women better mothers; and by insisting that education should not take children out of their homes, the author leaves the full range of those maternal activities open, that put into the hands of women some of the highest and most far-reaching duties, which the State can call upon its citizens to perform. So far then from cramping maternal instincts, their rightful and honored place in the organism of the State is vindicated to them.

The object, which Mary Wollstonecraft seeks mainly to accomplish by advocating national education is the introduction of co-education. Her plan for the establishment of national schools is as follows: The teachers are to be chosen by a select committee in each parish, to whom complaints of negligence can be made; if signed by six of the children's parents. Without distinction of sex or wealth, children under nine years of age are to be taught in schools absolutely free to all, and obliged to submit to the same discipline, or leave the school. In order to prevent any distinctions of vanity, she would even see the children dressed alike. But study is not to be made irksome to the little one; they are not to be confined to sedentary employment for more than an hour at a time; but much is to be taught them by way of relaxation. The school-room is to be surrounded by a large piece of ground, and here they are to be taught the elements of botany, astronomy and mechanics; for "many things improve and amuse the senses, when introduced as a kind of show, to the principles of which, dryly laid down, children would turn a deaf ear."[1]

She evidently anticipates in these sensible measures the modern Kindergarten.[2] She would also see the Socratic form of teaching by conversation introduced, as the best way of teaching children the elements of religion, history and politics. It is to be noticed, that she does not omit the study of religion in her plan for national education. After the age of nine, differentiation is to begin, natural aptitude and individual choice is to be taken into consideration; and while all remain together in the morning, to continue their studies, the afternoons may be devoted by boys to learning mechanical trades, by girls to learning to do housework and millinery. She would thus place industrial training also under national protection.

Co-education forms the central and well defined thought of the chapter on national education. In advocating the desirability of educating young people together, she tread on new ground; for at that time not even a limited practical experience offered foundation for theory. Yet, as she had claimed throughout, that the nature of reason is the same in all; and had denounced the system of female education, which ex-

1. P. 168.
2. Although it is now an educational common-place, the Kindergarten ("garden of children") was founded in 1837 by Friedrich Froebel, a German educator, to teach children aged four to six by way of games and play [*Editor*].

aggerated feeling and neglected the understanding, it remained to be shown, how that reason was to receive the training, that would enable woman to take her place by the side of man. Nothing could seem a simpler solution than co-education.

She did not hesitate, lest by advocating something new, she might destroy that, which had borne well the test of experience. There is a touch of sarcasm in the last sentence of the following appeal, which she makes to the French nation:

> Let an enlightened nation then try, what effect reason would have, to bring women back to nature, and their duty; and allowing them to share the advantages of education and government with man, see whether they will become better as they grow wiser and become free. They cannot be injured by the experiment; for it is not in the power of man to render them more insignificant than they are at present.[3]

Women had nothing to lose, and much to gain.

It is significant of the socialistic tendency of the demands of Mary Wollstonecraft, that she expects equality in education not through individual effort, but as a right granted by broad national policy. The only criticism that can be made to-day, is, that her demands did not reach far enough. She rightly demanded that primary schools should be national establishments; had she followed this to its logical consummation, she would have demanded, that higher education likewise should be sheltered by national institutions, open to rich and poor, man and woman, regardless of colour and creed. This would have been in accordance with the inherent tendency of the process of social development at the present time. She took the first step; in the midst of the second she halted. In sketching her plan for a system of national education, after speaking of primary education, she says: "The young people of superior abilities, or fortune, might now be taught, in another school, the dead and living languages, the elements of science, and continue the study of history and politics, on a more extensive scale."[4] This would make the right of entry, to the institutions for higher education, the privilege of wealth. Class distinctions would thus remain, to divide society into two classes, the educated and the uneducated. Equality of opportunity cannot be realized, where the mere possession of riches can secure one of the most influential privileges, that of education.

Mary Wollstonecraft is very moderate in her demands for the higher education of women. She was treading on unknown territory; for though the brilliant achievements of some of the women of her times might have fanned her hopes; yet, in her book, she resolutely looks away from the exceptional cases, and confines herself to the plain, dull average; and there she had nothing to inspire hope beyond the fact, that woman is in possession of reason, and that reason in its nature must be the same

3. P. 167.   4. P. 168.

in all. Her hints and suggestions are given largely with a view to fitting them for their position in the home; for it is her chief contention, that the ignorance, in which women are kept, tends to incapacitate the maternal character, and thus takes woman out of her sphere. The ignorance of women, she claims, renders the infancy of man a much more perilous state than that of animals. If it were only on this account, she deems the national education of women of the utmost importance. "In public schools therefore, to guard against the errors of ignorance, women should be taught the elements of anatomy and medicine, not only to enable them to take care of their own health, but to make them rational nurses of their children, parents and husbands."[5] They should be led to observe the progress of the human understanding in the improvement of the sciences and arts; "never forgetting the science of morality, or the study of the political history of mankind."

It might seem, in considering these special lines of study, which Mary Wollstonecraft recommends to women, that, after all, the distinction of sex is to enter education. She says nothing of a classical education, of the severe mental drill, which men must undergo. Expediency seems to be the motive that inspires her advice; she would have women trained to fulfil domestic duties, to be wise mothers. Even if this were the case, there would be a wide difference, between this end in view, and that of writers of her day, who merely sought to educate women in a way, that they might be pleasing to men. Does Mary Wollstonecraft merit the charge, that after she had fought sexual distinction in the realm of mind everywhere else, she leaves space here for the entering wedge?

It might seem so on the surface. Looking deeper, however, it appears that Mary Wollstonecraft had an insight into the needs of the human race, beyond that of many educationalists even of the present time. Her observations concerning higher education do not extend very far, but she insists on co-education throughout. She does not give a forecast of the college women of to-day, nor does she discuss the advisability of Medical Colleges for women, distinct from those of men. It is sufficient, that at a time, seventy-five years in advance of the first woman, who held her diploma as a medical practitioner, she possessed the optimism to say: "Women might certainly study the art of healing and be physicians as well as nurses."[6] Her remarks, which seemingly look to expediency only, indicate a perception, dim perhaps, and not fully enunciated, that after the whole range of educational advantages had been opened out to women, by means of co-education; and after individualism had thus received its just dues, in an unrestrained opportunity of choice, that then differentiation according to sex may begin, and that women, to a good degree, must specialize in the studies, that pertain to home-life. The study of sociology has opened out, in our own day, avenues of research, which seem specially inviting to women. Mary Wollstonecraft's

5. P. 177.   6. P. 148.

scant suggestions seem to point to this field of enquiry, as offering opportunity for investigation of both theoretical and practical nature. The true constitution of the family and its various functions, the bearing of domestic economy upon political economy, the prevention of crime, and many other social problems await their solution, to some extent, at the hands of women.

Mary Wollstonecraft left the widest scope of the self-assertiveness of the individual, but combines with this a full appreciation of the relation of the individual to the progress of the race. The individual must be subordinate to the process of development, that carries forward humanity; yet in serving the interests of the whole, he takes the path, that leads most readily to the furtherance of his personal welfare. This conception Mary Wollstonecraft has embodied in her views concerning the education of women; and has thereby given to her demands the character of reasonableness and applicability.

CAROLYN W. KORSMEYER

Reason and Morals in the Early Feminist Movement: Mary Wollstonecraft†

It is difficult to generalize about the theories at work in a social movement as broadly based and diversified as the women's rights movement of the nineteenth century, for its presuppositions, demands, even its goals changed and evolved during the century or so before women obtained the vote. Then, as now, the politics of the women's rights movement proceeded less from a systematic political theory as from a recognition of personal oppression and injustice. Naturally, as women became conscious of and actively dissatisfied with their place in the social order, their oppression as they perceived it was explained in the context of the prevailing ideas of the time, and, accordingly, prescription for change mirrored much contemporary political philosophy as well.[1]

One such "perceived oppression" was founded in the moral philosphy prevalent in England and America at that time. The connection between reason and morals which lies at the root of Locke's political philosophy and which enjoyed popular acceptance as well, was for women both a means of their oppression and a rallying point for the assertion of political

---

† Reprinted by permission of The Putman Publishing Group from *Women and Philosophy: Toward a Theory of Liberation*, ed. Gould and Wartofsky. Copyright © 1976 by Gould and Wartofsky.
1. This is perhaps most evident in the frequent appeal to the "natural rights" of women, a central concept of Locke's influential political philosophy.

It is also evident in the Declaration of Seneca Falls, itself patterned after the Declaration of Independence. [The Seneca Falls convention of 1848, organized by Lucretia Mott and Elizabeth Cady Stanton, marks the organized beginning of the nineteenth-century women's movement in America—*Editor*.]

equality.[2] Denied education and inculcated with the idea that they were frivolous, irrational creatures, the early feminists saw that the establishment of woman as a fully rational human being was one of the first steps towards political, legal, and social equality.

In this paper I shall explore some of the issues and arguments relevant to the subject of women, reason, and moral responsibility. I see this issue as one of the first theoretical questions to appear in feminist thinking of the early nineteenth century, though, needless to say, it represents only one aspect of the whole social movement. I have limited this study to the period between 1792 and 1848, dates which mark respectively the publication of Mary Wollstonecraft's A *Vindication of the Rights of Woman* and the Declaration of Sentiments and Resolutions presented at Seneca Falls, New York, a document which is commonly regarded as signifying the beginning of the organized women's rights movement in the United States.

Although Wollstonecraft was not herself a part of the women's rights movement (she died in 1797), her work was widely read and served as a reference for a number of active feminists in both England and America.[3] Additionally, in her work we find the questions of morals and reason treated with a depth of analysis less frequent in the later feminist writings. Accordingly, I have relied largely on her *Vindication* for the source of philosophical arguments advanced in behalf of feminism.

Wollstonecraft's general line of argument can be separated into three parts: (1) First and foremost, she argues that reason is essential for the development of moral character, whether that of a man or of a woman. (2) Then she presents a refutation of what I call the "separation of virtues" doctrine, then a popoular belief that there is a difference between "male" and "female" virtues. (3) In explanation of the position of women in society, she offers an argument based on the theory of associated ideas for "nurture" over "nature" as the cause of any deficiency found in the reasoning powers of females of the time. Wollstonecraft also points out an important inconsistency contained in the current theories about women and their moral character. With each of these aspects of her work, I have tried to indicate how her thinking fit into the popular beliefs of the day, and how similar ideas pervade the literature of the feminist movement of the nineteenth century in England and America. I shall discuss these issues more or less in order, and in concluding, I shall look back briefly from the perspective of the contemporary woman's

2. As far as I can ascertain, the eighteenth century philosophical debates over the foundation of morals, whether they are discovered by reason or perceived by a moral sense, and so on, had little or no effect on the question of the rationality of women and the political ramifications of this question. That the moral order was discoverable by reason, and that good moral judgment was only possible with developed rational abilities, seem to have been the theories that most affected women and feminism in the early nineteenth century.
3. Wollstonecraft's biographer, Eleanor Flexner, gives a broad account of her influence on feminists such as Frances Wright, Margaret Fuller, Lucretia Mott, Elizabeth Cady Stanton, and others. See Eleanor Flexner, *Mary Wollstonecraft* (Baltimore: Penguin Books, 1972), pp. 265–66.

movement for an evaluation of Wollstonecraft's work and of the struggle over the issue of morals and reason as an element in the philosophy of the early women's right movement.

In the eighteenth and nineteenth centuries, when the seeds of the women's rights movement first began to grow in England and America, it was the popular conception that men and women enjoyed different "spheres" of activity, and that their virtues—the character qualities and abilities they should strive to attain—were specifically tailored to these spheres. Considered too weak physically to venture into the world outside the home and too deficient in reason to make important decisions, the woman was relegated to the domestic sphere where, under the guidance and direction of her rationally superior husband, she tended house, raised children, and gave her family comfort and pleasure. Correspondingly, her "virtues" were an outgrowth of her sensitive, yielding nature: kindness, humility, gentleness, protectiveness, and so on.

Female nature and feminine virtues were often touted as the complement of male nature and masculine virtues, the two together making a perfect whole of human bahavior. For example, Rousseau states in *Émile,*

> A perfect man and a perfect woman should no more be alike in mind than in face, and perfection admits of neither less nor more.

> In the union of the sexes, each alike contributes to the common end, but in different ways.[4]

However, this notion of sexually distinct "spheres of activity" can in no way be construed as a doctrine of "separate but equal." Rousseau goes on to say,

> From this diversity springs the first difference which may be observed between man and woman in their moral relations. The man should be strong and active; the woman should be weak and passive; the one must have both the power and the will; it is enough that the other should offer little resistance.

> When this principle is admitted, it follows that woman is specially made for man's pleasure.[5]

Furthermore, as Aileen Kraditor has noted, the whole notion of proper activity being delineated by a "sphere," a term which implies limitation and confinement, really applies only to the woman, not to the man. "Strictly speaking, men have never had a 'proper sphere,' since their sphere has been the world and all its activities."[6] Woman's sphere and

---

4. J .J. Rousseau, *Émile*, trans. Barbara Foxley (New York: Everyman's Library), p. 322.
5. *Ibid*. Eva Figes, in chapter 4 of *Patriarchal Attitudes*, gives an interesting analysis of Rousseau's position on women, with some related remarks on Wollstonecraft (Greenwich, Conn.:

Fawcett Publications, 1970).
6. Aileen Kraditor, ed., *Up from the Pedestal* (Chicago: Quadrangle Books, 1968), p. 9. (The first section of Kraditor's collection deals with the subject of "spheres" of activity.)

the female virtues are to be considered more accurately as a glorification of a genuinely inferior social status, one which had to be attacked before even the first steps towards political and legal equality could be taken.

This time-honored notion of woman's place had significant political effects, for the acceptance of the existence of such a thing as a female sphere, so conceived, precluded any possibility of admitting women into full citizenship. Under the powerful influence of Locke and the political theorists who followed him, almost anyone interested in theories of citizenship and rights of the governed would also accept as a first principle the notion that a person derives natural and political rights through the possession of *reason*, that faculty which distinguishes human beings from the animals. Women, as a sex, were considered deficient in reasoning ability. It is reason, according to Locke, which enables one to discover the laws of nature—God's moral order—thus qualifying one as a participating member of society. So long as woman's reason was under suspicion, the early advocates of feminism could not make use of Locke's premise that "equals must have equal measure"[7] in order to lay claim to their natural rights, hitherto enjoyed only by a certain class of men. It was precisely with regard to reason, which defined the fully functioning citizen, that women were considered *un*equal. Lacking full use of reason, they could be unstable, capricious, wily, cunning, sensitive, and sentimental, and, it was thought, they had to be kept in the home for their own protection as well as for the good of society at large.

Mary Wollstonecraft attacked the notion of there being separate female virtues—a lesser feminine measure for virtue, adequate for women but not to be compared with the rationally-founded male virtue—as the first stage in her argument for the rationality and therefore the social equality of women.

Her attack on the notion of spheres of activity and female virtues focuses on what she regards as a logical fault in the very notion of there being two different standards for virtue. This fault is discoverable through analysis of the separation of virtues doctrine, which reveals it to be in fact a disguised form of relativism, a position as unacceptable to proponents of that doctrine as it is to Wollstonecraft herself.

Virtue and the exercise of virtuous conduct, Wollstonecraft holds with Locke, are to be attained only through the use of the reason. Reason is what she calls the 'primary human characteristic,' and virtue is its best achievement. Experience should combine with reasoning ability to produce the stable foundation of knowledge which is necessary for good moral judgment.[8] From these principles it follows that there can be only one kind of virtue, and that which passes as the female counterpart, based on sensitivity rather than on reason, is a sham and a contradiction.

7. John Locke, *Second Treatise on Civil Government*, chapter 2, #5. (Locke is quoting Hooker.)
8. Mary Wollstonecraft, A *Vindication of the Rights of Woman* (1792), ed. Carol Poston (New York: W. W. Norton and Co., 1987), p. 12.

. . . the perfection of our nature and capability of happiness, must be estimated by the degree of reason, virtue, and knowledge, that distinguish the individual, and direct the laws which bind society: and that from the exercise of reason, knowledge and virtue naturally flows, is equally undeniable, if mankind be viewed collectively.[9]

Since real virtue is only discoverable by reason, she argues, it is inconsistent to maintain that there is a different type of virtue for females which demands sensitivity, intuition, and obedience rather than reason and self-discipline. Not only is this type of "virtue" counterfeit, but also any attempt to set up a double-standard undermines the whole concept of virtue itself, making proper conduct and moral laws merely a relative matter. Taking the double-standard a step further, Wollstonecraft sees a danger that "virtue for women" and "virtue for men" will give way to "virtue for some people is not the same as for others," an unacceptably relativistic conclusion.[1] "If any class of mankind be so created that it must necessarily be educated by rules not strictly deducible from truth," she states, then "virtue is an affair of convention."[2] Only by means of a developed reasoning ability can one discover moral truths, thereby perceiving what virtue is and how to pursue it. One must conclude that there is only one measuring stick for both sexes: ". . . It is a farce to call any being virtuous whose virtues do not result from the exercise of its own reason."[3]

Having established that there is but one moral standard and it is based on reason, that the so-called female virtues founded on special sensitivity are not virtues at all, Wollstonecraft clears the way for approaching the question—Are women, then, in fact rational? Are they morally responsible human beings? In short, there are only two options:

Women are . . . to be considered either as moral beings, or so weak that they must be entirely subjected to the superior faculties of men.[4]

Needless to say, Wollstonecraft and the early feminists claimed the potential of full rationality and complete moral responsibility for women. But at the same time, they were sorely conscious of the damaging effects produced by the social forces acting on women. Surveying their general circumstances, (especially those of the women in the middle and upper classes), feminists were quick to observe that centuries of conditioning had in fact often produced a debased creature who conformed to the stereotype of misogynists. But that this condition in women was the effect of female nature was clearly false; by being excluded from positions which demanded the use of reason and moral responsibility, by being denied adequate education and experience, the frivolous "lady" of the nineteenth century was a product of definite, distinguishable social forces.

9. *Ibid.*
1. Wollstonecraft, pp. 26–27.
2. Wollstonecraft, p. 85.
3. Wollstonecraft, p. 21.
4. Wollstonecraft, p. 25.

Accordingly, the feminists demanded not only political and legal rights for freedom from the confinement of the domestic sphere; they also demanded to be accorded moral responsibility and the education and experience deemed necessary to carry out that responsibility. The catalog of commentary on this score is significant, for in being deprived of the development of their reason and thereby of their moral character, as they thought, the women of the late eighteenth and early nineteenth centuries felt they were being deprived of a defining part of their humanity.

In 1838 Sarah Grimke, American abolitionist and feminist, wrote that ". . . the noble faculties of our minds are crushed, and our reasoning powers are almost totally uncultivated."[5] Furthermore, man "has done all he could to debase and enslave her (woman's) mind; and now he looks triumphantly on the ruin he has wrought and says, the being he has thus deeply injured in his inferior."[6]

Perhaps the most systematic documentation of the abridgement of the rights of women which infringes on their ability to perform as morally responsible, fully human adults occurs in the Declaration of Sentiments and Resolutions proclaimed at Seneca Falls, New York, in 1848. Modeled on the Declaration of Independence, the document lists fifteen grievances and twelve resolutions, and fully seven of the total mention matters pertinent to morals, responsibility, and the exercise of both. Phrased as an accusation by womankind against her oppressor, mankind, the document declares that,

> He has made her, morally, an irresponsible being, as she can commit many crimes with impunity, provided they be done in the presence of her husband.[7]

(This grievance makes reference to the fact that for years women were denied legal recognition to such an extent that without legal identity separate from her husband's, a woman was not held responsible for crimes she committed in his presence or with his consent.)[8] The most critical aspect about the legal status of women, in the minds of the framers of the Seneca Falls Declaration, was the lack of responsible behavior expected of women. With no responsibility expected of them, they surmised, women would often fail to develop into mature adults.

5. Sarah Grimke, in Kraditor, pp. 86–87.
6. Sarah Grimke, quoted in W. L. O'Neill, *Everyone Was Brave* (Chicago: Quadrangle Books, 1969), p. 12.
7. Declaration of Sentiments and Resolutions, in Miriam Schneir, ed., *Feminism: The Essential Historical Writings* (New York: Vintage Books, 1972), p. 79. From our perspective in the contemporary woman's movement, this analysis of men as woman's prime oppressors appears superficial. The philosophy of historical materialism has probably been the greatest influence on the strengthening of the analysis of women's position in society. However, most of the early writers perceived man as the main cause of their situation, perhaps because he was the most immediate cause. Wollstonecraft mentions men as the cause of the problem twice, pp. 24 and 26. Here she remarks that men reap pleasurable benefits from the inferior status of women and therefore have much to gain by perpetuating that status.
8. Alice Felt Tyler, *Freedom's Ferment* (New York: Harper and Row, 1962, first published, 1944), p. 426.

The picture of woman as delicate, sensitive, and innocent was a way of viewing her as a perpetual child, and, as Wollstonecraft remarked, "Children, I grant, should be innocent, but when the epithet is applied to men, or women, it is but a civil term for weakness."[9]

Harriet Taylor Mill, Lucretia Mott, Emma Willard,[1] and many others allude time and again to the position of women in society as an enforced lack of moral responsibility, caused by "man-made restrictions (which . . . enervated the minds and powers of women."[2] Harriet Martineau, a visitor to America, observed in 1837 that,

> The morals of women are crushed. If there be any human power and business and privilege which is absolutely universal, it is the discovery and adoption of the principle and laws of duty. As every individual, whether man or woman, has a reason and a conscience, this is a work which each is thereby authorized to do for him or herself. But it is not only virtually prohibited to beings who, like the American woman, have scarcely any objects in life proposed to them; but the whole apparatus of opinion is brought to bear offensively upon individuals among women who exercise freedom of mind in deciding upon what duty is, and the methods by which it is to be pursued.[3]

It is not the case, then, that women are by nature less rational than men; rather, with their sex, reason has been "crushed" because of upbringing and education.

Wollstonecraft argued from the then-popular theory of *associated ideas* to explain how women's upbringing discouraged the development of powers of reason.[4] By this theory, the ideas which are temporally linked in childhood and adolescent experiences greatly shape the character, the moral stature, and the aesthetic proclivities of the adult. Wollstonecraft notes that early education is crucial to adult abilities, for it is then that the ideas are implanted which will serve as future guides in the powerful form of habits and propensities.

> When the ideas and matters of fact are once taken in, they lie by for use till some fortuitous circumstance makes the information dart into the mind with illustrative force that has been received at very different periods of our lives . . . Over these instantaneous associations we have little power, for when the mind is once enlarged by excursive flights or profound reflection, the raw materials will in some degree arrange themselves . . .

9. Wollstonecraft, p. 20.
1. Harriet Taylor, wife of John Stuart Mill, who inspired the ideas in his feminist tract *The Subjection of Women*; Lucretia Mott, Quaker reformer, abolitionist, and, with Elizabeth Cady Stanton, organizer of the Seneca Falls convention; Emma Willard, American educator who tirelessly traveled, lectured, and wrote about the cause of education for women [*Editor*].
2. Lucretia Mott, quoted in Tyler, p. 455.
3. Harriet Martineau, *Society in America* (1837),

Vol. 1 (New York: AMS Press, Inc., 1966), pp. 229–30. [Harriet Martineau (1802–76) was an English writer of severe Unitarian upbringing. Despite being ill for most of her life, she wrote for an income and succeeded well. She traveled to America in 1837, where she embraced the then-struggling, small abolitionist movement—*Editor*.]
4. For the classic exposition of the theory of the association of ideas, see David Hartley's *Observations on Man* (1749).

So ductile is the understanding, and yet so stubborn, that the associations which depend on adventitious circumstances, during the period that the body takes to arrive at maturity, can seldom be disentangled by reason.[5]

Since girls are not encouraged to develop the reflective powers of reason which could override and counteract the power of associated ideas, they are particularly vulnerable to them. Added to this is the kind of associations which their education permits:

Everything they see or hear serves to fix impressions, call forth emotions, and associate ideas that give a sexual character to the mind.[6]

If Wollstonecraft's appeal to associationism is now obsolete, the general thrust of her remarks—that education can explain thoroughly the significant social differences between men and women—is still quite alive.[7] Perhaps this is most true of her observations concerning the behavior the female learns to exhibit towards the male, (an aspect of that "sexual character of mind" mentioned above). Being dominated on account of their sex, and also being valued primarily as sexual beings, women are quick to see that it is only by exploiting their sexuality that they can effectively influence any particular decision. Little girls learn, observes Wollstonecraft, that reasoned, open actions are less effective than covert, flirtatious actions. Therefore from their earliest life to adulthood they are encouraged and molded into a position which is morally debasing.

This cruel association of ideas which everything conspires to twist into all their habits of thinking . . . receives new force when they begin to act a little for themselves; for they then perceive that it is only through their address to excite emotions in men, that pleasure and power are to be obtained.[8]

Given the strong and damaging force of the education of women, it is scarcely surprising that by adulthood they do not always have the same abilities as men. Complicating this fact, notes Wollstonecraft, women are generally economically dependent upon men, and must live off them by *charm*. a further incentive to remain the frivolous coquette, at least as long as beauty lasts.[9] In fact, the more astonishing thing is that women ever escape the effects of their upbringing at all:

5. Wollstonecraft, pp. 115–16.
6. Wollstonecraft, p. 117.
7. Wollstonecraft's discussion of the association of ideas at the beginning of Chapter VI calls up the quite modern discussions of the way we socialize children. The notions of what it is to be a girl or a woman are implanted virtually from birth onward and become, as Wollstonecraft says, "habitual slavery" [*Editor*].
8. Wollstonecraft, p. 117. Emma Willard, in 1819,
made a very similar observation: "A system of education, which leads one class of human beings to consider the approbation of another, as their highest object teaches, that the rule of their conduct should be the will of beings imperfect and erring like themselves, rather than the will of God, which is the only standard of perfection." (Kraditor, p. 81.)
9. Wollstonecraft, p. 141.

Educated in worse than Egyptian bondage, it is unreasonable, as well as cruel, to upbraid them with faults that can scarcely be avoided, unless a degree of native vigour be supposed that falls to the lot of very few amongst mankind.[1]

The conclusion is clear: it is society and men in society who perpetuate the customs which keep women in "worse than Egyptian bondage." Full moral responsibility must be granted to women, and to insure that responsibility, women must be allowed the kind of education that develops the use of their reason. Indeed, a change of this sort would not only benefit women, but society as well, for ". . . that society is formed in the wisest manner, whose constitution is founded on the nature of man . . ."[2] Since at present, society does not give a chance to half of humanity to develop fully, we can conclude that ". . . the most salutary effects tending to improve mankind might be expected from a REVO-LUTION in female manners . . ."[3]

So far, in examining the idea that women were considered deficient in their reasoning powers and therefore in their moral judgment, I have been emphasizing only one aspect of the theories concerning female morals that were important during the early years of the feminist movement. In fact, the theories affecting women were more complex than this, and, taken as a whole, can be seen to contain an important inconsistency. Since women were viewed as creatures whose moral nature could not depend for its foundation on rationality, sometimes they were regarded as totally amoral beings, if not actually evil. But most who adopted the notion of there being a female sphere of activity also maintained that women did have a moral nature, and sometimes even a spiritual superiority over men. Their virtue, however, was founded not in reason but in sensitivity and intuition.[4] Wollstonecraft refuted this combination of beliefs as inconsistent, but inconsistent or not, this "double-standard" of virtue had a profound social effect on those who lived under its aegis.

This confusing duality which pervaded the concepts of woman's character is in fact manifested in the Seneca Falls Declaration itself, giving that document the initial appearance of internal inconsistency. While for the most part it accuses men and society for making women beings who lack moral responsibility, as in the passages quoted earlier, later it makes reference to the current notion that indeed in some ways women were actually accorded moral *superiority* over men. ("That inasmuch as man, while claiming for himself intellectual superiority, does accord to woman moral superiority . . .")[5]

1. Wollstonecraft, p. 117.
2. Wollstonecraft, p. 12.
3. Wollstonecraft, p. 192. (It should be mentioned that Wollstonecraft's vision of revolution was rather different from ours today. One of the benefits of education for women, she believed, is that they would become better wives and mothers. She also felt that women are not the full equals of men, even though the measure of their virtue is the same. See p. 26)
4. Once again, the notion that women are moral through their sensitivity is not to be confused with the Moral Sense theory of the eighteenth century. (See Note #2, above, p. 286.)
5. Seneca Falls Declaration, in Schneir, p. 81.

This inconsistency is not a logical slip on the part of Stanton and Mott, framers of the document. It is a reflection of the paradoxical expectations operating on women at that time. As guardians of the domestic sphere, to women fell the task of rearing their children in the laws of God and decency. Woman's superior intuition and sensibility were supposed to grant her a moral and spiritual excellence; yet *at the same time* her deficient reason and poor cognitive ability were supposed to preclude the possibility of stable moral character! The mystified natural sentiments of woman, presumably, were supposed to take the place, as she attained wife and motherhood, of the reasoning abilities and self-discipline denied her in her education.

Claiming that moral responsibility was only possible through the development of good judgment and the reason, and the self-discipline necessary to exercise both, Mary Wollstonecraft focused on this paradoxical view of women as a major cause of their misery. Gentlewomen are brought up to be flirtatious, lively, pleasing, and unassertive, yet in marriage and motherhood they are expected to become suddenly the guides of morality and virtue, to manifest their 'natural sensitivity' and 'spiritual nature.' (Even though, with the same breath, those who exhort them to do so remind them that they must obey the superior reason of their husbands.) Wollstonecraft notes resentfully the unfairness of these expectations: ". . . How could Rousseau expect them to be virtuous and constant when reason is neither allowed to be the foundation of their virtue, nor truth the object of their inquiries?"[6] She also observes how this theoretical inconsistency has its practical consequences:

> And why is the life of a modest woman a perpetual conflict? I should answer, that this system of education makes it so. Modesty, temperance, and self-denial, are the sober offspring of reason; but when sensibility is nurtured at the expense of the understanding, such weak beings must be restrained by arbitrary means, and subjected to continual conflicts.[7]

This confusion in moral theory which, as Wollstonecraft argues, lies at the heart of the misguided separation of virtues into male and female, must have taken its toll on the women who lived under its contradictory credo. At least one historian, Carol Smith Rosenberg, has argued that the prevalence of hysteria, a broadly-conceived ailment that was not unusual among middle and upper class women in American in the nineteenth century, can be explained as the result of the conflicting demands made of women at that time—specifically, the conflict between an upbringing which taught women to be frivolous and dependent young ladies, and the subsequent expectation that, if necessary, they would bear heavy responsibility upon becoming wives and mothers.[8] It would

6. Wollstonecraft, p. 90.
7. Wollstonecraft, p. 82.
8. Carol Smith Rosenberg, from a lecture given at the State University of New York at Buffalo, Fall, 1972.

seem that Wollstonecraft was right, and that the reliance on natural sensitivity for the female virtues was an inadequate substitute for an education which prepared one for the realities of adult life.

The analysis of woman's distorting upbringing and its consequences, both social and personal, clearly was an important feature of the early feminist movement. In addition, the claim that women are innately as rational as men and the demand that they be treated as such formed the foundation for their revolutionary appeal, based like the demands of the liberal democratic social movements of the times, on the popular notion of "natural rights." "Equals must have equal measure," quoted Locke from Hooker. And all who are created equal are endowed with certain inalienable rights, continued Jefferson. With the assertion and the demonstration of their equal rationality and their equal responsibility, the feminists, appealing to their long-denied natural rights, demanded equal citizenship along with men.[9] It is safe to assume that the inconsistency of application of the principles of the American Declaration of Independence had occurred to women frequently in the early years of the nineteenth century, even before the Seneca Falls Declaration made those inconsistencies explicit. Harriet Martineau noted this anomaly in 1837:

> The democratic principle condemns all this as wrong; and requires the equal political representation of all rational beings . . . but it is interesting to inquire how so obvious a decision has been so evaded as to leave women no political rights whatever.[1]

Clearly, one way this "decision was so evaded" was through the denial that women were in fact rational beings.

Gradually, the conditions of women began to improve under law. After a series of state Married Women's Property Acts, they began to have a separate legal identity. Active women began institutions of higher learning for women, opening the doors for that 'exercise of reason' so long awaited. Eventually, of course, the crusade for women's rights simultaneously culminated and sputtered out with the extension of the suffrage to women.

That the "first" feminist movement did not achieve all its goals, that the vote was not enough, has been realized and analyzed now for some years. But it is perhaps not repetitive to direct our hindsight to an evaluation of this particular feature of the early years of the movement: to the preoccupation with moral responsibility and reason.

Clearly, this problem was perceived as an acute contributor to woman's oppression. But we should also ask the question: to what extent did the image of woman as irrational and irresponsible reach the heart of the oppression of *all* women? Mary Wollstonecraft stated at one point that

9. Shortly after the Seneca Falls Declaration, many feminists stopped justifying their equal rationality and simply demanded the right to equal political participation. (See Kraditor, Section III, Chapter 4.)
1. Martineau, p. 200.

indeed it was the main problem, for in her introduction she asserts her ". . . profound conviction that the neglected education of my fellow-creatures is the grand source of the misery I deplore."[2] However, by her own description, she is really writing for and about a certain class of women—of women of leisure who, for example, ". . . make up their faces for the day—five hours, and who could do it in less—do many spend in dressing, including preparation for bed, washing with Milk of roses, etc, etc."[3]

That she ignored the problems of laboring women is perhaps not surprising, even though in certain of her other writings she indicated an awareness of the troubles of those born to poverty and misfortune.[4] Most of her experience gave her the opportunity for close observation of women belonging to the middle and upper classes. Additionally, we should bear in mind that for some time after the advent of liberal democratic thought, not only the women but also the men of the laboring classes were considered to be lacking in rationality and therefore not candidates for full citizenship.[5]

It goes without saying not all women were oppressed by a belief that they were weak and delicate, demanding the guidance and protection of men. The women working in factories, the women who tended farms, the female slaves laboring in the fields all suffered more from other causes than from the problems presented by reason, moral responsibility, and the image of woman as irrational and frivolous.[6]

However, although the problems surrounding reason and morals may have been acute only for women of the more leisure classes, the struggles which they engendered attacked the degrading *stereotype* of woman at its root. If we can charge that political reform movements sometimes ignore the working classes, it is still more the case that popular sex stereotype does so as well. The image of woman which the early feminists fought, the social concepts of womanhood which kept them in a narrow and sometimes maddeningly unproductive sphere, were the product of the popular notion of a "lady," and not of a farmer's, a fisherman's, a miller's wife, nor of a female slave in the South.

Juliet Mitchell has stated that revolutionary ideas usually begin within or in relation to dominant ideology, and that it is the expected course of development for oppression to be articulated first by members of the middle or upper classes.[7] The arguments against spheres of activity, against the doctrine of the separation of virtues, and for the rational nature of woman and her natural rights as a citizen, perhaps are viewed most productively in this way.

2. Wollstonecraft, Introduction, p. 7.
3. From a letter from Mary to her sister, 1797, quoted in Flexner, p. 76.
4. Flexner, pp. 248–49.
5. C. B. Macpherson, *The Political Theory of Possessive Individualism* (Oxford: The Clarendon Press, 1962), Chapter 5, passim.

6. Probably the most dramatic contrast between the different kinds of social forces that affected women was demonstrated in Sojourner Truth's famous "Ain't I a Woman" speech, which can be found in Schneir's anthology.
7. Juliet Mitchell, *Woman's Estate* (Baltimore: Penguin Books, 1971), pp. 21–22.

Many new theories have developed within the contemporary woman's movement which, in some respects, supplant the old ones, (such as the substitution of analyses drawn from historical materialism for the earlier claims that men themselves were the sole source of oppression). In many ways, the subject we have been discussing is no longer a significant political issue. However, it would be inaccurate to claim that this early question has been entirely laid to rest. Although they speak in considerably diluted tones, there are still those who would claim that women's reason is less reliable than men's, or that it occurs in a different—perhaps even in an intuitive—manner.[8] Unfortunately, Mary Wollstonecraft's arguments, dated though they should be, have more than historical importance, for her particular battle has not altogether been won.

R. M. JANES

On the Reception of Mary Wollstonecraft's *A Vindication of the Rights of Woman*†

It is popularly assumed that Mary Wollstonecraft's *A Vindication of the Rights of Woman* was greeted with shock, horror, and derision when it appeared early in 1792, that the forces of reaction massed against this bold attempt to assert the equality of woman and spattered the Amazon with their pens. Her biographers have repeatedly asserted that the first reviews and recorded reactions to the work were generally favorable, but they have had little impact on the popular misconception. The reasons for that scholarly ineffectuality are obvious enough. Later in the decade, Wollstonecraft was vilified by the press, and for much of the nineteenth century hers was a name to brandish at feminists as evidence of the horrific consequences of female emancipation. The furious clamorings of 1798 quite overwhelmed the calm approbation of 1792 in both intensity and duration. Since most writers on Wollstonecraft and the *Rights of Woman* are concerned primarily with the tardy progress of female emancipation, they expect a negative response to her and her work and have less than an active interest in the peculiarites of late eighteenth-century social thought. But the reception of Wollstonecraft's work and that of her followers, Mary Robinson and Mary Hays, illuminates an interesting moment in the historical transformation of women's status. Those works, part educational, part psychological, part political, appeared when the contest for improvement of women's education and their status in the family had been largely won, and the contest for enlarged political, civil, social liberties was about to be joined. The

8. See, for example, Steven Goldberg, *The Inevitability of Patriarchy* (New York: William Morrow and Co., 1973), especially Section 4.

† From *Journal of the History of Ideas*, 39 (1978): 293–302.

progressive intellectual circles represented by the leading reviews reacted positively to demands for intellectual equality, improved education, and reformed manners. Demands for political participation by women or for changes in women's social behavior were regarded as unessential and absurd. Those elements of the works in question that corresponded to changes that had been in train for half a century were approved; those that marked out the direction of more drastic social transformations were rightly though disapprovingly remarked as revolutionary and visionary, if they were seen at all.

With one important exception, every notice the *Rights of Woman* received when it first appeared was favorable. The reviews were split along party lines. Periodicals of radical inclination, sharing Wollstone-craft's philosophical assumptions, sympathetic towards the rights of man and events in France, distressed by Edmund Burke's lack of consistency, approved the work. Enthusiasts of the rights of man, they did not greet the rights of woman with horror. Wollstonecraft had written for the *Analytical Review* since 1788. Joseph Johnson who had published both the *Analytical* and the book, reviewed it positively, of course, as did the *Literary Magazine*, the *General Magazine*, the New York *Magazine*, the *Monthly Review*, and the *New Annual Register*. These periodicals had also favorably noticed her *Vindication of the Rights of Men*, one of the first answers to Burke's *Reflections on the Revolution in France*. The single journal that had favorably reviewed her *Rights of Men* and ignored the *Rights of Woman* was the *English Review*.[1] Although periodicals less politically or more conservatively committed did not in the main choose to review the work, the *Critical Review* attacked it in two passionate installments.

The contents of the reviews favorable to the work indicate why it was ignored rather than virulently attacked by most of those opposed to the political assumptions Wollstonecraft held. Most reviewers took it to be a sensible treatise on female education and ignored those recommendations in the work that might unsettle the relations between the sexes. The *Analytical's* response was typical. The work was catalogued for the year not under politics, but under "political economy," and the reviewer observed that "in reality the present work is an elaborate *treatise of female education*. . . . If the bulk of the great truths which this publication contains were reduced to practice, the nation would be better, wiser,

---

1. *The English Review* clarified its position in supporting Mirabeau's *Treatise of Public Education*, which restated Talleyrand's view that women should be confined to a domestic education "in opposition to some modern philosophers, or rather what the Italians call *filosofas iri*, who would wish to put into soft female hands the rod of government, and the sword of justice," XIX (1792), 56. The *Gentleman's Magazine* had a good laugh over the *Rights of Men*: "We should be sorry to raise a horse-laugh against a fair lady; but we were always taught to suppose that the *rights of woman* were the proper theme of the female sex; and that, while the Ro-mans governed the world, the women governed the Romans" When the fair lady descended to her proper subject, the reviewer was not there to meet her. Both Wollstonecraft and the *Analytical* had anticipated the jocularity of the wits. *Gentleman's Magazine*, **61**, pt. 1 (1791), 151; *Analytical Review*, **12** (1792), 241–49, **13** (1792), 481–89; *Literary Magazine*, **1** (1972). 133–39; *General Magazine*, **6** (1792), 187–91; *New York Magazine*, **4** (1973), 77–81; *Monthly Review*, **8** (1792), 198–209; *New Annual Register* (1792), p. [298]; *Critical Review*, N.S. **4** (1792), 389–98, N.S. **5** (1792), 132–41.

and happier than it is upon the wretched, trifling, useless and absurd system of education which is now prevalent."[2] This ability to ignore the work's political implications crossed party lines. In an exchange between Horace Walpole and Hannah More,[3] neither of whom had read the book and both of whom had "been much pestered to read" it, Walpole told More that he had been "assured it contains neither metaphysics nor politics. . . ." When Walpole flung his memorable phrase "that hyena in petticoats" at Wollstonecraft, the occasion was a political provocation to which the *Rights of Woman* was irrelevant. He objected to her attack on Marie Antoinette in the *Historical and Moral View of the Origin and Progress of the French Revolution* (1794), and his phrase reciprocates Wollstonecraft's hostility and contempt towards the French queen.[4] As in later attacks on Wollstonecraft, Walpole's hostility was directed against the female republican writer, and not against the vindicator of the rights of woman. In 1792 in Walpole and in More's circle, there were those who managed to find the work innocuous as a political tract and valuable as an educational and critical one.

In approving the work, the reviewers endorsed the view that the character of women at the present time needed to become more independent, more rational, more equal to men in mind and spirit; and they indicated how widespread the assumptions of earlier educational reformers had become. As is so often the case with British reformers, the benevolent, improving impulse sought to ameliorate the condition of the sex, not to alter relative positions between the sexes. Her demands for change in woman's spiritual condition approved, Wollstonecraft's hopes for social change earned from most of her reviewers the general reservation that "several of her opinions are fanciful, and some of her projects romantic."[5] The differences were specified by the most feminist of the reviewers, William Enfield.

Enfield was a dissenting minister with impeccable credentials; he had been associated with the Warrington Academy, was the memorialist of John Aikin, Mrs. Barbauld's father, and was memorialized in his turn by Aikin's son, Dr. John Aikin. Reviewing the *Rights of Woman* in Ralph Griffiths' *Monthly Review*, he refrained from chiding Wollstonecraft for her "challenge to the ancient wisdom that considered women to be inferior men," and rejoiced that "how jealous soever WE may be of our *right* to the proud preeminence which we have assumed, the women of the present age are daily giving us indubitable proofs that mind is of no sex, and that, with the fostering aid of education, the world, as well as the nursery, may be benefited by their instructions." He included her in the class of "philosophers" and would not offend

2. *Analytical Review*, 12 (1792), 249; 13 (1792), 530.

3. Horace Walpole (1717–97), English politician, author of *The Castle of Otranto*, and one of the most famous letter writers of the time, had as one of his correspondents Hannah More, a noted

Bluestocking of the time [*Editor*].

4. *Horace Walpole's Correspondence with Hannah more, et alii*, eds. W. S. Lewis, Robert A. Smith, Charles H. Bennett, XXXI (New Haven, 1961), 370, 373, 397.

5. *Monthly Review*, 8(1792), 209.

her by styling her "authoress" (as the *Literary Magazine* had done). He copiously endorsed "the important business here undertaken . . . to correct errors, hitherto universally embraced, concerning the female character; and to raise woman, from a state of degradation and vassalage, to her proper place in the scale of existence, where, in the dignity of independence, she may discharge the duties and enjoy the happiness of a rational Being." The opinions that Enfield explicitly rejected are those that Wollstonecraft had anticipated would provoke laughter: the suggestions that women assume "an active part in civil government," that they abandon "the useful and elegant labours of the needle," and that the distinction of sexes be obliterated in social intercourse save where "love animates the behavior." The first and the second Enfield considered of little importance in improving the condition and character of women, the third impracticable outside of heaven. In spite of his retreat at those points where feminist opinions might make a practical social difference, Enfield did fortify the lonely outpost of a rational asexual ideal: "Both men and women should certainly in the first place, regard themselves, and should be treated by each other, as human beings," and he concluded his remarks with a wish that English possessed "some general term to denote the species, like Ανθρωπος and *Homo* in the Greek and Roman languages. The want of such a general term is a material defect in our language."[6]

Enfield's position both typifies the limitations of the response to the *Rights of Woman* and corresponds to the order in which reforms were to be achieved in the nineteenth and twentieth centuries. Women were to be better educated, more respectable, and more useful as doctors, nurses, teachers before they were to be admitted to civic participation. They would have colleges before they had the vote, and the vote before the question of obliterating behavioral differences between the sexes was raised again. The principal difference between the pro- and anti-feminist positions at the end of the eighteenth century and the beginning of the nineteenth was less their attitude towards future change than their attitude towards past formulations. The *Critical Review*, which produced the only attack on the *Rights of Woman*, was also the only review to maintain the essential inferiority and the necessary subordination of women.

That the *Critical* should have picked up the volume at all is surprising, although Derek Roper has pointed out that the review went through a moderately liberal phase between 1774 and 1805. Robinson, the publisher of the *New Annual Register*, who was to be fined in 1793 for selling Paine's *Rights of Man*, had become a partner in 1774 and exerted a moderating influence on editorial policies.[7] In spite of Robinson's association, the *Critical* reviewed Burke's *Reflections* favorably and scar-

---

6. *Ibid.*, 198, 209.
7. "The Politics of the Critical Review 1756–1817,"

Durham University Journal, **53,** N.S. 22(1961), 117–22.

ified both Wollstonecraft and Paine on the rights of man. In the *Rights of Woman* the *Critical* saw the revolutionary implications of the social recommendations more clearly than the liberal reviews. As a consequence, it rejected explicitly the feminist premise that there is no characteristic difference in sex, but at the same time it endorsed educational premises that would have seemed actively and aggressively "feminist" fifty years earlier. Most disturbing to the reviewer was Wollstonecraft's attack on the idea of a sexual character.

The reviewer favored educating women for the same objects Wollstonecraft had suggested: women should possess knowledge so as to be more suitable companions to their husbands, better tutors to their children, more useful members of society. They should be able to examine a subject coolly, compare arguments, estimate degrees of evidence, and trace the evolutions of the human mind. And Wollstonecraft is praised for the force and conviction that her arguments on this score carry. The point of difference was not the cultivation of women's minds, but the relative roles of the sexes and the psychological characteristics that are and ought to be peculiar to each. The author stood firm on the intellectual inferiority of women: no women exist or have existed who are the intellectual equals of men, and demonstrate the same strength of reasoning or reach of intuitive perception. Even if women should possess the abilities that men do, it is not desirable that they should exercise them: "and when all are strong, to whom must the weaker operations belong? The female Plato will find it unsuitable to 'the dignity of her virtue' to dress the child, and descend to the disgusting offices of a nurse . . .and the young lady, instead of studying the softer and more amiable arts of pleasing, must contend with her lover for superiority of mind, for greater dignity of virtue; and before she condescends to become his wife, must prove herself his equal or superior." The utilitarian base of the argument is comical enough: the tasks allotted women are so disagreeable that if women possessed alternatives, no one would do them; the child would stop[8] undressed, the weak unnursed. Contempt for feminine duties, fear of equality in relations between the sexes, conviction of the superiority of men and the masculine sphere of activity are all evident. At times the eighteenth-century fascination with polygamy seems to be lurking just under the surface of the prose, revelling in the grammar: we are told that "women [plural] are the companions of man [singular], and the companions of a rational creature should possess reason not totally uncultivated." Elsewhere the tendency to consider women as an undifferentiated herd and masculine achievement as singular turns up in the numbers used to refute Wollstonecraft's contention that women should have representatives in parliament: if they did, "the state would lose 10,000 useful domestic wives, in pursuit of one very

8. Remain or continue to be [*Editor*].

indifferent philosopher or statesman." Although he faulted Wollstone-craft for discussing modesty and carnal appetites too freely, the reviewer was not afraid that the work would promote sexual license. Quite the contrary: "The precepts are calculated to form such women as we hope never to see; such as we are certain would waste their days in joyless celibacy, their sweets upon the desert air."[9]

When the *Rights of Woman* first appeared in 1792, reviewers and readers alike agreed with its recommendations for reform in women's education. If we take "feminism" to mean anxiety for the education of women and the improvement of their minds, there did not exist an anti-feminist in England in 1790. If we take feminism to mean restlessness with the subordinate position of women and a vague desire that women should be possessed of more "liberty" and more consequence, then public opinion was divided between those who thought that women had quite enough liberty as it was and those who thought the rhetoric of submission inappropriate to relations between men and women. If we take feminism to mean demands for specific changes in women's civil disabilities, including the right to vote, Wollstonecraft herself barely qualifies, and her followers, Hays and Robinson, do not even make the attempt. But although Wollstonecraft stayed securely enough within the established boundaries of educational writing not to terrify her first read-ers, she ventured out of bounds often enough to exhilarate them.

As should now be commonly known, Wollstonecraft's reputation col-lapsed as a consequence of two separate events: the course of the rev-olution in France and consequent repudiation of the vocabulary of revolution in England; and Godwin's publication of her posthumous works, including *Maria Or the Wrongs of Woman* and his *Memoirs of the Author of a Vindication of the Rights of Woman*. When she died in 1797, generous obituaries appeared in the *Gentleman's Magazine*, the *Monthly Magazine*, the *European Magazine*, and *New York Magazine*.[1] When Godwin's *Memoirs* appeared the following year, they were picked up for review by far more periodicals than had taken up the *Rights of Woman* itself.

The *Memoirs* revealed that Wollstonecraft had borne a child out of wedlock and then been deserted by her lover (Gilbert Imlay), that she had pursued him and had attempted suicide on two occasions, that she had found consolation with Godwin and had engaged in sexual relations with him before marriage. This series of actions found no approval at the time from any political persuasion. The periodicals that had been favorably disposed towards the *Rights of Woman* united in wishing the *Memoirs* unwritten, unpublished, and unread. If the *Memoirs* were "a

9. N.S. 4 (1792) 390, 396, 393; 5, 139. The *Crit-ical* insisted on a characteristic difference in sex even against Catharine Macaulay Graham N.S. 2 (1790), 618.

1. *Gentleman's Magazine*, 68, pt. 2 (1797), 894; *Monthly Magazine*, 4 (1797), 232–33; *European Magazine*, 32 (1797), 215; *New York Magazine*, N.S. 2 (1797), 616.

singular tribute of respect to the memory of a well beloved wife,"[2] the vindication of adultery in *Maria* was scarcely more palatable. The most sympathetic readings of the *Memoirs* attempted to palliate her acts by attributing them to virtuous though mistaken motives. Having shared Wollstonecraft's political principles, this set of reviewers did not insist upon a necessary connection between her politics and her sexual divagations.

For those opposed to her politics, the *Memoirs* and *Maria* served up a delicious evidence of the consequences of Jacobin[3] principles in action. The anti-Jacobin attacks on Wollstonecraft took two forms: the merely scurrilous attack and the politically motivated scurrilous attack. The anti-Jacobin but professedly apolitical periodicals displayed the scandals in detail but paid little attention to her works. The life alone testified to the consequences of adhering to the "new order" and provided an example which, "if followed, would be attended with the most pernicious consequences to society; a female who could brave the opinion of the world in the most delicate point; a philosophical wanton, breaking down the bars intended to restrain licentiousness; and a mother, deserting a helpless offspring, disgracefully brought into the world by herself, by an intended act of suicide."[4]

The reviews founded for polemical purposes, the *British Critic* and the *Anti-Jacobin Review*, gave her publications more attention and distinguished themselves by a particularly nasty use of the argument ad feminam. To the clergyman conducting the *British Critic* (Archdeacon Robert Nares and William Beloe), she appeared "in the strongest sense, a voluptuary and sensualist but without refinement." As had the *Gentleman's Magazine*, they remarked the contrast between the *Rights of Woman* and Godwin's version of Wollstonecraft's last hours: "The reader of the Vindication of the Rights of Woman, will perhaps be surprised when he is informed, that, during her last illness, no religious expression escaped the author's lips. In that work, the grand principle is, that woman is not the inferior of man, but his equal in moral rank, walking along with him the road of duty, in which "they are both trained for a state of endless improvement."[5] With his version of the general proposition enforced by the *Rights of Woman* the reviewer has no quarrel, but it is clear that Wollstonecraft was led from the road of duty by the glimmerings of false philosophy. The *Anti-Jacobin* compared her to Mes-

---

2. *New Annual Register* (1798), p. [271]. The *Monthly Review* wisely considered the opinions on marriage and religion to be those of Godwin, not of his wife, **27** (1798), 321–24.
3. The Jacobins were the radical political clubs during the French Revolution. While at first moderate, they were finally responsible for the Reign of Terror and the ascendancy of Robespierre. "Jacobin" here means politically radical [*Editor*].
4. *European Magazine*, **33** (1798), 246–51. The original editor of the magazine was James Perry,

a Foxite, who left after the first year, 1782. By 1798, the chief publisher of the magazine was J. Sewell, who, though he belonged to the Association at the Crown and Anchor in the Strand which busied itself in the distribution of anti-republican propaganda, had dismissed the business of compilation and had prohibited political talk on his premises in 1792 (notice dated Dec. 31, 1792, **22**, last page).
5. *British Critic*, **12** (1798), 228–33.

salina,[6] denigrated the originality of her work, and isolated its political elements:

> Next succeeded her Rights of Woman, which the superficial fancied to be profound, and the profound knew to be superficial: it indeed had very little title to the character of ingenuity. Her doctrines are almost all obvious corollaries from the theorems of Paine. If we admit his principle, that all men have an equal right to be governors and statesmen, without any regard to their talents and virtues, there can be no reason for excluding women or even children.[7]

As had the *Critical* in 1792, the *Anti-Jacobin* located the vulnerability of the *Rights of Woman* in precisely those elements that account for the continuing interest in the work. The political features exaggerated for satiric purposes by eighteenth-century opponents are those isolated for praise by twentieth-century readers. Figure and ground have changed places.

To a considerable extent, it was the *Memoirs* rather than the *Rights of Woman* that shaped and colored Wollstonecraft's subsequent reputation. At the extremes of approval and disapproval were those like Godwin and the *Anti-Jacobin* who considered her acts an illustration of Jacobin morality in action. Between the ideologues were those like Matilda Betham who represented Wollstonecraft as an amiable eccentric who had refused to marry Imlay as a matter of principle, those who approved her principles and were embarrassed by her actions, and those who found both her life and principles reprehensible.[8] The range of attitudes has remained much the same from the beginning of the nineteenth century to the last quarter of the twentieth. The most obvious shift has been the replacement of moral disapproval by psychological disapproval: the lady was not evil, but certainly very odd, and not to be imitated.[9]

6. Messalina, the third wife of Roman emperor Claudius, was known for her profligacy and raw ambition. She seduced a married young man, was found out, and was executed at the age of twenty-six [Editor].
7. *Anti-Jacobin Review and Magazine*, 1 (1798), 94–102.
8. Mary Matilda Betham, *Dictionary of Celebrated Women* (London, 1804), 374–77. Betham's principal source was the *Analytical Review* which, with the *Monthly Mirror*, had waxed rhapsodic about the letters to Imlay and had acclaimed their author another Werther. *Analytical Review*, 27 (1798), 235–45; *Monthly Mirror*, 5 (1798), 153–57. The *Monthly Mirror* is most familiar from its attempt to do a "cover story" on Wollstonecraft in its second issue for which a portrait was engraved, 1 (1796), 131–33, but it was also conducted by Thomas Bellamy, hosier turned bookseller, who had conducted the *General Magazine*, one of the periodicals to review the *Rights of Woman* favorably on its first appearance. The *Critical Review* and *Gentleman's Magazine* disapproved of what they read, but were surprisingly restrained in their animadversions. The *Critical* even praised her genius and "undaunted and masculine spirit." *Critical*, N.S. 22 (1798), 414–19; *Gentleman's Magazine* 68, pt. 1 (1978), 186–87. More injurious was Alexander Chalmers, *General Biographical Dictionary*, rev. and enl., XVI (London, 1814), 54–55. That article followed the language of the *British Critic* in finding Wollstonecraft "a voluptuary and sensualist without refinement." Perhaps the pleasantest indication of the mix in attitudes towards Wollstonecraft appeared a few years later. Discussing the associations of Castletown Roche where Edmund Burke spent several of his earliest years, James Prior enumerated such luminaries as Essex, Raleigh, Spenser, and "the famed Mrs. Wolstoncroft," now in very respectable company: *Memoir of the Life and Character of the Right Honourable Edmund Burke*, 2nd ed. (London, 1826), I, 10.
9. The attacks on Wollstonecraft from the psy-

When the *Rights of Woman* first appeared, the attitude taken towards it varied directly with the political position of her reviewers, and the work was not generally regarded as politically significant. With the appearance of the *Memoirs*, the *Rights of Woman* came to seem more revolutionary than it had at first. Providing a vulnerable combination of sexual and political error, Wollstonecraft became the symbolic center for attacks on radical female writers. In certain circles, her name detached itself from her work and came to serve as a red flag for writers forgetful of what she had said. The influence of her name appears most strikingly in the reception accorded the works of her near followers Mary Robinson and Mary Hays.

Robinson's *Letter to the Women of England, on the Injustice of Mental Subordination, with Anecdotes* appeared in 1799 with the author disguised as "Anne Frances Randall," a self-proclaimed follower of Wollstonecraft.[1] The *New Annual Register, British Critic,* and *Critical Review* received the work without much hostility and without much respect. The *Critical* was admirably laconic in its complete notice: "Tolerable declamation in a cause which many will be inclined to support."[2] These reviews endorsed her educational recommendations and reserved judgment on the central question, the justice of mental (not social) subordination. The *Anti-Jacobin* took her off at more length, adverted as had all save the *Critical* to her being of "the school of Wollstonecraft," ironically emphasized Robinson's anecdote of the lady who shot her lover, and closed by reaffirming its purpose to root out the corruption the Wollstonecrafts spread in society. In effect, Robinson's work disappeared into the larger category dominated by Wollstonecraft's Amazonian figure.

In 1803 an anonymous work often attributed to Mary Hays, *A Defence of the Character and Conduct of the Late Mary Wollstonecraft Godwin* maintained with justice that Wollstonecraft's vilification was provoked by the passions raised by the revolution in France and by the asperity of tone adopted in the *Rights of Woman.* The author suggested that Wollstonecraft's tone had alienated many readers who would have been sympathetic to her views. If the work was by Hays, she knew whereof she spoke. She had abandoned work on her own feminist *Appeal to the Men of Great Britain in behalf of the Women* when the *Rights of Woman* appeared in 1792. In 1798, Johnson published her work anonymously. According to Claire Tomalin, the work found approval only at the *Analytical,* and like Wollstonecraft, Hays became "another butt for Tory sarcasm."[3] But Johnson's habit of anonymous publication to protect his

---

choanalytic point of view are familiar and have often been answered. Richard Cobb's comical hatchet job on Wollstonecraft as "impossible crazy lady" (*TLS*, Sept. 6, 1974, 941) has been severely rebuked by Janet M. Todd, "The Polwhelan Tradition and Richard Cobb," *Studies in Burke and His Time*, 16 (Spring, 1975), 271–78.

1. The *CBEL* lists the running title of Robinson's

Letter to the Women of England as a separate work, *Thoughts on the Condition of Women*, n.d.

2. *New Annual Register*, 1799, p. [275]; *British Critic*, 14 (1799), 682; *Critical Review* N.S. 27 (1799), 360; *Anti-Jacobin Review* 3 (1799), 144–46.

3. Claire Tomalin, *The Life and Death of Mary Wollstonecraft* (New York, 1974), 241.

authors and Hays' moderation of tone produced a paradoxical juxta-position. In the *Anti-Jacobin* for September 1800, Elizabeth Hamilton's *Memoirs of Modern Philosophers* was reviewed enthusiastically for show-ing "that *all* the *female* writers of the day are not corrupted by the voluptuous dogmas of Mary Godwin, or her more profligate admirers." The novel's heroine, Bridgetina Botherim, is a parody of Mary Hays, and in the November installment, the reviewer tells us that the novel contains "an excellent imitation of that vicious and detestable stuff which has issued from the pen of M - - y H - -s." Couched cozily in between, there appeared in October a long and generally favorable review of an anonymous work entitled *Appeal to the Men of Great Britain in behalf of the Women*. While the reviewer has learned to "look with a suspicious eye upon demands" for rights by "advocates of the new philosophy . . . whether proceeding from the pen of a *Paine* or a *Wollstonecraft*," this fair writer has no similar "sinister design" but advances a bold and fair specific appeal. Although the work contains some disputable prop-ositions, "there will nothing occur offensive to the feelings of delicacy, nor injurious to the interests of religion and morality."[4] Similarly fa-vorable though briefer readings were reported out by the *New Annual Register* and *Critical Review*, while the scorching attack was reserved for the *British Critic*, which assigned her to the party professing that "whatever is, is wrong" and charged her with illiteracy. As in 1792, the attitude towards a feminist work was shaped by the reviewer's perception of the writer's political stance, and in works afer 1792 the presence of the name Wollstonecraft was a frequent though not necessary clue to the writer's position. Hays's work, sufficiently moderate in tone to earn the epithet "impotent" from William Thompson,[5] was protected by its mildness from the *Anti-Jacobin*, but fell an arbitrary sacrifice to the *British Critic*, which attacked a set of political views and contemptuously dismissed the work's author as not worth correction, an indignity not visited upon Wollstonecraft, who was afforded much correction.

While Wollstonecraft did indeed suffer "stoning by the mob," the cause was not "the reasonable and noble idea of woman's place in the family" presented in the *Rights of Woman*. Nor was the cause her assertion that "the sexes were equal, [her demand for] educational op-portunities and even the franchise for women."[6] The stoning came well after the book and was not caused by a reaction to its specific content. Her educational proposals, when they were remembered, were widely approved. Her political and economic recommendations excited little negative or positive comment at the time of publication. The political hopes were too far from the possibility of realization to be seriously threatening, and the problem of work for women was a common theme when it concerned women of the lower classes or women educated

4. *Anti-Jacobin*, 7 (1800), 39–46, 369–76 (Ham-ilton); 150–58 (Hays).
5. *Appeal of One Half the Human Race, Women, against the Pretensions of the Other Half, Men, to retain them in Political, and thence in Civil and Domestic, Slavery* (London, 1825), vii.
6. "Modern Ideal of Womanhood" (excerpts from

Rights of Woman), in *A Library of the World's Best Literatures Ancient and Modern*, ed. Charles Dud-ley Warner, XXXIX (New York, 1897), 16131; Katherine B. Clinton, "Femme et Philosophie: Enlightenment Origins of Feminism," *Eigh-teenth-Century Studies*, 8 (1975), 283.

beyond their means of support.[7] The emphasis on motherhood that was so striking to the nineteenth-century reader received almost no direct attention from contemporaries. Motherhood was one of the duties to be performed by women in their endeavor to be respectable and useful; it was not yet an object of adoration. The element that came disturbingly close to men's bosoms was the attack on the sexual character of women, the denial that a peculiarly feminine cast of mind was desirable. Men who were glad to agree that mind is of no sex were not pleased to acknowledge that manners ought to be of no sex. The shift in the treatment of feminist works between 1792 and 1798 indicates the continuing approbation of improved education for women and the solidifying opposition to works that seemed to threaten the established relations between the sexes.

Compared to her followers, Wollstonecraft's particular contribution was to state and to enact the major topics of feminist discourse. In the positions she articulated and the life she led, she touched upon almost every topic that has since been raised. Everything is there. Consequently, the reading of her work has varied directly with the concerns of that movement for which she was the first in England to speak. Modern readers light upon her specific proposals for social change and her insubordinate and combative tone. Those elements, dimly discomfortingly visible and politely ignored at the end of the eighteenth century, have been spotlighted by changes in the condition of women. Wollstonecraft's emphases on education and character (the latter might, however, be construed as an early demand for "assertiveness" training) have faded into the background as those demands have been met by actual social change. Although the needs and interests of her audience have determined the reading of her book, there is no discrepancy between the purposes of the work in its original context and the uses to which it has been put. While the work's shape has been distorted, its intent has not been violated. One effect of the revival of the work, however, has been to distort the image present to its first viewers. Had Wollstonecraft argued specifically for the franchise, equal access to professions, equal treatment under the law, abolition of discrimination on the basis of sex, positions consistent with the book's argument but not developed, not central, or not present, her first readers might justly have thought her mad. Such recommendations would have borne no useful relation to the actual condition of women and the opportunities available to them. Instead, Wollstonecraft's abstract and general rhetoric provided for a variety of specific recommendations, and her specific recommendations were firmly in the forefront of eighteenth-century educational discussion, with some brief sorties to more dangerous terrain. Those elements of the work that modern readers tend to ignore ensured the work a respectful reception when it first appeared, and those elements that disturbed the work's first readers account for the continuing hospitality of its modern audience.

7. Mary Anne Radcliffe's *Female Advocate* (London, 1799) suggested restricting certain employments, such as toy and perfume sales, to women and establishing a magdalen to receive women; it was universally well received, though the *Critical* thought the style bad and the issues commonplace; N.S. **27** (1799), 479.

ELISSA S. GURALNICK

Radical Politics in Mary Wollstonecraft's A *Vindication of the Rights of Woman*†

Since its publication in 1792, A *Vindication of the Rights of Woman* has been treated almost exclusively as a feminist manifesto, a simple defense of women's rights. Although critics have generally allowed that the *Rights of Woman* enlarges upon the political tenets expounded in the *Rights of Men*, little attention has been paid to the relationship between the two documents. It has been as if the warning implied in the March 1792 issue of the *Analytical Review* has been carefully and universally heeded: "It might be supposed that Miss W. had taken advantage of the popular topic of the 'Rights of Man' in calling her work 'A Vindication of the Rights of Woman,' had she not already published a work, one of the first answers that appeared to Mr. Burke, under the title of, 'A Vindication of the Rights of Men.' But in reality the present work is an elaborate *treatise of female education.*"[1] As the *Analytical* reviewer seems to have wished, A *Vindication of the Rights of Woman* has never been thoroughly examined as a political tract, a radical critique of society from broad egalitarian premises.

Yet the *Rights of Woman* is a radical political tract, even before it is a radical feminist tract. In fact, the feminism that animates the *Rights of Woman* is merely a special instance of the political radicalism that animates the *Rights of Men*. To ignore this fact is to misconstrue much of the basic character of A *Vindication of the Rights of Woman*. It is to fail, as Wollstonecraft's critics have usually done, to understand the propriety of the work's apparent digressions into such tenuously related material as the tyrannical abuse of power by kings and the effeteness of their courts, or the detrimental effects upon society of the existence of a standing army and navy, or the mistakes of educators who would lead boys too early into an understanding of the vices of the world. And it is to underestimate as well the full extent of the social reform that Wollstonecraft envisions as necessary to ameliorate the condition of women in her society. A *Vindication of the Rights of Woman* cannot be properly interpreted except as a statement of political radicalism— more bold, more uncompromising, and more intelligently argued than the earlier *Vindication of the Rights of Men*.

Indeed, for all its spirit, the *Rights of Men* is not an impressive political document. It was conceived far too exclusively as a vituperative attack on the person and politics of Edmund Burke.[2] As the great British

† From *Studies in Burke and His Time* 18 (1977): 155–66.

1. *Analytical Review* 12 (1792): 248–49.
2. A perceptive analysis of style and rhetoric in the *Rights of Men* appears in James T. Boulton,

The Language of Politics in the Age of Wilkes and Burke (London: Routledge and Kegan Paul, 1963) pp. 167–76. Boulton shows that Wollstonecraft's criticism of Burke—whose style she finds too much marked by passion and imagination and too little spokesman for conservative public polity, and as an apparent deserter from the cause of freedom he had espoused in approving the American Revolution, Burke was a natural butt for Wollstonecraft, committed as she was to egalitarian principles. But in his *Reflections on the Revolution in France,* Burke had offended Wollstonecraft on more than philosophical grounds. With an injustice that she could not allow to go unnoticed, Burke had maligned the Reverend Richard Price—dissenting minister, political radical, and friend to Wollstonecraft from her days as schoolmistress in Newington Green. Price's sermon, *A Discourse on the Love of Our Country,* had served as the immediate provocation for the *Reflections,* and Burke had not concealed his scorn for the style or opinions of the eminent dissenter.[3] Wollstonecraft, only weeks after the publication of the *Reflections,* responded in kind, heaping on her opponent a wrath and a contempt she made no effort to disguise. Unabashedly, she characterized Burke as an unprincipled charlatan, given to wit above judgment, eloquence above honest simplicity, and opportunism above integrity.

In place of Burke's argument in defense of his political conservatism— an argument that Wollstonecraft thought to proceed from a spurious reliance upon supposed common sense[4]—Wollstonecraft offered an argument from reason. Reason tempered by passion, she contended, not only rejects Burke's appeal to tradition and the wisdom of antiquity, but also urges a spirit of revisionism founded on several clear truths: namely, that freedom is the birthright of all men; that the progress of virtue in civilization depends upon the equality of all men; that prescription and property are destructive of that equality and consequently injurious to the progress of virtue; that blind submission to authority is debasing to the men who kneel and ruinous to the men before whom the knee is bent. Elaboration of these truths vies with castigation of Burke as the principal focus of the *Rights of Men;* and the disorganization that follows from Wollstonecraft's divided purpose is compounded by the technique of free association that permits topic to succeed topic haphazardly throughout the text. In its incoherent organization, as in its rational and egalitarian premises, the *Rights of Men* looks ahead to its far more famous successor, *A Vindication of the Rights of Woman.*

The *Rights of Men* looks ahead, too, in the character of the figurative language that emerges from close reading of the text. Although Woll-

---

controlled by reason—is equally applicable to her own prose style in this emotional pamphlet. Boulton concludes that Wollstonecraft conveys the impression of being "a writer whose views were strongly felt and vigorously communicated; many of the strictures she directs at the *Reflections* are valid and telling; but the chief weakness is Wollstonecraft's inability to embody at all times in her prose those qualities of intellectual honesty and emotional discipline which she claimed were of

prime importance to a political philosopher. She condemns Burke and, by the same token, is herself condemned" (pp. 175–76).

3. Edmund Burke, *Reflections on the Revolution in France,* in *Works,* 6 vols. (London: Bohn, 1854), 2: 285 ff.

4. For Wollstonecraft's discussion of Burke's premises, see *A Vindication of the Rights of Men* (1790), ed. Eleanor Louise Nicholes (Gainesville: Scholars' Facsimiles and Reprints, 1960), p. 68.

stonecraft was not a dedicated or inventive user of metaphor or simile in her prose, she does appear to be struggling in the *Rights of Men* to discover a particular figure—one fit to describe the condition of men (and women) who have been made deficient in their humanity by reason either of undue wealth and power or of staggering poverty and abjectness. From the first pages of her answer to Burke, Wollstonecraft shows herself to be at once interested in this problem of dehumanization and incapable of describing it fully. She is not content to say of the rich, who "pamper their appetites, and supinely exist without exercising mind or body," merely that "they have ceased to be men." Groping after an expression harsh enough to describe their debasement, she calls them "artificial monster[s]," the deformed products of "hereditary property—hereditary honours." A vivid metaphor, but not, it seems, a satisfactory one; for it is never used again. Sixteen pages later, the rich are spoken of together with the uneducated lower classes, both emerging in description as vulgar "creatures of habit and impulse." The metaphor is ugly, particularly in its application to the poor, whom Wollstonecraft pitied; thus it, too, is abandoned. As the text proceeds, Wollstonecraft argues that sophistication, libertinism, servility, and depraved sensuality are unmanly; but she finds no comprehensive figure by which to represent that unmanliness.[5]

Not, at least, quite yet. But a figure is in the making—one that is at once startling and obvious, simple and extraordinary. That which is unmanly is, of course, womanly; and the realization that woman can be used as a general figure for the social and even political debasement of all mankind emerges sporadically but surely as the *Rights of Men* proceeds. As early as the third paragraph of the text, the possibility shyly obtrudes itself with Wollstonecraft's likening of a wit to a "celebrated beauty, [anxious] to raise admiration on every occasion, and excite emotion, instead of the calm reciprocation of mutual esteem and unimpassioned respect." Later, "luxury and effeminacy" are identified as the curses of the aristocracy, and "profligates of rank" are said to be "emasculated by hereditary effiminacy." As Wollstonecraft's attention turns to and from the special problem of woman's place in society—as woman becomes characterized as a flattered doll, vain, inconsiderate, intentionally weak and delicate, and designedly lacking in the "manly morals" of "truth, fortitude, and humanity"—the metaphor urges itself more strongly upon Wollstonecraft and reader alike. Although not so insistent or complex in this text as in the *Vindication of the Rights of Woman*, the figure does reach a kind of climax in the *Rights of Men* when Wollstonecraft attacks the quality of Burke's patriotism and piety: "You love the church, your country, and its laws, you repeatedly tell us, because they deserve to be loved; but from you this is not a panegyric: weakness and indulgence are the only incitements to love and confidence

5. Ibid., pp. 10–11, 12, 28, 42, 47, 50, 116.

that you can discern, and it cannot be denied that the tender mother you venerate deserves, on this score, all your affection."[6] Here in her description of the church as a weak, imprudent mother is the germ, already beginning to grow, of the figure which will animate and complicate the *Vindication of the Rights of Woman*, helping to make this later text altogether as radical in its politics as in its sociology.

For if the *Rights of Woman* is a political treatise, it is so primarily by virtue of the fact that Wollstonecraft consciously describes political as well as social realities in England through and by means of the social condition of the country's women. In his biography of Mary Wollstonecraft, Ralph Wardle notes that the central thesis of the *Rights of Woman* is "that women as well as men are entitled by birthright to liberty and equality, and that if their rights are withheld, they will deter the progress of civilization." Truly Mary enjoyed at least one flash of genius, and that came when she recognized the similarity between the plight of oppressed womankind and that of oppressed mankind, and concluded that the solutions were identical."[7] The flash of genius Wardle identifies is genius indeed, but not accurately described; for the similarity he notes is more complex than he allows. Oppressed womankind serves in the *Rights of Woman* not merely as a figure for oppressed and impoverished mankind, but as a figure for all men, high as well as low, who are implicated in social and political contracts which condone inequality of rank, wealth, and privilege.

Indeed, it is significant that in the *Rights of Woman* Wollstonecraft more often likens women to the rich and powerful than to the poor and weak, as would seem most natural. Women are oppressed, it is true; but their oppression is, ironically, the consequence of their privileged status as pampered creatures of whom no mental competence or moral intelligence is expected. As Wollstonecraft argues in the course of her exposition, "birth, riches, and every extrinsic advantage that exalt a man above his fellows, without any mental exertion, sink him in reality below them. In proportion to his weakness, he is played upon by designing men, till the bloated monster has lost all traces of humanity."[8] Speaking primarily of middle-class women, but warning that "the whole female sex are, till their character is formed, in the same condition as the rich," Wollstonecraft argues that women are born to indulgence, and powerful in the very weakness that is the beauty and cunning by which they lord it over the men who imprison them. Thus, women can be seen to "act

6. Ibid. pp. 4, 51, 97, 47–48, 52, 111–15, 112, 124.
7. *Mary Wollstonecraft: A Critical Biography* (Lawrence: University of Kansas Press, 1951), p. 157.
8. A *Vindication of the Rights of Woman, with Strictures on Political and Moral Subjects* (London, 1792), p. 91. A more readily available text— a reprint of the slightly revised second edition of the *Rights of Woman*—is the Norton Critical Edition, ed. Carol H. Poston (New York, 1987); in Poston's edition, the quotation is found on p. 45. All subsequent quotations from the *Rights of Woman* will be cited by two page numbers—the first a reference to the 1792 edition, the second a reference to Poston's. [Page references to the 1987 Norton edition are being supplied for this volume— *Editor*.]

as men are observed to act when they have been exalted by the same means." They are, in short, "either abject slaves or capricious tyrants"[9]— different sides of the same devalued coin.

So it is that Wollstonecraft can argue that women enjoy "illegitimate power" and receive "regal homage." They are like Turkish bashaws, like despots, like kings, like Roman emperors, like "vicegerents allowed to reign over a small domain"—and, conversely, all such tyrants are like women. When Wollstonecraft opines that

> it is impossible for any man, when the most favourable circumstances concur, to acquire sufficient knowledge and strength of mind to discharge the duties of a king, entrusted with uncontrouled power; how then must they be violated when his very elevation is an insuperable bar to the attainment of either wisdom or virtue; when all the feelings of a man are stifled by flattery, and reflection shut out by pleasure! Surely it is madness to make the fate of thousands depend on the caprice of a weak fellow creature, whose very station sinks him *necessarily* below the meanest of his subjects![1]

we can only understand that the regal character has been feminized in its degradation. Such is the inevitable conclusion to be drawn from the metaphoric pattern of the text.

That Wollstonecraft herself has drawn this very conclusion is evident from her discussion of the military. Soldiers, kings, and women, she contends somewhat disjointedly, are linked by similar, vicious characteristics. Soldiers, after all, by reason of their participation in a rigid military hierarchy, are types of the enslaved monarch: "Every corps is a chain of despots, who, submitting and tyrannizing without exercising their reason, become dead weights of vice and folly on the community." And every individual within every corps is characterized by womanly indolence, polished manners, and love of ornamental dress. Officers, especially, are "particularly attentive to their persons, fond of dancing, crowded rooms, adventures, and ridicule. Like the *fair* sex, the business of their lives is gallantry.—They were taught to please, and they only live to please." Lest we miss the point, Wollstonecraft concludes a long quotation from Rousseau—actually an extended comparison of the respective intellectual provinces of men and women—with the single comment. "I hope my readers still remember the comparison, which I have brought forward, between women and officers." Officers, we are made to realize, have been emasculated, womanized, by their exalted position within the body politic; and war has become "rather the school of *finesse* and effeminacy, than of fortitude."[2]

Emasculated, too, are the rich; for "wealth and female softness equally tend to debase mankind." Thus, the society of the great, like the society

9. Wollstonecraft, *Rights of Woman*, pp. 122/57, 92/45.
1. Ibid., pp. 38/21, 80/40, 115/54, 85/42, 119/56, 89/44, 98/48, 24–25/16.
2. Ibid., pp. 27/17, 43/24, 79/39, 132/145.

of women, is insipid. "Women, in general, as well as the rich of both sexes, have acquired all the follies and vices of civilization, and missed the useful fruit"; for both "neglect the duties of humanity"—women, by failing to cultivate their bodies and intellects for the benefit of their families; the rich, by failing to develop their physical and mental powers, in accordance with the laws of nature, for their own benefit and that of the state. Once again, Wollstonecraft drives home her point with a slyly framed quotation:

> When do we hear of women who, starting out of obscurity, boldly claim respect on account of their great abilities or daring virtues? Where are they to be found?—'To be observed, to be attended to, to be taken notice of with sympathy, complacency, and approbation, are all the advantages which they seek.'—True! my male readers will probably exclaim; but let them, before they draw any conclusion, recollect that this was not written originally as descriptive of women, but of the rich. In Dr. Smith's Theory of Moral Sentiments, I have found a general character of people of rank and fortune, that, in my opinion, might with the greatest propriety be applied to the female sex. I refer the sagacious reader to the whole comparison.[3]

The effeminate rich, like the effeminate military, enjoy social and political status at the expense of their own masculinity.

So natural is it for Wollstonecraft to argue that women enjoy the degradation of the exalted, that she rarely likens them to the truly abject. Occasionally, they are compared to the "mass of mankind"—"obsequious slaves, who patiently allow themselves to be penned up"; occasionally, their condition is likened to that of the poor. And in one outstanding instance, the wife who patiently drudges for her husband is said to be "like a blind horse in a mill." But characteristically, woman is described as a privileged slave, an underling comfortable in a debasement of which she herself approves. Thus, she is very much like a courtier who grovels before the king and, as a reward for his congeniality, enjoys himself a certain amount of groveling from others:

> From whence arises the easy fallacious behavior of a courtier? From his situation, undoubtedly: for standing in need of dependents, he is obliged to learn the art of denying without giving offence, and, of evasively feeding hope with the chameleon's food: thus does politeness sport with truth, and eating away the sincerity and humanity natural to man, produce the fine gentleman.
> Women in the same way acquire, from a supposed necessity, an equally artificial mode of behaviour.[4]

Woman is that saddest of spectacles—a human being of possible merit, defrauded of her potential and trivialized. And in so far as men are like

---

3. Ibid., pp. 108/52, 107/51, 129/60, 138/64, 122–123/57–58. 4. Ibid., pp. 109/52, 134/62, 144/67, 298–299/131.

her in their positions within the body politic, they too are defrauded and trivialized.

It is for this reason, no doubt, that Wollstonecraft so closely associates the betterment of woman's plight with the rise of the classless society.[5] Effeminacy—with all its implications of weakness, vanity, and amorality—must be banished from the state, and from all social and political institutions within the state, even as it is banished from individuals. The *Vindication of the Rights of Woman* cannot be a feminist document without also being a radical political tract, if only because Wollstonecraft perceives the private and public problems of her country to be inextricably related. "A man has been termed a microcosm; and every family might also be called a state," she asserts. "Public virtue is only an aggregate of private."[6] So long, then, as private virtue permits the indulgence and the debasement of woman, the state and all the individuals in it will suffer from a similar degradation.

It can thus be argued that Wollstonecraft does not digress from her subject when she turns her attention to what appear to be tangential matters. Although her text could be organized more coherently and the connections among her points stated more clearly, she does not willfully wander from her just domain. The conduct of parents toward children, of teachers toward pupils, of bishops toward country vicars, of military officers toward underlings, of monarchs toward subjects—these are all, after their fashion, types of the conduct of husbands toward wives; and as such, all bear examination and criticism. Even such "episodical observations" as those in which Wollstonecraft mourns the demise of the British hero or decries the vicious self-interest of the British statesman have their relevance. Such disgraces are intimately related to the paucity of virtue in British society, and virtue is condemned to moulder so long as woman is abused and happy in her abuse. As Wollstonecraft notes in her introduction to the *Rights of Woman*, "weak, artificial beings, raised above the common wants and affections of their race, in a premature unnatural manner, undermine the very foundation of virtue, and spread corruption through the whole mass of society!"[7] Women— especially those who are or who aspire to be ladies—are preeminently such beings; and the evidence of the corruption to which they contribute is as much Wollstonecraft's subject as the defense of their misappropriated rights.

Ultimately, it is the premise of Wollstonecraft's feminism that the establishment of women's rights must be allied to a complete transformation of society and the body politic. If the *Rights of Woman* seems less radical than such a premise would suggest, that is only because Wollstonecraft has had the tact merely to hint at the character society will assume when its transformation is complete. Reason, of course, will prevail; and a total leveling of distinctions among men (and women)

5. See, for instance, ibid., pp. 38/22 and 74/38.   7. Ibid., pp. 327–329/143–44, 5/9.
6. Ibid., pp. 411/177, 445/192.

will have been accomplished. More than any other end, Wollstonecraft desires the establishment of unexceptioned equality among all rational beings. She will allow a superior place in the order of things only to God, who merits homage by virtue of his wisdom and justice, not by virtue of his power. Even God himself cannot be a tyrant in Wollstone-craft's perfect society: he must be rational and virtuous, so that his character may serve as a foundation for human morality. Men, mean-while, must regulate their behavior "according to . . . common laws," recognizing a lesson in the fact that "the eccentric orbit of the comet never influences astronomical calculations respecting the invariable or-der established in the motion of the principal bodies of the solar system." Eccentricity—even the eccentricity of the hero or the genius—is, for Wollstonecraft, unnecessary and perhaps detrimental to the common good.

> It is not for the benefit of society that a few brilliant men should be brought forward at the expence of the multitude. It is true, that great men seem to start up, as great revolutions occur, at proper intervals, to restore order, and to blow aside the clouds that thicken over the face of truth; but let more reason and virtue prevail in society, and these strong winds would not be necessary.
>
> The welfare of society is not built on extraordinary exertions; and were it more reasonably organized, there would be still less need of great abilities, or heroic virtues.[8]

Three years later, in writing her history of the French Revolution, Wollstonecraft would return to this point, blaming the failure of the century's great social movement on those luminaries whose "patriotism expir[ed] with their popularity":

> It will be only necessary to keep in mind the conduct of all the leading men, who have been active in the revolution, to perceive, that the disasters of the nation have arisen from the same miserable source of vanity, and the wretched struggles of selfishness; when the crisis re-quired, that all enlightened patriots should have united and formed a band, to have consolidated the great work; the commencement of which they had acccelerated. In proportion as these desertions have taken place, the best abilities which the country contained have dis-appeared. And thus it has happened, that ignorance and audacity have triumphed, merely because there were not found those brilliant tal-ents, which, pursuing the straight forward line of political economy, arrest, as it were, the suffrage of every well disposed citizen.—Such talents existed in France: and had they combined, and directed their views by a pure love of their country, to one point; all the disasters, which in overwhelming the empire have destroyed the repose of Eu-rope, would not have occurred to disgrace the cause of freedom.[9]

8. Ibid., pp. 307/134, 372–373/162, 136/64.
9. *An Historical and Moral View of the Origin*   *and Progress of the French Revolution* (London, 1794), pp. 301–2.

If talent is to be an object of Wollstonecraft's respect, it must be employed for society's benefit by individuals indifferent to their own personal stake in the success they might achieve through largely individual endeavor. Talent, in other words—like wisdom, reason, and virtue—must be respected as an abstraction; and its possessors must be content to work for the common good without distinguishing themselves from the common man.[1]

How the perfect society of patriotic equals is to be established Wollstonecraft does not say, although there is evidence in the *Rights of Woman* that she believed its eventual establishment to be simply in the nature of things. "Every thing around us," she argues at one point, "is in a progressive state":[2] everything that survives the difficulties of existence develops from a weak and vulnerable infancy to a strong and dignified maturity. Society is no exception. In its infancy, it suffers the domination of an aristocracy that soon gives way, under the pressures of "clashing interests," to a monarchy and hierarchy; later, as civilization enlightens the multitude, the monarchy finds itself forced to maintain its unjustified power by means of a deception and a corruption which at once poison the populace and point out their own antidote—"the perfection of man in the establishment of true civilization."[3] Such, Wollstonecraft would later argue, was the experience of the French, whose

> revolution was neither produced by the abilities or intrigues of a few individuals; nor was the effect of sudden and short-lived enthusiasm; but the natural consequence of intellectual improvement, gradually proceeding to perfection in the advancement of communities, from a state of barbarism to that of polished society, till now arrived at the point when sincerity of principles seems to be hastening the overthrow of the tremendous empire of superstition and hypocrisy, erected upon the ruins of gothic brutality and ignorance.[4]

Nature, Wollstonecraft seems to assert, will provide for our own best interests in her own good time; we need only assist her by recognizing the character of those interests and working patiently on their behalf.

It is perhaps for this reason that Wollstonecraft poses so few practical solutions to the problems she identifies in the *Rights of Woman*. No measures she might suggest could possibly rival the wisdom of those measures that will naturally arise in the course of civilization's gradual development. Wollstonecraft need not attempt to incite revolution or even reform. She need only assist the slow, unalterable movement of

1. Early in the *French Revolution* (p. 7), Wollstonecraft announces the strength of her commitment to total equality among men by charging government with the responsibility of leveling natural inequalities: "Nature having made men unequal, by giving stronger bodily and mental powers to one than to another, the end of government ought to be, to destroy this inequality by protecting the weak." Essentially, she wishes to maintain the advantages which accrue to society from men of superior intelligence and training, while diminishing the disadvantages which arise from the social and political privilege usually accorded them.
2. *Rights of Woman*, p. 242/108.
3. Ibid., pp. 29–31/18–19.
4. *French Revolution*, pp. vii–viii.

progress by clarifying the character of those social problems which will demand solution in future years and by adumbrating the probable shape those solutions will take.[5] If, then, the *Rights of Woman* appears somewhat timid in the few proposals for reform that it offers, that appearance is largely misleading. As Wollstonecraft explains in the first chapter of her text, "Rousseau exerts himself to prove that all *was* right originally: a crowd of authors that all *is* now right: and I, that all will *be* right."[6] For Wollstonecraft, "all will *be* right" only when the whole of society has undergone a radical reordering. In the promise of that reordering lies the exteme political radicalism that is at once the premise and the sine qua non of *A Vindication of the Rights of Woman.*

MOIRA FERGUSON AND JANET TODD

[Feminist Backgrounds and Argument of *A Vindication of the Rights of Woman*]†

* * *

The British Background

The Rights of Woman responds to a literary tradition and to a changing social climate. Wollstonecraft does not mention the authors of the late seventeenth and early eighteenth centuries who wrote constructively about women's condition even if they did not anticipate her radical proposals. She does, however, mention and quote those who epitomize the tradition long dominant in English literature of denigrating women, possibly because these writers were better known and possibly because she wished to stress her own originality. Writers in this misogynist tradition usually both condemned women's frailty and archly praised it. Wollstonecraft is not amused at the sprightly satire of Pope and Swift, and she quotes with distaste from "To a Lady: Of the Characters of Women" in which women are termed "fine by defect." Her attitude is the same when she contemplates the unsatirical view held by one of her own sex of women as half-beings; Anna Laetitia Barbauld, so much admired in other areas, asserted that women were born "for pleasure and delight alone."[1]

---

5. Indeed, the example of the French Revolution would later evoke in Wollstonecraft a firm commitment to gradualism. In her history of Revolution, Wollstonecraft would argue that only an excessive degeneracy and tyranny of the aristocracy can justify a people's "having recourse to coercion, to repel coercion." For if the progress of reason is likely to bring about a melioration of conditions in government, "it then seems injudicious for statesmen to force the adoption of any opinion, by aiming at the speedy destruction of obstinate prejudices; because these premature reforms, instead of promoting, destroy the comfort of those unfortunate beings, who are under their dominion, affording at the same time to despotism the strongest arguments to urge opposition to the theory of reason" (*French Revolution*, pp. 69–70).

6. *Rights of Woman*, p. 22/15.

† From Moira Ferguson and Janet Todd, *Mary Wollstonecraft* (Boston: Twayne Press, 1984) 59–72.

1. Wollstonecraft, *The Rights of Woman*, p. 53. [Page references to the 1987 Norton edition are being supplied for this volume—*Editor.*]

In Wollstonecraft's day, various factors had modified the harsh literary view of women. The first was the abundance of female novelists like Fanny Burney, Charlotte Smith, Clara Reeve, and Elizabeth Inchbald, who presented heroines of moral if not always intellectual stature. Some of these novelists Wollstonecraft had reviewed for the *Analytical Review*, and she had been lavish in her praise whenever she discovered anything close to a satisfactory portrait of a woman.

A second factor was the growth of humanitarian and enlightened sentiment that drew attention to the poor, the weak, and the despised; all three categories included women. Wollstonecraft attacked this humanitarian sentiment in Burke when she believed it misdirected, but her own rhapsody on Price when she felt him misused reveals that she was not immune to its influence. Translated into the literary mode, humanitarianism became sentimentalism, a literary movement that made a heady combination of virtue and emotion. Sentimental pictures taught and moved, to tears if possible; they appealed especially to female readers, constantly told of their association with the heart, and they often included women in various postures of distress. In *The Rights of Woman* Wollstonecraft regards "with sympathetic emotion" her own picture of the mother of modest means surrounded with "smiling babes"; later she recollects "with pleasure" the pupil of a country day school returning "to recount the feats of the day close at the parental knee." In both passages the emotive effect comes from an extreme contrast with a vicious aristocratic system described immediately before. The effective humanitarian passage, whether on mothers, abused animals, or French queens, also relies on such sensational contrasts.

A third factor was the existence of the Bluestockings. This group of women, which included Hannah More, Elizabeth Carter, Elizabeth Montagu, and Hester Chapone, gained some position in a male world through combining piety, seriousness, and learning. But they wanted this position neither improved for themselves nor extended to others; Hannah More, for example, desired changes in the conduct rather than in the subordinate position of women, which she regarded as divinely appointed. Similar to Wollstonecraft in her emphasis on religion, she would have rejected Wollstonecraft's rationalist belief in the perfectibility of humanity on earth. Unfortunately, we have no specific comments from More on *The Rights of Woman*, for she refused to read the book, dismissing it as "metaphysical jargon." After Wollstonecraft's death she attacked the "presumptuous vanity dishonorable to their sex" of those "female pretenders" who advocated women's rights.[2]

Certainly the Bluestockings were not radical in their desires for women; yet through their intellectual and social stature, as well as their literary works, they helped form a tolerant climate of opinion concerning women.

2. Hannah More, *Strictures on the Modern System of Female Education* (London: T. Cadell & G. W. Davies, 1799), 2:20. For another example of the Bluestocking opinion, see Hester Chapone's *Letters on the Improvement of the Mind, Addressed to a Young Lady* (1773); *The Works* (Boston: Wells and Wait, 1809).

The Rights of Woman was thus received more favorably than it would have been earlier in the century or than it was in the next.

The major Bluestockings had little immediate influence on Wollstonecraft however, in fact, she seems to have read very few of the earlier women writers on her sex, radical or conservative. The exception of course is Catharine Macaulay, enthusiastically reviewed in the *Analytical Review* and acknowledged in Wollstonecraft's text.[3] Because of this accepted influence and because Macaulay's *Letters on Education* anticipate *The Rights of Woman* in so many respects, it is worth glancing at the two authors together.

In all essential ideas on women Wollstonecraft and Macaulay agree— politics, religion, and pedagogy. Both feel that the tyranny of men harms the mind and character of women, just as the tyranny of government scars a people. Both stress the value of learning for girls, believing that it contributes to rather than destroys piety and virtue. Like Locke, so important an influence on Wollstonecraft's early educational works, the two connect moral and intellectual education. They vigorously support coeducation on the grounds that separating the sexes during school years leads to a false peculiarly female standard for women. Again, both follow Locke in advocating outdoor physical exercise for girls and deplore the affected and pitiful image of frail women presented by male writers such as Burke and Rousseau. Wollstonecraft and Macaulay are also in accord when they contemptuously dismiss female accomplishments designed solely to render women sexually attractive, and they lash out against the harem mentality that allows this exclusive cultivation of the trivial. For each author, virtue is asexual and should be cultivated by men and women alike. They see the regeneration of society dependent on its treatment of women, and they believe together that women will take subtly and viciously what is not given to them as their right. They inveigh against women's status of civil nonentity and object to the practice of calling an inquiring female mind "masculine."

These are only a few of the ways in which Wollstonecraft and Macaulay agree in opinion and argument, and even a cursory reading of the *Letters on Education* will reveal many other striking similarities.[4] The differences of opinion mentioned in the review and confirmed by *The Rights of Woman* are slight, yet worth noting. Wollstonecraft emerges as more of a pragmatist in education and rationalist in religious matters than Macaulay, who depends for belief entirely on revelation. In her review she finds Macaulay's exacting reading list for the young rather optimistic, and she stresses that the prejudice concerning female chastity should be weakened only when women have been educated sufficiently to base virtue on rational principles. When Macaulay considers that

3. See selections from Catharine Macaulay on pp. 204–12 in this edition [*Editor*].
4. Other ideas Macaulay anticipated include the contradiction of exhorting women to good nature while providing them with examples of the power over men of sexual attractiveness and cunning; and the similiarity of men and women except in the area of physical strength. The latter idea was asserted by Macaulay and suggested by Wollstonecraft.

"*Example should* coincide with instruction," Wollstonecraft wryly exclaims: "True, O moralist!—But then thou shouldst educate two generations."

The main distinction between the two authors, however, is in form and style, not opinion. Far more than Macaulay, Wollstonecraft attacks the vices of women as they are, drawing from experience devastating pictures of contemporary women of the idle aristocracy and ignorant bourgeoisie. She is on the whole more forceful and audacious than her predecessor and it was in the energy of her expression that she was judged by reviewers to be most shocking.

The French Background

In revolutionary France, the country from which so much support might have been expected, Wollstonecraft had little precedent for her feminist views. The philosophers of the Enlightenment held orthodox ideas of women as weaker vessels and adjuncts of men, although they shared Wollstonecraft's belief that education can improve humanity.

Having destroyed most of the educational system of the old regime, the French revolutionaries tried to replace it with one more suitable for a new democratic and secular society. The preamble to the Constitution of 1791 stated that all institutions "which were injurious to liberty and equality of rights" and all "privilege" had been abolished. Title I of the Constitution put this positively regarding education in its proposal of "public instruction for all citizens."

The rights of men, including their right to education, clearly preoccupied the revolutionaries; only a minority of thinkers considered extending these rights to women. In the early years of the Revolution, some women exclaimed in pamphlets and petitions to the Assembly at the many peculiar grievances of their sex. They demanded, for example, that men be excluded from certain jobs so that women would have the right to work and would not be forced into idleness and prostitution. They asked for female education, civil rights for spinsters and widows, and reform of marriage laws seen as particularly harsh on women. One feminist journal even suggested women should be represented in the Assembly and that they should have sexual freedom equivalent to men's. Women established clubs in which they announced their demands and fashioned their ideas on equality. Yet although they occasionally appeared as a militant and separate force, these women almost always subordinated their demands to wider human considerations and their own good to the revolutionary society of which they were a part. Thus no single adequate document of any length came out of the Revolution to express the unique feminist position and desires.

The French works that most closely anticipated *The Rights of Woman* were by the Marquis de Condorcet and Olympe de Gouges. Both authors demanded improved education for women in addition to concerning themselves with political and economic rights. Olympe de Gouges based her feminist ideas on the *Declaration of the Rights of Man*, recently placed as preface to the Constitution of 1791. Although its proposals had seemed so universal in their application, she showed how women were excluded from them, how privilege had been retained for men, and equality denied to women. She advocated extending men's rights to women. Many of her ideas were similar to Wollstonecraft's, but less insistently expressed and less realized by example.[5]

In *Letters to a Citizen of New-Haven* (1788) and *On the Admission of Women to the Suffrage* (1790) Condorcet proposed full educational rights for women.[6] His proposal was taken up but vastly modified by Talleyrand, who presented his *Report on Public Instruction* in September 1791.[7] This plan was designed to fulfill the requirements of education in Title I of the Constitution, and it bore out Gouges' statement that women were not included in the general rights, for it made hardly any provision for their education. According to the plan, girls were to be educated with boys until the age of eight; thereafter they were to remain at home in domestic employment.

Much of Talleyrand's report was rejected by the committee set up to bring about a national education, and in April 1792 Condorcet in his *Report on Education* reiterated the importance of female education.[8] He did not suggest coeducation at the primary school level except where a town was too small to support two schools, and he failed to deal with women's more advanced education, promising to devote another report to their training in general. He did provide a practical reason for the education of women that was similar to Wollstonecraft's: women were the principal trainers of children in the home, and many families were headed by widows.

According to a letter written in February 1793, Wollstonecraft herself was working at that time on a plan of education for the French committee on education.[9] There is no record that she completed or presented this interesting document, but she would no doubt have gone beyond Condorcet in arguing for coeducation at all levels and for a syllabus as broad for girls as for boys.

When she was working on *The Rights of Woman* in 1791, Wollstonecraft was probably unacquainted with Olympe de Gouges, Condorcet, or any other French feminist writers. She knew, however, of Talleyrand's *Report* and the importance of its author, and its official nature must

5. Olympe de Gouges, *Declaration des Droits de la Femme et de la Citoyenne* (1791), reprinted in *Women in Revolutionary Paris 1789–95*, ed. Darline Gay Levy, Harriet Branson Applewhite, and Mary Durham Johnson (Urbana: University of Illinois Press, 1979).
6. Jean Antoine, Marquis de Condorcet, *Oeuvres complètes*, ed. A. Condorcet O'Connor and M. F. Arago (Paris: Firmin Didot Frères, 1847–49).
7. For a description of this document, see Crane

Brinton, *Lives of Talleyrand* (New York: Allen & Unwin, 1936).
8. The *Report* is printed in *French Liberalism and Education in the Eighteenth Century*, trans. and ed. Francois de la Fontainerie (New York: McGraw Hill, 1932). For a discussion of Wollstonecraft and Condorcet, see *Shelley and His Circle*, 4:872–76.
9. Wollstonecraft to Ruth Barlow, February 1793, *Shelley and His Circle*, 4:866.

have suggested to her how little the French Revolution was truly affecting the subordinate status of women. To change this situation by influencing Talleyrand was the immediate, stated aim of *The Rights of Woman*.[1] There is, however, no evidence that it succeeded in this or affected by any other means the pedagogy of the Revolution.

The Argument with Rousseau

As *The Rights of Men* responds to Burke's *Reflections*, so *The Rights of Woman* in great part responds to Rousseau's *Émile* with whose general ideas on education she seemed so much in agreement when writing *Original Stories*, despite her need to change the gender of the pupils.[2] Wollstonecraft had a larger polemical aim than to refute a single author, but certainly much of her argument arose from her scorn of Sophie, whom Rousseau held up as exemplary for womankind. Wollstonecraft had, however, learned much from Rousseau and she greatly admired his humanitarianism and liberal sympathy. Certainly in his opposition to tyranny and orthodoxy he was her guide and model, and in a letter to Imlay she later admitted, "I have always been half in love with him."[3] Perhaps, then, the fierceness of her attack on his view of women derived from her deep sympathy with his character and with his other ideas; she was angry that a man so admirable should now seem to be so far astray.

Wollstonecraft quotes Rousseau at length in her book, expressing her outrage at his opinion of women as totally subordinate to men and at his educational scheme that would fit females only for such a role. She emphasizes virtue and reason throughout in an attempt to correct Rousseau's view that young women need only cultivate those qualities that make them alluring to men.

In the early pages of *The Rights of Woman* Rousseau is already one of those authors who tend "to degrade one half of the human species, and render women pleasing at the expense of every solid virtue (oo)." Constantly, he is invoked as the holder of opinions Wollstonecraft finds anathema; these include the idea that weakness in women is useful as a pretext for yielding to a natural appetite without violating romantic modesty, and the belief that girls from birth are naturally fond of adornment and gossip. Rousseau's woman is seen as a "fanciful kind of *half being*," one whose duties are directed only outward and who can work only through manipulating the passion of men.

By Chapter 5 Wollstonecraft is ready to deal at length with Rousseau as a writer who has "rendered women objects of pity, bordering on

1. According to Wollstonecraft's Advertisement, *The Rights of Woman* was intended as the first of two volumes; the legal and political situation of women was to have provided material for the second. This second volume was never written, and none of Wollstonecraft's later books provided a sequel, although the unfinished novel, *The Wrongs of Woman*, came closest to it in its concern for the legal inequality of men and women and for the particular injustices suffered by the poor.
2. Rousseau's view of women was complex and varied from work to work. Wollstonecraft was concerned only with the picture presented in *Émile*.
3. Godwin, *Posthumous Works*, 1:155.

contempt." As she summarizes it, Rousseau's argument in *Émile* is that women ought to be weak and passive because they are physically weaker than men; they should be subordinate to men, to whom they must render themselves agreeable. To compensate for this dependence and inferiority, women have been given the facility to excite desire, through which men are made dependent. Female weakness enhances desirability and women are therefore quite right to glory in it.

Rousseau asserts that the most important quality in a woman is good nature or sweetness of temper. Yet he appears to contradict this later when he considers that subtlety or animal cunning and sexual attractiveness are the only advantages of women to compare with men's physical strength and intellect. Wollstonecraft notes his contradiction, and laments the unhappy confusion it creates in the minds of women who are exhorted to cultivate good nature and yet are surrounded by examples of the success and power of cunning and seductiveness.

Having proved that men and women differ physically, mentally, and emotionally, Rousseau of course proposes different educational schemes for the sexes: "The education of the women should be always relative to the men," he asserts bluntly. "To please, to be useful to us, to make us love and esteem them, to educate us when young, and take care of us when grown up, to advise, to console us, to render our lives easy and agreeable: these are the duties of women at all times, and what they should be taught in their infancy (ooo)." A harsh statement of male superiority, it is rendered outrageous by the insistance of the pronoun "us"; the author and his fellows pronounce definitively on women, the eternal other and object.

Continuing, Rousseau argues that physical development in boys is the development of physical charm whereas in girls it is the development of personal charm. In this way, adulthood extends its shadow over childhood. Because of their dependence girls must early learn restraint, since they will be subject to exercising it all their lives and must become used to doing so. This, in Rousseau's view, should not be difficult, because "a state of dependence being natural to the sex, they perceive themselves formed for obedience."

The commonplace nature of Rousseau's ideas emerges when Wollstonecraft discusses the works of Fordyce and Gregory, popular English educators who shared Rousseau's view of women's derivative nature. Again virtue and intelligence are useful only insofar as they attract men, and are a hindrance where they do not serve this end. The attacks on male writing about women that fill Chapter 5 reflect Wollstonecraft's view of the persuasive power of pedagogical and ethical works, especially when they reinforce an already widespread notion. Rousseau, termed in *The Wrongs of Woman* "the true Prometheus of feeling," is especially dangerous just because he is, like Burke, so powerful and emotional a writer. The pen on the side of prejudice is a lethal weapon.

The Argument of The Rights of Woman

Against the bias that gives birth to its own evidence, Wollstonecraft asserts the rights of women, especially to an education that would render them beings worthy of respect or at least immune to prejudice. Repeatedly, she stresses not equality of the sexes but the right of women to prove this through increased opportunities and independence. Although she provides rational bases for her arguments, they are in the main founded on religion; in Wollstonecraft's view, the degraded situation of women affronts the God who created men and women in his own image. To trivialize immortal souls through degrading reason becomes a most heinous crime against humanity.

Wollstonecraft fuses her rationalism and optimistic Christianity: reason becomes a proof of God and of human immortality. She argues from the belief that women possess reason and that this reason emanates from divinity and supports virtue. Although the quantity may vary, it is the same quality in all people: "The perfection of our nature and capability of happiness, must be estimated by the degree of reason, virtue, and knowledge, that distinguish the individual, and direct the laws which bind society: and that from the exercise of reason, knowledge and virtue naturally flow, is equally undeniable (14)."

In spite of the existence of reason in everyone, the women whom Wollstonecraft saw around her were certainly in her view inferior to men, both morally and intellectually. Moral inferiority has come from the idea of relative morality (so well expressed by Rousseau), which considers that women should order their conduct not to align it with absolute ethical standards but to please men. To this end, reason has been uncultivated in women, while sensibility or emotionalism has been allowed to grow excessively, to the point where it becomes lascivious indulgence. Virtue, to which people must aim, is seen as a balance through reason between restraint and emotion. So by concentrating only on the emotions, women have been cut off from rational virtue, a quality further obscured for them when female virtue is defined solely as sexual fidelity. Intellectual inferiority has come from faulty education that has termed unnatural any signs of robust thinking in women and has shut them out from any strenuous intellectual pursuits.[4]

The first page of Wollstonecraft's introduction well expresses the destructive process that renders women worthless creatures and then educates them accordingly:

> The conduct and manners of women, in fact, evidently prove that their minds are not in a healthy state; for, like the flowers which are planted in too rich a soil, strength and usefulness are sacrificed to beauty; and the flaunting leaves, after having pleased a fastidious eye, fade, disregarded on the stalk, long before the season when they ought

---

4. Wollstonecraft required intellectual vigor in women, not only so that they might enter some of the male professions, but so that they could be come better wives and mothers. Domestic virtue was, in her view, a product of intellect.

to have arrived at maturity.—One cause of this barren blooming I attribute to a false system of education, gathered from the books written on this subject by men who, considering females rather as women than human creatures, have been more anxious to make them alluring mistresses than affectionate wives and rational mothers; and the understanding of the sex has been so bubbled by this specious homage, that the civilized women of the present century, with a few exceptions, are only anxious to inspire love, when they ought to cherish a nobler ambition, and by their abilities and virtues exact respect. (7)

Clearly, the panacea for women's ills is education. It must, however, be education in reason, not the traditional triviality.

Pedagogy was one of the concerns of the century, and many debated whether a national education was desirable and feasible. Some saw it as the answer to a complexity of social and psychological ills, but William Godwin opposed it for boys and girls because he felt that education should be given only where it was actively sought and should never be imposed.[5] Wollstonecraft looked to the state for education of both sexes, since she felt it was the right of all. The universal education she envisioned was limited to the elementary level, after which some should proceed into vocational training according to their sex; the more able and affluent of both genders should continue with their education. She stressed the need for day schools that would complement a loving home. Her brief look at the boarding school of Eton had convinced her of the viciousness of the boarding system as practiced in England, where it reinforced both class and sex prejudices.

With education suitable for their class, women would, in Wollstonecraft's view, be able to support themselves adequately or fulfill themselves in their traditional role of wife and mother. Properly educated, they could prove themselves intellectually and morally equal to men; if they were neglected, such equality remained a hypothesis. The need for female education was a need also of society as a whole; unless the intellectual condition of women improved, there could be no further social advance for humanity.

To relate the subjection of women to the subjection of men under an arbitrary authority, Wollstonecraft cleverly brings together women and soldiers. Because both receive a deficient and harmful education, both often display the same characteristics. Because they are subordinated and because they enter the world prematurely, both have superficial knowledge, shallow characters, and a love of gallantry. What is said of soldiers can apply to women as well: "Society . . . as it becomes more enlightened, should be very careful not to establish bodies of men who must necessarily be made foolish or vicious by the very constitution of their profession." The profession of women, which their present education serves, is to be mistresses; but, like soldiers, women usually

---

5. Godwin considered dangerous the alliance of government and education that a national education presupposed. It would, he believed, lead to the reinforcement of established prejudice.

fill their function only for a very short period of their lives. In a stroke of genius that enforces her argument, Wollstonecraft compares the most "masculine" group of men with the most "feminine" group of women. Thus she makes her point about education and suggests the distortion behind the sexual labels: "Where is then the sexual difference," she demands, "when the education has been the same?'

Her Own Experience

Before she published *The Rights of Woman*, Wollstonecraft wrote to her friend William Roscoe that she was working on a book in which she herself would appear "head and heart."[6] Both are displayed when she treats the various classes of women, the pampered aristocrat, the bourgeois housewife or teacher, and the working woman or outcast.

Wollstonecraft reserves the harshest criticism in her book for the aristocratic woman who exists at the apex of two false systems of values, class and sex. Such a woman is marred by the effects of unjust privilege, both real from her upper-class position and illusory from her status as an object of sexual gallantry. She is both a parasite on society and its victim. As in *The Rights of Men*, here Wollstonecraft's hatred for this type of woman is certainly informed by her feelings toward Lady Kingsborough, the only aristocrat whose life she could have known intimately. Wollstonecraft came to the Kingsboroughs after her strenuous time at Newington Green as an independent, self-supporting and self-defining woman. The contrast between Lady Kingsborough and herself must have been keenly felt, the more so since it was not a simple contrast of passive dependence and active independence. In Wollstonecraft's letters, Lady Kingsborough was criticized not only for feminine passivity but also for her assumption of authority. In her Wollstonecraft encountered a harder problem than when she regarded the domestic woman of the middle class, and she responded harshly. In her writing, aristocratic women were mere animals, weak and depraved beings, fitting inmates of a seraglio. Clearly, she felt it useless to urge such women to take more care of their children or act as rational beings; the social situation that allowed their existence needed changing.

The horrors encountered by laboring women and servants, later forcibly illustrated in *The Wrongs of Woman*, are little discussed in *The Rights of Woman*. Wollstonecraft did, however, consider the plight of fallen women, a new group in her theoretical writings; she recommended that people treat them in an enlightened way and that their seducers maintain them:

> I cannot avoid feeling the most lively compassion for those unfortunate females who are broken off from society, and by one error torn from all those affections and relationships that improve the heart and mind.

It does not frequently even deserve the name of error; for many innocent girls become the dupes of a sincere, affectionate heart, and still more are, as it may emphatically be termed, *ruined* before they know the difference between virtue and vice:—and thus prepared by their education for infamy, they become infamous. Asylums and Magdalenes are not the proper remedies for these abuses. It is justice, not charity, that is wanting in the world! (71)

Wollstonecraft was not the first woman to plead for this group, but she was one of the first to make the problem part of a larger sexual and social condition and the fallen woman one of the victims—rather than the only victim—of social values. That she required justice rather than charity is a measure of her distance from *Original Stories*, where charity was often the only response to misery. Her knowledge of the working class cannot have been great, but her experience with the Bloods must have taught her how thin was the line between respectability and disgrace, between genteel and coarse poverty. Fanny Blood's sister crossed this line and ended in the workhouse, and the possibility of doing the same must have worried the Wollstonecraft sisters after the abduction of Eliza, when they anxiously discussed whether they could subsist on painting and sewing.

In depicting the middle class, Wollstonecraft had her own experience to draw on most fully. She had tried many of the routes open to women who could not or would not be dependent on their families. She had been a companion, a school teacher, and a governess. The liberality and kindness of Joseph Johnson had opened for her a profession rarely available to women, and her experience was so atypical that she did not suggest it as commonplace. In fact, she had little to say on the subject of the middle-class woman and employment, although she did in passing deplore the male intrusion into the traditionally female occupation of midwifery. She was more concerned with changing attitudes of women to allow them to see in their professional, intellectual, or domestic work the same possibility for fulfillment as men saw in theirs.

Like *Mary, A Fiction*, *The Rights of Woman* springs from Wollstonecraft's experience and does not escape its paradoxes: romantic love is seen as both a delusion and the "concomitant of genius"; an unhappy marriage is good for the children when contrasted with a passionate one, but disastrous when contrasted with one based on domestic friendship; sensibility marks the humanitarian and the languishing female. Such paradoxes reveal that right conduct is far from simple. Reason and its aid, education, are needed in large amounts for people of both sexes to make necessary fine judgments. If there is one absolute in the book that allows for no contradiction it is the need for reason in this situation. Chapter 1 opens with the ringing assertion that humanity's preeminence over animals is in reason, and the final chapter ends with an impassioned pleas for the rights of reason for women.

In her own life in 1791 and 1792 Wollstonecraft needed the reason she praised, and her cry for it grew not only out of her past but out of her present. She was thirty-two, still in a way isolated, unloved, and, although famous, unappreciated. Over the months Fuseli had come to stand for the intellectual stimulation and the emotional warmth she required, and her infatuation had grown apace. While writing her book she was exhilarated by her own courage in love and literature; when she finished, however, she sank into the restlessness and dissatisfaction that so often plagued the dependent women she described. "Her pen was palsied," Johnson later told Godwin. "You know the cause."

Certainly the intensity of her passion for Fuseli must have come from her years of repressed emotion, her often exaggerated care of an importunate family. It sprang too from female dependence on the social forms that she castigated in *The Rights of Woman*. A passionate act that affronted these forms was so horrifying that everyone recoiled from it and branded the woman an outcast. When Wollstonecraft knocked on the door, announced to his wife she could no longer live without Fuseli, and begged to be admitted into the family, she committed such an act. After her rejection she had little to do but leave for a liberated France. There she tested the theories of *The Rights of Woman* in her own life and for a time sadly depicted in herself the picture of the subservient female, trained deeply in sensibility, not self-respect.

* * *

MITZI MYERS

Reform or Ruin: "A Revolution in Female Manners"†

Charting domestic reformation in 1798, the *Annual Register* maintained that the French Revolution had "illustrated the connection between good morals and the order and peace of society more than all the eloquence of the pulpit, and the disquisitions of moral philosophers had done for many centuries." An early adherent of the view that the English grew Victorian as the French turned republican, this journalist sketches a cultural turnabout from the alarmingly prevalent "levity and licentiousness of French manners" in the upper ranks and the fashionable circles who mimicked them to reverence for religion, marriage, and domesticity as the guarantors of social cohesion.[1] The *Register* thus

† From Studies in *Eighteenth-Century Culture* 11 (1982): 199–216.
1. *The Annual Register; or, a View of the History, Politics, and Literature, for the Year 1798*, 2nd ed. (London: W. Otridge, 1806), p. 229. For evidence that French noblewomen self-consciously adopted domesticity as a similar response to revolutionary upheaval, see Margaret H. Darrow, "French Noblewomen and the New Domesticity, 1750–1850,"

Feminist Studies, 5, no. 1 (Spring 1979), 41–65. Darrow argues for "an explicit, causal relationship between political developments and familial change," p. 57. Even before the war, middle-class English travelers were prone to contrasting Parisian ladies "enslaved by fashion" with their own enlightened domesticity; for a typical example, see *The Works of Anna Laetitia Barbauld*, ed. Lucy Aiken (London: Longman, 1825), II, 103.

summarizes the interconnected topics of the escalating reform or ruin polemic which is a distinctive strand in the decade's ideological warfare, motifs milked for all they were worth not only by reactionaries, but also by reformers of every persuasion, from radicals to Evangelicals.[2]

Among these interlocking themes, woman's role is stellar. Long-term cultural and economic shifts—expanding female education, the increasing impact of middle-class ethics and affluence, the rise of Evangelicalism—united with the explosive hopes and fears kindled by the French Revolution to make woman's influence and activities a matter of grave concern. In the new climate of moral seriousness engendered by the complex (and complexly used) example of dissolute France, the female population was recognized as vital to the nation's well-being. If the decay of states resulted from a general depravity of manners, woman provided a focal point for moral regeneration. Indeed, of all the dangers menacing England, none, claimed that busy pamphleteer John Bowles, was so destructive to the "social machine" as female modesty sacrificed to Gallicized aristocratic fashion, "a much more formidable enemy than Buonoparte himself." Bowles's obsession with feminine manners stems from the (supposedly) "obvious and indissoluble connection, which Providence has been pleased to establish between female chastity and the welfare and safety of civil society," a link endlessly rehearsed from the *Anti-Jacobin* and the *British Critic* to scores of novels.[3] Women moralists too called for "a revolution in female manners," for a reconstituted domestic ideal, as a key means of preserving and purifying the country, but, converting problem into opportunity, they maneuvered the issue with an adroit and ambitious mastery which far outstrips the simplistic hysteria of such male reactionaries as Bowles.[4] This essay explores representative female writers' exploitation of moral reform as a woman's issue, challenging the stereotypical opposition of the ideologies of domesticity and feminism and suggesting some ways of reading, some revisionist strategies for decoding the period's mentorial advice.

"Changes of Times, and Fashions, still demand / New Lessons to instruct the Female Band," remarked one mid-century conduct book writer.[5] No period more aptly illustrates his observation than the revolutionary decades, which witnessed an energetic proliferation of both

2. See Richard A. Soloway, "Reform or Ruin: English Moral Thought during the First French Republic," *Review of Politics*, 25, no. 1 (Jan. 1963), 110–28; and *Prelates and People: Ecclesiastical Social Thought in England, 1783–1852* (London: Routledge and Kegan Paul, 1969), pp. 26–45, for an overview of the motif epitomized in John Bowdler's title of 1797—*Reform or Ruin: Take Your Choice!*
3. John Bowles, *Remarks on Modern Female Manners, as Distinguished by Indifference to Character, and Indecency of Dress* (London: F. and C. Rivington, 1802), p. 12; *A View of the Moral State of Society, at the Close of the Eighteenth Century,*

Much Enlarged, and Continued to the Commencement of the Year 1804, with a Preface Addressed Particularly to the Higher Orders (London: F. and C. Rivington, 1804), p. 37.
4. Mary Wollstonecraft, *A Vindication of the Rights of Woman, with Strictures on Political and Moral Subjects*, ed. Carol H. Poston (1792; rpt. New York: W. W. Norton, 1987), p. 45 (and also p. 192). [Page references to the 1987 Norton edition are being supplied for this volume—*Editor.*]
5. Thomas Marriott, *Female Conduct: Being an Essay on the Art of Pleasing. To be practised by the Fair Sex, before, and after Marriage. A Poem, in Two Books* (London: W. Owen, 1759), p. 79.

radical and conservative directives to women. The conventional interpretation of the new lessons for females in that time of convulsive change has recently been reiterated by Lawrence Stone, whose formulation follows closely that of Maurice Quinlan forty years since. Quinlan's pioneering inquiry into how Victorianism antedated Victoria locates the nineties as a "turning point in English social history," the era when a conservative corpus of manners was fathered by reaction to the revolution and mothered by educators like Hannah More who lauded a newly created standard of womanly excellence, the "model female." Quinlan reads the *Rights of Woman* as sui generis, a radical call for female self-assertion which leagued all other preceptors against the rebel Wollstonecraft. Stressing the importance of extreme femininity and urging women to be a species apart, they called upon their audience "to accept [woman's] subordinate position and to stake all upon the bargaining power of . . . sexual attraction. It was to be," says Quinlan, seriously misrepresenting their stance, females' "one forte, guarded by rules of decorum and made mysterious by the disguise of frailty."[6]

The Family, Sex and Marriage, Stone's massive study of English domestic history, similarly confers a symbolic value on More's popularity. Stone draws a sharp dichotomy between woman's status in the eighteenth-century ambience of "affective individualism" ("relative" equality, companionate marriage, sexual permissiveness) and her devaluation and subordinance in the Evangelically fueled resurgence of patriarchalism which he finds characteristic of the nineteenth. The remarkable success of More's fictionalized conduct book *Coelebs in Search of a Wife* (1808)—it sold eleven editions in nine months, thirty before More's death[7]—Stone believes, "marks the end of an era in husband-wife relations: the Amelia Rattles were out, the Lucilla Stanleys were in." (Since More's anti-heroine Amelia is "boisterous," a "hoyden," "a mass of accomplishments . . . without one particle of mind, one ray of common sense, or one shade of delicacy," any student of eighteenth-century feminine exemplars must wonder when she was ever in.)[8] *Coelebs*, says Stone, "celebrates the ideal woman . . . devoted in domestic duties, religious, modest in dress, silent unless spoken to, deferential to men, and devoted to good works." The brand "new ideal of womanhood" iconized in More's Lucilla "involved total abnegation, making the wife a slave to convention, propriety, and her husband." For Stone, late-eighteenth-century feminism thus "died a swift and natural death, not

6. Maurice J. Quinlan, *Victorian Prelude: A History of English Manners, 1700–1830* (1941; rpt. Hamden, Conn.: Archon Books, 1965), pp. 69, 143.

7. M. G. Jones, *Hannah More* (1952; rpt. New York: Greenwood Press, 1968), p. 193. Henry Thompson, *The Life of Hannah More: with Notices of her Sisters* (London: T. Cadell, 1838), p. 2, notes that *Coelebs* was even translated into Ice-landic.

8. Lawrence Stone, *The Family, Sex and Marriage in England, 1500–1800* (New York: Harper and Row, 1977), p. 668; Hannah More, *Coelebs in Search of a Wife, comprehending Observations on Domestic Habits and Manners, Religion and Morals*, in *The Complete Works of Hannah More* (New York: J. C. Derby, 1856), II, 356–57.

to be revived again until the twentieth century."[9] More recently and more demeaningly yet, Lynne Agress's *The Feminine Irony* indicts en masse late eighteenth- and early nineteenth-century women writers as "devil's disciples" for perpetuating a "passive, inferior, feminine stereotype" rather than protesting the second-class standing they inherited from an imperfectly illumined Enlightenment.[1] Again, More is the premier villain; Wollstonecraft, the lonely exception.

Modern scholarship, then, myopically reproduces the anti-Jacobin opposition of More and Wollstonecraft, the contrast between the bishop and the hyena in petticoats epitomized in Walpole's letters or Richard Polwhele's *The Unsex'd Females*.[2] Rightly emphasizing the ferment over womanhood seething in the nineties, Quinlan and Stone reincarnate as new what were old standards, familiar favorites in the conduct book repertoire of femininity, while failing to consider the positive redirections factored into the ostensible traditionalism of reformers like More. Conversely, overaccenting Wollstonecraft's iconoclasm obscures the degree to which her demands are typical of a wide spectrum of women writers. In the nineties, in fact, female educators of every stripe—from radicals like Catharine Macaulay Graham, Wollstonecraft, Mary Hays, and Anne Frances Randall (who was probably Mary Robinson), to moderates like Clara Reeve, Maria Edgeworth, Anna Laetitia Barbauld, Priscilla Wakefield, and Mary Ann Radcliffe, to religionists like Sarah Trimmer, More, and Jane West—vigorously attacked the deficiencies of fashionable training and values. In their different ways, they seek to endow woman's role with more competence, dignity, and consequence. Downgrading the ornamental and pleasing to magnify the useful and moral, they dwell on the disjunction between functional education for ethical living and the current "phrenzy of accomplishments" geared merely to seduce success in a disadvantageous marriage market.[3] Female instructors in general were increasingly prodding their auditors to take responsibility for realizing their own potential, to become self-improved, albeit modest, mistresses of their own—and the nation's—destiny. Such women, gently or stringently reformist in orientation, had female co-workers, discreet rebels among the horde of novelists overtly preoccupied with propriety, and notable male contemporaries like the Evangelical Thomas Gisborne as well as numerous nineteenth-century successors.

Situating these variant models of female reform within a theoretical

9. Stone, pp. 668, 342. In view of Stone's presentation of More as the arch-propagandist of repression, it is surprising to find her described elsewhere in the text (p. 352) as a "feminist educational reformer."

1. Lynne Agress, *The Feminine Irony: Women on Women in Early-Nineteenth-Century English Literature* (Rutherford, N.J.: Fairleigh Dickinson University Press, 1978), pp. 172, 16.

2. *Horace Walpole's Correspondence*, ed. W. S. Lewis, Robert A. Smith, and Charles H. Bennett,

XXXI (New Haven: Yale University Press, 1961), 397; Richard Polwhele, *The Unsex'd Females: A Poem* (1798; rpt. New York: Garland, 1974), pp. 35–36 n. [For a selection from Polwhele's poem, see pp. 235–37 in this edition—*Editor.*]

3. Hannah More, *Strictures on the Modern System of Female Education, with a View of the Principles and Conduct prevalent among Women of Rank and Fortune* (1799; rpt. New York: Garland Publishing Co., 1974), I, 62.

context based on current work in social anthropology offers a more sensitive and nuanced approach than clichés of bifurcation reducing most women to passive victims, to mindless mouthpieces of patriarchal attitudes. Edwin and Shirley Ardener's analysis of dominant and muted groups draws attention to the subtleties and ambiguities of belief systems generated by the culturally inarticulate.[4] Subordinate groups like women must shape their world views *through* the dominant models, transforming their own perceptions and needs as best they can in terms of received frameworks. If women's alternative or counterpart models are not acceptably encoded in the prevailing male idiom, female concerns will not receive a proper hearing. Women's ways of ordering, of making significant their situation, must thus be carefully disinterred from the dominant structures which muffle them. Even though female models of reality and desire mostly follow the ground rules, their unique deviations from the norms make a woman's world of difference. Women's interpretations of their roles are not fully coincident with men's. If writers enjoin the primacy of familial duties, as do both More and Wollstonecraft, they may yet invest women's roles with powerful, even subversive meanings quite different from conventional ascriptions of weakness and public insignificance. Since female models characteristically operate in terms of strategically redefining and rescripting traditional markers, the linguistic surface of such sexual pronouncements must be carefully scrutinized for imperfect integrations, submerged conflicts, covert messages—for all the meanings which hover interstitially.

Not only do the texts of prescriptive works demand solicitous sifting, but their contexts, their membership in wider ideological movements, also require investigation. In an important essay focusing modern reexamination of Evangelicalism, for instance, Gerald Newman persuasively questions the orthodoxy of such polemicists as More, concluding that they did "much more indeed to subvert the established order than to uphold it" and that the neopuritans "should be regarded as moral and social revolutionaries."[5] Masters and mistresses of propaganda specializing in fifth column tactics, they obeyed the injunction to be "wise as serpents, and harmless as doves," infiltrating and undermining the traditional order from within through their genius for organization and for manipulation of public opinion. The revised view of Evangelicalism as a militant vanguard of emergent middle-class consciousness convincingly demonstrates how diverse anti-French political strategies (whether anti-old or anti-new regimes) mutated into a much broader social and moral critique of aristocratic mores and modes, paving the way for progressive nineteenth-century liberalism. To downplay political hostilities and connect middle-class groups seldom considered together is to illuminate the pervasiveness and the ideological significance of reformist ethics as an

---

4. Shirley Ardener, ed., *Perceiving Women* (London: Malaby Press, 1975), pp. vii—xxiii.
5. Gerald Newman, "Anti-French Propaganda and British Liberal Nationalism in the Early Nineteenth Century: Suggestions toward a General Interpretation," *Victorian Studies*, 18, no. 4 (June 1975), 401.

agent of the class redistribution of moral authority necessary for fundamental social change.[6]

Although Newman cites "the puritanical strictures on upper-class habits laid down equally by Mary Wollstonecraft and Hannah More," he does not pursue his insight to probe the intersection of moral reform, class tension, and gender consciousness.[7] Yet, despite the fulminations Wollstonecraft occasioned (and these derived even more from her checkered life than from her work), what most strikingly emerges from close interrogation of competing radical and Evangelical domestic ideologies is the similar psychological and emotional dynamic, the unexpected congruence of the ideals and programs expressed in such politically polar works as Wollstonecraft's *Rights of Woman* (1792) and More's *Strictures on the Modern System of Female Education* (1799), *Coelebs's* thematic precursor. (The same might be said for the works of the radical Mary Hays and the orthodox Jane West.) "It is amazing," observed their contemporary Mary Berry, studying More and Wollstonecraft in tandem, how much the two "agree on all the great points of female education. H. More will, I dare say, be very angry when she hears this."[8] No doubt, for More emphatically refused to read Wollstonecraft and thought her a dangerous malcontent.[9] Nevertheless, the parallels between the two texts extend far beyond their mutual insistence on the radical renovation of female education and manners as prerequisites to a moral restructuring of society.

6. Matthew 10:16; see Newman, "Anti-French Propaganda," pp. 385–418; Ford K. Brown, *Fathers of the Victorians: The Age of Wilberforce* (Cambridge: Cambridge University Press, 1961); Bernard Semmel, *The Methodist Revolution* (New York: Basic Books, 1973); Michael Hennell, "A Little-Known Social Revolution," *Church Quarterly Review*, 143 (Jan.–March 1947), 189–207; V. Kiernan, "Evangelicalism and the French Revolution," *Past and Present*, no. 1 (Feb. 1952), pp. 44–56; G.F.A. Best, "The Evangelicals and the Established Church in the Early Nineteenth Century," *Journal of Theological Studies*, n.s. 10, pt. 1 (April 1959), 63–78; and "Evangelicalism and the Victorians," in *The Victorian Crisis of Faith: Six Lectures*, ed. Anthony Symondson (London: SPCK, 1970), pp. 37–56; Ernest Marshall Howse, *Saints in Politics: The "Clapham Sect" and the Growth of Freedom* (London: George Allen and Unwin, 1953); Charles I. Foster, *An Errand of Mercy: The Evangelical United Front, 1790–1837* (Chapel Hill: University of North Carolina Press, 1960); Kathleen Heasman, *Evangelicals in Action: An Appraisal of their Social Work in the Victorian Era* (London: Geoffrey Bles, 1962); Ian Bradley, *The Call to Seriousness: The Evangelical Impact on the Victorians* (London: Jonathon Cape, 1976); Standish Meacham, "The Evangelical Inheritance," *The Journal of British Studies*, 3, no. 1 (Nov. 1963), 88–104; Harold Perkin, *The Origins of Modern English Society, 1780–1880* (London: Routledge and Kegan Paul, 1969), esp. pp. 280–

90; Muriel Jaeger, *Before Victoria* (London: Chatto and Windus, 1956), pp. 31–52; David Spring, "The Clapham Sect: Some Social and Political Aspects," *Victorian Studies*, 5, no. 1 (Sept. 1961), 35–48; "Aristocracy, Social Structure, and Religion in the Early Victorian Period," *Victorian Studies*, 6, no. 3 (March 1963), 263–80; and "Some Reflections on Social History in the Nineteenth Century," *Victorian Studies*, 4, no. 1 (Sept. 1960), 55–64; Asa Briggs, "Middle-Class Consciousness in English Politics, 1780–1846," *Past and Present*, no. 9 (April 1956), pp. 65–74. Brown's assessment differs from others cited, but his analysis of Evangelical strategy is to the point. Stone and Randolph Trumbach, *The Rise of the Egalitarian Family: Aristocratic Kinship and Domestic Relations in Eighteenth-Century England* (New York: Academic Press, 1978), argue that the eighteenth-century English aristocracy was already beginning to embrace the domestic ideal, but upper-class laxity and levity remained an article of faith in middle-class reformist rhetoric.

7. Newman, "Anti-French Propaganda," p. 402, n. 28.

8. *Extracts of the Journals and Correspondence of Miss Berry from the Year 1783 to 1852*, ed. Lady Theresa Lewis (London: Longmans, Green, 1865), II, 91.

9. *Memoirs of the Life and Correspondence of Mrs. Hannah More*, ed. William Roberts (London: R. B. Seeley and W. Burnside, 1834), II, 371.

Wollstonecraft's enlightened womanhood and More's doctrines of Evangelical femininity, her authoritative codification of woman's sphere, responsibilities, and powers, demonstrate alike the extent to which reformist educators had assimilated and were purveying the ascendant bourgeois ethic sanctifying useful industry and family, an ideology which was at that historical juncture for the most part progressive, criticizing, not celebrating the status quo.[1] But at the same time—and this is a crucial point—female moral reformers were recasting that ethic in women's terms for women's benefit, suiting to their own needs the general middle-class protest against aristocratic license and inutility and inflecting bourgeois modes to fit the feminine sphere of endeavor. Moral reform, radically or Evangelically permuted, offered such activist ideologues a body of legitimating imperatives and a vocabulary for venting female dissatisfaction and rendering telling critiques of a society governed by worldly libertine males, as well as for formulating counterpart models based on middle-class female values and priorities. For them, to reform is to reform. Applying the corrective insights stimulated by woman's unsettled status in a transitional era, they ask what constitutes the good society and how women can further it. Significantly, their social strictures both partake of and subtly subvert certain constituents of the bourgeois nexus. Proponents of the humanizing values associated with home, they do not endorse domesticity as decorative gloss or quiescent retreat. Rather, they interpret domestic culture as proffering active roles, constructive channels through which women can aid in revitalizing the world to conform to the values of home, not the materialistic marketplace. Defining domesticity in terms of social responsibility, they negotiate available ideologies into habitability.

Combatants for the allegiance of their increasingly leisured, marginally educated countrywomen, Wollstonecraft and More both strive to replace the regnant ideal of pliant, unproductive urbanity with socially functional middle-class models. Had More looked into Wollstonecraft, she would have discovered an analysis of contemporary female frivolity, incompetence, and maldirected energies, of "weak and wretched" women, commensurate with her own, as well as a similar idealistic myth of what properly fortified female minds might accomplish: a more respectable and powerful status underscoring women's need for purposeful, nationally significant work (whether charitable or paid) and endowing them with weighty authority as mothers and educators, a reordering of the state through the wise nurture of children, a reining in of male behavior and attitudes to a chaste and modest single standard.[2] The "ideal of

---

1. For progressive bourgeois ideology, see Isaac Kramnick, "Religion and Radicalism: English Political Theory in the Age of Revolution," *Political Theory: An International Journal of Political Philosophy*, 5, no. 4 (Nov. 1977), 505–34; and "Children's Literature and Bourgeois Ideology: Observations on Culture and Industrial Capitalism in the Later Eighteenth Century," in *Culture and Politics from Puritanism to the Enlightenment*, ed. Perez Zagorin (Berkeley: University of California Press, 1980), pp. 203–40. I am grateful to Professor Kramnick for allowing me to read the latter in manuscript.

2. The quoted phrase is from *Rights of Woman*, p. 7.

passive womanhood" frequently attributed to the Evangelicals is very much a misnomer.[3] For at the heart of both More's and Wollstonecraft's works lies a pattern of female domestic heroism, an image of activity, strength, fortitude, and ethical maturity, of self-denial, purity, and truth. It is God, however differently envisioned, who empowers what are essentially revivified spiritual ideals. If life is probationary, an education for immortality, then woman is not mere flesh for male consumption, not a being delimited by sexual attraction (as Quinlan would have it), but a creature of rationally educable mind and aspiring soul, a potent spiritual agent whose most exigent duties are personal improvement and social regeneration.

Both women thus challenge popular conduct book recommendations for feminine training and behavior—hide your wit, your learning, your health—and define themselves in opposition to the usual arts of flattery, dissimulation, and manipulative pleasing, signal women's restiveness in their elegant niche and implicitly querying Stone's optimistic conclusions about eighteenth-century female status. Indicting what they call the Mohammedan view of woman as docile matter catering to masculine appetite (perhaps best exemplified in Rousseau's Sophia), they claim homage not to charm and modish graces, but to mind and moral excellence. They deplore a female education fixated on the body and senses, for moral reform entails mental enlargment, a puritan work ethic of the mind. Finding women's brains and morality in a state of ill repair, both prescribe a regimen of rigorous ethical and intellectual cultivation to exercise the faculties of readers starved on elegant abstracts, vitiated by "stupid novelists" and artificial male gallantry. They go in for "dry tough reading" and bracing character formation.[4] If they appropriate bourgeois stress on motherhood, they infuse the evolving ideal with spiritual and mental backbone and public import, each writer transforming the parable of the talents into an exemplum of maternal heroism and power.[5] If they push the middle-class virtues of accountability, diligence, discipline, and order, they also deride social emulation and self-indulgence to preach a genuine upward mobility—that of the soul. More does not hew to the orthodoxly genteel line on woman's role any more than does Wollstonecraft, nor is her "new ideal" wholly retrograde. She inculcates not passive submission, but reasoned acquiescence to established custom, and that only up to a point. As with Wollstonecraft, and with comparable important consequences, her ultimate frame of reference is non-secular. Evangelical spiritual egalitarianism, like feminism, offers a path to autonomy and transcendence of sex. It is no

3. By, for example, David Monaghan, "*Mansfield Park* and Evangelicalism: A Reassessment," *Nineteenth-Century Fiction*, 33, no. 2 (Sept. 1978), 230.

4. *Rights of Woman*, p. 183; *Strictures*, I, 165.

5. Matthew 25:14–28; see *Rights of Woman*, p. 51; *Strictures*, I, 52–53; for the evolution of analogous patterns of moral motherhood in America,

see Linda K. Kerber, "Daughters of Columbia: Educating Women for the Republic, 1787–1805," in *The Hofstadter Aegis: A Memorial*, ed. Stanley Elkins and Eric McKitrick (New York: Alfred A. Knopf, 1974), pp. 36–59; and Ruth H. Bloch, "American Feminine Ideals in Transition: The Rise of the Moral Mother, 1785–1815," *Feminist Studies*, 4, no. 2 (June 1978), 101–26.

accident that both like to cite that fruitfully ambiguous verse "be not conformed to this world."[6]

Each preceptor in her own way is a reformer who works to extend female agency through the moral revision of conventions. Wollstone-craft's radicalism, for example, is firmly embedded within the bourgeois paradigm. Modifying middle-class domesticity to fit her own purposes, she creates an alternative, potentially revolutionary female ideology within a scaffolding of cultural givens. Like such other mentors as Jane West, she makes an initial point of addressing not ladies, but "those in the middle class, because they appear to be in the most natural state." For men at least, the necessity of exertion ensured the "notorious" conse-quence that "the middle class contains most virtue and abilities." But its women "ape the fashions of the nobility," fall prey to "factitious manners" imported from aristocratic France, and, exasperatingly, all yearn to be "ladies. Which is simply to have nothing to do." In fact, she concludes, her own "observation with respect to the middle rank, the one in which talents thrive best, extends not to women." Since static women will halt all progress, the *Rights of Woman* is designed to remedy this unhealthy enervation by guiding them back to nature, reason, and virtue, to the "severe duties" and "domestic pleasures" of Wollstonecraft's desideratum: "more observant daughters, more affectionate sisters, more faithful wives, more reasonable mothers—in a word, better citizens." She tirelessly contrasts duty and diversion, the life style of enlightened domesticity and elite gallantry. Women are to shun the stigmata of the frivolous great world—dress, pleasure, and sway—relishing instead the "minutiae of domestic taste," the "simple grandeur" of "dignified do-mestic happiness."[7] Pointedly reversing aristocratic attributes—sensual-ity, indolence, luxury, privilege—the new woman's world projected by middle-class radicalism exalts modesty for both sexes, serviceable work, education, and, above all, mothering.

Wollstonecraft asserts (if sometimes without elaboration) many claims integral to modern feminism, suing for coeducation, economic inde-pendence, legal equality, and freer access to jobs and professions, yet, despite her often inflammatory rhetoric, the core of her manifesto re-mains middle-class motherhood, a feminist, republicanized adaptation of the female role normative in late eighteenth-century bourgeois notions of the family. Nature enlists women to fulfill "peculiar duties": "the rearing of children, that is, laying a foundation of sound health both of body and mind in the rising generation, has justly been insisted on as the peculiar destination of woman." In accordance with this female destiny, women are naturally "susceptible of the attached affections." Indeed, though Wollstonecraft derides sexual virtues and sentimental

6. ". . . but be ye transformed by the renewing of your mind," Romans 12:2; for examples, see More, "An Estimate of the Religion of the Fashionable World," *Works*, I, 297; *Strictures*, II, 194, 239; *Collected Letters of Mary Wollstonecraft*, ed. Ralph M. Wardle (Ithaca and London: Cornell Univer-sity Press, 1979), p. 118.

7. *Rights of Woman*, pp. 9, 57, 75, 56, 147, 76, 10, 150, 166, 191.

propaganda casting all women in one languid mold, she also affirms, taking for granted the female's primary responsibility for child care, that "whatever tends to incapacitate the maternal character, takes woman out of her sphere." No more than More (or, for that matter, Mill) does she aspire to pluck most women out of their families or dissever them from their relative duties.[8]

On the contrary, Wollstonecraft aggrandizes, heroizes the maternal mission, elevating woman's status by making her familial roles the linchpin of a new society. Although she does not suggest that woman's only possible place is the home, motherhood provides a pervasive rationale for better education, as well as for civil existence and work. The more enlightened understanding women acquire, the more they will take to those offices nature annexes to their gender. As "active citizen,' the average woman will advance the common welfare by managing her family, educating her children, and assisting her neighbors, also standing ready for work outside the home to facilitate family maintenance if necessary. In thus carrying out her communal obligations, she eludes the spirit of degrading dependence and self-respectingly earns her keep, while also developing her own autonomous moral character. Like Mill, Wollstonecraft has recently been faulted as a feminist theorist for failing to challenge the nuclear family as an institution or to question its constraints on female life. Her acceptance of natural sex roles, of rationalized marriage and motherhood as public service in the national interest, it is argued, limits her application of egalitarian principles to women. But for Wollstonecraft, nature and reason validate the bourgeois family as a key corrective to the sins of an oppressive, class-bound establishment. Only through training generations of reform-oriented citizens can the "pestiferous purple" of rank and riches ultimately be exorcized. Her vision of radical progress, of "public freedom and universal happiness," depends on the private virtue nourished by chaste fathers and "patriot" mothers. Marriage civilizes man, families school humanitarian republicans, and domestic affections cement the general good.[9] Her radical politics operates through the militant moral posture inherent in middle-class ideology.

Intent on reinventing bourgeois domestic conventions in women's

8. *Rights of Woman*, pp. 167, 189, 166, 177, 63.
9. See *Rights of Woman*, pp. 151, 169, 5, 146, 18, 6, 4, 192, 158, 144. The importance and comforts of being a mother are also thematically stressed in Wollstonecraft's unfinished last novel, written after she herself had become one. See, for example, the strong statement on p. 154, *Mary, A Fiction and The Wrongs of Woman*, ed. Gary Kelly (London: Oxford University Press, 1976). For critiques of Wollstonecraft's values, see Virginia Sapiro, "Feminist Studies and the Discipline: A Study of Mary Wollstonecraft," *The University of Michigan Papers in Women's Studies*, 1, no. 1 (Feb. 1974), 178–200; and Nancy M. Theriot, "Mary Wollstonecraft and Margaret Fuller: A Theoretical Comparison," *International Journal of Women's Studies*, 2, no 6. (Nov–Dec. 1979), 560–74. For similar criticism of Mill, see Susan Moller Okin, *Women in Western Political Thought* (Princeton: Princeton University Press, 1979), pp. 226, 30. Elissa S. Guralnick, "Radical Politics in Mary Wollstonecraft's A *Vindication of the Rights of Woman*," *Studies in Burke and His Time*, 18 (Autumn 1977), 155–66, stresses Wollstonecraft's radicalism, but also observes that the text offers no practical political program. [Guralnick's essay is reprinted on pp. 308–17 in this volume.]

favor, Wollstonecraft elides any possible antagonism between their "first duty . . . to themselves as rational creatures" and their next "as citizens, . . . that, which includes so many, of a mother." The text cancels conflict between individual autonomy and corporate duty in declaring, for instance, that "the being who discharges the duties of its station is independent." Such configurations illuminate Wollstonecraft's argumentative and emotional logic, revealing how her expressivism was tempered by and shaped through current models of public belief. Critic of sexual stereotyping though she was, Wollstonecraft's feminism is very much conditioned by and justified in terms of revisionist bourgeois ideology, that idyll of a harmonious and socially productive domesticity which haunted her imagination and punctuates her text. On the one hand, even the eighteenth-century's foremost female radical equates private need and public contribution, demands no rights without concomitant duties. Her translation of feminism into the language of social purification and spiritual endeavor demonstrates the female strategy of self-assertion through virtue, of being good as potential power. "I will be *good*, that I may deserve to be happy," she was to write in the greatest psychic crisis of her life.[1] On the other hand, Wollstonecraft's tailoring of her conceptual framework shows how female marginality clarifies moral insight, evolving dynamic models of resistance within a dominant superstructure.

If Wollstonecraft's new society predicates the ultimate deletion of the great as a class (servants and the poor perdure—their lot is commiserated with but not resolved), More embarks on a reclamation project. A firm believer in the efficacy of example to chasten or corrupt, she shepherded the *ton* toward social helpfulness and the "almost sacred joys of *home*." "Reformation must begin with the GREAT," she intones, or the reformer merely throws "odours into the stream while the springs are poisoned." Lamenting that the "middle orders have caught the contagion" of fashionable emulation and that "this revolution of [their] manners" has almost rendered obsolete the adage " 'most worth and virtue are to be found in the middle station,' " she scolded women of rank and fortune into trading their lazy Frenchified habits for the strenuous exertion of feminine influence in her *Strictures*, while establishing a voguish pattern of bourgeois domestic culture in *Coelebs*. Like Wollstonecraft, she posits a reform or ruin dichotomy, attesting women's potency to undermine or save their country. They bear, in More's view, special civil and social responsibilities. Yoking gender and regeneration, she proclaims that educated women's moral force, by example and exhortation (she herself was a formidable model), can resurrect society on a Christian basis. *Strictures*, for instance, opens with an invigorating evocation of female power, urging women to its "most appropriate" exercise:

---

1. *Rights of Woman*, p. 145; *Collected Letters*, p. 233. For an idyllic bourgeois vignette, see *Rights of Woman*, pp. 142–43.

"to raise the depressed tone of public morals." Trafficking in mere manners is a "low mark, a prize not worthy of their high and holy calling."[2] Her terminology of moral reform insists on female agency; her works comprise a practical, comprehensive program for converting the standard *topos* of feminine influence from pacifying sham to redemptive fact. Not only must patricians embrace middle-class and Christian values, but men, forsaking aristocratic male honor, must also accede to the feminization of their ethos in the name of Jesus.[3] More's conflation of Christian and feminine virtues to female advantage cuts two ways, enduing women with quiet strength and courage and weaning men from their lax codes to that of the domestic milieu. She adjures females to self-discipline, but the worldly latitude forbidden them is not allowed to men either and what is good for women is also salutary for men.

More's subsumption of the feminine in the Christian is the root of her pious, public-spirited tour de force. Supplely preserving conventional appearances, she gives them a new direction, not only investing woman's traditional province with national relevance but also expanding her sphere. In line with general Evangelical professionalization, she ennobles woman's work into a vocation: "the profession of ladies . . . is that of daughters, wives, mothers, and mistresses of families." But women are not, cloistered, to renounce the outside world. Rather, following More's incessant emphasis on active virtue, they are to broaden their nurturing and reformative functions: the "superintendance of the poor" is "their immediate office"; *"charity is the calling of a lady; the care of the poor is her profession."*[4] More inoculates everyday routine with aggressive virtue: women must not only discountenance vice, for example, but debar the guilty rake from society. One historian of feminism remarks that, "without in the least intending" it, devout women like More and Sarah Trimmer who mapped out new female fields were really fomenting mid-Victorian feminist revolt.[5] She had in mind More's manifold philanthropical contributions, both personal and authorial—what might be labeled social feminism—but in fact the drift of More's explicitly conservative message is toward a liberating reworking of feminine ideology. She avers not only women's capability to define their own sphere—an issue of autonomy however bounded that sphere—but also their fitness for ethical stewardship. A partisan of her sex amply possessing Evangelic tactical shrewdness, More was a female crusader infinitely more successful than Wollstonecraft or any other competitor. She furbishes her goals in palatable form and hones those ideals paid cultural lip service

2. "Sensibility: An Epistle to the Honourable Mrs. Boscawen," *Works*, I, 35 (cf. *Strictures*, II, 161); "Thoughts on the Importance of the Manners of the Great to General Society," *Works*, I, 274; *Strictures*, I, 62–63, 4–5.

3. For examples of strictures on male honor and of the conflation of Christian and feminine virtues, see "Fashionable World," *Works*, I, 284, 288–89;

and "Preface to the Tragedies," *Works*, I, 504–5.

4. For Evangelical professionalization, see Bradley, pp. 156–78; *Strictures*, I, 97, 98, 117; *Coelebs*, *Works*, II, 372.

5. Ray Strachey, *"The Cause": A Short History of the Women's Movement in Great Britain* (1928; rpt. Port Washington, New York: Kennikat Press, 1969). p. 13.

to achieve her own ends, playing within the rules of the game while taking on the substantive reorganization of the dominant male culture's beliefs and values. Underneath its discreet surface, a More text is alive with submerged power, not that derived of dominance but a positive power of ability, competence, energy—a negative power of refusal, the right, indeed duty, to say no to custom, on Christian grounds of course. (A complete analysis of the complex rhetorical counterpoint through which she manages to convey female power while upholding sexual complementarity and deftly sidestepping impropriety would require a separate essay.) Rhythmically alternating the systole of ingratiating genuflection and the diastole of combative assertion, it is also predictably rife with latent contradictions and undrawn conclusions.

Yet More clearly offered much to her readers—a diet of "wholesome occupation, vigorous exertion, and systematic employment" seasoned by "rational and domestic enjoyments."[6] The comment of a young American attuned to nuance is instructive: "what an important sphere a woman fills! how thoroughly she ought to be qualified for it—but I think hers the more honourable employment than a man's for all men feel so grand and boast so much—and make such a pother about their being lords of the world below . . . oh every man of sense must humbly bow before woman. She bears the sway, not man as he presumptuously supposes."[7] Outlining the advantages of separate spheres, of women's role as "lawful possessors of a lesser domestic territory," More persuasively infuses their domestic vocation with social and political resonance. Nor is the Evangelical view of marriage she presents a regression to patriarchy. If she likes to talk of mutual dependence, she is a firm advocate of companionate marriage. Her heroine Lucilla Stanley may be too good for modern tastes, but she is indisputably a woman of character, a wife to be consulted, not dictated to. Participating in "all the dignity of equality," she is "not only the associate, but the inspirer of [Coelebs's] virtues"—his "coadjutress," "directress," and "presiding genius."[8] More's stress on philanthropy also spoke to female needs, as Wilberforce's reflection on the improved status of unmarried women indicates: "formerly there seemed to be nothing useful in which they could naturally be busy, but now they may always find an object in attending the poor." His diagnosis is echoed more ambivalently by that astute observer Lucy Aiken (Mrs. Barbauld's niece), who traced the overexuberances of the charitable "rage" to More, but knew "no one circumstance by which the manners, studies, and occupations of Englishwomen have been so extensively modified, or so strikingly con-

6. *Strictures*, II, 126, 201.
7. Mehitable May Dawes (Goddard), diary entry for June 12, 1815, quoted in Nancy F. Cott, *The Bonds of Womanhood: "Woman's Sphere" in New* *England, 1780–1835* (New Haven and London: Yale University Press, 1977), p. 99.
8. *Strictures*, II, 22; *Coelebs, Works*, II, 306, 372.

tradistinguished from those of a former generation." They were, she thought in 1842, a hardier, more active lot.[9]

Female activity and usefulness are indeed More's forte. Accepting constraints, she construes them as moral heroism, delivering the expected, but on her own terms: let girls "not be instructed to practise gentleness merely on the low ground of its being decorous and feminine and pleasing, and calculated to attract human favour," as the male conduct book writers she sardonically paraphrases counsel, but "on the high principle of obedience to Christ . . . a perfect pattern of imitation." The "divine Alchymy" of vital religion dilates female prerogative, licenses therapeutic moral imperialism, for in religion women are men's full equals, in truth their superiors and guides. Christianity generously reimburses women for earthly handicaps (a topic on which More can be tart) and opens a lawful avenue to achievement. More's Christian heroism is daily, domestic, full of small private amendments with public reverberations—requisite for men but peculiarly suited to the women whose ascriptive meekness and charity Christianity so strikingly ranks above society's rougher male standards.[1] In her pre-Evangelical days, More had likened women to fine porcelain vases on high shelves, but 1799 pleaded for "a patriotism at once firm and feminine for the general good," for the "young Christian militant" who could "awaken the drowsy spirit of religious principle." When, in an England trembling before "the most tremendous confederacies against religion and order, and governments, which the world ever saw," More pronounced religious rebirth the one thing needful, it is not surprising that she tapped a receptive female constituency eager to believe that on their influence depended "the very existence" of civilization, that the "dignity of the work" to which they were summoned was "no less than that of preserving the ark of the Lord." Doing the good work of moral reform, they enrolled as Providence's agents.[2]

Moral reform, then, was the complex issue of the day, and it was preeminently a female issue, witnessing the dialectic through which women, enmeshed in ideologies, use cultural definitions to try to shape their own lives, partly complying with and partly taking charge of their

9. Wilberforce is quoted in Jaeger, p. 29; *Memoirs, Miscellanies and Letters of the Late Lucy Aikin: Including Those Addressed to the Rev. Dr. Channing from 1826 to 1842*, ed. Philip Hemery Le Breton (London: Longman, Green, Longman, Roberts, and Green, 1864), pp. 421–22, 435. According to Mrs. Barbauld, philanthrophy was a full-blown fad by 1813; see her *Works*, II, 107–8. For recent documentation of the rage, see. F. K. Prochaska, "Women in English Philanthropy 1790–1830," *International Review of Social History*, 19, pt. 3 (1974), 426–45; and Barbara Corrado Pope, "Angels in the Devil's Workshop: Leisured and Charitable Women in Nineteenth-Century England and France," *Becoming Visible: Women in*

European History, ed. Renate Bridenthal and Claudia Koonz (Boston: Houghton Mifflin, 1977), pp. 296–324.
1. *Strictures*, I, 143, 138; II, 30–41, 93. Wilberforce's view of women parallels More's in his very popular *A Practical View of the Prevailing Religious System of Professed Christians, in the Higher and Middle Classes in this Country, Contrasted with Real Christianity*; 6th ed. (London: T. Cadell and W. Davies, 1798), pp. 445–47.
2. "Essays on Various Subjects, Principally Designed for Young Ladies," *Works*, I, 550 (More did not, perhaps significantly, include this 1777 work in her 1830 edition.); *Strictures*, I, 4–6, 83, 54; II, 97.

destinies. However amenable to variant subplots, it both testifies to female agency and ratifies woman's socially functional centrality. Though their remedies differ in many details, Wollstonecraft and More each diagnose England's moral—and almost mortal—illness in analogous terms. Perceiving a society infected with fashionable corruption, both preach a militantly moral middle-class reform grounded in women's potentiality. Delineating a female vision of the world, they put familial experience first. It is certainly true that conservatives identified feminists and male radicals who dared to reassess family structure and the relationship between the sexes as a threat. Terrified of collapse on the home front, they shored up domestic verities to strengthen the nation for its external battles. As the *Annual Register* spelled out, "The grand spring and cement of society is, the divine principle of love, branching forth from conjugal into parental, fraternal, and filial affection, an attachment to kindred, neighbours, countrymen."[3] Because domesticity and patriotism were thus inextricably joined, women, sex, and the family were thematic obsessions of anti-Jacobin polemic. The foundations of national morality were laid in private families: the home was found of civic virtue, custodian of social stability, bulwark against political subversion. But radicals like Wollstonecraft (and Hays) were equally anxious for a renovated domestic ideal: marriage, says Wollstonecraft, is the "cement of society," the "foundation of almost every social virtue." For each side, then, woman's role as "chaste wife, and serious mother" is pivotal.[4]

Both More and Wollstonecraft also avow the wider warrant of female example to effect national change and spur women to "labour by reforming themselves to reform the world."[5] Anti-sensuality, pro-chastity, both orchestrate modesty, self-control, and purity as human values rather than primarily feminine ones. Women were no longer to be merely the customary refiners of manners and the victims of those duplicitous manners, not the votaries of love, but the reformers of male and female morals alike and the beneficiaries of those reformed morals. Seeking to remodel traditional sexual codes and ethical systems to satisfy the needs of the time, radicals and Evangelicals alike were assailing the double standard of aristocratic French gallantry and immorality, espousing moral reform for all classes and sexes. Such alternative (but not mutually exclusive) domestic ideologies as More's model of Evangelical femininity and Wollstonecraft's rational womanhood are parallel, even symbiotic, female responses to political upheaval, attempts to take advantage of national unease to repattern domestic life through new schematic images of social order. Both were part of the larger and eventually successful bourgeois campaign to rehabilitate a degenerate culture through propaganda for enlightened domesticity and societal reform. If the demands of such radicals as Wollstonecraft for equal political rights were premature, their demands for forceful female social leverage and for freedom

3. *The Annual Register . . . for . . . 1798*, pp. 229–30.

4. *Rights of Woman*, pp. 165, 71, 28.

5. *Rights of Woman*, p. 45.

from sexual exploitation were not. From the positive perspective of moral reform, the doctrines of femininity are more profitably viewed not as the unequivocal opposite of feminism in the nineties, but rather as a perhaps necessary precondition to, a stage of preparation for, nineteenth-century feminism.

MARY POOVEY

[A *Vindication of the Rights of Woman* and Female Sexuality]†

* * *

In October 1791 Mary Wollstonecraft informed her new friend, William Roscoe, that she had begun sitting for the portrait he had commissioned. "I do not imagine that it will be a very striking likeness," she apologized playfully; "but, if you do not find me in it, I will send you a more faithful sketch—a book that I am now writing, in which *I* myself . . . shall certainly appear, head and heart."[1] The "sketch" was *A Vindication of the Rights of Woman* (1792), and, as this letter suggests, Wollstonecraft's second political tract proves that during the preceding year she had progressed considerably in her ability to understand not only political issues but also her own place within them. In discovering that her most natural allies in the debate conducted in *The Rights of Men* were women (and not, as that work suggested, either liberal bourgeois males or the poor), Wollstonecraft was more nearly able to come to terms with the emotionalism that disrupted that argument; in learning to harness her emotion and by recognizing its fellow in the emotionalism of other women, she seems to have begun to perceive that the problem that had always undermined her self-confidence was collective rather than personal.

The first of Wollstonecraft's breakthroughs in *The Rights of Woman* was the insight that individual responses are, first and foremost, responses to situations and that, in a telling way, what made the middle-class woman into a Proper Lady was her "situation." Women, like the rich, are "swallowed up . . . *localized* . . . by the rank they are placed in, by *courtesy*."

Women, commonly called Ladies, are not to be contradicted in company, are not allowed to exert any manual strength; and from them the negative virtues only are expected, when any virtues are expected,

† From Mary Poovey, *The Proper Lady and the Woman Writer*, pages 69–81. Reprinted by permission of the author and The University of Chicago Press.
1. *Collected Letters of Mary Wollstonecraft*, ed.
Ralph M. Wardle (Ithaca and London: Cornell University Press, 1979), pp. 202–3, 6 October 1791. All references in text and notes will be to this edition (cited as *MWL*), with page number and date.

patience, docility, good-humour, and flexibility; virtues incompatible with any vigorous exertion of intellect.[2]

"Rest on yourself," Wollstonecraft replied to the request for advice from the young author Mary Hays, for special danger awaits the woman writer who, accustomed to "courtesy," can be placated by meaningless praise. "An author, especially a woman, should be cautious lest she too hastily swallows the crude praises which partial friend and polite acquaintance bestow thoughtlessly when the supplicating eye looks for them" (*MWL*, p. 219; 12 November 1792).

Wollstonecraft's second important realization in *The Rights of Woman* was that the attitudes and expectations that perpetuate female weakness are institutionalized by the very texts that purport to be "authorities" and even by the values encoded in language. Women respond to local situations as Proper Ladies because from their childhood on they are instructed to conceive of themselves according to masculine assumptions of what "feminine" behavior is. Thus one major cause of the "barren blooming" that Wollstonecraft discerns in women is "a false system of education, gathered from the books written on this subject by men who, considering females rather as women than human creatures, have been more anxious to make them alluring mistresses than affectionate wives and rational mothers" (p. 7). By teaching women to understand themselves solely by men's judgments, to submit to the restraint of propriety, and to pursue their educations only with regard to man's happiness, these male "authorities"—and the women who echo them—have deprived women of the opportunity for self-exertion and, therefore, of the possibility for self-improvement.

The ideal paradigm of maturation that Wollstonecraft introduced in *The Rights of Men* obviously demands an educational program diametrically opposed to this feminine cultivation of "negative virtues." Her assumption here, which anchors the praadigm, is that all human beings are equal in their fundamental capacity to reason; discriminatory education should thus be eliminated because it is detrimental to the improvement of humanity as a whole. Women, as women, have been denied the "rights of man"; they have lost their legitimate position within the collective noun through an education that has denied them maturity.[3] In order to combat this assumption of essential difference and to break down the behavior that institutionalizes it, Wollstonecraft asserts that women, as a social group, have much in common with other, largely male groups, Her basic strategy is to emphasize the similarities between female behavior and that of other groups: the wealthy (pp. 187, 191), soldiers (p. 23,) wits (p. 56), and Dissenters (p. 194). Arguing "from analogy," she then asserts that it is reasonable and morally requisite

2. *The Rights of Woman*, p. 58. [All subsequent references will appear in the text and will refer to this edition—Editor.].
3. For a discussion of this aspect of *The Rights of* *Woman*, see Janet M. Todd, "The Language of Sex in A *Vindication of the Rights of Woman*," *Mary Wollstonecraft Newsletter* 1, no. 2 (April 1973): 10–17.

to teach women to recognize their essential affinities with men. Only then will women perceive the crucial relationship between their private actions and the welfare of society at large (p. 183). Only when women are considered—and consider themselves—human beings rather than sexual objects, only when their education develops rather than suppresses their reason, only when they are granted the legal equality they by nature deserve, will they be able to contribute to the overall improvement of humanity. Wollstonecraft insists that her argument is not based on special interest; because she is intent on effacing all sexual discrimination, she declares herself "disinterested" and claims to speak with the neutral voice of the species, "the firm tone of humanity" (p. 3).

Perceiving her own voice as the generalized, ideal voice of collective humanity relieves Wollstonecraft of much of the insecurity that marked *The Rights of Men*. She claims that her admonitions now have the widest possible base; they transcend the charge of egotism or self-interest, and they derive their authority from the instances of reason that, as she continues to argue, are everywhere evident. This position gives Wollstonecraft the confidence to embark on the course of direct confrontation she advocated but did not pursue in *The Rights of Men*. In *The Rights of Woman* she is finally able to identify and aggressively challenge the "authorities" she holds most responsible for female education: Rousseau, and conduct-book writers like Drs. Gregory and Fordyce.

The root of the wrongs of women, according to Wollstonecraft, is the general acceptance of the idea that women are *essentially* sexual beings— or, as Rousseau pharses it, "a male is only a male now and again, the female is always a female . . . ; everything reminds her of her sex."[4] Wollstonecraft's response to this sexual characterization of women is simply to reverse the charge: not *women*, she argues, but *men* are dominated by their sexual desires; *men's* insatiable appetites are the root of both economic inequality and social injustice. Arguments about women's "natural" inferiority, then, are only men's rationalizations for the superior social position they have unjustifiably seized, and their talk of "natural" female wantonness is merely a cover for the sexual appetite that men both fear and relish in themselves. Rousseau is the "sensualist" Wollstonecraft attacks most sytematically for indulging in "voluptuous reveries": "Rousseau declares that a woman should never, for a moment, feel herself independent, that she should be governed by fear to exercise her natural cunning, and made a coquetish slave in order to render her a more alluring object of desire, a *sweeter* companion to man, whenever he chooses to relax himself" (p. 25). Thus Rousseau's "discovery" of the "natural law" governing women, she charges, is simply a creation of his own repressed desire:

> Rousseau respected—almost adored virtue—and yet he allowed himself to love with sensual fondness. His imagination constantly prepared

4. Rousseau, *Émile*, trans. Barbara Foxley (New York: Dutton/Everyman, 1974), p. 324.

inflammable fewel for his inflammable senses; but, in order to reconcile his respect for self-denial, fortitude, and those heroic virtues,
which a mind like his could not coolly admire, he labours to invert
the law of nature, and broaches a doctrine pregnant with mischief
and derogatory to the character of supreme wisdom. [P. 42]

Rousseau, as a "voluptuous tyrant," simultaneously rationalizes his own
sensuality and gratifies it, and, at the same time, he punishes the being
who tempts him to this self-indulgence by making her responsible for
sexual control. Here Wollstonecraft is very close to perceiving how a set
of beliefs can be generated from or adopted because of local needs and
psychological imperatives. Moreover, she intuits the dynamics of repression and compensation at work in this production: as forbidden longings
are censured, sexual desire erupts in another, more permissible form:

All Rousseau's errors in reasoning arose from sensibility. . . . When
he should have reasoned he became impassioned, and reflection inflamed his imagination instead of enlightening his understanding.
Even his virtues also led him further astray; for, born with a warm
constitution and lively fancy, nature carried him toward the other sex
with such eager fondness, that he soon became lascivious. Had he
given way to these desires, the fire would have extinguished itself in
a natural manner; but virtue, and a romantic kind of delicacy, made
him practise self-denial; yet, when fear, delicacy, or virtue, restrained
him, he debauched his imagination, and reflecting on the sensations
to which fancy gave force, he traced them in the most glowing colours,
and sunk them deep into his soul. [Pp. 90–91]

The imagination, far from being the moral faculty philosophers like
Adam Smith described, becomes the agent of vicarious gratification; and
when the imagination becomes "debauched" in the name of virtuous
self-denial, the artist seduces his reader as he indulges himself: "And
thus making us feel whilst dreaming that we reason, erroneous conclusions are left in the mind" (p. 91).

Although Wollstonecraft's most direct attack centers on Rousseau and
the conduct-book writers, in footnotes and asides she challenges a much
more intimidating cultural "authority"—John Milton.[5] Wollstonecraft
knows that Milton's portrayal of Eve's "sweet attractive grace, and docile
blind obedience" (p. 19) stands behind Rousseau's Sophie. Milton, she
implies, is as much a "sensualist" as Rousseau. He acknowledged that
Eve is formed precisely in the image of Adam's innermost desires, made
"thy likeness, thy fit help, thy other self, / Thy wish, exactly to thy
heart's desires" (*Paradise Lost* 8. 450–51). Wollstonecraft therefore asserts that Eve, as sensuality incarnate, with her "wanton ringlets" and

---

5. For a discussion of the role Milton plays in the
writings of other nineteenth- and twentieth-century women, see Sandra M. Gilbert and Susan
Gubar, *The Madwoman in the Attic: The Woman*
Writer and the Nineteenth-Century Literary Imag-
ination (New Haven: Yale University Press, 1979),
pp. 187–212.

"coy submission" (*PL* 4. 306, 310), her "glowing cheek" and "tresses discompos'd" (*PL* 5.10), stands as commentary not on woman but on the men from whose imagination she sprang—from Milton's Adam and, before him, from Milton himself. With anger restrained only by her veneration for Milton, Wollstonecraft cites the words the poet placed in Eve's mouth as evidence against him:

> To whom thus Eve with *perfect beauty* adorn'd.
> My Author and Disposer, what thou bidst
> *Unargued* I obey; So God ordains;
> God is *thy law, thou mine*: to know no more
> Is Woman's *happiest* knowledge and her *praise*.
> [*PL* 4. 634–38; Wollstonecraft's italics]

It is significant that Wollstonecraft cannot attack Milton directly. Of all the cultural "authorities" she engages, Milton is clearly the most imposing, not only because of his preeminence in the English literary, political, and religious traditions but because of the special veneration accorded to Milton by Johnson's London circle. The fact that she can record her outrage against Milton only by allusions and by italicizing words in a quoted text (as in the passage just quoted) suggests the extent to which she is still reluctant to take her aggression to its logical extreme.

From the disguised but ever-present force of male desire, Wollstonecraft charges, all the evils that oppress women follow. Kept in a prolonged mental childhood to enhance the "innocence" men find so appealing, women are denied access to the personal experience necessary to the formation of a strong "human character" (p. 114). She clearly sees the paradox inherent in this deprivation: denied all challenging encounters and education, women are actually trapped within experience—the narrow domain of their own personal, *sensual* experience. Consequently incapable of "generalizing ideas, of drawing comprehensive conclusions from individual observations" (p. 54), women become obsessed with immediate impressions and gratifications. Because men indulge *their* sensual desires, women, trying to please, become slaves to their own senses and thus hostage to every transient emotion. Far from being the beneficiaries of "sensibility," women are actually the victims of feeling:

> Their senses are inflamed, and their understandings neglected, consequently they become the prey of their senses, delicately termed sensibility, and are blown about by every momentary gust of feeling. . . . Ever restless and anxious, their over exercised sensibility not only renders them uncomfortable themselves, but troublesome, to use a soft phrase, to others. All their thoughts turn on things calculated to excite emotion; and feeling, when they should reason, their conduct is unstable, and their opinions are wavering. . . . By fits and starts they are warm in many pursuits; yet this warmth, never concentrated into perseverance, soon exhausts itself. . . . Miserable indeed, must

be that being whose cultivation of mind has only tended to inflame
its passions! [Pp. 60–61].

Wollstonecraft cannot deny that women are, for the most part, satisfied
with the sensual gratification of male attention. And, because they are,
they participate in men's voluptuous designs. By internalizing "false
notions of beauty and delicacy" (p. 117), they cultivate that "sexual
character" of the mind that actually strengthens their chains. Women
embrace their inessentialness; thoughts of men continually occupy their
minds; they seek out lovers whose ingratiating manners flatter their self-
images; they are content to derive their identities from their relationships
to men—as "daughters, wives, and mothers" (p. 26). No wonder, Wollstonecraft laments, that men accuse women of intellectual superficially
and sensual self-indulgence. Indeed, Pope's maxim that "ev'ry Woman
is at heart a Rake" is not only a man's wish-fulfilling projection but a
self-fulfilling prophecy as well (p. 117). If women do not always rest
content within this masculine fantasy of power and self-indulgence, their
violations are at best indirect and surreptitious. Cunning is the resort of
the powerless who would not lose the illusion of power, and tyranny
over her helpless servants and children serves to vent an oppressed woman's wrath.

So intent is Wollstonecraft to reject the prevalent stereotype of women
as *all* sexuality that she comes close to arguing that women have *no*
innate sexual desires at all. Repeatedly she implies that female sexuality
is only a learned response to *male* sexuality, a strategy unconsciously
adopted in order to win the emotional acceptance that women really
want. "Men are certainly more under the influence of their appetites
than women," she flatly states (p. 137). What seems like sexual desire
in women is actually either "sympathy" or disguised vanity:

> The sexual attention of man particularly acts on female sensibility,
> and this sympathy has been exercised from their youth up. A husband
> cannot long pay those attentions with the passion necessary to excite
> lively emotions, and the heart, accustomed to lively emotions, turns
> to a new lover, or pines in secret, the prey of virtue or prudence. I
> mean when the heart has really been rendered susceptible, and the
> taste formed; for I am apt to conclude, from what I have seen in
> fashionable life, that vanity is oftener fostered than sensibility by the
> mode of education, and the intercourse between the sexes, which I
> have reprobated; and that coquetry more frequently proceeds from
> vanity than from that inconstancy, which overstrained sensibility nat-
> urally produces. [P. 65]

Promiscuity and repression surely exist; yet Wollstonecraft is at pains to
argue that such responses to sexual agitation are rare and, if the euphemism "*over-strained* sensibility" is significant, unnatural. It should not
surprise us that Wollstonecraft goes on to describe an ideal marriage as
one without passion ("a master and mistress of a family ought not to

continue to love each other with passion" [p. 30]), and she asserts with apparent assurance that women will easily be able to transform sexual desire into the more "serious" and "austere" emotions of friendship (p. 130).

Yet the closer we read Wollstonecraft's *Vindication*, the clearer it becomes that her defensive denial of female sexuality in herself and in women in general is just that—a *defense* against what she feared: desire doomed to repeated frustration. Contrary to her assertions, Wollstonecraft's deepest fear centers not on the voraciousness of male sexual desire but on what she fears is its brevity. Thus, while she can insist that "in the exercise of their maternal feelings providence has furnished women with a natural substitute for love," this substitute turns out to be necessary because, inevitably, the "lover [will become] only a friend" (p. 152). The devoted mother she describes proves to be a "neglected wife," driven to seek from her children the gratification that her "unhappy marriage" no longer provides. And the heroism of the self-sacrificing widow, which she celebrates, turns out to be barren and decidedly equivocal: "Raised to heroism by misfortunes, she represses the first faint dawning of a natural inclination, before it ripens into love, and in the bloom of life forgets her sex. . . . Her children have her love, and her brightest hopes are beyond the grave where her imagination often strays" (pp. 50–51).

Such repression is necessary, Wollstonecraft implies, because, far from being the learned response she asserts it is (and wishes it were), female sexuality is actually as demanding as male sexuality; perhaps it is even more urgent. In two remarkable passages Wollstonecraft betrays the fact that she shares the moralists' anxiety about female appetite. The first passage begins with an indictment of indecorous eating habits. Men are the worst offenders on this score, but, she acknowledges, "some women, particularly French women, have also lost a sense of decency in this respect; for they will talk very calmly of an indigestion. It were to be wished that idleness was not allowed to generate, on the rank soil of wealth, those swarms of summer insects that feed on putrefaction, we should not then be disgusted by the sight of such brutal excesses" (p. 137). While Wollstonecraft's scorn for the idle rich accounts for part of her venom here, her subsequent association of the "refinement of eating" with "refinements of love" more fully explains her vitriolic language. She goes on to describe female voluptuaries as "the slaves of casual lust . . . who are, literally speaking, standing dishes to which every glutton may have access" (p. 138). Clearly her disgust embraces both sexes here, for she is indicting sexual desire itself: "The depravity of the appetite which brings the sexes together," she argues, or "sensual gust," is dignified only when "the feelings of a parent mingl[e] with an instinct merely animal" (p. 138).

In a second telling passage, however, Wollstonecraft implies that female sexuality might even be more voracious—and hence more blame-worthy—than male desire. In a final attempt to denigrate the appetite she feels increasingly unable to deny, Wollstonecraft argues that platonic "feeling" provides a gratification that is superior to sexual pleasure. "What are the cold, or feverish caresses of appetite," she asks, "but sin embracing death, compared with the modest overflowings of a pure heart and exalted imagination?" (p. 192). The personification here is Wollstonecraft's final embedded allusion to *Paradise Lost*. The scene to which it refers, in book 2, culminates in Milton's first image of female procreation. Death is the son of Sin by Satan; the incestuous coupling of Sin and Death produces innumerable Hell Hounds, which prey upon their mother in a hideous cycle of painful procreation: "These yelling Monsters," Sin laments,

> hourly conceiv'd
> And hourly born, with sorrow infinite
> To me, for when they list into the womb
> That bred them they return, and howl and gnaw
> My Bowels, thir repast.
>
> [*PL* 2. 796–800]

However, in her allusion to this Miltonic image, Wollstonecraft makes one significant alteration. In *Paradise Lost* the ghastly cycle of birth and death is the result of a rape, which Sin graphically describes to Satan:

> I fled, and cri'd out *Death*;
> Hell trembl'd at the hideous Name, and sigh'd
> From all her Caves, and back resounded *Death*.
> I fled, but he pursu'd (though more, it seems,
> Inflam'd with lust than rage) and swifter far,
> Mee overtook his mother all dismay'd,
> And in embraces forcible and foul
> Ingend'ring with me, of that rape begot
> These yelling Monsters.
>
> [*PL* 2. 787–95]

Wollstonecraft's Sin, however, seems much more obliging; indeed, syntactically, *she* is the aggressor: "sin embracing death." Almost parenthetically, and almost certainly unconsciously, Wollstonecraft betrays her fear that female desire might in fact court man's lascivious and degrading attentions, that the subordinate position women have been given might even be deserved. Until women can transcend their fleshly desires and fleshly forms, they will be hostage to the body—a body that in giving birth originates death, that in demanding physical satisfaction makes itself vulnerable to frustration and pain.

The suspicion Wollstonecraft reveals here that female appetite might be the precipitating cause of women's cultural objectification also helps account for her vehement disgust with female physicality. Abhorring those "nasty, or immodest habits" that girls in boarding school acquire, she goes on to attack, in surprisingly vitriolic language, the "gross degree of familiarity" that "sisters, female intimates, or ladies and their waiting-women" exhibit toward one another (p. 127). She cautions all girls to wash and dress alone, lest they take up "some still more nasty customs, which men never fall into. Secrets are told—where silence ought to reign; and that regard to cleanliness . . . is violated in a beastly manner" (p. 128). It is difficult to know exactly what Wollstonecraft is referring to here; her insistent delicacy may result from some personal memory or a general revulsion from eighteenth-century girls' boarding-school conditions.[6] But, whatever the original offense, it is clear that her disgust involves female bodies and female desires—and all the ramifications of sexuality that she does not want to think about here.

For most late eighteenth-century writers, such an attack on female sexuality would have centered, at some point, on the imagination, for that faculty was generally understood to be the "*source* of sexual feeling."[7] Certainly Wollstonecraft's ambivalence about imagination in *The Rights of Men* leads us to expect this. But here she is careful to distinguish between imagination, which directs an individual's desire toward spiritual gratification, and "appetite," which fixes his or her attention on sensual objects. Essentially, Wollstonecraft is desexualizing imagination so that she can explain how a substitute gratification can satisfy sexual desire. Echoing eighteenth-century moralists, she characterizes imagination in sexual terms (it is a "vigorous" principle, "panting after" its object in "eager pursuit"); but its ultimate function is to "absorb every meaner affection and desire" as it leads the individual toward the happiness that is profoundly "not material" (p. 74). That Wollstonecraft continues to use sexual imagery to describe this substitute happiness suggests, however, that she is at least dimly aware that religious consolation *is* a substitute gratification. "True voluptuousness must proceed from the mind" (p. 192), she argues, but intellectual "voluptuousness" is an image that proclaims the primary of the senses. Wollstonecraft intends to strip the maturation process completely of its sexual character; but if she succeeds in making the sexes equal, she fails to eliminate the sexual component that is the source of her ongoing anxiety.

In her attempt to shore up her character, to control the emotional energy that threatened to explode her political argument in *The Rights of Men*, Wollstonecraft has turned her argument outward. The result is a more perceptive analysis both of ideology and of her own position within it. But while her basic assumption—that women are primarily reasoning rather than sexual beings—enabled her to create a self-image sufficiently strong to attack prejudices and practices that traditionally had wholly silenced women's voices in political discussions, her inability

---

6. Nina Auerbach also discusses Wollstonecraft's anxiety about the "subtle sexual contagion" of women's schools. See her *Communities of Women: An Idea in Fiction* (Cambridge, Mass.: Harvard University Press, 1978), pp. 14–15.

7. See Patricia Meyer Spacks, "Ev'ry Woman is at Heart a Rake," *Eighteenth-Century Studies* 8, no. 1 (Fall 1974): 38.

to acknowledge or fully assimilate the profoundly unreasonable longings of her own emotional or physical being caused her to weaken the argument she had so effectively begun. For Wollstonecraft does not extend to women the same insight she used in exploding Rousseau's euphemisms and evasions; that is, she does not develop the idea that either women's characteristically volatile sensibility or her own scheme for emotional gratification might be a sublimation of sexual energy. In order to sidestep the investigation of sexuality that this insight would necessitate—and the admission of "weakness" it would entail—Wollstonecraft repeatedly turns her argument away from every potentially dangerous acknowledgment that women have sexual or physical needs.

We can see one consequence of this evasion in her own use of euphemisms and circuitous phrasing. Whenever Wollstonecraft approaches a subject that arouses her own volatile emotions, her language becomes both obscure and abstract; she shuns concrete nouns as if they were bodies she is trying to cover over. In fact, she will fully indulge her feeling only when its object is physically absent or unidentified. Even then she uses artificial and abstract rhetoric to generalize her emotion and to idealize the provocative situation. Her celebration of modesty is a particularly clear example of the results her abstractions could produce:

> Modesty! Sacred offspring of sensibility and reason!—true delicacy of mind!—may I unblamed presume to investigate thy nature, and trace to its covert the mild charm, that mellowing each harsh feature of a character, renders what would otherwise only inspire cold admiration—lovely!—Thou that smoothest the wrinkles of wisdom, and softenest the tone of the sublimest virtues till they all melt into humanity;—thou that spreadest the ethereal cloud that, surrounding love, heightens every beauty, it half shades, breathing those coy sweets that steal into the heart, and charm the senses—modulate for me the language of persuasive reason, till I rouse my sex from the flowery bed, on which they supinely sleep life away! [P. 121]

Wollstonecraft's celebration of "mellowing," "smoothing," "melting," and "shading" suggests the extent to which she is attempting to dematerialize her subject. Perhaps an even more revealing text is the one in which she defines "human rapture." Here the emotion is twice removed from its physical object and it is described in poetic clichés notable primarily for their imprecision and immateriality. The "rapture," predictably, is not for the physical person but only for "whatever had touched the person"—the glove or slipper, for example—of "an absent or lost friend":

> A shadowy phantom glides before us, obscuring every other object; yet when the soft cloud is grasped, the form melts into common air, leaving a solitary void, or sweet perfume, stolen from the violet, that memory long holds dear. [P. 124]

Although Wollstonecraft repeatedly professes to admire clarity, this image not only describes obscurity but is itself purposefully vague. Only in such a "fairy ground" of spiritual relationships and in such abstract and impersonal language can she allow herself to imagine intense feeling, for in this immaterial context desire can be neither sexual nor literal nor demanding of satisfaction.

An even more severe consequence of Wollstonecraft's refusal to acknowledge female sexuality is her reluctance to consider women as a group capable of achieving solidarity or taking the initiative for social reform. Because she considers the root of culture's values to be *men's* sexual desire, she continues to portray social reform strictly in terms of individual men's acts of self-denial and self-control. Certainly her understanding of the determinate relationship between the individual and institutional or historical forces is more sophisticated in *The Rights of Woman* than in *The Rights of Men*. In it she explicitly acknowledges, for example, the limited efficacy of individual effort (especially in education; see pp. 21, 157) and the necessity for societywide changes in legal, political, and employment policies (see pp. 145, 147, 148). But when she calls for change, her summons always encourages an alteration in *individual*, particularly *male*, attitudes. "Let men become more chaste and modest" (p. 11), let the nobility "prefer" the practice of reason (p. 22), let "mankind become more reasonable" (p. 56); only then can social change begin. The terms used may pass as generic nouns and pronouns, but they most frequently designate males. Wollstonecraft is generally *not* challenging women to *act*. When she calls for a "revolution in female manners" (p. 45), for example, she is not advocating a feminist uprising to overthrow manners but rather a general acquiescence in the gradual turning that the word "revolution" was commonly taken to mean in the eighteenth century. Women are simply to wait for this revolution to *be* effected, for their dignity to *be* restored, for their reformation to *be* made necessary. The task is primarily men's, and it involves not confrontation but self-control. Wollstonecraft defers her discussion of legal inequality to the promised second volume (which she never wrote) because, in her scheme, social legislation is less effective than individual self-control. And in *The Rights of Woman*, Wollstonecraft emphasizes independence rather than equality both because she conceives of society as a collection of individual attitudes rather than legal contracts and because she imagines relationships to be fundamentally antagonistic rather than cooperative. The major antagonism, however, is not against an external force but against one's own self—against fear and, especially, against desire. This idea, of course, is actually only a generalization of the behavior traditionally advocated for women; it is the Protestant ethic stripped of its component of personal assertion and material reward.

It is partly because Wollstonecraft so thoroughly distrusts her own sexuality that she rejects a female speaking voice in *The Rights of Woman*. While occasionally she speaks self consciously as a woman ("in the name of my sex" [p. 150]), more frequently she distinguishes between herself and "them" ("I plead for my sex—not for myself" [p. 3]); "I do not wish them [women] to have power over men; but over themselves" [p. 62]). At least once she speaks "as man with man," but even then she aspires not to a masculine voice but to a voice totally unconscious of sexuality. Here she is adopting Rousseau's definition of men and simply bringing the definition of women in line with the implicit asexual ideal. "Men are not always men in the company of women, nor would women always remember that they are women, if they were allowed to acquire more understanding" (p. 123, n. 7). Occasionally she addresses women, but both her formal, self-consciously rhetorical address and her condescension distance her from her natural allies: "Hapless woman! what can be expected from thee . . . ?" (p. 97); "O ye foolish women! . . . ignorant ye are in the most emphatical sense of the word" (p. 180). Wollstonecraft clearly wants most of all to distinguish herself from all sexual categories so as to attain a neutral voice. She speaks comfortably "as a philosopher" and "as a moralist" (p. 34), but in her most cherished self-image she speaks to her "dear contemporaries" as "a fellow creature," using the "firm tone of humanity" (pp. 92, 150, 3). She even dramatizes herself as achieving a stance of almost Miltonic "disinterestedness":

> Let me now as from an eminence survey the world stripped of all its false delusive charms. The clear atmosphere enables me to see each object in its true point of view, while my heart is still. I am calm as the prospect in a morning when the mists, slowly dispersing, silently unveil the beauties of nature, refreshed by rest. [P. 110]

Despite the natural tropes, this description actually characterizes the speaker; *she* is as "calm as the prospect" cleansed of mists, and *hers* are the "unveil[ed] . . . beauties." In this ideal, disembodied state, Wollstonecraft transcends her femaleness—and with it, presumably, the agitations that make her female heart, now still, cry out.

From her evasions and her aspirations, it seems clear that the price Wollstonecraft felt her new profession exacted was her female sexuality. This was a price she thought she was more than willing to pay; for if the ideal writer has no sex, he or she is therefore free from both the body's limitations and its demands. Adopting this characterization of the writer could theoretically protect Wollstonecraft from the painful vacillations of feeling she had alternately repressed and indulged during her youth. At the same time, this persona allowed her a certain amount of social self-confidence, especially in Joseph Johnson's circle, where feminine graces seemed to be irrelevant and such women as Anna Barbauld were acknowledged as intellectual equals by being criticized as such. But it also, of course, blinded Wollstonecraft to crucial emotional and physical needs—needs that were increasingly demanding attention. That she could mistake her growing passion for Henry Fuseli for a purely "rational desire"—even to the point of proposing, to his wife, that she,

Wollstonecraft, should join the Fuseli household—attests to the extent of her self-deception and to the power of the desire she tried to philosophize away. Although it made her famous, *The Rights of Woman* did not provide Wollstonecraft with the "stability of character" to which she aspired. Late in 1792, after Fuseli had rejected her advances, she found herself again painfully self-divided, her "heart" once more at war with her beloved reason. "I am a strange compound of weakness and resolution!" she wrote to Joseph Johnson.

> There is certainly a great defect in my mind—my wayward heart creates its own misery—Why I am made thus I cannot tell; and, till I can form some idea of the whole of my existence, I must be content to weep and dance like a child—long for a toy, and be tired of it as soon as I get it. [MWL, p. 221; c. late 1792]

Whether or not Wollstonecraft was correct in deducing a fundamentally nonsexual human essence is, of course, beside the point, for the tensions in her argument demonstrate that, even in her own terms, she had not resolved the complexities of the issue, either theoretically or practically. Clearly, simply to recognize the structure of sexual oppression and inequality, as Mary Wollstonecraft did, was not sufficient to achieve genuine freedom. Remaining a prisoner of the category she most vehemently tried to reject, she allowed what looked like an externalization of rage to return remorselessly to herself. The frustrations behind the contradictions evident in *The Vindication of the Rights of Woman*, her strongest polemic, would be dispelled only when she found a way to allow the writer and the woman to speak with one voice.

Mary Wollstonecraft—
A Chronology

1759	27 April. Born in the Spitalfields district of London, second child and first daughter of Edward John Wollstonecraft and Elizabeth Dickson.
1763–8	The Wollstonecraft family moves to Epping; Barking, Essex and Beverly, Yorkshire where the father tries, in each place unsuccessfully, to establish himself as a gentleman farmer.
1774	Family returns to Hoxton, a suburb of London, Mr. Wollstonecraft having failed at farming.
1775	Wollstonecraft meets Fanny Blood, the woman who will become her soulmate.
1776	Family moves to Langharne, Wales.
1777	Family returns to the London suburb of Walworth, where Mary and Fanny live near each other.
1778	Mary Wollstonecraft takes employment as a companion to Mrs. Dawson of Bath; during her tenure also visits in Southampton and Windsor.
1780	Wollstonecraft returns home to nurse her dying mother.
1782	Mrs. Wollstonecraft dies; Mary's sister Eliza marries Meredith Bishop; Mr. Wollstonecraft remarries a woman known only as "Lydia" and returns to Wales; and Mary goes to live with Fanny and her family, where her needlework helps to maintain the struggling Blood family.
1783	Birth of Eliza and Meredith Bishop's daughter.
1784	Wollstonecraft, having been summoned by Mr. Bishop, goes to attend her sister Eliza who is seemingly deranged after the childbirth. Mary secretly removes Eliza to Hackney, then Islington, convinced that her sister's mental breakdown resulted from cruel usage by her husband. A legal separation is obtained for the Bishops, but the mother does not have custody of her child, who dies before age one year.
	Mary and Eliza Wollstonecraft and Fanny Blood open a school in Islington, moving it later to Newington

Green where they are joined by Everina, the third Wollstonecraft sister. Newington Green offers Wollstonecraft the friendship of Reverend Richard Price, famous liberal of the period; she is also introduced to Dr. Samuel Johnson.

1785   Fanny Blood goes to Lisbon to marry Hugh Skeys. Soon pregnant, she sends for Wollstonecraft to be with her at the birth of her child, and, at Mary's arrival, Fanny is already in premature labor. She dies in her friend's arms 29 November, the baby dying soon after.

1786   After her return from Portugal Wollstonecraft finds the school in financial trouble and closes it.
Writes *Thoughts on the Education of Daughters*, her first book.

Takes job as governess to elder daughters of Viscount Kingsborough of Mitchelstown, County Cork, Ireland, residing briefly at Eton before her removal to Ireland where she observes at firsthand one of the oldest and most famous public (what would be called in America "private") preparatory schools.

1787   Goes with Kingsboroughs to Dublin, thence to Bristol, where she is dismissed from their employ by Lady Kingsborough.

Returns to London, determined to make her living by her pen.

1788   Joseph Johnson, her publisher and friend, releases her first novel *Mary, a Fiction* and her children's book, *Original Stories from Real Life*, as well as her translation from the French of Jacques Necker's *Of the Importance of Religious Opinions*.

Begins writing for the *Analytical Review*, a monthly just established by Joseph Johnson and Thomas Christie.

1789   Johnson publishes her anthology *The Female Reader*, under the pen name "Mr. Creswick"; no copy of this collection has yet been located.

1790   Johnson publishes her translation from the German of Christian Salzmann's *Elements of Morality*; publishes (anonymously) *A Vindication of the Rights of Men*, the first published response to Edmund Burke's *Reflections on the Revolution in France*.

1791   Second edition of *A Vindication of the Rights of Men* appears, this time with the author's name.

Wollstonecraft moves to new quarters in Store Street.

Begins work on *A Vindication of the Rights of Woman.*

1792   Publication of *A Vindication of the Rights of Woman;* a second, revised and corrected edition appears later the same year.

Leaves for Paris alone in December.

1793   Meets Gilbert Imlay, American explorer, author, and entrepreneur.

Moves from Paris to the outlying suburb of Neuilly for safety in the revolution-torn country.

In September, moves back to Paris, is registered as Gilbert Imlay's wife at the American embassy for the protection which American citizenship would afford her.

1794   Joins Imlay in Le Havre in February.

14 May. Fanny Imlay born.

Imlay returns to Paris, soon followed by Wollstonecraft and Fanny; then he returns to London and the mother and her baby stay on in Paris alone.

Publication of her *Historical and Moral View of the Origin and Progress of the French Revolution.*

1795   Wollstonecraft and Fanny return to London.
Tries to commit suicide but attempt is discovered by Imlay.

In June, leaves as Imlay's business envoy on a trip to the Scandinavian countries, accompained by Fanny and Marguerite, the child's nurse.

In October, discovering that Imlay is living with an actress, attempts suicide a second time by jumping off Putney Bridge.

1796   Publication of *Letters Written during a Short Residenc in Sweden, Norway, and Denmark.*

Meets William Godwin for the second time; Wollstonecraft and Godwin become lovers.

1797   29 March. Mary Wollstonecraft and William Godwin married at Old St. Pancras Church; the couple entertain guests jointly at No. 29, the Polygon, but work in separate quarters during the day.

30 August. Mary Wollstonecraft Godwin born.

10 September. Mary Wollstonecraft dies of puerperal

("childbed") fever and is buried five days later in churchyard of Old St. Pancras Church.

1851   Percy Florence Shelley moves the remains of Woll-stonecraft and Godwin to Bournemouth to rest beside their daughter (and his mother) Mary Wollstonecraft Godwin Shelley.

Selected Bibliography

There have been some important strides in Wollstonecraft bibliography in the decade between 1975 and 1985. Ulrich Hardt's critical edition of A *Vindication of the Rights of Woman* (Troy: Whitston Publishing, 1982) provides an offset' of the first edition of 1792 into which are clearly inserted or footnoted variant readings from the second 1792 edition, the final edition, Hardt claims, over which Wollstonecraft would have had any control. In addition, the book is heavily annotated for the student reader, although perhaps overannotated for the more experienced reader.

Ralph M. Wardle's *Collected Letters of Mary Wollstonecraft* (Ithaca: Cornell UP, 1979) is a milestone and has at last provided scholars and students with a single repository of all Mary Wollstonecraft's letters. There is ample annotation and a clear chronological arrangement of the letters, and the editor is one of the first—and the best—Wollstonecraft scholars in America.

Finally, Janet M. Todd's *Mary Wollstonecraft: An Annotated Bibliography* (New York: Garland Publishing, 1976) recapitulates all the available Wollstonecraft material through 1976 in a list that runs to 727 items. Concise comments on nearly each selection point to the most useful material. The bibliography proper is preceded by an introduction that glances at the whole history of Wollstonecraft criticism by categories.

The first section of the following bibliography lists Mary Wollstonecraft's works, including modern reprints when applicable. The second section lists suggested critical and biographical material that should be useful for those interested in further study of Mary Wollstonecraft and of A *Vindication of the Rights of Woman* in particular.

MARY WOLLSTONECRAFT'S BOOKS

Thoughts on the Education of Daughters: with Reflections on Female Conduct, in the more important Duties of Life. London, 1787.

Mary: A Fiction. London, 1788. Available in an excellent modern annotated edition with an introduction by Gary Kelly. London: Oxford UP, 1976.

Original Stories from Real Life, with conversations, calculated to regulate the affections, and form the mind to truth and goodness. London, 1788.

Translation of Jacques Necker's *On the Importance of Religious Opinions.* London, 1788.

The Female Reader; or Miscellaneous Pieces, in Prose and Verse; Selected from the Best Writers, and Disposed under Proper Heads; for the Improvement of Young Women. London, 1789. Available in a modern facsimile with introduction by Moira Ferguson. Delmar: Scholars' Facsimiles and Reprints, 1980.

Translation of Madame de Cambon's *Young Grandison.* London, 1790.

A *Vindication of the Rights of Men, in a letter to the Right Honourable Edmund Burke.* London, 1790. Available in a modern facsimile with introduction by Eleanor Louise Nicholes. Delmar: Scholars Facsimiles and Reprints, 1975.

Translation of Christian Gotthilf Salzmann's *Elements of Morality for the Use of Children.* London, 1790.

A *Vindication of the Rights of Woman, with Strictures on Political and Moral Subjects.* London, 1792. Several modern editions exist, but particularly recommended is the introduction by Miriam Kramnick to the Penguin edition (1982).

An Historical and Moral View of the Origin and Progress of the French Revolution: and the Effect It Has Produced in Europe. London, 1794. Available in facsimile reproduction with an introduction by Janet M. Todd. Delmar: Scholars' Facsimiles and Reprints, 1975.

Posthumous Works of the Author of A Vindication of the Rights of Woman. Ed. William Godwin. London, 1798. Includes *The Wrongs of Woman, or Maria; a Fragment; Letters to Imlay; The Cave of Fancy; Fragment of Letters on the Management of Infants.* Available in a modern reprint with an introduction by Gina Luria. New York: Garland Publishing Co., 1974. Wollstonecraft's second novel, *The Wrongs of Woman, or Maria* unpublished in her lifetime, is available in modern editions. Especially recommended is the annotated edition by Gary Kelly. London: Oxford UP, 1976.

The Emigrants. London, 1793. (Attributed to Mary Wollstonecraft by Robert R. Hare. See Hare's edition published by Scholars' Facsimiles and Reprints. Gainesville: 1964.)

BIOGRAPHICAL AND CRITICAL STUDIES

Benedict, Ruth. *An Anthropologist at Work*. Ed. Margaret Mead. Boston: Houghton Mifflin, 1959. Benedict's unpublished essay on Wollstonecraft is found here.

Bouten, Jacob. *Mary Wollstonecraft and the Beginnings of Female Emancipation in France and England*. Amsterdam: 1922; Philadelphia: Porcupine Press, 1975. Suggests intellectual influences on Wollstonecraft's thought.

Flexner, Eleanor. *Mary Wollstonecraft*. New York: Coward, McCann and Geoghegan, 1972. Adds new material and gives sound discussion of Wollstonecraft's ideas.

Ferguson, Moira. *First Feminists: British Women Writers 1578–1799*. Bloomington: Indiana UP, 1985. Excellent compilation of Wollstonecraft's precursors, well-introduced.

———. "Mary Wollstonecraft, and Mr. Cresswick." *Philological Quarterly* 62 (Fall 1983): 4–23.

Guralnick, Elissa. "Rhetorical Strategy in Mary Wollstonecraft's *Vindication of the Rights of Woman*." *Humanities Association Review* 30 (1979): 174–85.

Janes, Regina. "Mary, Mary, Quite Contrary, or Mary Astell and Mary Wollstonecraft Compared." *Studies in Eighteenth-Century Culture* 5 (1975): 121–39.

Kelly, Gary. "Mary Wollstonecraft as Vir Bonus." *English Studies in Canada* 5 (1979): 275–91. An insightful article that argues that Wollstonecraft got her rhetorical stance for writing A *Vindication of the Rights of Men* from Quintilian by way of Fuseli. Has implications for the *Rights of Woman* as well.

Kelly, Joan. "Early Feminist Theory and the *Querrelles des Femmes*, 1400–1789." *Signs* 8 (Autumn 1982): 4–28.

Lloyd, Genevieve. *The Man of Reason: Male and Female in Western Philosophy*. Minneapolis: U of Minnesota P, 1985. Relevant background to Mary Wollstonecraft.

Martin, Jane. *Reclaiming a Conversation: The Ideal of the Educated Woman*. New Haven: Yale UP, 1985. Contains a substantial section on Mary Wollstonecraft.

Myers, Mitzi. "Mary Wollstonecraft's *Letters Written . . . in Sweden*: Toward Romantic Autobiography." *Studies in Eighteenth-Century Culture* 8 (1978): 165–85. Deconstructs Wollstonecraft's writing and shows how she writes to discover herself with, once again, implications for the *Rights of Woman*.

———. "Politics from the Outside: Mary Wollstonecraft's First *Vindication*." *Studies in Eighteenth-Century Culture* 6 (1977): 113–22. Excellent summary of the ideas in Wollstonecraft's *Vindication of the Rights of Men*, which deepens understanding of her later work.

Nussbaum, Felicity. "Eighteenth-Century Women." *Studies in Burke and His Time* 19 (1978): 223–31. A major review essay.

Paul, Charles Kegan. *William Godwin: His Friends and Contemporaries*. Boston, 1876.

Paulson, Ronald. *Representations of Revolution*. New Haven: Yale UP, 1983. Chapter 3 treats Wollstonecraft along with Burke and Paine in a trenchant discussion of the French Revolution.

Peabody, Josephine Preston. *Portrait of Mrs. W. A Play in Three Acts with an Epilogue*. Boston: Houghton Mifflin, 1922.

Pennell, Elizabeth Robins. *Mary Wollstonecraft Godwin*. London, 1885.

Preedy, George R. [Mrs. Gabrielle Campbell Long]. *This Shining Woman*. London: Collins, 1937.

Prior, Mary, ed. *Women in English Society, 1580–1800*. London: Methuen, 1985. Essays covering a wide range of subjects clarifying what life was like for women before and during Wollstonecraft's time.

Rendall, Jane. *The Origins of Modern Feminism: Women in Britain, France and the United States, 1780–1860*. London: Macmillan Publishers Ltd., 1985.

Rogers, Katharine M. *Feminism in Eighteenth-Century England*. Urbana: U of Illinois P, 1982.

Roper, Derek. "Mary Wollstonecraft's Reviews." *Notes and Queries* 5 (1958): 37–38.

Sunstein, Emily. *A Different Face*. New York: Harper & Row, 1975. An appreciative, psychological approach to Wollstonecraft's life.

Taylor, G. R. S. *Mary Wollstonecraft: A Study in Economics and Romance*. London: Martin Secker, 1911. A good example of the romanticization of Wollstonecraft's life.

Theriot, Nancy. "Mary Wollstonecraft and Margaret Fuller: A Theoretical Comparison." *International Journal of Women's Studies* 2 (1979): 560–74.

Thiebaux, Marcelle. "Mary Wollstonecraft in Federalist America." *The Evidence of the Imagination*. Ed. Donald H. Reiman, Michael C. Jaye, and Betty T. Bennett. New York: New York UP, 1978, 195–235.

Todd, Janet. "The Biographies of Mary Wollstonecraft." *Signs* 1 (1976): 721–34. A useful rundown of the whole list of biographical efforts.

———. "The Language of Sex in A *Vindication of the Rights of Woman*." *Mary Wollstonecraft Newsletter* 1 (1973): 10–17.

———. "Mary Wollstonecraft: A Review of Research and Comment." *British Studies Monitor* 7 (1977): 3–23. Surveys and assesses information available up to 1975.

————. "The Polwhelan Tradition and Richard Cobb." *Studies in Burke and His Time* 16 (1975): 271–77.

Tomalin, Claire. *The Life and Death of Mary Wollstonecraft*. New York: Weidenfeld and Nicolson, 1974. Good information on Wollstonecraft's stay in France, with some new documents and information.

Wardle, R. M. "Mary Wollstonecraft, *Analytical* Reviewer." *PMLA* 642 (1974): 1000–9.

Wilson, Arthur M. "Treated Like Imbecile Children." *Women in the Eighteenth Century and Other Essays*. Ed. Paul Fritz and Richard Morton. Toronto: S. Stevens, 1976. 89–104. Wilson sees A *Vindication of the Rights of Woman* as "a benchmark in England."

NORTON CRITICAL EDITIONS

DATE DUE

DEMCO 38-297